To Char[...]
with my compliments —
Ron Moran

Inconstant Companions

Inconstant Companions

Archaeology and North American Indian Oral Traditions

Ronald J. Mason

THE UNIVERSITY OF ALABAMA PRESS

Tuscaloosa

Typeface: Bembo

∞

The paper on which this book is printed meets the minimum requirements of American
National Standard for Information Sciences-Permanence of Paper for Printed Library
Materials, ANSI Z39.48–1984.

Library of Congress Cataloging-in-Publication Data

Mason, Ronald J.
    Inconstant companions : archaeology and North American Indian oral traditions /
Ronald J. Mason.
        p.   cm.
    Includes bibliographical references and index.
    ISBN-13: 978-0-8173-1533-7 (cloth : alk. paper)
    ISBN-10: 0-8173-1533-0 (alk. paper)
    1. Indians of North America—Folklore. 2. Indians of North America—History. 3. Oral
tradition—North America. 4. Ethnohistory—North America. I. Title.
    E98.F6M28 2006
    305.897—dc22

2006008288

Contents

Preface

This book addresses a fundamental historiographical problem in archaeology, history, and anthropology generally but most especially when those disciplines are practiced in cross-cultural contexts. Although my focus is on North America, this problem is global. When an archaeologist excavates traces of a society with which some modern native people claim affinity and for which they assert possession of traditional historical knowledge, the scientific results may diverge sharply from the traditional knowledge claims. In such cases, who is to be believed? Why one and not the other? Must it be a zero-sum game? That problem, while long-standing, has grown to critical proportions and heightened decibel levels since the political decolonization of much of the non-Western world following the Second World War. This is the issue popularly encapsulated in the question and, simultaneously, challenge: "Who controls (or owns) the past?"

On the face of it, that question is absurd. The past is beyond control. It is exempt from ownership. It is extinct. The challenge, however, is another matter. Notwithstanding some societies' denials of the pastness of the past, examples of which will be met in the following pages, what is really being asked in this question/challenge is, "When disagreements arise, whose version of the past is to be preferred?" This in turn involves the compound question, "For whom, by whom, and for what purpose?"

This has been a difficult book to write. And some will likely conclude the same about reading it. It will also be judged controversial. Doubtless many who simply scan its pages to see whether they might want to read it will decide not to, finding it opinionated in a direction not their own, frequently requiring close attention, and sometimes discomforting. It is most assuredly out of step with the current vogue to find equal value in "different ways of knowing"—that is, to regard adherence to canons of evidence and rules of logic developed in the West as intolerable "hegemonic trespass" on non-Western epistemic traditions. An unfortunate but inevitable consequence of being out of step is treading on toes. When and where I have done this has been incidental to pushing an argument onto grounds already occupied. Not a few of the possessors of those toes are persons I esteem and regard as friends. I trust they know me well enough to see no personal malice where none is intended.

Cognizant of the risk I take in forearming potential critics of what I have to say in this book, I nevertheless owe it to all readers to state my professional expertise and acknowledge my relevant shortcomings. I am a liberally educated anthropologist of long field, museum, and college teaching experience and have special research interest in the archaeology and ethnohistory of North America's native people, particularly those south of the Arctic and east of the Rocky Mountains. I am not a Homeric scholar nor a classical archaeologist. Neither am I a biblical historian, an Africanist or Oceanian ethnographer, a Norse epic or Serbo-Croatian ballad specialist, a psychologist of memory, an expert in documentary exegesis, nor a folklorist. In these fields I claim no more than amateur status and acquaintance with some of their practitioners. I have also done extensive reading in those fields—not all of it to be recommended for sheer pleasure—and have found in their combination insights I regard as indispensable in dealing with some of the issues intrinsic to the relations between oral traditional histories and those revealed by scientifically informed historiography. A little knowledge, it has sometimes been said, is a dangerous thing. To which I would add, none is even worse.

In pursuing these matters, I have greatly benefited from advice, criticism, and encouragement from a number of individuals who, while not always in agreement with my opinions, went out of their way to respond helpfully to my requests for information or special services. Whatever errors and other shortcomings may be found in what follows are my responsibility alone. Those to whom I am especially indebted are Matthew Ansfield, Donald Bahr, James A. Brown, William A. Chaney, Charles E. Cleland, James A. Clifton, Glynn Custred, Frederica de Laguna, Charles Garrad, Jeff Grathwohl, William Green, Robert L. Hall, June Helm, Dale R. Henning, Alice B. Kehoe, Nathan S. Lowrey, George P. Nicholas, Peter N. Peregrine, Terry L. Rew-Gottfried, Robert J. Salzer, George R. Saunders, Lynn S. Teague, Alexander von Gernet, Jere Wickens, James V. Wright, and most of all my wife and colleague, Carol I. Mason.

Although they were not directly connected with the writing of this book, I want to express my indebtedness to my early mentors and friends, too many of whom, alas, can no longer be thanked in person, for persuading me by their example of the indispensability of an archaeology integrated with the rest of anthropology and liberal education: Dorothy Cross, Loren

C. Eiseley, J. L. Giddings, Jr., Ward H. Goodenough, James B. Griffin, Samuel Noah Kramer, J. Alden Mason, George I. Quimby, Froelich G. Rainey, William A. Ritchie, Linton Satterthwaite, Jr., and John Witthoft.

Finally, it is a pleasure to express my gratitude to the Department of Anthropology and the administration and staff of Lawrence University for unstintingly providing the facilities for postretirement research and writing and to Judith Knight and the editorial and production staff of the University of Alabama Press for their splendid performance in ushering my manuscript into print.

Inconstant Companions

I

Introduction

A Southern Ute Indian once observed to the ethnographer Marvin Opler, "Everything moves on and is lost. . . . For nothing can stop. Nothing is left of those days but my story and your words. Nothing remains behind" (Opler 1940:119). From another age and another continent is the Latin adage "Verba volant, scripta manent" (what is said vanishes; what is written remains [Coward in Alexandre Dumas's *La Reine Margot,* 1997:496n101]). In short, the spoken word flees before time while the written transgresses it. Unless even the most esteemed utterances are captured in writing, they are inevitably annihilated with the passing of generations, however much the later try to snare the echoes of the earlier and reproduce what they think they heard. Writing, at least, shares with archaeological remains a greater, even if unequal, portion of durability. The latter survive even the extinction of languages, written or not. But they do so at the price of less immediately grasped intelligibility.

Until the end of the fourth millennium B.C., when writing began in Mesopotamia, and later still in Egypt, China, and a few other parts of the world, "histories" were verbal. Because of limited compass of social needs and capabilities and the fact of finite human memory, those accounts of the past linked proximate to current generations in ascending sequences at the cost of mythologizing more remote ancestors as they slipped from personal recollections. In the greater part of the world, not excluding the majority of people in those lands where literacy eventually came to claim a stake, this limitation prevailed for additional thousands of years. But another, implicit, history, probably rarely rationalized as such, was passed across the generations in the form of the mores and folkways as well as the inherited language of each society. And this was enough for the social and psychological needs of people before the rise of complex societies with fissioning social roles, proliferating statuses, and the emergence of religious, political, and other educated elites or clerisies. In most such societies, as ascertained by archaeological and ethnohistorical evidence, lives were shorter than their later realized potential and cultural change was commonly sluggish. For most of humanity's career, each generation's experiences were pretty much what its forebears had been, even if for each individual those experiences loomed large under the concentrated attention engendered by limited horizons and short tenure. In the grand scheme of things, not much happened to foster a chronology beyond "when mother was a girl," "when our grandfather killed the crazy man," "before the old chief's house burned down," or "in the dream time." And in a great many, and perhaps most, such societies, time was circular. What went before comes again.

Only in historical recency in Mediterranean environs, culminating in Western Europe and among its paradigm-sharing acolytes as they arose in other parts of the world, was this fundamentally parochial, essentially pragmatic, repetitively inclined, and contracting temporality usurped. This was made possible by the rise of a specialized, ultimately professional, coterie that gradually developed the idea of an objective purview of the human past while struggling to acquire the enabling means. That reach often exceeded grasp does not detract from the unique breach with all previous conceptions of history this usurpation represented. The new means affording that reach, and breach, were precipitated out of the Renaissance and its rejuvenated interest in Classical Greece and Rome, the Age of Discovery, the Reformation, and the Enlightenment. These were followed by developments in philology and historical linguistics; the birth and dawning recognition of the implications of stratigraphic and historical geology, paleontology, and evolutionary biology; and innovations in the posing of historical (*sensu stricto*), anthropological, and folkloric questions. Seeing connections among these phenomena encouraged the search for maximum agreement among independent types of evidence or, equally critically, failures of anticipated convergences that might signal error. The greater the redundancy of the former, or the fewer of the latter, the higher the confidence researchers could place on their conclusions. Together, and in conjunction with mathematics, psychology, physics, chemistry, and their sister disciplines, this coalition of intellectual enterprises has attained preeminence in the study of the world, its inhabitants, and their history. In both historical and contemporary global perspectives, as Ernest Gellner (1988) has argued at length, through a kind of cultural ecological natural selection, Western science and historiography have achieved a hitherto and elsewhere unparalleled independence from religious and other extraneous considerations in the pursuit of objective knowledge. Although that independence and resulting reliability is considered by some critics as more a matter of degree than of kind, the magnitude of that degree challenges the pragmatic relevance of the criticism (see Carneiro 2000:74–82; Kuznar 1997:17–65, 148–152, 159–172, 213–219; Rescher 1997).

But for a concatenation of reasons, that hard-won freedom from extraneous constraints on scientific and historical inquiry has lately come under critical and even hostile challenge once more. Although those reasons include legitimate intellectual concerns, such as the influence of class and gender bias on theory and praxis, others are of a more mundane character embedded in a general reaction against perceptions of unfair allocations of wealth, authority, and power in contemporary society. Of most immediate relevance here is "anti-colonial" or "anti-neo-colonial" resentment of archaeology's, anthropology's, and Western historiography's perceived privileged epistemological status vis-à-vis that of other claimants to historical knowledge. This resentment, building on an inchoate but growing public sense of guilt over past treatment of native peoples, has attracted enough political support to affect legislation having pragmatic consequences. With significant numbers of archaeologists and other anthropologists counted among its supporters, the most dramatic example of that success to date in the United States has been the passage and implementation of the Native American Graves Protection and Repatriation Act, usually referred to by the acronym NAGPRA. Whatever its virtues—an inexhaustible topic of controversy in itself—this governmental action has also brought about unintended results of a more questionable and even dangerous character. Not least among them has been the obfuscation of critical distinctions between what is and what is not knowable about the indigenous American past and the roles of archaeology and oral traditions in addressing that issue.

This book examines these and related matters, among them the arguments of many of my professional colleagues, as well as Native Americans, who are concerned with recapturing for oral histories and, most critically, oral traditions a reinvigorated voice, if not the pivotal role anciently enjoyed in the depiction of histories in nonliterate societies. Notwithstanding undoubted merits, some of their proposals invite restoration of the justifiably superseded (e.g., Biolsi and Zimmerman 1997; Kehoe 1998:212–214; Thomas 2000; Wylie 2002:242–244). As I hope to show, such a restoration would be counterproductive as well as contrary to the very freedom of inquiry its proponents espouse. Thus science and systematic historiography, never totally at home in popular culture whose largesse otherwise helps sustain them, today find themselves cajoled, not always gently, to acknowledge as legitimate types of knowledge claims the repudiation of which has been indispensable to their present attainments.

Nevertheless, categorical denial that historical information is to be found in the traditions of oral or formerly oral societies is no more defensible than unqualified claims to the contrary. Either pronouncement assumes a priori what cannot be known in advance of investigation. Before such an undertaking, however, one must be prepared for the likelihood that mixed, ambiguous, or uncertain results will be more common than definitive ones. There are several reasons that recommend such an expectation. Most obviously, archaeologists and historians cannot expect the annals of oral or folk societies to parallel their own ideas of historical assumptions, standards of evidence, logical structure, type of contents, or mode of exposition. Indeed, what counts as proof or justification for believing recountings of the past varies among societies. Furthermore, accounts of former times in nonliterate societies and in archaic stages of literate ones typically include stories of incredible events and fantastic characters, so much so as to dishearten many a researcher from trying to disentangle possible fact from borderline plausibilities accompanied by patent fiction. Of course, the employment of adjectives like *incredible* and *fantastic* or comparable superlatives reflects the plausibility judgments of persons of a modern, literate, scientific bent, not those of the tradition tellers. But it is incumbent on the former to acknowledge that others reared in different cultures may have quite divergent understandings of when those adjectives are appropriate. While people everywhere make distinctions between the extraordinary and the commonplace, the criteria they employ are not necessarily universal. Similarly, terms like *history, plausibility,* or *science,* or their closest analogs, are not likely to be semantically equivalent across all cultural frontiers.

Although discussed at great length in the following chapters, these fundamental anthropological facts are preliminarily raised here because they are obscured, glossed over, and even ignored in some archaeological publications reviewed in this volume. A traditional story of world beginnings or tribal migrations recited as a meant-to-be-believed truthful "history" by a respected community elder is not to be demeaned because it would fail to pass muster as academic "history." The two are different enterprises whether or not they exhibit areas of convergence. It thus should be understood that the uses of the aforementioned adjectives and nouns in what follows conform to standard English-language usage except where context or explicit exception signals otherwise.

In advance of more extended treatment later, an initial explication of the dichotomy *oral history/oral tradition* will be useful for what follows. The first of these terms is applicable to verbal testimonies having a maximum time depth limited by the recollections of the oldest living member of a society; they are attestations of personally witnessed things and events. Oral traditions, however, are heirlooms of accumulated memories; purporting to maintain the remembrances of ancestors no longer around to speak for themselves, they thereby are intrinsically more inviting of cautious reception by prehistoric archaeologists. Like written or documentary history, oral histories and oral traditions are usually distinguished *by their curators* from fiction. Unfortunately, as already mentioned, it is not always clear to outsiders of any of these genres just how and where to draw the line between fact and fiction.

Even though it is the case that movements to "reform" archaeology by "broadening" its purview through the incorporation of "traditional" knowledge or "other ways of knowing" about the past are represented in different nations around the world, my main focus is on North America above the Rio Grande, the region I know best. But because most of the seminal studies of oral traditions and genealogies, the nature of orality, the impact of writing on historical thinking, social and verbatim memory, the structure of myths, the classification of folktales, and much else germane to understanding the North American material have been made in Europe, Africa, and other parts of the Old World, a good deal of information from those other regions is necessarily included in the presentation that follows. Much of this will doubtless be as unfamiliar to the student of native North American societies as it was to me when I first developed an interest in the relationship of archaeology and oral traditions. I hope it will prove as fascinating to the reader as I have found it to be.

Salient in at least this latter region is the demand levied on archaeologists via NAGPRA and other federal, state, or provincial mandates, and by tribal officials on reservation lands, to consider aboriginal oral traditions as encapsulating historical content—in the modern Western sense of that term—even if purportedly disguised in metaphorical, figurative, or allegorical language (see Chapter 2). That many of these officials and agencies represent political power and command the purse strings of cultural resource management (CRM) archaeology, by far the majority type of archaeological field projects, amplifies the decibel level of their involvement somewhat above that of cerebral discourse. This fact tends to rivet attention.

My principal concerns in this study are those assertions of oral tradition historicity, how they are to be evaluated, and what role they should play in archaeological reconstructions of the Native American past. By way of introducing those concerns, I want to emphasize that I do not challenge the legitimacy of the former *in their own cultural contexts.* Nor am I averse to the right of Indians or archaeologists or anyone else to appeal to indigenous myths, legends, or other traditions for possible insights into historical or prehistorical questions—provided, that is, that justification for such appeals is couched in terms compatible with the intelligibility requirements of Western historiography. Furthermore, I have no wish to deny Indian claims that their own historical perspectives are equally valid with, or even superior to, those deriving from the Euroamerican scholarly tradition, *insofar as such claims are understood as bound to the indigenous milieu of which they are a part.* However, I do most emphatically quarrel with conceding such equality, let alone superiority, in the context of archaeological and historiographic theory and practice. Indeed, I argue for their decided inferiority *in that milieu.* Lest this contrast be misunderstood as simply a facile reassertion of the doctrine of cultural relativism, I do mean to assert the epistemological superiority of the Western or Euroamerican achievement in reconstructing human (and indeed, universal) history over all its predecessors and contemporary would-be rivals. The former is and does what the latter are not and cannot do: it is critically reflexive and evidence-bound, and it is capable of comprehending the others in their own terms while concurrently deconstructing them in a search for whatever of their component elements may be testable by independent methods. For this very reason, I take claims to the contrary as requiring close inspection and, where based on rational grounds and not the nihilistic dogma of "our history is as true as anybody else's," the courtesy of challenge. Of course, Western science and historiography, particularly as represented in modern archaeology, are neither error-free nor capable of addressing every question students of the human past would like to pose. Limited and flawed as they are, they nonetheless provide the surest access to that past yet devised if something more is wanted than "preservation" of cherished traditional versions of it. Apropos of this observation, Roger Anyon and his coauthors (1997:80) are quite right and unwittingly supportive of this view when they complain of archaeology that it "has little meaning to Indians as a way to enhance oral tradition itself within a traditional cultural context." How could it? The two pursue separate purposes.

Some Examples of Archaeology and Oral Traditions at Cross-Purposes

In 1999 the U.S. Department of the Interior's National Park Service released a public relations publication entitled *The Federal Archeology Program 1996–97, Secretary of the Interior's Report to Congress.* Under the "overall guidance" of Francis P. McManamon, chief archaeologist and manager of the federal program, the report was meant both to serve a popular audience and to constitute "a credible document" (Andrews and Flanagan 1999:67). It must be understood in those terms—that is, simultaneously simple and worthy of public acceptance. Among its contents is a brief commentary by Sharon Hatch on pictographs in the Falls Creek Archaeological Area in

Colorado administered by the Forest Service. This informs readers that site managers and archaeologists "didn't know anything about the traditional significance of the images," which generally are difficult to date and which occur in an area that had been occupied over nearly a thousand years, but that modern Indians do. How they do is left unsaid, as are reasons for believing them. Nevertheless, according to the writer, advisors from 26 different tribes and the New Mexico Indian Tourism Association, representing nearly as many separate languages drawn from among a good half dozen linguistic phyla or macro-families, were able to provide "information on clans, migrations, and events expressed in the symbols." Whose opinions took precedence in so variegated an assemblage of "advisors"—one could hardly expect unanimity—is not reported. Nevertheless, the advisors also said that "traditional oral history should inform all interpretation," although (some of?) "the images contain sensitive information." Readers are assured this advice will be followed. The conclusion is drawn that "tribal elders and traditional advisors . . . *are our best, and only, teachers*" (Hatch 1999; emphasis added).

Elsewhere, Patricia A. Dean and Clayton F. Marler (2001) argue for the incorporation of Shoshone spirituality in archaeological theory and practice. While they acknowledge variability in Shoshone beliefs and behaviors (not least as exemplified by the "heterogeneously composed" Wind River Shoshones), they urge researchers to follow their example in employing such beliefs and behaviors in their interpretation of archaeological remains. The earnestness of their recommendation notwithstanding, the three discrete examples they cite from their own work, involving the recovery of a bundle of cropped human hair, a cradleboard, and some unspecified human remains, should be thought of as equivalent to experiments in need of completion and replication rather than as tested prescriptions worthy of adoption. What they offer are ethnographic analogies that may or may not have anything to do with their archaeological discoveries. They point out interesting possibilities but pay insufficient attention to interpretive traps. Greater familiarity with the extensive literature on problems of analogical reasoning in archaeology, reams of which were written in the last several decades of the twentieth century, might have helped them avoid some of those traps. Interested readers might wish to consult a useful review of many of the issues in that literature since published by Alison Wylie (2002:136–153).

Most saliently in this case, information about the age or ages of the archaeological discoveries is not provided in Dean and Marler's discussion, not even the crude distinction between historic and prehistoric. Nor is any justification advanced for invoking as relevant historical and ethnographic

Shoshone soul beliefs in "enhancing" understanding of the archaeological finds, other than the implication that because the pertinent sites are located in southeastern Idaho those people must somehow be implicated. Did no other native people ever use that territory? Operationally, the authors presume not. They advise that, following laboratory studies, prehistoric *potsherds* from other sites in the same region should be returned for reburial to the sites from which they came, such reburials to be accompanied with "appropriate prayers and rituals" of the Shoshone. This "enhanced appreciation for Shoshone spirituality" is offered as an example of "collaborative research" between archaeologists and Indians and as a possible way to reconcile conflicting cultural values.

In a previous publication I volunteered "easy"—that is, not to be dismissed without more credible counterarguments—examples of insights contemporary or historically reported Native Americans can sometimes provide investigators about otherwise unobtainable "meanings" of certain classes of archaeological features. The examples chosen were identifications of a particular subset of large petroforms or stone outline figures found on the northern plains (Mason 2000:249). As reported by Thomas F. Kehoe and Alice B. Kehoe (1959), firsthand knowledge claims of elderly native informants and information derived from even older but similar second-hand accounts in ethnographic and historical documents attributed various of the figures to Blackfoot, Crow, Mandan, and Sioux makers. Moreover, those same testimonies sometimes even specified what certain "monuments" had been intended to signify. In the absence of contradictory information, these "identifications" seemed worthy of tentative acceptance.

Although not constituting a blanket rebuttal of the foregoing attributions, a more recent, if brief, report by Carlos German (1998) of the Saskatchewan Museum of Natural History on his involvement in the "repatriation" of such stone outline figures in that province introduces a strong caution. In addition to the information that contemporary First Nations people hold all petroform sites as sacred, whether or not archaeologists regard the Saskatchewan examples specifically as prehistoric, they also consider the individual rocks composing them to be "living, animate objects." Despite this consensus, German learned that "traditional knowledge concerning their [the petroforms'] function range[s] from commemorative memorials to special events or individuals; monuments for marking burials, territorial boundaries, or battles; or directional markers to water sources or places of (physical or spiritual) safety."

Discovering disagreement among American Indians or anybody else about this or that is hardly news. But if more than opinion surveys are sought, more than opinions are required to separate grains of historical fact from folkloric chaff. Relying on evidentially unsupported beliefs in such matters, while of indubitable value to folklorists and to ethnographers trying to see the world as their informants do, is otherwise than by happy accident a wasteful diversion in the search for a trustworthy past. Whose opinions should command respect in the absence of external data suitable for ranking them? Much of this book is concerned with that problem and the sometime failure of archaeologists to confront it. Of course, archaeology is not alone in the resulting discomfort, as many an ethnographer can attest.

Who, for instance, may rightfully claim residential priority at the Fort Belknap Reservation established as recently as the late nineteenth century on and south of the Milk River in north-central Montana? Gros Ventres or Assiniboines? Members of the two tribes have lived there since then. In her study of the reservation's modern descendants of the people originally settled there, ethnographer Loretta Fowler (1987) encountered strongly, and apparently honestly, held contradictory views about who was first at that locale. Even though sometimes representing themselves to themselves as well as to the outside world as one people, most residents on the reservation alternately also think of themselves as Gros Ventres or Assiniboines, even though intermarriages, including with whites, are and have been common for several generations. Notwithstanding many intertwined family lines, even today Fowler, as an outsider, was impressed by their cultural differences. Among the differences subsisting between them, *as perceived by the people themselves,* were self-congratulatory "observations" on one's own tribal superiority vis-à-vis the other in personal dependability, industry, charity, morality, spirituality, respect for the old traditions, and, among still other things, history. With regard to the latter, each tribe has its own "here first" story insisting on its primacy as original inhabitants of the reservation and on its having welcomed and succored the late-coming and in-need-of-support other (Fowler 1987:197–232). Each group's claim is of course "verified" by its own oral traditions. Any outside historian or ethnographer who would rely exclusively on those sources of information would simply hit an impasse. Or something more disturbing, as in the following.

Amy Dansie (1999), in a sensitive essay on some of the dilemmas frustrating would-be reconcilers of Western scientific and traditional Native American epistemologies, specifically in the contentious arena of NAGPRA negotiations, prefaces her own face-to-face encounter with that "something more disturbing" when she writes: "One thing I have learned to face is that Indian people who hold to traditional understandings of the universe do not agree with my culture's definition of reality. The physical facts I accept as valid evidence of time, physical appearance, genetic relationship, cultural affiliation, and historic continuity of human populations around the planet are rejected by some Native Americans in favor of a view that the creator made each group of people independently, and that they never moved from their place of origin. I do not believe it is disrespectful to doubt such assertions that are simply not defensible in the real world of human history." Now the "something more disturbing": "At a major consultation meeting with the Northern Paiute and Shoshone in November 1997, I tried to ask about the abundant documented evidence of their own oral history which included battles between the Paiute and other people in the Lahontan Basin. *I was told that those stories were not the real Paiute history, only lies told to white people. They could not share their sacred knowledge to explain why these stories, steadfastly maintained as fact until nine years ago, were not real anymore.* I understand open defiance of science, but not at the expense of factual history" (Dansie 1999:31–32; emphasis added).

One would like to think this last experience, while not unique in the annals of anthropology, would be relatively rare. That complication apart, it is the recurring matters of divergence in how people in different societies think about historical knowledge—rather than particularistic emphasis on the details of past happenings, although some of these will receive some notice in later chapters—that more imperatively command attention.

In 2000 I published an article in the journal *American Antiquity* on the several arguments students of American Indians typically employ for and against the incorporation of native oral traditions in the reconstruction of culture histories. These arguments include, accompanied here by my abbreviated criticisms in that article in parentheses, for the pro side:

1. Oral traditions are as valid as scientific statements about the past and should be treated equally with them (but the first are sanctioned by heritage, the second by critical reasoning and empiricism);
2. Even nonliterate people are bound to know their own histories better than outsiders can (but with respect to oral tradition, their reciters do not "know" their ancestors' histories but only what they have been told by their proximate progenitors);
3. Because they are emic phenomena, oral traditions are not challengeable on their own grounds and should be accepted as evidence accordingly (evidence of what? Of course, *on their own cultural grounds* they are inviolable to external challenge, whereas they surrender that inviolability when intruded into scientific discourse);
4. Whole blocks of past time are known exclusively through oral traditions (in that case, whatever traditions assert is unverifiable, unfalsifiable, and worthless *as history*);

5. Verbal and written accounts of the past are equally valid, each simply addressing differing "realities" ("reality," by definition is a unity, totality, actuality; that some people may have different ideas about what is "real" is another issue, but one that does not confer equal ontological value to those different ideas);

6. In those areas where archaeology and oral traditions overlap, their combination offers a richer view than either can alone (it is, of course, intrinsically interesting to compare varying visions of the past, especially so where they are independently testable—as in the case of the Ridge Ruin investigation [McGregor 1943; Mason 2000:251–252]);

7. Because archaeology grew out of the Western cultural tradition, it is by its nature ethnocentric and should be augmented or even replaced by "alternative histories" (this charge commits the genetic fallacy of confusing epistemological issues in historiography with the facts of cultural history; that aside [and linked to the foregoing pro argument 6] there is undoubted value in the reminder that different perspectives can enhance understanding of "what happened in history").

In addition to the pro assertions (and condensed rebuttals) just reviewed, the negative arguments in my article may be briefly summarized as follows:

1. Contingent as they are on memory, the veracity of oral traditions must be regarded as highly dubious;

2. Oral traditions reflect the concerns of their contemporary reciters more than conditions and events of the past (societies require stories that meet present needs, not the arcane curiosity of pedants);

3. Oral traditions are emic and thus, *on their own grounds,* largely impervious to external challenge (this is a somewhat expanded statement of the initiating affirmation in pro argument 3 [above], there fallaciously employed in justifying claims to evidential parity with scientific evidence);

4. Typically, parts if not all of oral traditions are regarded by their believers as sacred, not to be freely accessed by outsiders having purposes potentially at odds with the tradition keepers; the enforcement of this linkage puts blinders on researchers.

Much of what follows discusses these arguments at greater length, sometimes expanding them to encompass additional perspectives deserving more scrutiny than was possible in the earlier publication. These and related points of contention no longer command only academic attention. Growing interest in them, linked as they are in the wider public with issues of civil liberties, minority rights, and religious versus educational and scientific freedoms—as in the evolution/creation science or intelligent design tussles, NAGPRA issues, and the Kennewick Man controversy (the latter two discussed below)—is well attested in lay as well as professional publications. Besides archaeology, the fields of ethnology, social anthropology, sociology, social psychology, history, political science, and, increasingly, jurisprudence and public policy are also affected. But inasmuch as I am here addressing the archaeology–oral tradition relationship primarily, I have confined myself as much as possible to that arena. That this intention will here and there be breached is a consequence of the wider worlds of political and economic interests sometimes intruding themselves into what ideally should be independent of them. Conversely, the reader will detect occasional extrusions from other scholarly discussions having broader ramifications. The two tend to coexist, as the obverse and reverse faces of a coin.

For instance, archaeologist David Hurst Thomas (2000), in an attempt to bridge the sometimes opposed interests of archaeologists and Indian traditional-culture guardians, asserted that those oppositions "cannot be seen as a simple conflict between modern science and traditional religion." Whether he meant the adjective *simple* to signify the nonexistence of the issue as so stated or, more complexly, that it is not the only one, Thomas (2000:257) is unequivocal in stating his belief that what is at stake is "a struggle for control of American Indian history." He is sympathetic to assertions by certain Indians and their confederates that the discipline of archaeology has resulted in "scientific desecration of Indian spiritual life" and "has robbed the Native American people of their history and their dignity" (Thomas 2000:257). Fundamentalist Christians and Moslems, among others, make similar complaints about science generally, I would add.

In atonement for these alleged sins of his profession, Thomas proffers an olive branch of terminological and other concessions, concessions that those of his colleagues who find the charges overblown rhetoric are unlikely to endorse. Explicitly conceded are (1) a role for Indians, whose possession or lack of archaeological qualifications is not addressed, in determining how his discipline should be redefined (Thomas 2000:xxxv); (2) the appropriateness of unnecessarily contemptuous jargon by some Indian traditional-culture activists and even certain archaeologists in characterizing as "the archaeological party line" the deservedly long-held, but now quite properly challenged, thesis that the earliest inhabitants of the New World were the makers of Clovis projectile points (Thomas 2000:168); (3) that Indians must "recapture their own language, culture, and history" from "non-Indian historians and anthropologists" who, according to the former's revanchist-style reasoning, have stolen them by studying them (Thomas 2000:xxxiv); and (4) that archaeologists should acquiesce in the censoring of certain words in their technical vocabulary when, as in the cases of "Anasazi" and "prehistoric," for instance, some Indians find them offensive. For this latter reason, as well as his willingness to grant historical veracity carte blanche to Indian oral traditions, Thomas avows that "except for direct quotes from historical sources, you'll not find the word 'prehistoric' anywhere in this [Thomas 2000] book." After all, he unqualifiedly affirms, "most tribes maintain rich oral traditions, which describe in detail their remote past" (Thomas 2000: 206). How those details are known and just how remote is that past are as unaddressed as the warrants for their reliability. Equally unremarked is the irony intrinsic to the thievery charge in the third complaint. That irony is essentially identical to what Alexander von Gernet (2000:106) has noted in another context: "Curiously, Aboriginal intellectuals who see the use of oral traditions by Western historians as a form of cultural appropriation have themselves appropriated the discourse of Western postmodernism to make the argument."

Thomas's views, for all their concessions, are relatively moderate in the ideologically inflamed crisis of late twentieth–early twenty-first century anthropology and social thought. More radical positions have been staked out by critics within and outside of archaeology currently inveighing against what they see as the intolerable hegemony of inhumane ("cold") Western scientific thought over humane (presumably not cold) Native American thought (e.g., Allison 2000; Cook-Lynn 2001; Custer 2001a, 2001b; V. Deloria 1997a, 1997b; Jamieson 1999; Stapp and Longenecker 2000a, 2000b, for just a few recent examples of this genre).

The less egregious stance Thomas has taken is shared by a substantial number of academic and cultural resource management archaeologists and other interested commentators. Among them are proponents of what is coming to be called "indigenous archaeology," whereby traditional American Indian beliefs are somehow to be melded with science in the practice of a new archaeology (e.g., Echo-Hawk 1997, 2000; Watkins 1998, 2000; Whiteley 2002). Although the broad aims of such scholars are similar, they have not attained unanimity in just how to go about achieving them. Given the philosophical and methodological difficulties in doing so, let alone the emotional freight often accompanying contemplation of the effort, this is hardly surprising (see the exchanges among Allison [2000], Stapp and Longenecker [2000a, 2000b], and Watkins [1998], denouncing the elevation of the scientific method to primacy in archaeology, and Clark [1998], Funk [2001], and Lepper [2000], defending it). What has been put forward to date in support of rapprochement between contending advocates of culturally distinct "ways of knowing" is often platitudinous (be respectful and look for common ground), intellectually bankrupt (archaeologists have stolen Indians' pasts; any belief about the past is as good as any other), or an earnest mixture of sense and nonsense, thus rendering concise appraisal premature. But some of the stumbling blocks are clear enough. They are both daunting and, if ignored, as they often are, dangerous. They will be encountered in numerous metamorphoses in the following pages. They have cropped up, with varying degrees of critical evaluation, in recent collaborative publications examining the strained relations between archaeologists and other anthropologists and Indians (e.g., Biolsi and Zimmerman 1997; Dongoske et al. 1997; Dongoske et al. 2000; Nelson and Kehoe 1990; Nicholas and Andrews 1997; Schmidt and Patterson 1995; Swidler et al. 1997).

Certain of Joe Watkins's proposals, put forward by a man who is both a professional archaeologist and an American Indian, illustrate something of the tension between wants and means. Like Thomas, Watkins characterizes the relations between archaeologists and Indians as "a war over the heritage of that [Native American] world." The two sides "are battling over the physical and spiritual control of one of America's earliest inhabitants [Kennewick Man]." Watkins (2000:180) says, "Perhaps this is one of those battles that archaeologists [but evidently not Indians] need to reexamine." The proper resolution of this "war," Watkins suggests, is for Western science, by which he specifically means archaeology, to accept an increased presence of extraneous restraints on accustomed freedom of inquiry and to "blend" itself with "non-Western beliefs concerning the philosophy of the past." Watkins caricatures archaeology as "an esoteric science" that "neatly sorts pot shards and arrowheads into even rows" and forgets that the people who made those things were real people—something that he says Indians, contrary to many of their oral traditions, I would point out, never forget. Archaeology's lack of "a spirit of humanity" can be corrected by the development of indigenous archaeology. That new discipline "refuses to be 'objective' and embraces the emotional [component?], one that pursues not 'truth' but understanding" (Watkins 2000:180–181). Asserting that archaeologists are not "passionate" (one wonders how many professional meetings Watkins has attended) and like only "cold facts" as opposed to Indians' liking for "things outside of the demonstrable world," Watkins (1998:23) argues that science and religion are "intertwined" and that "neither should exist without the other." His faith-based archaeology is emphatic in averring the nonexistence of such a thing as "disinterested evaluation of knowledge claims" (Watkins 1998:23). But this is a fallacious assertion; by rejecting the possibility of objective—disinterested—knowledge, the author has removed any rational grounds for accepting his own arguments.

Indigenous archaeology, whether of the Watkins variety or some other, will have Indians controlling when, where, and how archaeological research is to be conducted on Indian lands, an authority they already largely exercise by law; Indians will be encouraged to become professional archaeologists, presumably of the indigenous persuasion; and Indian control of museum collections will be expanded, a development already well under way by virtue of NAGPRA, especially as its provisions have been interpreted by the National Park Service of the Department of the Interior and the U.S. Army Corps of Engineers (see below). In the new archaeology, Indian oral traditions about tribal pasts apparently are to be respected as containing a core of historical truth, although often metaphorically disguised, comparable to what is found in Western scientific or historiographic writings. Despite Watkins's sincere appeal for scientific archaeologists and the upholders of traditional knowledge to work together as much as possible for their common advantage, an appeal no sensible person could reject, its implementation is another matter. Sovereign irreconcilabilities (e.g., Indians are descendants of hominids that evolved in the Old World versus their having been created in America) must either be surrendered or a modus vivendi of agreeing to disagree openly accepted. It is hard to escape the conclusion that the archaeology in "indigenous archaeology" will be subordinated to the "greater good" of reforming itself into what might be called an ideological social service, one compatible with cherished Native American attitudes and beliefs. (See Anyon et al. 1997:85–86 and Sheridan 2002 for instances of how, by restricting scholars' access to oral traditions and other information, even when collected with the support of federal grant money, the possibility of exposing incompatibility between science and tradition is disallowed a priori.)

That these tensions between scientific archaeology and Native American traditional knowledge in reconstructing the prehistoric past are of more than arcane concern is illustrated by the contemporary intrusion of political pressure and even governmental mandates into the relationship. Two especially conspicuous recent examples, one still ongoing, show how scientific knowledge can be subordinated to those intrusions in areas of public policy and the investigation of irreplaceable bioarchaeological remains in a case in which such knowledge would otherwise be unchallenged. Equally to be regretted in these examples is the exploitation of indigenous oral traditions, aided and abetted by some of their own guardians, to serve purposes properly those of Western historiography for which traditional narratives were never intended and which, when pressed into service, are caricatured thereby.

The first of these instances concerns prehistoric Pueblo (Anasazi) ruins in the Southwest. Ostensibly on the basis of their tribal legends, tales unsupported, indeed sometimes contradicted, by archaeological, linguistic, and ethnohistoric information, the National Park Service determined that the Navajo Indians are "culturally affiliated" with Anasazi archaeological remains, at least with respect to Chaco Canyon National Park (Nicastro 2000). Thereby, the Navajos were granted a privileged voice in matters of Anasazi site curation and repatriation of sacred and other items of cultural patrimony not their own. This decision was made after consultation with a small panel of Indians, archaeologists, bureaucrats, and other private citizens known as the NAGPRA Review Committee (for background, see Bray 2001 and King 1998; for animadversion of that law and its likely consequences, Clark 1998; for their defense, Watkins 1998). The Hopi Indians, a known Anasazi cultural descendant tribe, were understandably outraged at this travesty. Their representative to the NAGPRA committee, Leigh Kuwanwisima, complained to it that "we were surprised by the park's determination that a non-puebloan tribe is culturally affiliated with Hopi puebloan ancestral remains. . . . When you begin to mix in political elements, you do not do justice to the law" (quoted in Nicastro 2000:70).

The second example is the infamous case of Kennewick Man, the approximately 9,000-year-old skeleton eroded out of the bank of the Columbia River in Washington in 1996. Well-preserved human remains of this antiquity are rare and can provide invaluable information on an otherwise hardly known population of the earliest Americans (Chatters 2001). Almost as soon as news of the discovery became known, and before more than preliminary inspection of the bones and the site could be definitively expanded, Indian traditional-culture advocates demanded both the cessation of any studies that might be under way and custody of the remains in order to rebury them. The Army Corps of Engineers, having responsibility for navigable waters, peremptorily stepped in, took possession of the bones, and reburied the site in such a way as to severely limit if not destroy any possibility of future scientific excavation. This was done in the face of legislation then known to be pending in Congress to protect the site. The Department of the Interior, also exercising jurisdiction in the affair, responded to Indian pressure and scientists' complaints by joining with the Corps to store the bones and restrict scientific access to both bones and site pending legal resolution of the issues. At the same time, potentially physically contaminating religious rites were permitted to be held over the bones by groups of Indians as well as Euroamericans claiming some sort of Medieval Scandinavian religious connection to Kennewick Man. Following prolonged negotiations with the government agencies, and against Indian wishes, a few archaeologists and biological anthropologists were given permission to conduct further tests on the human remains, although not as freely and extensively as they would have liked or as the age of the remains made desirable. At various times the bones were stored, and some misplaced, in a local sheriff's lockup, and they were transported to the Washington State Museum where, under tight security, these further studies took place. The Interior Department's National Park Service took it upon itself to decide what scientists could and could not participate.

A coalition of five regional Indian tribes had quickly formed following the discovery to make their will known and to press for the prohibition of scientific studies. They did this notwithstanding the news, widely publicized, that Kennewick Man's skull was at first thought to be that of an early nineteenth-century white man or, subsequently, that the skull bore a greater resemblance to early, in the sense of ancient, Pacific rim inhabitants than to modern Native Americans and that there was an absence of associated cultural evidence that might suggest affiliation with any existing tribes or their likely ancestors. Clearly, some of the more militant traditional-culture defenders in the coalition saw an opportunity to create a cause célèbre embarrassing to the larger culture's accustomed authority.

Finding himself in an uncomfortable position attendant on the national publicity the dispute had generated, Bruce Babbitt, Secretary of the Interior in the Clinton administration, at last came to a decision. In a letter to the Corps of Engineers, Babbitt announced that his advisors had persuaded him that "the geographic and *oral tradition* evidence establishes a reasonable link between these remains and the present-day Indian tribe claimants" (quoted in *Science* 2000; emphasis mine)! By this letter the Secretary reopened the door to Indian possession and reburial of those remains. This attempted resolution of the problem was promptly challenged in court by a small group of archaeologists and physical (biological) anthropologists (Custred 2000, 2002). After six years of legal wrangling and the compilation and exhaustive review of 22,000 pages of administrative record, the District Court for the District of Oregon found for the plaintiff scientists against the Corps of Engineers and the Interior Department (Opinion and Order Civil No. 96-1481-J). However, this ruling was appealed by the concerned tribes. Alan Schneider, lead attorney for the scientists, thereupon estimated another two to seven years for a final resolution of the case, during which time he assumed no further studies of the remains would be allowed (American Committee for Preservation of Archaeological Collections [ACPAC] 2002). On February 4, 2004, a three-judge panel of the U.S. Court of Appeals for the Ninth Circuit upheld the original court ruling. This latest legal decision (D. C. No. CV-96-01481-JE [No. 02-35994]), which for a while appeared to possibly face further appeal either to a larger panel of Ninth Circuit judges or to the Supreme Court itself (Lepper 2004:19), has instead been threatened with potential obsolescence via a further research-restricting amendment to the NAGPRA law introduced in the Senate Indian Affairs Committee by John McCain of Arizona (ACPAC 2005; Holden 2005). At the time of this writing it remains possible that further years will be added to the antiquity of Kennewick Man before his legal fate is sealed and his potential contributions to ancient American history will either be released for what they have to say or, to that history's detriment, will be forbidden expression altogether.

An Umatilla religious leader who has also served on the NAGPRA Re-view Committee, in a tribal position paper published in the *Tri-City Herald* newspaper on October 27, 1996, wrote: "If this individual [Kennewick Man] is truly over 9,000 years old, that only substantiates our belief that he is Native American. From our oral histories, we know that our people have been part of this land since the beginning of time. . . . Some scientists say that if this individual is not studied further, we, as Indians, will be destroy-ing evidence of our own history. We already know our history. It is passed on to us through our elders and through our religious practices" (quoted in Watkins 2000:136–137).

The foregoing quotations are the words of two late-twentieth-century literate persons occupying important positions and having available to them expert advice and boundless sources of information. They are not pre-Columbian or serfdom-bound Medieval illiterates isolated in their own time and place, thereby barred from the knowledge of the modern world. With respect to the latter quotation, I am reminded of Walter Ong's (1982: 53) thought when contemplating a similar rote reaction to new situations by a young illiterate peasant in the former Soviet Union: "There is no way to refute the world of primary orality. All you can do is walk away from it into literacy." That peasant had an excuse. But, as just seen, literacy is not enough. Its potential requires exercise. As with biblical fundamentalists, the ultimate source of knowledge to Indian traditionalists cited by the Umatilla religious leader is self-contained and independent of external authority. It stands on its own (see also Anyon et al. 1997:78, 80–82, and Echo-Hawk 1997:89 on this point). Thereby science cannot possibly bar people from adhering to their convictions. Reciprocally, however, it would seem proper for those same tradition holders to respect the right of others to exercise *their* belief in another sort of knowledge: that resulting from scientific in-quiry, one unfortunately crippled by hindered access to the kinds of data peculiar to *its* needs—"Render therefore unto Caesar the things which are Caesar's; and unto God the things that are God's" (Matthew 22:21). Of course, the extenuating circumstance of political expediency can be invoked, at least in Babbitt's case. But if it is, this is further condemnation of the intrusions of extraneous interests into the conclusions of what should be free inquiry.

It will be apparent from the foregoing that some of the issues dealt with in this volume are likely to elicit strong emotional responses from many people in addition to—I hope not instead of—stimulating intellectual consideration. Given these politically correct times, this is as understandable as it is unfortunate. I have accordingly tried to indicate that I hold traditional beliefs to be worthy of respect when and as each is situated within its own milieu. Someone raised in, say, traditional Aleut culture cannot be expected to think like a contemporary logician teaching at a university any more than a Jesuit theologian would reason like a fundamentalist Protestant. These different modes of thought are all interesting and each legitimate on its own premises. Hackles are raised, however, when one infringes on the territory of another. Nevertheless, that is unavoidable when science trespasses onto sensitive areas already occupied by a metaphysical ancien régime. And where the trespass is sanctioned by superior intellectual competitiveness— that is, the intruder outperforms the intruded upon—acclaim is apt to be temporarily partial, with resentment making up the difference.

Just as the oral traditions of a particular society deserve respect for what they are, they risk losing that due respect when taken out of their original context and proffered as a surrogate for something missing in another one. In science and modern historiography, for example, the absence of physical evidence of a flood at an archaeological site is not made up for by a flood myth in the culture of a people thought to be descended from the original occupants of the site, while that evidential lack will probably be of little or no interest to the myth believers. Similarly, the presence of flood deposits at the site would neither be negated by the absence of a flood myth nor, for traditional belief holders, alter their allegiance to the truth value of the myth. The presence or absence of *both* physical evidence and flood tradition may or may not be taken as indicative of reciprocal corroboration, depending on the compatibility and weightiness of other relevant considerations. In the absence of such considerations, the compatibility of flood deposits and flood story, or the compatibility of their equal absence, simply implies the possibility of mutual corroboration without certifying it. There may have been numerous floods in the area of the site, but not the one featured in the myth. The Pima story of the great flood alleged to have overwhelmed the prehistoric Hohokam culture and the culture hero Elder Brother in Arizona comes to mind (see Mason 2000:252–253; Teague 1993:443–444). Even without accessibility of independent sources of information, it is of course quite possible that some elements in oral traditional histories are in

fact true. But bereft of either verifiability or falsifiability, they are historically valueless.

The limited capability of myths and other oral traditions to adapt to
alien sources of information without transforming themselves in the process
is not unvarying. But it is a palpable concern to would-be guardians of traditional cultures. Roger Anyon and his coauthors (1997:78, 83–84) put it
bluntly: "Archaeologists are interested in learning about the past. Native
Americans are interested in maintaining the cultural traditions they inherited from their ancestors who lived in the past." These same cultural guardians assert the limited usefulness if not irrelevance of archaeology with respect to oral traditions even while arguing just the reverse for archaeology
(Anyon et al. 1997:78, 80–82). Although these writers do not speak for all
Indians, they do represent a major and growing faction, especially among
those who put themselves forward as spokespersons for the Native American and/or the penitentially reformed archaeological "communities." Science and folk belief are always uneasy cohabitants of history.

The following chapters will explore this uneasiness. They will confront
sense and nonsense in the past and present of archaeological and oral traditional versions of cultural history, especially as they have been and are urged
into alliances ostensibly aimed at the creation of more inclusive "multivoiced" renderings. Although my focus is on North America, I have concentrated on those culture areas I know best or for which I have been able to
locate particularly coherent accounts in the works of others. To the best of
my ability, I have not slighted areas or problems because I found them uncomfortable to deal with or because I thought they might present data and
arguments that would contradict what I believe to be otherwise true and
defensible. I have attempted to treat with fairness reasoned points of view
not my own and even unreasoned ones held by those whose conditions of
life exempt them from the censures properly owed the more educationally
credentialed. Nor have I hidden or attempted to sugarcoat for the easily
offended my commitment to the science and scientific historiography that,
beginning in the West, but since diffused over most of the world, I regard
as far and away superior to any and all other "ways of knowing" about the
world—ways, that is, that are not concerned with such things as spiritual
values, artistic "truth," national or ethnic celebration, communion with nature, or self-realization.

Because of unclear thinking and slippery usage regarding the term *history*, the next chapter explicitly focuses on its definitions and relevance to
archaeology in which a simple misunderstanding of intended meaning can
easily lead to reading at cross purposes to the writing. The following chapter
explores the topic of memory—individual recollections, with special atten-

tion paid to allegations of verbatim recall, as well as what are sometimes called "cultural," "social," or "collective" memories. Memory, of course, among its many functions, carries the weight of oral tradition. And, among the latter's manifold services are those of sovereign preserver, transmitter, and interpreter of a society's past. When, in those services, however, oral tradition is also entertained, usually by outsiders, as addressing history in the sense of a chronicle amenable to testing for reliability by universal (non-ethnocentric) standards, its Achilles heel is exposed.

Enlisting the previously considered dimensions of history and memory, attention is directed in the succeeding chapter to critical examinations of the three examples of "historically reliable" oral traditions with which I am usually confronted in conversations with friends and colleagues and that, in one form or another, are standard fare in many an archaeological or ancient history textbook. While only one of these specimens touches on the Western Hemisphere (that of the Norse discovery of North America) and the other two concern the Trojan War and certain stories bearing on biblical archaeology, all raise issues relevant to oral traditions and archaeology everywhere, including aboriginal America. After all, the "histories" in these three cases had each been orally related for generations before their transmutations—if not transmogrifications—into the written versions by which we know them. Then, after an examination of the cross-culturally established characteristics of oral traditions as a genre, the remaining chapters explore particular instances of the enlistment of indigenous North American stories about the past in attempts by scholars to augment the always partial evidence of their own disciplines. These conclude with a few words about possibilities of rethinking, adherence to critical standards of logic and evidence evaluation, and endorsement of an already growing movement whereby local historical sensibilities and universal scientific historiography might approach a modus vivendi. Readers will also encounter in these pages examples of Indian and non-Indian traditions having little or no direct, or at least immediately obvious, connection with archaeological or other historical investigations. But each such case harbors serious implications potentially pertinent to those that do.

2

On History

Anyone at all familiar with contemporary intellectual currents must be aware of a widely shared philosophy of radical relativism that denies to all observers, presumably excepting those who articulate that philosophy, the ability to make genuine contact with anything external to themselves. The a priori conclusion of this belief is futility in the search for anything that is not hopelessly distorted by the entrapments of culture, time and place, ideology, and, not least, personal idiosyncracies. If there is a real world "out there," how are we ever to know it? We sit, like Plato's cave dwellers, with our backs to that world (assuming it exists) and speculate on the meaning of its shadows. Note Plato's dates: 427?–347 B.C. He thought he knew a way out of the dilemma. Halfway around the world and a trifle later another philosopher, Chuang Tzu (369?–286 B.C.) posed the puzzle in its most intimate terms thus: "Once Chuang Chou dreamt he was a butterfly, a butterfly flitting and fluttering around, happy with himself and doing as he pleased. He didn't know he was Chuang Chou. Suddenly he woke up and there he was, solid and unmistakable Chuang Chou. But he didn't know if he was Chuang Chou who had dreamt he was a butterfly, or a butterfly dreaming he was Chuang Chou. Between Chuang Chou and a butterfly there must be *some* distinction" (Watson 1964:13).

It must provide comfort to many besides those holding a cyclical view of history to recognize in its modern guise the return of an ancient predicament rather than the birth to innovating thinkers of an idea never thought of before. In its current incarnation, the problem of the relationship of observer to object has become critical in more fields than abstract philosophy. Sociocultural anthropology and literary studies are possessed by the quandary and seem especially eager to surrender all claims to objectivity. And so is much of the historical discipline. The now modish relativism that started out a century ago as a sensible precaution against naive ethnocentrism, and presentism, has been deprived of its rightful value through misuse. Thus exists the current sometime despair—and in some quarters, barely disguised celebration—over the alleged impossibility of writing history that is objective. Once again the old Rankean goal of determining "what really happened" in the past (implying as it does the historian's ability to escape entrapment in his or her own place and time) and seeing things as they once were has been declared dead (for useful, discipline-crossing discussions see Collingwood 1946; Dray 1993; Gellner 1985, 1988; Gibbon 1989; Harvey 1966; Kuznar 1997; Meyerhoff 1959; Nagel 1986; Novick 1988; Rescher 1997; Salzman 2002; Trigger 1989; von Gernet 2000; Wylie 2002).

Of course, the past can only be imagined and never be revisited in any literal sense (although that would be contested by some non-Western peoples holding cyclical views of time or otherwise subscribing to the recurrence of past characters and events in the present and future). And any individual imagining the past cannot escape all the coils of self-interest and contingencies of time, place, personal status, and current ethos. This is as true of chemists, physicists, and other "hard" scientists (Kuhn 1970) as it is of historians, archaeologists, sociologists, literary scholars, or anybody else. How could it be otherwise? But they are not thereby bereft of any possibility of knowing something genuine about the world around them—or even of the ability to correct mistaken notions of the world before their own time (e.g., apposite my comments on Troy in Chapter 4, see Herbert Butterfield [1981:189–190] on the remarkable Lancelot Voisin de la Popeliniere and *his* 1599 views on the alleged post-Homeric Trojan diaspora). Indeed, the very limitations of contingency make possible some degree of reliable apprehension of the world by reducing to something less than overwhelming the influx of perceived signals it emanates. The paleontologist and evolutionary biologist George Gaylord Simpson, in some of his public lectures, observed that natural selection necessarily ensured something other than spurious contact with at least a part of the world external to the individual organism. While we do not and do not need to experience the rich olfactory world of canines, we are aware of the existence of that world and can measure or otherwise characterize it through indirect means. And there are parallels to Simpson's biological observation in the cultural realm. Bruce G. Trigger, citing V. Gordon Childe, has invited attention to the negative potential for human societies of critically limited apprehension of the world *as it really is* (my emphasis). They both have taken note that "human beings adapt to environments not as they occur in nature but as they perceive them to be. Yet, if perception and reality were too discordant, natural selection would quickly eliminate such societies" (Trigger 1989:378).

Reflexivity is a term much in vogue in contemporary social science and literary studies. As most generally used, it labels as prerequisite to minimally biased contemplation of other people, especially people in societies colonized in some manner by one's own, whether living or dead, a rigorous critique of the self-serving interests, prejudices, and ethnocentrisms that can obscure the observer's vision of the "Other." How much of what the anthropologist or historian reports is an ethnocentric or otherwise situational delusion? A projection of his or her assumptions? An imposition of the outsider's construction on to the "Other?" The outsider's view, by definition, can never be identical to the insider's. Therefore, how much of what is reported is in some meaningful sense genuinely out *there*? As discussed by Philip Salzman (2002), some current versions of these useful questions are carried to such extremes that they imply or openly assert the impossibility of objective knowledge of other people or other times. The goal of objectivity, by this view, should be abandoned in favor of a "perspectivist" surrender that ultimately relegates observation and understanding to musings in self-contemplation: the "Other" is not what it is, it is only what we think it is. The concreteness of the "Other," by this strategy, becomes lost in the process of self-interrogation. However, one of anthropology's self-justifications has long been the light that knowledge of other cultures throws on one's own. It is the possibility of sometimes making *objective* distinctions between what "they" think and what "we" think that makes that anthropological claim more than platitudinous and that saves reflexivity from nihilism.

Making a fundamental distinction between Native American and Western or Euroamerican ideas about the nature and course of history has long had currency in anthropology. For example, Charles Hudson (1966) makes that distinction in contrasting "folk history" and "ethnohistory." He uses as his model for that distinction the linguist Kenneth Pike's (1954–1960) dichotomy of "emic" and "etic," after "phonemic" and "phonetic" analyses of languages. In the first, it is the native speakers' recognition of meaningful sound categories that is sought by the analyst. While native English speakers in Kaukauna, Wisconsin, say *bo-at,* they are referring to what other English speakers elsewhere call a *boat,* the difference in sound value conveying no significance vis-à-vis the referent. In phonetic recording, the analyst will hear some sounds the native speaker usually is unaware of. The phonological difference in this example is real, and thus important for phonetic transcription, but it carries no phonemic weight, such as the sound value whereby *b* is distinguished from *c* in the words *boat* and *coat,* respectively. Hudson analogously characterizes folk history as emic history, that is: " 'folk history' . . . denote[s] the historical beliefs of other societies and cultures." It renders what "really happened" in the past as understood by narrators in those other societies and cultures "as judged by *their* sense of credibility and relevance." "Ethnohistory," on the other hand, is an etic enterprise that aims "to reconstruct, using all available materials, what 'really happened' in terms that agree with *our* sense of credibility and *our* sense of relevance" (Hudson 1966:53–54; last two italics mine). Both kinds of history are important. Understanding how members of an American Indian tribe or an aboriginal Australian band or a Polynesian chiefdom or an African kingdom see their own history is incumbent on archaeologists as anthropologists. Those "interior" views of a people's history are as critical to understanding other societies as is their kinship and political organization or their subsistence practices. In one way or another they are a component of every ethnography worthy of the name. To be respected for what they are, such emic or folk histories should not be forced into the foreign mold of etic history or ethnohistory, or vice versa. To do so risks violation of the integrity of each. Sometimes, however, and this is where opportunities and not just troubles reside, the two visions of history overlap, thus offering the possibility of what might metaphorically be called binocular historical vision. I shall return to this prospect in some of the following chapters.

Illustrating his contrast between folk history and ethnohistory, Hudson draws on Nicholas Gubser's 1965 recording of Nunamiut Eskimo or Inuit oral traditions and histories and his discussions with the Nunamiuts about them. Those people divide their history into three categories (my paraphrasing):

1. *Itchaq imma*—the days before the oldest remembered generation of relatives. This time deals with the creation of people and animals and the transformations of things. Although some of these recountings are thought to be *unipquaq* (just imaginative stories), most are regarded as *koliaqtuaq* (true stories). Among the latter are tales of how Raven brought light to the people.
2. *Ipani*—the recent past of personal remembrances; events experienced by the informant or by persons known to him or her. Creation and transformation stories sometimes said to have occurred in this time are generally regarded by people as simply imagined. There are, for instance, disagreements over shamans actually transforming themselves into other things. But a story of a particular shaman escaping enemies by turning himself into a sparrow hawk is regarded as true.
3. *Ingalagaan*—a hazy time between and having elements of the first two.

As indicated by Gubser and by Hudson, there are different standards of credibility regarding evidence considered as appropriate in category 1 narrations as opposed to those in category 2. Hudson (1966:56) points out that many of the category 2 stories (those that would likely be labeled oral histories in modern parlance) would be regarded as credible in ethnohistory, while none in category 1 would pass the test regardless of Nunamiut insistence on their veracity.

Long before the emic-etic terminology came into use, Robert Lowie (1915) had stressed the critical distinction between native histories and those of his own cultural tradition, finding the former to be essentially value-less *as historical sources.* When challenged by such anthropological colleagues as Alexander Goldenweiser (1915), Roland B. Dixon (1915), and John R. Swanton (1915), the latter two having earlier provoked Lowie by what he saw as historiographic naïveté in their treatment of Indian traditions, a judgment apparently concurred with by several of his other colleagues, Lowie relented just enough to admit native histories as possible sources for ideas that might occasionally be worth following up (Lowie 1917). But he insisted that when Indian traditions purported to say anything about events antedating, roughly, the middle of the nineteenth century they were either superfluous (what could they tell that was not already evident from language studies, historical records, or archaeological data?) or untrustworthy, not to say unusable, because of their characteristic failure to disentangle ordinary things and events from the fantastic: talking animals, for instance, or transforming shamans, the dead returning to life, and bison spending winters at the bottoms of lakes. Such stories were irrelevant to any scientific reconstruction of Indian history.

Basing part of his discussion on Lowie's famous denial of historicity in American Indian oral traditions, the folklorist Richard M. Dorson (1972: 203) added an insightful further consideration to that question:

> Lowie argued that primitive man [this was not then the pejorative term it has since become] cannot distinguish between a trivial incident and a major fact worthy of remembrance. With so revolutionary a fact as the introduction of the horse, the Nez Perce tradition errs seriously, while the Assiniboine connect the horse with a cosmogonic hero-myth. The Lemhi Shoshoni possess no recollection of the visit of Lewis and Clark, but do relate a mythical encounter between Wolk ["Wolf (or Coyote)"] as father of the Indians and Iron-Man as father of the Whites. The Indian's historical perspective can be said to match that of the illiterate peasant who describes the European war from his own personal observation. As for the accuracy of migration legends, the chances are one in four (or six, if earth and sky are included) that they will guess right the direction of their travel. Even entirely pos-

sible trifling stories of wars and quarrels are now shown, by their geo-graphical distribution, to be folklore and not fact. Therefore [quoting Lowie (1917)], " . . . as we cannot substitute folk-etymology for phi-lology, so we cannot substitute primitive tradition for scientific his-tory." Hence "Indian tradition is historically worthless."

Lowie's and Dorson's positivist stances in the foregoing statements and Hudson's forthright folk history/ethnohistory dichotomy are helpful, if partial, entrees into some difficult issues that confront the pursuit of histori-cal knowledge across cultural and temporal boundaries. As will be seen in later pages, philosophical and methodological problems continue to beset students of humanity's past and present careers. The philosopher Thomas Nagel (1986:9) has provided one of the clearest statements of the perspec-tive best suited to the consideration of those problems:

> It is necessary to combine the recognition of our contingency, our finitude, and our containment in the world with an ambition of tran-scendence, however limited may be our success in achieving it. The right attitude in philosophy is to accept aims that we can achieve only fractionally and imperfectly, and cannot be sure of achieving even to that extent. It means in particular not abandoning the pursuit of truth, even though if you want the truth rather than merely something to say, you will have a good deal less to say. Pursuit of the truth requires more than imagination: it requires the generation and decisive elimi-nation of alternative possibilities until, ideally, only one remains, and it requires a habitual readiness to attack one's own convictions. That is the only way real belief can be arrived at.

I am concerned here with history: what it is and how we get at it and are justified in thinking we have got it right or, more modestly, are able at least to determine that others have got it wrong. In this discussion, history and historians are not defined exclusively by access to and use of written rec-ords; "prehistory"—simply, the time before writing—falls within this pur-view as well. Indeed, much of geology, paleontology, paleobotany, and even astronomy fully qualify as history ("the historical geology of the Llano Es-tacado," "a history of the gastropod *Lecanospira* in the Ordovician Beek-mantown formation," "sequencing the rise of the early bryophytes," "evo-lution of the solar system"). But the history to be examined here is limited to human history, most especially as unfolded in aboriginal North America. The tools for investigating that more limited compass include archaeology as well as written records and, of course, ethnography, biological anthropology, linguistics, and oral histories and traditions. Unequal in trustworthiness in specific instances or in general utility, their combination has the advantage of potential redundancy or, equally important, of raising alarms when found to be incongruous.

What happened in history? Apart from the initial considerations briefly raised at the beginning of this chapter, so seemingly straightforward a question is instantly complicated by the fact that the term itself is widely called upon to serve at least two different, if related, functions. Those functions, easily distinguished in the abstract but difficult to disentangle in practice, bedevil historians and their critics. The same word refers to both the product of what historians do and the object of their attention—that is, what is believed to have happened in the past and what actually did. The two do not necessarily coincide. A few words on this conundrum as a sort of brush-clearing preparation for the main purpose of this essay may help to clarify important issues if not resolve them to every reader's satisfaction.

On one hand, as just seen, history is understood as describing and making intelligible *the past* in writing or, in nonliterate societies, in speech. History in this sense is statements of opinion or belief about what happened in times gone by. Thus *histories* differ slightly to radically in scope, premises, and procedures (that is, in their historiographies), as well as in their conclusions, from society to society, place to place, and time to time, and even between status groupings in any given society. Commonplace assertions reflecting this meaning of history are "we have our history, you have yours," "history is written by the winners," and "ideology writes history." Whatever credibility may be granted diverse histories qua history, their narrators may consciously or not also serve interests more current to their own time in the celebration of cultural identity and the justification of social, economic, and power differentials. Thus, crucial to this first use of the term *history* is the inescapable position of the history writer or history teller in his or her own time and place (hence the indispensability of measured reflexivity). History is the present reflecting on the past and doing so with the implication if not declaration of a true, not a fictional, relation. Words like *story, fable, myth,* and *legend* tend to be used instead of *history* where uncertainty, falsehoods, and half-truths are acknowledged as intractable. Of course, when and where—or even if—these distinctions are warranted is contentious ground. And this ground is especially contentious when the indigenous histories of oral societies in places like the Americas, Oceania, and Africa are compared with the histories of the same peoples written by Western historians. Recently published thoughtful discussions of the resulting tensions and how to address the issues they raise, even if sometimes mistaken in my opinion, are by Robert Borofsky (2000), Richard Bradley

(2003), Julie Cruikshank (1998, 2002), Philip J. Deloria (2002), Greg Dening (2000), Clara Sue Kidwell (2002), Peter Nabokov (2002:126–149), Marshall Sahlins (1985), Peter M. Whiteley (1998, 2002), and Alexander von Gernet (1996). Still others, including some not so thoughtful but influential nonetheless, are cited elsewhere in this volume and/or in Mason (2000).

The second sense or meaning of history referred to earlier is the declared realm of the past tense: the ever-receding accumulation of everything preceding the present. History in this sense is meant to signify what actually took place in times past irrespective of our knowledge or ignorance of it. History is that "certain stratum of reality which historians make it their professional business to study" (Dray 1993:1). It is constituted of the world as it formerly was. Today, segments of that former reality *may be known* (Caesar was assassinated in Rome in 44 B.C.; George Armstrong Custer died at the Battle of the Little Bighorn on June 25, 1876, Crazy Horse did not); *not known,* even if in principle potentially knowable (New Madrid–scale earthquakes struck the Ohio Valley in Late Archaic times [remember: trilobites really had once existed even though that fact became known only hundreds of millions of years after their extinction, and dinosaurs had also once existed before the fact of our knowing—but not so late as to have coexisted with humans, so-called creation science and Vine Deloria, Jr., notwithstanding]); or inherently *unknowable* (it was the flight of the losing faction in a blood feud that first induced a crossing of Beringia to the New World). Understood in these terms, history is intrinsically independent of the historian and is in no way reflective of personal, social, or cultural perspective or ignorance (see Trigger 1989:379–382). As circumstances, actions, and events slip from the fleeting present to become the past they are forever completed, finished, extinguished ("All the king's horses, and all the king's men . . . "). In this sense, history falls in the set of "*intransitive* objects of knowledge" described by Guy Gibbon in his discussion of "realist" archaeology. These are "the real things and structures, mechanisms and processes, events and possibilities of the world which are for the most part quite independent of us and invariant to our knowledge of them" (Gibbon 1989:144).

No longer extant, what happened in history is inaccessible to observation, let alone repeal or alteration. That being the case, how can something that no longer exists be known to have existed and made an object of study? The former existence of anything can only be inferred from something in the present. A surrogate or model of that now extinct "certain stratum of reality" has to be created from the surviving debris of that former reality, be it in the form of rock strata, fossils, physico-chemical residues, documents, oral histories and traditions, ruins, artifacts, or clues embedded in linguistic, anthropometric, genetic, or social and cultural data. From such clues and their manipulation in imagination is a surrogate of the past (a history in the first sense) constructed. But this would-be replica is not to be mistaken, although it often is, with history in the second sense—that is, the once real thing that no longer exists (see Dray 1993 and Fischer 1970 for trenchant examples).

Histories, hereafter to be understood in the first sense as models of or surrogates for the past, vary in their quality. Good histories—good, that is, by the criteria of critical historians, archaeologists, and others, not by those appropriate to reciters of local verbal legacies (the latter, of course, have their own standards of "goodness")—differ from poor ones in a number of ways. These include the degree to which they conform with the strongest recovered evidence and how they are interpreted by cogent thinking in the light of surviving related phenomena, analogs, agencies, and processes observable in the modern world (e.g., the uniformitarian principle in geology). But even the best of histories are uneven. They must also be forever incomplete, if for no other reasons than inescapable limitations of data and perspective. New information and rethinking of old arguments inevitably force reappraisals of what historians thought they knew or believed they had presented in the most compatible (or least disjunctive) way with current information and tested methods of analysis. Even though the actual past will never—can never—be recaptured with complete fidelity in attempted reconstructions of it, historians must aim for such a result in the hope of getting a bit closer to that goal than their predecessors. They must do so in the certain knowledge of uncertain success. That the task is unendingly difficult and the aim exceeds the grasp is warrant enough to be wary of histories that represent themselves as inerrant or that rely on unnecessary assumptions, untestable hypotheses, or paranormal phenomena.

Just how, then, is a historian or archaeologist not ensnared in the coils of radical reflexivity, thoroughgoing cultural relativity, or nihilist species of deconstructionism or postmodernism to assay the possible relevance of American Indian—or any other people's—oral traditions in the reconstruction of culture histories? To what degree, if at all, can they and the dominant Western historiography address the same questions? The historicity of statements about the past, that is, their being considered accurate or truthful rather than erroneous or fanciful, is of course a judgment that will often be rendered differently among the world's cultures. Privileging the Western perspective over any of the others can and frequently does invoke charges of unfairness, naive or even intentional ethnocentrism, or worse: "hegemonic trespass," "a power play with political inequality," "neocolonialist presumption," "racism," "arrogance"—these latter being charges that immediately foreclose rational communication. But howsoever that may be, the traditions that scholars are apt to encounter in their historical researches among oral peoples are the products of societies that rarely had the need, let alone the luxury of resources, to support the development of free inquiry into such arcane matters as critical history. It is part of the unique legacy of the Western experience to indulge the principle, howsoever inconsistently the praxis, of this kind of undertaking. Thus, Philip J. Deloria (2002:16), remarking on similarities and differences between Western and American Indian historiographies, makes the important point that "native oral histories [within which he includes oral traditions] have their own social and cultural legitimacy outside of academic judgments, which have often been less concerned with meaning and context and more focused on verifiable facticity." And in another part of the world (Polynesia) a comparable observation is stressed in Greg Dening's sensitive account of how two different historical traditions colored perceptions of the first meeting, in 1767, of Englishmen (aboard HMS *Dolphin*) and Tahitians. In that account, the need for an independent touchstone is revealed in Dening's admission that "how the natives saw the Strangers is, *by any standard of objective discourse,* nothing more than informed guess" (Dening 2000:118; my emphasis). Both of these quotations expose the analyst's ultimate need, however committed to some form of cultural relativism short of nihilism, for a standard by means of which historiographic intelligibility may be made to comprehend alien "histories." That historiography that concedes the least to unexamined premises and agencies is the closest approximation to that independent touchstone.

Different "ways of knowing" history cannot be ascribed equal ontological weight without jettisoning intelligibility. Some come to prevail and expand across cultural frontiers while others retract and expire. This may be due simply to disparities in political or economic power among societies, as Michael S. Nassaney (1994) and many others have argued and is doubtless true in many cases of colonization, or it may also or instead reflect the superior ability of certain conceptualizations of the past to withstand critical scrutiny and answer more questions. As already stressed, there have to be some contingently independent intellectual grounds for the latter succession to occur. Peter M. Whiteley (2002:405–406), a strong defender of the value of Native American oral traditions in studying their pasts (specifically, in his case, that of the Hopis), implies the existence of such an extracultural dimension when he employs the term "*legitimate* oral tradition," thereby inferring the existence of its opposite (my emphasis). His willingness to entertain epistemological restraints on the anthropological doctrine of cultural relativism evidences itself as follows: "Over-emphasis on hard science risks neglecting vital evidence that might greatly enhance explanation of the past. But free-for-all relativism, where each account is as good as any other and is only accountable to criteria of judgment ('my grandfather told me, so it must be true') unsusceptible of evaluation means an interpretive Tower of Babel. Philosophically speaking, differing accounts of the past must intersect in certain important respects, or they are not accounts of the past, but of something else" (Whiteley 2002:406).

The same writer, however, is less than consistent in his warnings about an interpretive Tower of Babel. In his disturbing study *Rethinking Hopi Ethnography,* detailing the near impossibility of conducting anthropological research in contemporary Hopi Indian communities, Whiteley laments in an endnote the cautious treatment by archaeologists, whom he blatantly stereotypes, of indigenous Hopi and other Pueblo historiographies. In doing so he thereby seems to overlook his own warnings of Babelian confusions as well as the resentment of the Hopis and others at what they see as appropriation by outsiders of their knowledge "property rights," an issue he had previously and at length taken pains to explore. He writes: "Archaeologists, for example, in both their theory and praxis, have more often than not systematically excluded the knowledge and interpretations of living Pueblo descendants—as they have with non-Western indigenous peoples worldwide. The intellectual grounds for exclusion, particularly in the now old 'new archaeology,' exalt cold 'scientific analysis' of mute material remains over indigenous oral histories: Natives need not apply. To me, at least, this seems an appalling interpretive error (as well as a morally indefensible act in a genuinely plural society), cultural varieties of historicity notwithstanding" (Whiteley 1998:236n32; also Whiteley 1997:202–203n30).

But one of the dilemmas facing investigators who would look to oral traditions for information helpful in interpreting archaeological remains arises from the very quality typical of such traditions that some of their students find most appealing:

> By identifying the multiple, often quarreling interest groups within any society [e.g., local communities, lineages, clans, non-kinship sodalities], and by making each of their claims the measure of any given history's intended relevance or "scale" (rather than abstract concepts of time or genres of narrative), we arrive at oral tradition's defining benefit and unending pleasure: multiple versions. Ultimates and absolutes belong to the gods; it is as hopeless to search for any single, authoritative ur-narrative as it is to look for paradise [Nabokov 2002:47].

Within the cultural world of the Hopi Indians of Arizona, as religious historian Armin Geertz points out, one looks in vain for a single authoritative account of their Four Worlds myth of tribal emergence "because there is no such complete version. Each clan jealously guards its own version as being autochthonous and complete in its own right. . . . These clan traditions are mutually incompatible, and accounts— even within a single clan, especially from other mesa villages—are conflicting" [Nabokov 2002:48, with internal quotation from Geertz, "Reflections on the Study of Hopi Mythology" (Vecsey 1990:130)].

It is hardly surprising in so inherently contentious a field of inquiry as how to make sense of multicultural conceptualizations of history, especially as the field is presently enmeshed in accusatory and defensive politics and moralistic posturing, that even the most earnest investigators can sometimes find themselves trapped in contradictions while trying to reconcile logically irreconcilable points of view. A particularly curious one is Peter Nabokov's treatment of Alfred L. Kroeber's 1951 verdict on the historicity of Arizona-California Mohave narratives of their past. A summary of the latter's view has also appeared in the work of William C. Sturtevant (1966: 26–27). Nabokov writes:

No matter how concrete their inventories of old place names and accounts of migrations and intertribal warfare were, when anthropologist Alfred Kroeber evaluated Mohave narratives around the turn of the twentieth century, he likened them to the sort of "pseudo-history" he found in the Book of Mormon. This verdict was sealed when Kroeber discovered that to the Mohave these stories of ancient beginnings, clan movements, and epic battles received their stamp of historical veracity through the "power dreams" (*sumach ahot*) received by individual tale-tellers. First and foremost, Mohave national identity and homeland were dreamed and sung realities. They emerged in the era of supernatural ancestors such as Frog, Serpent, and Buzzard, whose homes and exploits were commemorated in place names. Then human ancestors claimed these places, amalgamated them into a sacred geography, and through more dreaming and singing maintained communication with Frog and Buzzard's parallel plane of existence [Nabokov 2002:127–128].

Nabokov approvingly cites the views of Robert K. Thomas, Vine Deloria, Jr., and Alfonso Ortiz on the meaning of history for Indian people, especially the latter's stricture that Indians have (or believe they have [cf. Bradley 2003:226]) an insoluble bonding with places (mountains, canyons, rivers, etc.) and history in its fully indigenous, that is, ethnocentric, sense. The native "meanings" of history "[are not] irrelevant to the historian's task if he or she is to represent a given tribe's view of reality accurately and fully" (Ortiz quoted in Nabokov 2002:131–132; brackets are the latter's). This quotation is inarguably basic anthropological doctrine. It is one of the discipline's fundamental charges to attempt to understand history or any other phenomena from the emic ("insider's") perspective, insofar as that is possible. From that perspective, Julie Cruikshank (2002:18) is right in maintaining that "the issue of how much historical accuracy Homeric poems, Icelandic sagas, Tlingit oratory, or Tagish life stories contain is really beside the point if we understand their contribution as providing social memory, however adequate or inadequate." But that perspective and that contribution do not preempt others. They do not address the issue of how indigenous people's conceptions of history are to be articulated with those by means of which modern Western historians and, especially, archaeologists, do their work. Thus, without attempting to solve this dilemma, Nabokov, to put it charitably, simply suggests that Kroeber was ethnocentric in likening Mohave "historical" narratives to what he (Kroeber) regarded as Mormon pseudo-history. Nabokov's rebuke is ambiguous, however. Is the point of the rebuke that the Book of Mormon is "pseudo-history" (Nabokov does not defend it against that charge) but the Mohave narratives are not? It can hardly be the reverse in view of Nabokov's stressing the concreteness of old Mohave place names and accounts of migrations and battles, even though dreamed, in which case Nabokov is as guilty of ethnocentrism as Kroeber is implied to be. Or is it that neither, in Nabokov's opinion, is any less factual than history in the Euroamerican scholarly sense of Kroeber? But then, given his previous reference to history in oral societies as having no veridical content beyond that locally granted it by various scales of group self-interests, it is difficult to know wherein Kroeber is to be deemed more deficient than his critic.

Although I do not believe it was original with him, Leslie A. White enjoyed describing history in conversation and class lectures as "one damn thing after another." Encompassing not only an immeasurable number of "things" but also an infinity of perspectives from which they were witnessed as well, history, as in William H. Dray's earlier cited "certain stratum of reality," can only be known indirectly. Furthermore, to acknowledge that it can be known only partly is a colossal understatement. The salience of such limitations increases when cultural boundaries are crossed. The historiographies of oral societies present special problems if the products of their sovereign exercise are to be enlisted to help answer questions posed by Western historians or archaeologists. Indeed they are often mutually incomprehensible. To lessen the potential violation of historical science canons of evidence and argumentation—but at the sometimes necessary sacrifice of the enlisted other's beliefs and conventions—certain cautions must be observed.

Preconditional to the use of indigenous narratives in historical studies by Western-trained scholars are (1) the assumption that what is to be used from those narratives is susceptible in principle to testing—that is, that it is a matter of ascertaining historical likelihood, not religious, emotional, folk, or poetical "truth"—and (2) acceptance of the scientific method as the means whereby conclusions are sought. Rejecting the first axiom obviates the second and removes the problem from serious consideration. Accepting the first but rejecting the second does the same. Both preconditions are necessary even though, because of inadequacies either of relevant data or in thinking about them, they are not guarantees of correct conclusions. But at least the possibility of reaching such conclusions remains if deficiencies of information or thought are reduced by continuing research.

A corollary of these preconditions is the refusal to consider supernatural, paranormal, or other unverifiable agencies, beings, processes, and so on, however great or small, as causes or influences admissible in scholarly explanation. Much popular opinion to the contrary notwithstanding, few scholars would agree with the public testimony of a recently deceased football champion that Indians were created with a superior gift "to sneak up on people," that Joseph Smith really did find gold tablets inscribed with the prehistory of the New World in a New York hill, or that the current preeminence of the United States is owing to divine plan. Such assertions that defy human capabilities or that invoke conditions, events, or forces that preclude verification or falsification merit no consideration except as psychological and cultural phenomena, themselves inviting of scientific investigation. And so it is with analogs of similar ontological status in other cultures when they may be proffered as historical data. They, too, must withstand scrutiny under the lights of the axioms just invoked. Imperatively, fabulous creatures, powers, and events incompatible with the foregoing strictures must be rejected out of hand. While some readers "may decry some of these scruples and protest that there are more things in heaven and earth than are dreamt of in my philosophy" (the philosopher Nelson Goodman paraphrasing Hamlet), "I am concerned, rather, that there should not be more things dreamt of in my philosophy than there are in heaven or earth" (Goodman 1955:39).

Unknowingly anticipating some of Goodman's more philosophical strictures, almost half a century earlier Robert Lowie had sought to safeguard anthropology from stepping into a maze he considered best not entered. Specifically, he inveighed against the use of oral traditions in attempting to

reconstruct American Indian cultural histories. Oral traditions, he maintained, could offer nothing of a historical nature not more readily and less
ambiguously obtainable by scientific means. Besides, whatever tatters of historicity survived in those tales he regarded as compromised beyond re-
demption by their intimate involvement with spirits, gods, talking animals,
preternatural ancestors, and the like. Lowie viewed them as superfluous to
the writing of cultural history, intrinsically unreliable, and subversive of
methodological rigor: "We cannot safely reject as mythical that part of a
tradition which conflicts with our conception of physical possibility and
retain the remainder as correct" (Lowie 1915:598).

Still, notwithstanding Lowie's stricture, one reiterated in different terms
by Edmund R. Leach (1954:265–268) and Barbara J. Price (1980:161–164,
175–178), eminently among others, it is a Siren urge to suspect that vestiges
of historical fact may adhere to even fantastic stories. There is no way of
dealing with the lure of that urge except to rely on hunch or prejudice and
take one's chances or, preferably, to rely on adherence to the preconditions
introduced earlier and on judgment informed by a general knowledge of
the oral tradition genre. This must be coupled, of course, with as detailed a
familiarity as possible with the content and context of the particular case
being considered.

That possibly true history, that is, history that would stand up to critical
examination if relevant information were available for scrutiny, may indeed
survive in traditional accounts, although frequently disguised by metaphor
and interlaced with clearly fictional elements, cannot be flatly discounte-
nanced. Many scholars will quickly point to a number of examples in support of this contention. Especially prominent among those examples are
Schliemann's tracking down of a physical Troy by reading Homer, the use
of Icelandic sagas to search out the Norse discovery of America, and, of
course, some of the findings in the field of biblical archaeology. These not
only combine fact and fancy, they also have the virtue for the purposes of
this book of having been orally composed and transmitted long before their
commitment to writing. Their examination confers the additional benefit
of hopefully foreclosing possible charges of anti-Indian prejudice.

After a necessary exploration of the nature of memory, the phenomenon
upon which much of oral tradition stands or falls, the question of the historicity of those three Old World representatives is presented for consideration in Chapter 4. Issues raised there will then be seen to bear on the relevance of archaeology and critical historiography generally to assessing the
historical content of traditional narratives anywhere, those of indigenous
America not least among them. Before turning in these directions, however,
an origin narrative of the Catawba Indians of South Carolina and two his-

torically recent traditions from the Western (Teton or Lakota) Sioux of the Great Plains, one a rebuttal of the other, will serve as conclusion to the present chapter and a useful introduction to those that follow.

On Catawba Origins

In his discussion of the consequences of the introduction of Old World diseases among the Catawba Indians in the Southeast, James H. Merrell describes a phenomenon by no means limited to those unfortunate people. Many other tribes suffered comparable losses. Specifically:

> Survivors of these horrors were thrust into a situation no less alien than what European immigrants and African slaves found [when coming to grips with a strange new world]. The collected wisdom of generations could vanish in a matter of days if sickness struck older members of a community who kept sacred traditions and taught special skills. When many of the elders succumbed at once, the deep pools of collective memory grew shallow, and some dried up altogether. In 1710, Indians near Charleston told a settler that "they have forgot most of their traditions since the Establishment of this Colony, they keep their Festivals and can tell but little of the reasons: their Old Men are dead." Impoverishment of a rich cultural heritage followed the spread of disease. Nearly a century later, a South Carolinian exaggerated but captured the general trend when he noted that Catawbas "have forgotten their ancient rites, ceremonies, and manufactures" [Merrell 2000:30].

Unfortunately, for a number of reasons including those just recited, nothing substantive is known of Catawba traditional history before and during the early Colonial period. Compounding the natives' loss of that information was the lack of most colonists' interest in recording whatever bits and pieces of it might have come to their attention. Detailed written accounts of orally transmitted Catawba traditions relate to later times, and with limited exceptions *their* recording was largely postponed to the first half of the twentieth century. These later renderings of the Catawba past embrace unverifiable matters as well as a few historically factual events that occurred from the time of recording back to the mid-eighteenth century. They also include essentially timeless "just-so" tales (how ground squirrels got their stripes, and so on) and stories about remote Catawba ancestors, the "ancient people," in a mythic world. An example of the former is the verbal listing in 1937–1938 by Sam Blue, at that time tribal chief, of the Catawba head chiefs going as far back as the "great chief" Haigler, killed by the Shawnees in 1762 or 1763 (Speck 1938:8n23; Speck and Schaeffer 1942:564–566). Impressive as this listing appears to be (Merrell 1989:262–263, 368n132), it must be remembered that there existed concurrent documents that could have been accessed by literate Indians or their white acquaintances and by means of which memory could be refreshed.

The second kind of stories, those about the "ancient people," were indeed refreshed, albeit in a different sense. Thus, for example, were pigs and horses introduced to pre-European-contact ancestors. Because stories linking them "came from the Nation's elders rather than someone else," they were apt to be believed. This was true of all stories having "the sanction of tradition whether they were traditional by scholarly standards or not; they belonged to the ancient people even if those people never would have recognized them" (Merrell 1989:271). Memory—social or collective memory in this case—like nature, abhors a vacuum. The Catawbas, like other people, filled that vacuum with new memories and traditions in satisfaction of altered needs. Not least among those needs was reaffirming connections with the tattered past.

In 1853 Henry R. Schoolcraft quoted at length from an anonymous manuscript recording what he took to be an authentic Catawba account of that tribe's early history. Entitled *Memoir of the Catawbas* (Schoolcraft 1851–1857:3:293–296), that same document has since been partly reproduced by Douglas Summers Brown (1966:29–31), who identifies its author as Philip Edward Pearson. Written about 1842 at the request of the then-governor of South Carolina, Pearson's *Memoir* is credited by Brown (1966:37), however many its "minor [*sic*] inaccuracies and embellishments," as being "an honest record of the Indians' own account of themselves." Brown devotes almost a dozen pages to subsequent criticisms of the manuscript's historical reliability (Brown 1966:27–38). Nevertheless, she (yes, *she*) argues against dismissing it. Her reasons rest upon the document's age, the argument that "it gives information not found elsewhere," and the fact that the origin story it contains is the same, "with some variations," as that given to a prominent churchman, one Bishop Gregg, by the Cherokee-Catawba leader William Thomas (Brown 1966:28n2, 37).

The age of a document is of itself as equivocal to assessing its credibility as is the observation that some part of what it contains is unique and otherwise unknowable. Invoking compatibility with an independent source of relevant information, on the other hand, is more inviting of serious consideration. However, inasmuch as it was this same William Thomas who supplied Schoolcraft with Pearson's rendering of the tradition (Schoolcraft 1851–1857:2:343), the question arises of Thomas's supporting testimony being pseudo-confirmation, dependent on prior knowledge of its contents. Schoolcraft both alluded and referred to that manuscript-memoir in the second volume of his multivolume study (Schoolcraft 1851–1857:2:86 and 343), and he quoted it at length in the following volume (Schoolcraft 1851–1857:3:293–296). This was a decade later than Pearson's *Memoir* is believed to have been written and deposited with the government of South Carolina, from which Thomas obtained the original or a facsimile.

The memory underlying *Memoir of the Catawbas* is in a curious state of double jeopardy. Pearson, its author, "fond of antiquarian researches and preserving legendary lore," was ostensibly committed to writing a Catawba oral tradition he had garnered from now unknown and doubtless fast disappearing sources. At the time of the *Memoir's* composition, the Catawba population of barely over a hundred souls was but a shadow of the thousands that had existed in the seventeenth century (Rudes et al. 2004:310; Swanton 1952:92). Unfortunately, his manuscript recording the Indian memories he had heard was later destroyed in a fire, and he was forced to rely on his own memory to recreate what he had originally written (Brown 1966:28, 30).

Briefly, according to Pearson's rewritten version, the Catawbas were indigenous to Canada. There, however, they lived under intolerable pressure from their "hereditary enemies," the now French-armed Connewangas, identified as Senecas by Schoolcraft. Finally, goaded beyond endurance, about 1650 they fled their homeland by the remarkable feat of crossing "the St. Lawrence, probably near Detroit." They then headed to eastern Kentucky where they turned on and defeated the pursuing Connewangas. Following this victory, the tribe divided. One faction remained there, ultimately to be absorbed into the Chickasaws and Choctaws. The other migrated to Virginia, thence to South Carolina where, after an epic battle with the resident Cherokees that resulted in the combined deaths of over 2,000 warriors, peace was made and the invaders settled down on Cherokee-ceded land (Brown 1966:29–31; Schoolcraft 1851–1857:3:293–296).

As with many other traditional histories—oral especially, but not excluding written—it is always possible to pick out as historical otherwise confusing bits and pieces of narrative. Not infrequently, such identifications are "recognized" by attributing to them metaphorical disguise which, once deciphered, facilitates their manipulation to fit with independent data. Thus James Mooney (1894:69–70) was willing to credit *Memoir of the Catawbas* with genuine content in its assertion of implacable Catawba-Iroquois enmity, a serious Catawba-Cherokee altercation, and settlement on the Catawba River with the Broad River to the west as the border between the latter two tribes. Most of the rest of the tale he found "absurd." Brown (1966:33–38) adds her own pro and con arguments to this evaluation. Certainly today, even though the origins of the Catawbas remain obscure in many ways, there is no archaeological or ethnohistorical support for a Canadian homeland. In fact, it now appears likely that the Catawbas were the product of coalescence of a number of small, previously autonomous tribes and bands such as the Esaws, Sugarees, Shuterees, and Saxapahaws. Other groups, not all speakers of a Siouan language, let alone of the Catawban variety, came and went over the ensuing years. The Catawbas as historically known probably emerged not much before 1700, about the same time that saw the formation of the Creek confederacy (Merrell 1989:92–133).

Most archaeologists today derive the late prehistoric ancestors of the historical Catawbas and related groups from what Charles Hudson (1990:67) has labeled the "*nouveau arriviste*" Mississippian paramount chiefdom of Cofitachequi. This was the name both of a major town and a vast "province" in central and northwestern South Carolina when visited by Hernando de Soto in 1540 and Juan Pardo in 1566–68. The shadow of Old World disease was then already upon the land, for that great chiefdom was in rapid decline owing in part to unprecedented population losses undercutting its social, ideological, and economic foundations. While some authorities have equated Cofitachequi with Kasihta, a Muskogean-speaking tribe and one of the divisions of the Creeks (e.g., Swanton 1922:215–225), others imply, if they do not state, that the province of Cofitachequi was predominantly Siouan (Catawban) speaking (e.g., Rudes et al. 2004:301). This view is reinforced by their chronological linking of population estimates for Cofitachequi and the Catawbas (Rudes et al. 2004:310, Table 1). Hudson (1990: 115n47) disputes equating the Mississippian town and province with Kasihta, the latter being a known Lower Creek town. Most likely, he maintains, Cofitachequi was a multilingual society: "Eastern Muskogean languages were spoken in the principal towns of the chiefdom of Cofitachequi, but these towns exercised power and influence over towns in which other languages, such as Catawban, were spoken" (Hudson 1990:68). These latter views, if correct, most economically point to the survivors of the Cofitachequi collapse as among the likely proximate forebears of the Esaws, Sugarees, and others and thus of the historical Catawbas, rooting them, as it were, in their historically recorded southeastern homeland.

And Whence Came the Lakota Sioux?

Unlike the foregoing Catawba account or the historical traditions of the Central Siouan tribes to be discussed in Chapter 9, the derivation narratives of the western Great Plains–dwelling Lakota or Teton Sioux in the nineteenth century had relatively little to say regarding remote origins in faraway places. Among important exceptions to this generalization, however, was the belief of some Lakotas in a trans-Mississippi fountainhead of their people in the not very distant past, perhaps in Minnesota and Wisconsin. An influential proponent of this tradition was the Oglala war leader Red Cloud, many of whose modern descendants maintain the same belief (Lazarus 1991:417). But, in fact, until the last half of the 1800s, recorded traditions of the Oglalas, Brules, Hunkpapas, and other Lakota tribes were essentially silent about geographical origins, or they simply implied that those peoples had always lived where they were when whites first encountered them in their nineteenth-century "homelands." It was not until the middle of that century that the now famous Black Hills specifically received explicit attention in this regard. Their "sacredness" and generative role as original and immemorial homeland of the Lakota people have since, especially in the twentieth and twenty-first centuries, become articles of faith to perhaps most Lakotas (Bordewich 1996:103–106, 222–235; DeMallie 2001b:794; Lazarus 1991:417). Indeed, this elevation to canonical status has become a prominent gospel in the wider phenomenon of Indian assertions of American genesis (e.g., V. Deloria, Jr. 1997a:57, 81, 232, among many others).

Among the difficulties in linking Lakota origin traditions to an archaeological trail is the historical recency of their authors in their "immemorial" homeland. Nevertheless, considering those difficulties is not only pertinent to the subject of this book. It is prudent in view of currently fashionable—and now legally mandated—admonishments that museum curators particularly meld traditional folk histories with pasts predicated on critical scholarship (see the previous chapter on NAGPRA and related legislation).

In his recorded December 5, 1944, interview with his biographer-editor John G. Neihardt, the Oglala longtime Roman Catholic catechist and since-celebrated traditional holy man, Black Elk, ostensibly recollecting a bit of ancient history, recounted that his people's ancestors originally had lived by an ocean. Having also been a one-time performer with Buffalo Bill's Wild West Show in Europe, it is unlikely that he meant Lake Superior or any other fresh body of water when he said this. Some time after vacating this home by the ocean, Black Elk related, the ascendancy of humans over animals was established by the outcome of a race held at "the heart of the earth." This locale he described as a "promised land," for which the Indians were admonished to seek. He thought it probably was the Black Hills (Black Elk in DeMallie 1984:307–310).

Even though Black Elk's mention of the Black Hills was not until 1944, DeMallie (1984:309–310, 2001b:794) credits it as supporting evidence that a century earlier "stories were also told identifying the Black Hills as the site of creation of humankind." However, the holy man's words are ambiguous.

It is unclear whether he meant that humans had been created in that place or more simply that they had there been awarded dominance over animals as the result of the aforementioned race as well as being given knowledge of the bow and arrow. These benefits were bestowed by the "Thunder-beings" on the primeval culture hero Red Thunder, during whose life the great contest is said to have occurred.

Regardless of Black Elk's ambiguity, the vehemence with which some prominent modern Sioux spokespersons dismiss overwhelming evidence pointing to their forebears as historically recent invaders rather than im-memorial inhabitants of the Black Hills and neighboring tracts in western South Dakota, eastern Wyoming, and northwestern Nebraska is little short of daunting. Without questioning the sincerity of most holders of this po-sition, its popularity is also dramatic testimony to the role of pragmatic self-interest. In this instance, calculation of the best strategies to pursue land and monetary claims overrides preoccupation with factual accuracy in the re-production of the past. Tellingly, the evidence so dismissed includes that of Red Cloud himself and a number of famous nineteenth-century Sioux cal-endar keepers in addition to that of non-Sioux Indian and white narrators who actually witnessed much of that invasion or whose parents or grand-parents did. Good summaries are to be found in DeMallie (1980:44–45, 2001a, 2001b), Hassrick (1964), Hyde (1937), and White (2000). Indeed, the Lakota chief Black Hawk (not to be confused with the more famous Sauk leader) openly boasted at the 1851 Fort Laramie Treaty Council that "these lands [that is, portions of Sioux-claimed territory that the United States government wanted returned to other tribes] once belonged to the Kiowas and the Crows, but we whipped these nations out of them, and in this we did what the white men do when they want the lands of the Indians" (quoted in Lazarus 1991:18).

The earliest record of the Sioux in the Black Hills, Richard White points out, is in a pictographic calendar, or "winter count," for the year 1775 or 1775–76 (White 2000:547, 558n17). This record is frequently cited by many others as well (e.g., Bordewich 1996:104; DeMallie 2001a:731; Hass-rick 1964:61; Lazarus 1991:429; and, initially, Mallery 1886:130). The rele-vant native document is one of the Corbusier-collected winter counts pub-lished by Garrick Mallery (1886:127–146 and Plates XXXIV–LI). The celebrated nineteenth-century Oglala chief American Horse claimed serial authorship of this calendar for his grandfather, his father, and himself. As personally explained to Mallery, American Horse related that the initial pictograph referred to the year 1775–76, when Standing Bull, the great-grandfather of his contemporary namesake, "discovered" the Black Hills (Mallery 1886:130 and Plate XXXIV). A separate winter count by Cloud

Shield places this event in the following year (Hyde 1937:23). In the American Horse history for the year 1814–15 is recorded the collapse of Sioux-Kiowa peace talks (Mallery 1886:135 and Plate XL). Another winter count, that of Iron Shell, commemorated the same year, naming it "Crushed a Witapahatu's [Kiowa's] Head" (Hassrick 1964:9, 306). This killing by a Sioux wrecked the proposed peace. Shortly thereafter the Kiowas were expelled from the Black Hills. Hassrick (1964:61) says that the Sioux had already essentially defeated both the Kiowas and the Cheyennes by 1805. Certainly by 1825, the Sioux, specifically the Oglalas and Brules, had driven the Kiowas as well as the Crows from the Black Hills, thus taking sole possession by right of conquest (White 2000:551).

As assessed by Raymond DeMallie (in Walker 1982:111–121), and alluded to in the present work (see Chapters 8 and 10), the winter count calendars of the Lakotas and some other Plains tribes are fascinating combinations of pictographic symbols, brief written commentaries—in either or both Indian and English orthographies on the animal skin and paper documents themselves—and recorded explanations of their meanings by their creators, descendants, or other persons presumed to be knowledgeable. They provide invaluable insights into what and how events were perceived and selected for representation by the calendar keepers as they sought to preserve mnemonic reminders of personal, family, band, community, or tribal history. As such, they vary enormously in scope, detail, intelligibility to others, and verifiability. Points of compatibility among several winter counts and agreement with independent sources of information help to establish the sometime fact of genuine historicity. These usually have to do with references to such occurrences as devastating visits of epidemic diseases, abnormally severe winters when people starved and even "crows fell," and unusual celestial phenomena like eclipses and meteorite showers. An example of the latter occurred in 1833 and was recorded on a Kiowa winter count (see Chapter 10).

There are many exceptions to compatibility, however. For example, the American Horse winter count and one by No Ears exhibit approximately 75 percent instances of failures of agreement or simple mutual relevance (DeMallie in Walker 1982:115–117). With idiosyncracies inherent in the drawing and in the "reading" of mnemonic figures, it is not surprising that original meanings often were lost with the deaths of their makers or that uniform results have often escaped their later would-be decipherers. George Hyde, drawing on his own experiences and those of Charles A. Eastman, an educated Santee Dakota medical doctor and collector of oral histories and traditions among the Sioux people in the late nineteenth and early twentieth centuries, was respectful but skeptical of the historical accuracy of any interpretation of pictographs purporting to record events going back more than sixty years from the then present (Hyde 1937:ix, 54n9). "From the Oglalas who are now living," Hyde wrote, "nothing very useful can be obtained on the history of their people back of the year 1850 . . . This is not poor memory; it is the frailty of human nature" (Hyde 1937:ix).

Hyde's comments on Sioux memory expose the Achilles' heel of even pictographically assisted orally transmitted pasts. That the winter counts could be aids to memory is not to be doubted. Nor, however, is their role as stimuli to imagination. Distinguishing the two among mixed conventionalized and individualized ideograms could hardly be straightforward, uninfluenced by more immediately pressing interests of their "readers." As simultaneously potential sources of genuine as well as spurious history they, like verbally propagated past reflections in general, invite both the respect and suspicion that Hyde, Eastman, Walker, DeMallie, and others have accorded the winter counts. Memory, as those students came to realize, and as the next chapter will show, is not and never has been an inert recorder of time's passage.

3

On Memory

Whether prompted by mnemonic aids such as painted bison hides, wampum belts, items in a medicine bag, the rhythm of chanting, or verbal prodding by listeners who know something about the matter, oral histories and traditions, by the fact of their orality, are artifacts of memory. As such, they are hostage to the eternal argument between memory's tenacity and its fickleness. The passage of time, changing family or national fortunes, and innumerable other factors subtly or brazenly intrude into that argument. Memory can no more escape "the slings and arrows of outrageous fortune" than can its human carriers. It adapts to the affairs of its time and place even while conserving some connections to earlier times and the same or other places.

Psychologists studying memory have recognized for some time that their subject is multidimensional. This is even clearer now than it was in the days of Frederick Bartlett, Hermann von Ebbinghaus, Sigmund Freud, William James, and the other pioneers of the field. Memory acquisition, preservation, and retrieval have been found to vary by type of memory, for example, short-term store, long-term store, episodic, semantic, procedural, cognitive, motor. Furthermore, time, experience, bias, culture, and other variables have been shown to be as indispensable to understanding memory as neurophysiological or other biological factors. Some recent discussions of this multidimensionality may be found in Bower (2000), Neisser (1982), Neisser and Hyman (2000), Parkin (1993), and Tulving and Craik (2000).

Of special relevance to the role of memory in oral traditions is the dichotomy Endel Tulving labeled *episodic* and *semantic* memories. As succinctly characterized by Alan Parkin (1993:39–40), the former is made up of "an individual's autobiographical record of past experience," whereas the latter embraces "our knowledge of language, rules, and concepts"—*and traditions,* I hasten to add. Episodic memories may be trivial, as in my remembering having had an underripe banana this morning, or momentous, as in my standing in a silent crowd with my father in early morning darkness on a railroad embankment in Holmesburg, Pennsylvania, to see President Roosevelt's funeral train on its way to Hyde Park. I will doubtless forget the banana episode as quickly as one does most such inconsequential incidents. But other things and events linger a lifetime in episodic memory, even some I do not regard as being as important as that experience in Holmesburg. Semantic memory, vis-à-vis the foregoing examples of episodic memory, stores and makes available to consciousness the generalized knowledge without which discrete bits of experience would have little or no meaning. It enables me to know what a banana is (a yellow tropical fruit that comes in bunches and so forth). By means of semantic memory, I understand what a funeral train is, where Holmesburg is located, who President Roosevelt was. These two kinds of memory interact in complex and not fully understood ways. There is a vast difference between an individual's first witnessing the performance of, say, a baptism and his or her knowing what that ceremony means. A common experience of ethnographers on an initial visit to a foreign community is puzzlement, perhaps disbelief, and even fear. The sudden realization of his or her alien status is called "culture shock." Simply put, it is only when the accumulation of episodic memories of discrete events is translated into semantic memory—the process whereby the particular loses some of its uniqueness and becomes integrated into generalizations—that the initial shocks of incomprehension are replaced by understanding and by knowledge.

A widely held belief credits important, especially dramatically important, events as being more reliably fixed in memory than is true of the more mundane. Their veracity is apt to be challenged only in the face of contradictory evidence or as the remembered event slips ever further back into remoter time. Even though intuitively sensible, there are so many instances of the failure of personal "dramatic" memory to withstand critical examination that this should give pause to anyone who would appeal to it in any particular case as being self-evident.

A powerful example of the shortcomings of such memories was revealed in the January 1946 proceedings of the Joint Congressional Committee Investigation on the Pearl Harbor tragedy. In sworn testimony before that committee, as summarized by the historian Gordon W. Prange (1982:712–713), a potentially history-changing meeting took place in late March 1941 between Admiral Husband E. Kimmel, Commander-in-Chief, United States Pacific Fleet, headquartered at Pearl Harbor, Hawaii; Captain William Ward (Poco) Smith, Chief of Staff, Pacific Fleet; and Captain Ellis M. Zacharias, commander of the cruiser *Salt Lake City* and a highly respected naval intelligence expert and student of Japan. At that meeting, Captain Zacharias said he advised Admiral Kimmel that if Japan decided on war with the United States "it would begin with an air attack on our fleet on a week-end and probably a Sunday morning." He remembered then predicting (correctly, as it turned out) the probable route of carrier-launched attackers and, further, that the enemy task force would make an immediate retreat following the attack. In reply to the admiral's request for advice on how to protect Pearl Harbor against such a possible attack, Captain Zacharias urged daily air patrols out to 500 miles along the approach he thought the Japanese would use, advice that for whatever reason was never acted upon. The captain claimed, and appeared to exhibit, a clear memory of all of this in his testimony to the investigating committee. Admiral Kimmel's memory of the meeting, however, was ambivalent. Captain Smith flatly contradicted Zacharias's account. Prange (1982:713) states, "So here we have two honorable, intelligent, and experienced officers telling contrary stories [only five years after their meeting and concerning one of the potentially most critical insights into what went wrong in preparedness to safeguard naval and military assets on Oahu from the strong possibility of a Japanese attack]. This situation is by no means unique in the Pearl Harbor problem, but this particular incident is one of the most nagging. And there it rests to this day." And this serious disparity of memories—memories in which some self-serving, if unconscious, bias doubtless played a role— belongs to *oral history,* not *oral tradition,* with the latter's even greater vulnerability to the erosion of authentic remembrance and reconfiguration by the unconscious substitution of the spurious.

Here is another example of oral history from the same period as the foregoing. This one is drawn from the first volume of Arthur M. Schlesinger, Jr.'s (2000:xiv) autobiography:

As a historian, I well know the fallibility of memory. I remember lunching one day with Dean Acheson when he was writing his superb memoir, *Present at the Creation.* He seemed more than usually wrathful. "I had a most disconcerting morning," he said, calling urgently for a dry martini. "I was writing about the decision in 1941 to freeze Japanese assets in the United States"—the decision that, we now know led the Japanese to attack Pearl Harbor. "I have the most vivid memory of the meeting in President Roosevelt's office. The President was sitting at his desk; Cordell Hull [the secretary of state] was sitting opposite him; I was in a chair by the Secretary's side. I can close my eyes and see the scene," he said, closing his eyes. "But my damned secretary,

Miss Evans, checked the record and found that Mr. Hull had the flu and was off in White Sulphur Springs recuperating. He wasn't at the meeting at all. I can't believe it."

Free-wheeling raconteurs—and Acheson was one of the best—improve their tales until telling reorganizes reality. Conscientious memoirists—and Acheson was one of the best—check the record [Schlesinger's brackets].

Still another specimen of the need for caution in crediting oral history with more stand-alone reliability than it deserves may be examined in Ulric Neisser's (1981) insightful comparison of John Dean's testimony before Congress about Watergate-related conversations in the Oval Office and what was later discovered to have been recorded on the infamous Nixon tapes. This particular case lays bare the consequences of the sometimes "frayed wiring" connecting episodic and semantic memories, even in a man celebrated for his "unusual" powers of detailed recollection. Individual conversations, not surprisingly, turned out to have been remembered, or disremembered, in the wider contexts of their personal, political, and legal enmeshment.

Here is a fourth and last example, this one drawn from ethnographic research in the northern plains and also entangled with an event that, while not as world-shaking as Pearl Harbor, the decision to freeze Japanese assets, or the denouement of a national scandal, was dramatic enough for its narrator-participant to presumably remember it accurately. This is a story in two versions recorded by Robert H. Lowie, probably the foremost twentieth-century student of the Plains Indians, a scholar who wrote his doctoral dissertation on their mythology, and who was, as previously noted (Chapter 2), a prominent skeptic of the latter's historical value. Lowie, of course, had records to check. His Crow informant did not. The story is called *A Battle with the Dakota* (Lowie 1942:19–22; reprinted in Du Bois 1960:145–148 and Dundes 1965:262–264).

In 1910 Lowie purchased a Crow "sacred" shield from its owners Yellow Brow and his father. A few years later Lowie got Yellow Brow to recite the shield's history, a recitation that concluded with a description of a battle with the Dakotas, an engagement in which the shield repelled those ancient enemies. Less than 20 years later Yellow Brow related the "same" story. While many of the details from the earlier account were retained in the later, such as the names of some of the participants (e.g., Wants To Die, Double Face, Young White Buffalo, Plays With His Face), the noticeable nervousness of Double Face before the battle, and his wanting to sing certain sacred songs in addition to those of the Big Dog Society, there also were a number of interesting discrepancies. Paramount among these was the omission of any reference to the shield and the substitution of the Cheyennes for the Dakotas. A new character makes an appearance in the second version of the story: one Dangling Foot, who is killed along with a small body of Crows. The first account given to Lowie may have been meant to assure him of the value of the shield, although such a motive would seem to have been more appropriate before or at the time of purchase. However that may be, the shield's importance had been obliterated in the later account of the battle. In the context of this story's reproduction, Lowie's observation that "it has been recognized for some time that individual storytellers within a tribe vary appreciably in their rendering of a tale" qualifies as something of an understatement vis-à-vis historical reliability.

The forensic psychologist Elizabeth Loftus would probably find little surprise in the foregoing vignettes. As a memory researcher often called upon to serve as an expert witness in criminal trials, she is intimately familiar with the discrepancies that frequently reveal a divorce between the actuality of events and their remembrance. She and other students of the mutations to which memory is subject in sober normal people—from the repetition of petty rumors to such more serious matters as childhood memories of sexual abuse and eyewitness recollections of murder—have learned due caution in accepting at face value what people think they remember.

> Memories don't just fade, as the old saying would have us believe; they also grow. What fades is the initial perception, the actual experience of the events. But every time we recall an event, we must reconstruct the memory, and with each recollection the memory may be changed—colored by succeeding events, other people's recollections or suggestions, increased understanding, or a new context.
>
> Truth and reality, when seen through the filter of our memories, are not objective facts but subjective, interpretative realities. We interpret the past, correcting ourselves, adding bits and pieces, deleting uncomplimentary or disturbing recollections, sweeping, dusting, tidying things up. Thus our representation of the past takes on a living, shifting reality; it is not fixed and immutable, not a place way back there that is preserved in stone, but a living thing that changes shape, expands, shrinks, and expands again, an amoebalike creature with powers to make us laugh, and cry, and clench our fists. Enormous powers—powers even to make us believe in something that never happened.
>
> Are we aware of our mind's distortions of our past experiences? In most cases, the answer is no. As time goes by and the memories gradu-

ally change, we become convinced that we saw or said or did what we remember [Elizabeth Loftus in Loftus and Ketcham 1991:20].

The examples of limited memory reliability just reviewed refer to the most common genre of memory acquisition: memory as a kind of echo of an individual's life experiences. Such memories are automatically produced and are not the result of conscious or intentional design. In a sense, memories simply happen. Their later recall, according to the studies of psychologists and psychiatrists, is much less instantaneous and potentially more convoluted than their initial genesis, as just indicated in the quotation from Loftus (see also Loftus and Loftus 1980; Offer 2000; Rubin 1995). Police and lawyers and judges learned long ago not to confuse the memories of plaintiffs, defendants, and witnesses—eyewitnesses not excluded—with what really happened or with the true facts under contention. As anyone who has ever been involved in courtroom procedures knows, wading through ambiguous and contradictory sworn testimonies of participants who "remember just as if it was yesterday" can be a tortuous experience and one not guaranteed to result in certain resolution.

Psychologists also have long been interested in finding ways to experiment with the social transmission of memory under controlled conditions. How can the accuracy of memory retention or loss be objectively explored in situations in which people tell one another stories they in their turn have received from yet others? How selective is such memory processing? Are there cultural variables that need to be factored in? Answers to questions like these are, or should be, of interest to students of oral traditions, whether or not they seek to use personal testimony or the folklore of groups of people, as in myths and legends, in historical studies. Combining psychological and ethnographic (especially folkloric) methods and data has shed some interesting, if still limited, light on these queries. Likewise illuminating have been studies of the diffusion of rumors (e.g., Allport and Postman 1947; Rosnow 1991), even if only to indicate how their operation differs from the intrinsically vertical transmission of information, and misinformation, in oral traditions.

One of the earliest and most influential of such social psychological explorations was published as "Some Experiments on the Reproduction of Folk Stories" in the journal *Folklore* by Frederick C. Bartlett (1920 [reprinted in Dundes 1965:247–258]). Later, that same author published one of the most influential books ever written on the study of memory (Bartlett 1977 [first published in 1932]). In the *Folklore* article he reported on investigations using 20 University of Cambridge undergraduates ("subjects"). Bartlett designed two quite different but complementary protocols employing American Indian and African folktales. These were short and simple. The first experiment, called "the method of repeated reproduction," had each subject read the same folktale and then periodically attempt to reproduce it from memory after variable lapses of time. Although there were some interesting results of this experiment, perhaps especially the tendency of many subjects to retain some of the minor details of the stories they attempted to reproduce at the expense of more important contents (Bartlett called this phenomenon "the persistence of the trivial"), they were less dramatic to students of folklore and other oral traditions than those of the second experiment. This one, called "the method of serial reproduction," was initiated by having a single subject read twice an American Indian or African folktale and then, after some 15 to 30 minutes, try to reproduce it from memory in writing. This attempted reproduction, not the original folktale, was given to a second subject who, after two readings and another 15- to 30-minute interval, tackled the job of writing down what he or she remembered of that first reproduction. This second reproduction was shown to a third subject who in turn attempted to reproduce *it*—and so on to the end when the twentieth subject wrote down the remembered version written by subject 19. Needless to say, a good deal had dropped out, been added, or been distorted by the end of the chain of reproductions. Bartlett, anticipating this, of course, was mainly interested not simply in the fact or even magnitude of cumulative change but in investigating just how change took place and in developing some general principles of change in the process of down-the-line person-to-person story transmission.

Criticisms of this pioneering work, particularly with regard to its possible implications for folklore studies and the temporal integrity of oral traditions generally, followed in short order and have continued on and off ever since its publication (for a fine and succinct review of some of this reaction see Alan Dundes's introduction to his reprinting of Bartlett's study [Dundes 1965:243–247]). Among the most cogent criticisms leveled at this innovating study was that the subjects *read* and *wrote* their reproductions of the folktales, whereas in the societies from which the tales had been taken they were *orally* transmitted and *aurally* perceived. Serious questions arise from the implication that visual and auditory memories are formed, stored, and recalled in identical ways. Certainly the conventions of reading and writing differ from those of listening and speaking, with the former typically being more formal, measured, edited, and polished. People just do not think and express themselves in the same way in the two forms of communication.

A second objection concerned the disconnection between the subjects and the folktales they read. The Cambridge students were not culturally ac-

climated to the world in which the stories were born and had meaning. As
the students and the stories did not share a common heritage, the stories
were alien to their understanding. One suggestion for improving such studies would have the subjects exposed to tales at home in their own environment, for example, stories concerning the University of Cambridge itself.
Closely linked to this consideration is the sociological contrast between a
group of individuals brought together to participate for a limited time in a
class situation and the more interpersonally linked members of, say, a lineage, clan, or tribe coming together to listen to words that concern them at
least in part by virtue of their common membership.

The folklorist Walter Anderson (cited in Dundes 1965:245–246) pointed
out that, unlike the subjects in Bartlett's experiment, the narrators of folktales typically would have heard several tellings of their tales, and from more
than a single source. This, he argued, would operate to act as a check on
accumulating errors. Anderson set up his own serial experiment in his German university, independently giving three subjects the same "short obscure" German legend. Each of these subjects then passed on their reproductions to a second subject, and so on through three independent chains of
transmission, concluding in each case with the eleventh reproduction. In
Dundes's words, "Anderson found that the three end products were similar
to Bartlett's final versions in that they revealed degenerative change. Anderson concluded that even with a comparison of the final versions from each
of the three chains, it was impossible to reconstruct the original version
exactly." But Anderson, alas, also employed writing instead of verbal communication in his experiment. And he failed to act on his own observation regarding multiple sources for the stories narrators recounted. Dundes
(1965:245) criticized both him and Bartlett for being ignorant of, or failing
to take into account, the likelihood that the huge difference in the intervals
between receiving and transmitting the stories (a half hour and a day in the
experiments, years in the societies of origin) is an important fault that ne-
glects to deal with a possibly crucial independent variable.

The Africanist anthropologist Siegfried F. Nadel (1937), inspired by Bartlett's experiments, set out to control the cultural variable by using African
students and a "folktale" he himself wrote based on Nupe and Yoruba stories. As summarized by Dundes (1965:269–270) in a precis in his *The Study
of Folklore,* Nadel gave the tale to 40 boys, half of them Nupes, the rest
Yorubas, and had them attempt to reproduce it from memory. He discovered that cultural differences were even more apparent in the results than
individual variation. For example, the Nupe reproductions were not only
freer and less exact than the Yorubas' but they also contrasted with the latter in paying more attention to matters of time and place than to the un-

folding of the story's plot. Although, as in any such exercise, the context was artificial—and context affects performance—it is no great leap of faith to infer that normally transmitted oral traditions are likewise susceptible to differences in cultural conventions. While such an inference seems hardly in need of justification beyond more than a cursory glance at a few of the world's mythologies, such simple controlled experiments as those just briefly reviewed, even with their flaws, have yielded independent data and pointed to a direction in need of following.

The Influence of Writing on Memory

As creative and distorting as memory so frequently is, in certain and not always understood circumstances it is also impressively capable of accurate retention of reams of detailed information. Indeed, human life as we know it would be impossible without that capability. And that retentive accuracy operates selectively with trivial matters as well as with the crucial. Just why and how memory delivers accurate recollections with respect to one situation or set of matters and not another is a lively and continuing field of psychological inquiry.

Memory can be trained. The training can be automatic and effortless— indeed virtually unconscious—as in little children who seem readily to absorb verbatim along with their native language simple counting-out rhymes and ditties like "Eenie Meenie" (Rubin 1995). Or the training can be deliberate and rigorous, as with actors learning their lines, students studying a foreign language, opera singers developing their repertoires, or devotees learning to recite sacred texts. In either situation, of course, there is always individual variation in the speed and degree of accuracy of memorization.

Some feats of accurate memorization are truly prodigious. The most extreme of these feats—*if at all accurately reported*—are awesome indeed, verging as they do on the preternatural. "In the 1984 *Guinness Book of Records*," Hunter (1985:226) reports, "the record listed under 'human memory' is the recital from memory of the 6666 verses of the *Koran* in 6 hours, the correctness being checked by 6 Koranic scholars who followed the recitation." The same writer, a psychologist with research interest in memory, further notes reports of the verbatim memorization of all 77,932 words in the Arabic *Koran* specifically, "by countless people, many of whom have no understanding of the Arabic language outside of the *Koran*" (Hunter 1985:226). Walter J. Ong (1982:65–66) similarly calls attention to claims of the word-for-word recitation by Brahman teachers or gurus and their students in India of the lengthy and complexly worded *Vedas* or Hindu sacred texts. In another often-credited example of lengthy verbal recall, the previously cited

psychologist Ian M. L. Hunter instances the celebrated memory of Lord
Macaulay. If not in the same class with those just cited, the latter is certainly
noteworthy. Already known for his ability to recite verbatim great swaths
of the Shakespearean corpus and half at least if not all of the 10,565 words
of Milton's *Paradise Lost,* "He was always willing to accept a friendly challenge to a feat of memory. One day, in the Board-room of the British Museum, Sir David Dundas saw him hand to Lord Aberdeen a sheet of foolscap,
covered with writing arranged in three parallel columns down each of the
four pages. This document, of which the ink was still wet, proved to be a
full list of the Senior Wranglers [undergraduates] at Cambridge, with their
dates and colleges, for the hundred years during which the names of Senior Wranglers had been recorded in the University Calendar" (Trevelyan
1876:2:178–179; also quoted in Hunter 1985:227–228). Such a tour de
force of memorization of sheer trivia—something of a quite different order
from recalling the structured interdependent texts of the *Koran* or the *Vedas*
or the works of playwrights and poets—is difficult to credit without sub-
stantiation. Hunter does not indicate whether anyone actually checked Macaulay's list for its accuracy, so I checked the source myself in Trevelyan and
found that no one had, or at least that Macaulay's biographer made no mention of such a test had it been made (Trevelyan 1876:2:178–179). The story
may nevertheless be true, but unverifiable as it is, it is hardly as credible as
the evidential data Hunter otherwise musters for his controlled investigations into lengthy verbatim recall.

But it is both disheartening and amusing, after this citing of Lord Macaulay's alleged inerrancy of memory, to take note of Henry Adams's estimate, in 1895 in the *American Historical Review,* of at least 30,000 factual
errors in Macaulay's *History of England* (cited in Jordy 1952:130). Anthropological, folkloric, and historical as well as psychological literature has led too
many researchers astray by the uncritical valuing of unverified accounts of
human memory. While probably most people claim to know, or know of,
individuals having extraordinary ability to exactly remember things that
happened long ago or to recall with word-for-word exactness conversations
overheard or texts read months, years, or even decades previously, they would
also agree that such individuals are rare. And they are probably much rarer
than people think.

On the basis of data collected from psychometric analysis, experiments in
cognitive psychology, ethnography, and historical and biographical sources,
Hunter argues that true, especially lengthy, verbatim recall, often referred to
as "tape-recorder memory," is much less common than usually credited and,
when it can be investigated and confirmed, it exists in only special circumstances (Hunter 1984, 1985). Those special circumstances include not only

the extraordinary motivation of the aforementioned actors learning their lines and novitiates committing sacred texts to memory but most of all *the presence of a written text*. Hunter's ethnographic data are drawn from others' fieldwork in parts of Europe (especially Yugoslavia and Hungary), Africa, and Oceania (Micronesia), as well as from cross-cultural examinations of historiographic differences between literate and primarily nonliterate societies. While ethnographic samples can always be improved, those consulted by Hunter constitute a respectable body of reliable data that generate powerful implications for comparable studies in other parts of the world and other periods of time.

"Tape-recorder memory" or lengthy verbatim recall (LVR), as Hunter defines it, is in fact not very lengthy. The "tape" in the "recorder" turns out to be astonishingly short. To qualify as lengthy verbatim recall, a remembrance must consist of a minimum of 50 (!) words, and those words must exactly duplicate the original words claimed to be remembered, and they must be in precisely the same order. Synonyms and paraphrases are not acceptable as evidence of verbatim recall. Of special interest to would-be users of oral traditions as sources of historical information, lengthy verbatim recall, as Hunter appears to have demonstrated, is text-dependent both for its genesis and its survival. In his own words, "the human accomplishment of lengthy verbatim recall arises as an adaptation to written text *and does not arise in cultural settings where text is unknown*. The assumption that nonliterate cultures encourage lengthy verbatim recall is the mistaken projection by literates of text-dependent frames of reference" (Hunter 1985: 207; italics mine).

How, it might be asked, does one test for lengthy verbatim recall in non-literate people? In the absence of a written text as a check there was no practicable or reliable way until the historically recent development of word-for-word accuracy in stenographic writing or, best of all, the even more recent invention of the portable battery-powered tape-recorder (see Henige 1982). The classicist/philologist Milman Parry and his student Albert B. Lord, with the latter innovation in their young hands in the short middle years between the two World Wars, revolutionized the study of the structure and mode of recall of contemporary and thus indirectly also ancient, oral traditions. In doing so, they likewise exposed the scholarly and popular myth of the ubiquity and length of verbatim memory to be found in primarily oral societies and among illiterates in otherwise literate ones (Lord 1960; Parry 1971; Parry et al. 1974; Peabody 1975).

Parry and Lord worked with illiterate Serbo-Croatian balladeers widely celebrated for their astonishing ability to recite (sing) famous oral traditions. Many of their ballads were reputed to be old—some were alleged to date back as far as the 1389 battle of the Serbs and Turks at Kossovo, and they ran to hundreds, thousands, and even tens of thousands of words. The ballad singers claimed absolute word-for-word fidelity in every performance they gave. They believed they possessed true verbatim recall. Some even said they were able to repeat without a single error all the lines of a lengthy ballad they had heard only once. Listeners in the taverns where they performed and much of the general public were inclined to so credit them. When Parry and Lord and their assistants tape-recorded repeated performances of the "same" ballads by the same singers, however, it was immediately obvious that each performance was in fact unique. Except for the general story line, names of particularly important places and characters, short stock phrases, and traditional epithets, every repetition of a ballad was in essence a new composition, different from both predecessor and successor. As the psychologist David C. Rubin (1995:7) put it, in citing Parry and Lord's discoveries in his own major contribution to memory research, "Singers may report that they repeat a piece word for word, but their actions do not support their claim." Indeed, they do not even think of "words" the way literate people do:

> Man without writing thinks in terms of sound groups and not in words, and the two do not necessarily coincide. When asked what a word is, he will reply that he does not know, or he will give a sound group which may vary in length from what we call a word to an entire line of poetry, or even an entire song. The word for "word" means an "utterance." When the singer is pressed then to say what a line is, he, whose chief claim to fame is that he traffics in lines of poetry, will be entirely baffled by the question; or he will say that since he has been dictating [to the researchers] and has seen his utterances being written down, he has discovered what a line is, although he did not know it as such before, because he had never gone to school [Lord 1960:25].

The word *verbatim* is much abused, as Hunter, Lord, Parry, and others have pointed out in the preceding pages. *The Oxford English Dictionary* (second edition) defines it as an adverb meaning "word for word; in the exact words"; as an adjective: "corresponding with, or following, an original word for word"; and as a substantive: "a full or word-for-word report of a speech." Notwithstanding dictionary definitions and common usage occasionally conforming therewith, it is apparent that the term or its functional equivalents (as in "precisely" or "exactly" recalled or recited) are often employed even when in fact there are no grounds to assert anything more than an assumed rough similarity to an original utterance. I and others of my age cohort have known innumerable friends and acquaintances, I once among them, who swore—vehemently swore, when challenged—that they remembered exactly and word-for-word what Ilsa (Ingrid Bergman) asked of the piano player in the classic film *Casablanca:* "Play it again, Sam. Play 'As Time Goes By.'" But she didn't. What she said was, "Play it once, Sam. For old time's sake. Play it, Sam. Play 'As Time Goes By.'"

As shown by the following two examples, this indiscriminate usage often keeps company with the intuitively appealing fallacy, all too commonly accepted by archaeologists and ethnographers, and even historians and classicists (of all people!), that preliterate and later nonliterate people in otherwise literate societies had (and have) superior memories to those of citizens of modern, literate polities. This alleged superiority is usually attributed to the special need of societies without writing to compensate for its absence by fostering more rigorous attention to the development of extended and exact recall among its members and by honoring those who so excel. The pervasiveness of this fallacy makes more understandable the ready attribution by many otherwise worldly interrogators of "verbatim" recall to tribal "elders." The curators of oral—as opposed to literate—societies' histories, it is argued, surely must keep their memories honed by their repetitive exercise before a demanding audience, many of whose members know the stories recited if not all the details. Lineage and clan ancestors are to be remembered not only because it is respectfully owed them but also because ramifying rights and obligations are entailed in such knowledge—and in the acknowledgment by others of its authenticity. Particular pains to keep the record straight are supposed to be absolutely obligatory among genealogists in chiefdoms and kingdoms. Legitimacy is less apt to face challenge when proximate and more remote ancestors can be summoned in memory to attest it. Lacking writing, the genealogist's reciting of lines of descent is critical. Not least, of course, is the assumption and exhibition of reliable memory in religious and curing ceremonies—they are not necessarily distinguishable—in which accuracy and correct step-by-step procedures are regarded as mandatory if they are to be efficacious. War honors are to be remembered. The entirety of a nonliterate people's conception of themselves and the universe is carried in and can be retrieved only from memory. Aided only by such mnemonics as they may have devised, such people have nothing else. Their memories, it is assumed, must therefore be better than those of literate folk. So goes the reasoning. Scholarly dissertations along these lines are not difficult to find. I cite a particularly explicit instance of this type of argument from the work of the distinguished student of the Icelandic sagas Peter Hallberg, as translated by Paul Schach:

For people nowadays it must certainly seem odd that narratives which fill several hundred printed pages should have been memorized and transmitted practically verbatim from one generation to the next. But in former times, when the art of writing was unknown or at best known to very few, conditions must have been far more favorable for oral tradition than in our day. A person was simply compelled to store in his memory all sorts of facts and figures which one today can look up in books. The Icelandic Law Speaker, for example, was originally supposed to recite the entire body of law at the General Assembly during his three-year period of office. The very purpose and intention of remembering something must formerly have strengthened memory and recollection in a manner different from today, when there are so many possibilities of relieving one's memory. It also seems reasonable that the concentration required for memorization could have been much greater in an older, more primitive and more homogeneous society than in our modern, complicated culture with its tremendous and continuous piling up of new material through books, newspapers, radio, television, etc. But in the old Icelandic community there may perhaps have existed other special conditions favoring a reliable oral tradition. One often senses in the sagas a remarkable concern that certain deeds should really be remembered and reported. An episode in *Egils saga* describes how Kveld-Ulfr and his son Skalla-Grimr with their followers "clear" one of the king's ships they come upon. They kill all men on board except two or three, the ones they regard as least important. In return these have to tell what men were on board and what their errand was. Then they are released and ordered to betake themselves to the king and to report accurately to him what had happened and which opponents of his had carried out the deed. The thought of renown after death can for the characters in the sagas be a powerful incentive to do their utmost . . . They already see themselves, so to speak, in the light of history [Hallberg 1962:51–52].

Ironically, only a few pages later in the same publication, the author undercuts his own arguments. He defers to the scholarly judgment of the saga analyst Sigurthur Nordal when he agrees with him that "thus in a number of crucial points the supporting framework of the action of *Hrafnkatla* has been proven to be fictitious, and consequently the belief in the historical reliability of this saga collapses" (Hallberg 1962:67). And therefore: "Admittedly the question of history versus fiction, oral tradition versus individual authorship has not been answered once and for all by Nordal's contribution. He himself has demanded emphatically that each saga must be examined individually with regard to its historical veracity, its sources, and its treatment of subject matter. But when *Hrafnkatla,* regarded as among the historically most reliable sagas, is exposed as a work of fiction, one must be on guard against alleged historical tradition in other cases, too" (Hallberg 1962:67).

Although it may be true that there are and were individuals capable of accurately reciting from memory lengthy portions, or indeed all, of certain of the Icelandic sagas in their written or published form, there is little warrant for assuming anything comparable when those sagas existed in preliterate form in Greenland and Iceland (see Chapter 4). Once committed to writing, the sagas ceased to be the living, adapting narratives they had been in previous generations of retelling. Leaving aside transcribers' would-be emendations, such history as the earliest surviving manuscript commemorates can be at best no more than the embalming of the latest rendition of a lineage of tales.

Here is the second example of the combining of alleged verbatim recall and the attribution of superior memories to nonliterate peoples. After concluding that two of the characteristic limitations of oral traditions generally are deficiencies in or even lack of chronology and relative infrequency of truly independent means of confirming what they affirm about past events, Jan Vansina acknowledges the fact of some exceptions. A North American example he cites (Vansina 1985:189) comes from the ethnographic and ethnohistorical work of Gordon M. Day (1972) with the St. Francis Abenaki Indians in southwestern Quebec. Peter Nabokov (2002:76) also enlists this frequently cited study in support of the sometime historical reliability of oral traditions not dependent on documentary sources.

Between 1959 and 1963 Day recorded two Abenaki oral traditions and discovered an unpublished manuscript relating events that had taken place 200 years earlier. In 1759, immediately before the British triumph at Quebec and the end of the French and Indian War, Major Robert Rogers and his celebrated Rangers attacked and destroyed the French-allied Abenaki village of St. Francis. The two oral traditions and the manuscript, the latter dated 1869 and containing "observations made at St. Francis" and some "family traditions of the raid," are said to be compatible with both English and French records of the attack. Furthermore, they yielded additional information that could only have been known to the Indians themselves—insider information that, if true, offers a resolution to a puzzling discrepancy between the British and French accounts of the number of Indians killed (200 versus 30, respectively). According to that information, between Rogers's locating and then reconnoitering the unsuspecting village and launching his pre-dawn assault, an unknown Indian member of his force, protected by darkness and keeping himself out of plain view, managed to warn one of its residents and, through her, to warn others to flee. Not realizing that his surprise had been compromised and that many Indians had already escaped into the surrounding woods in advance of the attack, Rogers may simply have estimated the number who likely would have died in their houses when he burned the town. Day relates the interesting possibility that the single Indian of Rogers's command lost in the attack, a man Rogers merely identified as a Stockbridge, may have been the one who had given the warning to the Abenaki woman or girl. After the attackers had left the scene, returning villagers came across a badly wounded stranger who identified himself as a "Mahigan." Knowing he was about to be killed by the enraged survivors, the helpless man begged that he first be baptized. Unaware that he might have been their mysterious benefactor, they mockingly allowed him to choose a Christian name before "baptizing" him with an ax.

Day records that the first of the two accounts he was told was from an elderly woman. She had learned the story when a young girl from her old aunt. The aunt had been told the story when she was a girl from her grandmother, who had been a little girl at St. Francis when Rogers' Rangers attacked. These transmissions, Day (1972:103) stresses, have "brought us the story of an eye-witness to a 1759 event in only two steps." He continues, "The second tradition was obtained from an elderly man who had it from his grandmother, who was born in 1830 and had known persons who were alive at the time of the raid" (Day 1972:105).

> These traditions often touch the historical record at certain points. At these points, they usually coincide with the historical record or are at least compatible with it, and of course go on to present new statements about the event, which, if true, enlarge our knowledge of it. This congruity with history must increase our confidence in the traditions where it is not the result of acquaintance with history, *a thing to be watched for in a literate community.* That is, the validity of the oral tradition is enhanced by its goodness of fit with the historical data. But the phenomenon which struck me was the frequency with which the traditional statements solved puzzles created by the partial coverage of the documents and the frequency with which the data of history and the data of tradition taken together form a congruous and more believable whole. This phenomenon I have chosen to call *oral tradition as complement*" [Day 1972:100; first italics mine].

Day's assertion that "acquaintance with history," by which he means knowledge of the past informed by written material, is absent in this case is challengeable on grounds he himself provided. In addition to the 1869 manuscript previously mentioned, that same year saw the publication in Montreal of a *History of the Eastern Townships* that contained an account, "curiously garbled" though it might have been, of the Rangers' withdrawal from St. Francis (Day 1972:102–103). That the St. Francis Abenakis were not all illiterate, at any rate beginning at least as early as 1773, is indicated by their starting to send some of their sons in that year to Dartmouth College (Day 1972:99). Was knowledge of what was contained in that manuscript and especially in that publication regarding the most traumatic event in the community's history unknown to or not talked about by the descendants of the original participants? Were the oral traditions truly virginal, innocent of all contact with written sources? In view of the foregoing, prudence advises that the case for pristine orality in this instance is suspect. At best, it is no more than a possibility.

Not even that can be said for Day's belief in old Abenakis, and eastern Algonquians generally, "carefully and deliberately training young children until some of them knew the old stories *verbatim*" (Day 1972:103; my emphasis). Following this statement of faith is the transcription of the first oral tradition of the raid, that of the elderly woman. This contains the presumptively verbatim words spoken two centuries earlier to the young woman or girl by the unknown Indian: "Don't be afraid. Friend. I am your friend, and those enemies, those strange Iroquois, they are there in the little woods [planning] that when all [the Abenakis] leave for home they will kill them all, their husbands, and burn your village, and I come to warn you" (Day 1972:103; his brackets). Two pages later, in a discussion of the second of the raid traditions, that given by the old man, "*the exact words of the warner are recalled*" (my italics). These are: "My friends, I am telling you. I would warn you. They are going to exterminate you" (Day 1972:105).

Social Conditioning of Remembering

There is another dimension to the use of memory in reconstructing history beyond whatever can be shown to be its innate limitations in the human species. Already alluded to in some of the foregoing examples, it is the social context within which memory operates, and it is critical in the contemplation of oral traditions considered as history. Following their examination of chiefly genealogies of the West African Tiv and Gonja peoples, Jack Goody and Ian Watt were able to show how memory, as socially manipulated in oral traditions, can be a useful, indeed sometimes essential, medium for validating the claims of new generations of leaders. So employed, such genealogical memories "serve the same function that Malinowski [1926:23, 43] claimed for myth; they act as 'charters' of present social institutions rather than as faithful records of times past" (Goody and Watt 1968:33). History via orality rather than literacy has its advantages, at least for those who come out on top. In Hawaii, as throughout Polynesia generally, chiefly genealogies reflected the interests of their sponsors, elevating, for example, a junior family line to more senior status by emphasizing higher-ranking ancestors at the expense of the less exalted: "Genealogists were called the wash-basins of the *ali'i* [chiefs] in which to cleanse them [that is, their genealogies]" (Linnekin 1997:13, quoting the Hawaiian historian David Malo).

Genealogies are not the only products of oral traditions to be "washed." Excluding perhaps brief formulaic utterances repeated at short intervals, the reciters of oral histories, traditions, myths, and legends, including those regarded as sacral, inevitably introduce changes in what they transmit, whether they intend to or not. Although such tradition-purveyors in oral societies may be convinced that their recitals of such material exactly recapitulate the "original" versions to which each was exposed—which versions were not necessarily the same—their own memory-based renditions and those of their successors inescapably shift with each performance. Notwithstanding their dedication to authenticity and convictions of exact replication of what they seek to transmit unaltered and true, the immutable mutates:

> Statements are often made about verbatim oral memorization of the Vedic hymns in India, presumably in complete independence of any texts. Such statements, so far as I know, have never been assessed in view of the findings of Parry and Lord and related findings concerning oral "memorization." The Vedas are lengthy collections and old, probably composed between 1500 and 900 or 500 B.C.—the variance that must be allowed in possible dates shows how vague are present-day contacts with the original settings in which grew the hymns, prayers, and liturgical formulas that make up these collections.
>
> . . . In the wake of the recent studies of oral memory . . . questions arise as to the ways in which memory of the Vedas actually worked in a purely oral setting—if there ever was such a setting for the Vedas totally independent of texts. Without a text, how could a given hymn —not to mention the totality of hymns in the collections—be stabilized word for word, and that over many generations? Statements, made in good conscience by oral persons, that renditions are word for word the same, as we have seen, can be quite contrary to fact. Mere assertions, frequently made by literates, that such lengthy texts were retained verbatim over generations in a totally oral society can no longer be taken at face value without verification. What was retained? The first recitation of a poem by its originator? How could the origi-

nator ever repeat it word for word the second time and be sure he had
done so? . . .

In point of fact, the Vedic texts—on which we base knowledge of
the Vedas today—have a complex history and many variants, facts
which seem to suggest that they hardly originated from an absolutely
oral tradition.

. . . oral memorization is subject to variation from social pressures.
Narrators narrate what audiences call for or will tolerate. When the
market for a printed book declines, the presses stop rolling but thousands of copies may remain. When the market for an oral genealogy
disappears, so does the genealogy itself, utterly [Ong 1982:65–67].

Jack Goody's decades-long studies of African material have added enormously to contemporary understanding of the structures of oral literatures
everywhere (e.g., Goody 1972, 1987; Goody and Watt 1968). They have
helped substitute more substantive empirical measurements in place of subjective impressions in the assaying of the relationship between such compositions and individual and collective memories. His African findings are
certainly in essential agreement with Walter Ong's cautions regarding the
value of much scholarly, as well as popular, crediting of staggering feats of
verbatim oral memory in recitations of the Hindu Vedas (Goody 1987:110–
122, 167–190). The latter, of course, even had the advantage of a vastly
longer association with writing than was true of the peoples among whom
Goody has worked.

West Africa, where Goody has concentrated his field efforts, is home to
an impressive number of lengthy, complex *myths* (in Goody's typology, oral
compositions usually in poetic form and considered sacred) and *epics* (usually in prose and not considered sacred). One of the former is called the
Bagre of the LoDagaa people of Ghana (Goody 1972, 1987:79–81, 86–91,
94–96, 99–105, 167–177). Despite its length (one of the versions Goody
recorded consists of some 12,000 lines of verse and required close to eight
hours to recite), all performances of the Bagre—they are as much ceremonies, with dancing and music, as recitations of the myth—are regarded by
their performers and audiences as exactly the same. Because he was able to
experience parts of several Bagre performances and to record another entire
recitation, this time by tape recorder as opposed to the earlier hand transcription, Goody (1987:88) demonstrated that the claim of repeated exactness appeared to refer more to a general structural similarity rather than to
verbal accuracy. Speakers condensed, reinterpreted, elaborated, and even deleted elements, themes, and story lines in addition to word and line substitutions, often apparently unaware of the spontaneity they and their audi-

ences engendered. They were not tape recorders on "playback" mode. They *interacted* with their audiences. One gets the impression from Goody's descriptions that sympathetic inventiveness as much as memorization—*and* what I would call quasi-memorization—produced each oral edition. In fact, examples of prolonged verbatim recall from previous performances of the Bagre were far fewer than Goody had anticipated when he began his research. The exactness of repetition he found had mainly to do with order of ceremonies and intention to honor a spirit of authenticity while eliciting approval. These findings appear to be compatible with those derived from others' studies of the long epic poems (which "poems" are in fact usually prose) of the Fang, Mongo-Nkundo, Fulani, and Bambara peoples to which Goody makes reference.

Reading another eminent Africanist and contributor to the scholarly study of oral literature and the role of memory in its perpetuation, Ruth Finnegan, reinforces many of Ong's and Goody's conclusions while adding other considerations that bear on them. The context of the following brief quotations is her concern with stories and storytelling for purposes of amusement, moral tales, initiation and other ceremonial rituals, family and national histories, and origin myths and other grand oral traditions that, while supposed to be true, may not always be universally believed. Investigating this latter consideration may demand inquisitorial skills usually lacking in collectors of oral literature. Indeed, the question seems rarely to be raised, Goody excepted. That aside, it will be obvious by now, both from the foregoing and the following quotations, that faltering memory is not the single parent of variation and change in oral literature and specifically the oral traditions in which history is supposed to reside.

A further point about too much dependence on typologies here is that this under-emphasizes one of the most striking characteristics of much oral literature—its flexible and unfixed quality. This applies particularly in the case of prose. In the actual narration of stories—and the actual narration is what matters in oral literature—there is very often no fixed wording, and the narrator is free to bind together the various episodes, motifs, characters, and forms at his disposal into his own unique creation, suited to the audience, the occasion, or the whim of the moment. The same point has been well made by Ruth Benedict in the context of American Indian (Zuni) stories [Finnegan 1970:328–329; see my Chapter 5, this volume, for discussion of Benedict's work].

Contrary to the assumptions of many writers, the likelihood of stories having been handed down from generation to generation in a wordperfect form is in practice very remote. This whole concept, in fact, is much more plausible in the case of *written* than of oral literature. As already remarked . . . one of the main characteristics of oral literature is its verbal flexibility . . . so that even if the basic plot did, in a given case, turn out really to date back centuries or millenia—and in one sense it is a truism that all stories (written or unwritten) have already been told—this would be only a very minor element in the finished work of art produced in the actual telling. The verbal elaboration, the drama of the performance itself, everything in fact which makes it a truly *aesthetic* product comes from the contemporary teller and his audience and not from the remote past [Finnegan 1970:319].

Socially sanctioned (more formally, "institutionalized") memories, while perhaps convincing to those without inclination to question them, or simply not having access to means of appeal, can be complicating hindrances to free recall of past events. These may be obvious, or they may be more subtle, as in the unconscious conditioning of individual recall by cultural factors: the press of what the sociologist Maurice Halbwachs, early among others, called "collective memory" or "the social frameworks of memory" (Halbwachs 1992; see Schwartz 2000 for its relevance to political biography). "Instead of viewing collective memory as the past working its will on the present," as Peter Novick (1999:3) puts it, "Halbwachs explored the ways in which present concerns determine what of the past we remember and how we remember it."

Collective memory, as Halbwachs used the phrase, is not just historical knowledge shared by a group. Indeed, collective memory is in crucial senses ahistorical, even anti-historical. To understand something historically is to be aware of its complexity, to have sufficient detachment to see it from multiple perspectives, to accept the ambiguities, including moral ambiguities, of protagonists' motives and behavior. Collective memory simplifies; sees events from a single, committed perspective; is impatient with ambiguities of any kind; reduces events to mythic archetypes. Historical consciousness, by its nature, focuses on the historicity of events—that they took place then and not now, that they grew out of circumstances different from those that now obtain. Memory, by contrast, has no sense of the passage of time; it denies the "pastness" of its objects and insists on their continuing presence [Novick 1999:3–4].

Neither Halbwachs (nor Coser, his editor and translator) nor Novick was primarily concerned with oral societies, of course. Their observations on collective memory nevertheless have even more cogency with respect to the latter because of the absence of written records to serve as checks. One must always be aware that oral traditions, when taken as free sources of historical information, are in fact impaled on the twin horns of memory and social servitude. Many of the memories people have, of course, are idiosyncratic—unique to each individual. But these are not the stuff of collective memory, except perhaps on the essentially ephemeral and small scale of immediate family experience. Neither do they seem to figure in the development of oral traditions. These latter draw their inspiration from collective memory and doubtless in turn have reciprocal influence. In terms of memory, if oral traditions track any history, it is one of memories of memories, each in their turn in thrall to retrogressively once-contemporary social needs. Where there are no extramural checks on such memories, they must inevitably lead in an accelerating regression to historical indeterminacy.

Robert Hall, with some of whose work I take issue elsewhere in this book (e.g., Chapter 8), has sensitively, indeed poignantly, reflected on the tragedy of pasts extinguished in actuality and eroded in memory, even if he has felt less constrained thereby than have I in proposing reconstructions. His words seem a fitting conclusion to this essay:

> In *Black Elk Speaks* [Neihardt 1979] Black Elk explains to John Neihardt that the spirit world "is the real world that is behind this one, and everything we see here is something like a shadow from that world." The same philosophy [shades of Plato!] applies nicely to culture history. The historical past was real, but the evidence that survives of it can be distorted and disconnected, like a shadow cast on a field of rocks. The evidence includes traditions often imperfectly transmitted between generations; ceremonies whose symbolism has changed to become supportive of new values; origin myths naturalized to new locations; ceremonial objects whose full significance was known only to elders who have died; the bones of Indians whose deaths silenced personal stories that still await telling; buried artifacts that speak of technologies long forgotten; and earth constructions that speak of rituals long abandoned [Hall 1997:169].

4

Norsemen, Trojans, and Ancient Israelites

With the advantage of individual and collective memory studies freshly in mind and with the purpose of demonstrating the nonparochial character of other issues at stake in juxtaposing archaeology and oral traditions, the present chapter invites critical attention to three of the most famous Western traditions that are widely believed to harbor hefty components of historical veracity. These examples survive *in the form we have come to know them,* of course, because of the fortunate intervention of writing. They enjoy two other advantages for my purpose. They are well known and are seriously regarded, even sacredly so in the ultimate case, by a great many informed people. Finally, it is precisely the fact of their being Western, of having sprung from cultural hearths independent of Native America, that makes them germane, qua traditions, to understanding something of the latter's oral traditions as *they* bear on archaeological reconstructions of cultural pasts.

An obvious difference between these Western and American Indian traditions lies in how and by whom they came to be written down. Whereas the former were part of the oral inheritance of those who recorded them, most of the latter were not. It may thus be argued that comparisons between the two are obscured by the introduction of a foreign cultural/linguistic filter between oral fount and written transcript that obtains in one case but not the other. How important is this complication? It does raise the possibility of an additional source for error.

Even though most recorded Indian oral histories and traditions came from their own lips, their translation into an alien language rendered in an introduced medium must prompt questions about fidelity to the originals, as most ethnographers have long been aware. And as some Native Americans themselves complain, that European cultural/linguistic filter through which their mythologies and other traditions must pass on their way to recording changes them. In transmission they are apt to become stilted, lose much of their original vitality, and may be significantly altered in meaning. Ironically, taken at face value, this complaint sabotages the insistence of many critics who argue that archaeologists should do more to incorporate Indian oral traditions in their work. Chapter 5 examines some of these problems. Suffice it to suggest here that some considerable portion of the deficiencies Native Americans complain of are in fact intrinsic to any and all attempts to convert what is sometimes called oral literature into written form, whether or not the intrusion of a foreign cultural/linguistic filter plays a part. Indeed, it may be questioned whether the latter is wholly absent in the cases of the Old World traditions examined in the present chapter. Certainly some of the Israelite legacy derived from the non-Semitic Sumerians. And neither ancient Greek nor Old Icelandic are the languages by which most modern readers know the *Iliad* and the *Odyssey* or the Norse sagas, respectively. Moreover, it is the American Indian's traditions that at least sometimes had the advantage of initial conversion into literary form by linguistically trained students. This fact in itself suggests that the pertinence of the alien filter objection in the American cases, while viable, is likely weaker than its assertion.

The Icelandic Vinland Sagas

Oral accounts about lands west and southwest of the freshly established Norse settlements in Greenland, stories committed to writing by later generations in Iceland, are often cited as exemplars of the power of oral traditions to preserve history. For Peter Hallberg's ambivalent endorsement of historical reliability in the Icelandic sagas generally see the previous chapter. The two traditions pertinent to the discovery of America reside in *Saga of the Greenlanders* and *Saga of Erik the Red* (Hreinsson 1997:1:1–32; Magnusson and Palsson 1966; Thorsson and Scudder 2000:626–674). The first of these recorded versions is believed to have been composed and committed to writing in about A.D. 1200; the second in about 1260 (Wahlgren 1986:96). Because the originals no longer exist, however, the sagas survive only in later copies whose fidelity to their disappeared predecessors ought not be taken at face value. In the words of two of the translators of these sagas: "It must always be borne in mind that the Icelandic sagas were never museum pieces, embalming for all time a literary act; they were living things, and later generations thought nothing of adapting or re-writing them to suit changing taste" (Magnusson and Palsson 1966:31).

The oldest copy of *Greenlanders' Saga* ("a copy of a copy of an oral account" [Wahlgren 1986:91]) was written sometime between A.D. 1382 and 1395; the two earliest versions of *Erik's Saga* date from the early 1300s and the late 1400s, respectively, and they fail to agree between them in many particulars as well as in style (Magnusson and Palsson 1966:29–31). They also differ in major ways from *Greenlanders' Saga*. Commenting on the larger corpus of Icelandic sagas generally (*Islendinga sogur*), which he characterizes as "fictionalized accounts" of the Viking Age, even though they retain some historical facts, Robert Kellogg attributes their writing mainly to the thirteenth and fourteenth centuries, some 300 years after the events that inspired them (in Hreinsson 1997:1:xxx, xlii, and in Thorsson and Scudder 2000:xviii, xxxv [Kellogg's *Introduction* is identical in both publications]).

According to *Greenlanders' Saga*, five "follow-up" voyages, one aborted because of bad weather, came on the heels of the accidental sighting of America near the end of the tenth century A.D. by the thereafter insignificant Bjarni Herjolfsson, who, while claiming to have seen previously unknown lands, some with large trees and other appealing resources, made no landfalls. A few years later Leif Eriksson set out from Greenland to explore these sightings. From north to south he named the discovered lands Helluland (probably Baffin Island), Markland (probably Labrador), and Vinland. The location of the latter is much disputed on philological, botanical, and other grounds. Although Newfoundland is in contention for that identification because of its Viking-age site at L'Anse aux Meadows, some saga authorities opt for New England or even Long Island as more likely (Sigurdsson in Thorsson and Scudder 2000:626–634; Wahlgren 1986). However that is finally resolved, at some place in Vinland, perhaps at L'Anse aux Meadows at the northern tip of Newfoundland's great western peninsula, Leif established his temporary quarters (Leifsbudir). It was near that place, wherever it was, that his elfish German companion Tyrkr found the grapevines and grapes that have generated disputation ever since. The northern limits of the wild grapes that figure so prominently in the Vinland stories lie well to the south of Newfoundland, and the proposal that *vin* refers to something other than true *grapes* is still controversial (Wahlgren 1969, 1986).

After Leif's expedition returned to Greenland, each of his two brothers made their own western voyages. Thorvald Eriksson was able to find Leifsbudir, explored farther afield, had the first encounters with the native people of the new land (*Skraelings*), was killed, and thus became the first white man to be buried in America. The other brother, Thorstein, failed in his attempt to find the new lands and was forced to turn back because of storms and fog. Thorfinn Karlsefni, says *Greenlanders' Saga*, was the next to visit Vinland. He also found Leifsbudir, overwintered two years there, traded with and had fights with the Skraelings (in one of which a bellowing bull frightened them off), and had his wife, the tenacious twice-widowed

Gudrid, present him with a son, the first white child born in America. The last attempt to establish a colony in the new world was that of Freydis Eriksdottir, Leif's illegitimate half-sister, and her husband Thorvard. This expedition, which some authorities believe is pure fiction (Wahlgren 1986), made it to Vinland only to destroy its chances at permanency by internal divisions and mass murders instigated, and even committed in the case of the female victims, by Freydis herself.

Erik's Saga relates only two sailings across the Davis Strait to North America following the first sightings of land, which were accidental and this time credited to Leif Eriksson, not Bjarni Herjolfsson. As in *Greenlanders' Saga,* Thorstein Eriksson fails in his attempt to duplicate his brother's achievement, let alone to make landfall. The great adventure, therefore, is that of Thorfinn Karlsefni. He leads a company of three ships loaded with 160 people—including Leif's other brother Thorvald (credited, it will be recalled, with his own expedition in *Greenlanders' Saga*)—and cattle and other provisions necessary for a colonizing effort. Unable to locate Vinland, Thorfinn and his party find and settle in a place they called Hop, a locality also blessed with grapes, "wild wheat," and good timber. There are encounters with the Skraelings (the bellowing bull makes another appearance with the same beneficial result) and with a uniped! Two Skraeling boys are captured by the Norsemen and, despite the freshness of their meeting and the mutual unintelligibility of their languages, tell them a fascinating story about processions of men in white garments carrying banners. The saga closes with abandonment of the settlement and return to Greenland.

What is one to make of all of this? The stories are filled with fabulous reports beyond those few I have mentioned in these synopses: a dead man coming back to life; a doppelganger who appears at Leifsbudir; a pair of impish Scottish slaves (one can imagine renaming them Papageno and Papagena) who merrily go exploring by themselves into the interior of the new lands and return with grapes and grain for their masters; the conjuring up of a whale to allay the would-be colonists' hunger; prophecies about the futures of yet unborn descendants, prophecies that, of course, come true; and so forth. The famed Norwegian Arctic explorer Fridtjof Nansen himself would accept none of this except as "rousing fiction" (Wahlgren 1986:27). He has had a lot of company.

With the discoveries of Norse artifacts in Arctic Canada and excavations at the site of L'Anse aux Meadows in northern Newfoundland (A. S. Ingstad 1977; H. Ingstad 1964, 1969; McGhee 1984; Morison 1971:32–80; Wahlgren 1986), philologists, historians, and archaeologists now have independent reason to credit the sagas with some historical credibility (McGovern 1981; Morison 1971:32–80; Wahlgren 1969, 1986). This is true whether or not the island of Newfoundland is in fact wholly or only partly Leif Eriksson's Vinland or L'Anse aux Meadows is Leifsbudir. That that site is Norse is now beyond question. Nevertheless, the history in the sagas is entangled with the patently spurious. As one scholar puts it: "While not contemporary with the events they describe or written as deliberate histories like *Landnamabok,* such historical fiction [*Greenlanders' Saga* and *Erik's Saga*] probably still embodies some authentic traditions. While we would be unwise to base a reconstruction of Sherman's campaign on *Gone With the Wind,* the novel reflects some aspects of ante bellum society in transition" (McGovern 1981:294).

The Norse explorations to Vinland are believed to date between the end of the tenth and the beginning of the eleventh centuries. Voyages to northern Greenland, Markland, and Helluland appear to have continued for several more centuries. Thus some two to two and a half centuries of strictly oral tradition carried the historical weight of the Norse discoveries in Vinland until unburdened onto writing in Iceland. As previously noted, the original manuscripts have long since disappeared. A further one to two centuries intervened before the writing of the oldest surviving copies. Summed up, the hiatus between purported events and their reporting in extant documents provided opportunities for distortion and loss that are sobering. These add to cautions other writers have pointed to with respect to yet other representatives of the genre, themselves having nothing to do with anything as extraordinary as Norse in America: "when *Hrafnkatla,* regarded as among the historically most reliable sagas, is exposed as a work of fiction [which the quoted writer, following Sigurthur Nordal, believes to be a justified conclusion], one must be on guard against alleged historical tradition in other cases, too" (Hallberg 1962:67).

Nevertheless, Erik Wahlgren, a skeptic about L'Anse aux Meadows being the site of Eriksson's attempted settlement but not about its identification as Norse, and himself inclined to seek Leifsbudir further south, makes the important point: "American patriotism apart, a main reason for this [earlier preoccupation with New England as the place to look for Vinland] was of course the mention in the sagas of *grapes* and *grapevines,* without which detail searches for Vikings below the Canadian border would have lacked persistence, *while without the sagas themselves no one would have looked anywhere at all*" (Wahlgren 1986:121; last set of italics mine).

It does no injustice to the trenchancy of the foregoing proposition to suggest that the archaeological discoveries of Norse artifacts as well as of Inuit carvings apparently influenced by Norse contacts in Arctic Canada would, sooner or later, have stimulated awareness among prehistorians of the possibility of making similar finds in areas to the south, even if the sagas had never existed. But, of course, and this is the main point, the sagas do exist, and they played the initial role leading to the now unchallenged demonstration of a Norse presence in pre-Columbian America.

The Search for Homer's Troy

In perhaps the most celebrated claim of archaeological investigations vindicating oral traditions—as those traditions are preserved in writing, of course—Heinrich Schliemann is believed to have located the fabled city of Troy, Homer's "Ilios," by using Homer as his guide. Notwithstanding his confusions over the most appropriate level at the multicomponent site of Hissarlik in Anatolia, the consensus of scholarly opinion has come to endorse his geography. I am not here concerned with the long history of controversy over the fieldwork, let alone Schliemann's personality, matters that have been delved into at length by many others more competent to pass judgment than I am (e.g., Calder and Traill 1986). This essay focuses, rather, on issues of possible historicity in Homeric Troy and the Trojan War and their relationship to archaeological data.

Currently the weight of scholarly judgment is that the oral traditions out of which emerged the *Iliad* and the *Odyssey* had been recited (sung) for the some five or five and a half centuries between the estimated dates of the Trojan War and the form given them by Homer. The former datum is circa 1250 B.C., according to Manfred Korfmann, the latest excavator at Hissarlik (Drews 1993:10n6); the latter datum sometime between perhaps 735 and 700 B.C. (Latacz 2004:3; Luce 1998:12; Wood 1985). Homer's versions must have been committed to writing at that time or directly thereafter. Thomas Martin's (2000:38) estimate for this consummation is compatible, if a little less precise; he suggests sometime in the last half of the eighth century B.C. Alphabetic writing is now known to have been in increasingly wide use in Greece by the end of that same century (Luce 1998:12–13).

The original orality of the two great poems is convincingly attested by internal evidence and comparative studies of the genre elsewhere, most impressively by the work of Milman Parry and his student Albert Lord in their analyses of Homer in the light of their groundbreaking studies of unwritten Serbo-Croatian heroic songs (Lord 1960; Parry et al. 1974; see also Foley 1990; Kirk 1976; Nagy 1996; Shrimpton 1997). However, that little or no time elapsed between Homer's compositions and their enshrinement in writing is virtually certain. Indeed, "the preservation of the epics in the form given them by Homer would hardly have been possible without the aid of writing" (Luce 1998:13). Current estimated chronologies are supportive of Luce's contention.

Nevertheless, as the history of Homeric scholarship and as Bronze Age archaeology have shown, the poems are of debatable consequence for establishing the historicity of the stories about Troy. Certainly, Homer's geography of Troy fits best with that of the archaeological site of Hissarlik, and many of the later Greeks and Romans accepted the identification of the place, a fact in itself that must have influenced Schliemann in deciding where to focus his efforts. The Troy in Schliemann's mind was Homer's— that of Priam, Agamemnon, Helen, Achilles, Hector, and the others. It is this latter that has traditionally been meant in discussions of Troy and the search for an archaeological "confirmation" of the Trojan War.

Even with likely earthquake and unambiguous excavational destruction at Hissarlik allowed for, signs of combat and slaughter on a scale commensurate with that described in the *Iliad* have proven equivocal. Projectile points, pieces of armor, scattered and hacked skeletal remains, and so on, even allowing for after-battle scavenging and retrieval of bodies by both besiegers and besieged, have long struck skeptics of Homer's description of the Trojan War as disjunctively rare (Schliemann 1881:603–606; Wood 1985:228). Even when such items have been found, stratigraphic or associational provenience has not always been clear. On the other hand, until very recently, "Troy" meant the "citadel," the walled eminence dominating the site of Hissarlik. This fortress supposedly housed the city's royal household and government. Only since 1988 has large-scale excavation under the direction of Manfred Korfmann been undertaken in the "lower city," where the majority of the population lived. These more humble but more extensive precincts have been discovered to also have been fortified with walls and even a trench cut into bedrock. It is in these new excavations where the previously puzzling dearth of projectile points has been rectified (Latacz 2004:15–49). Among its other functions, this much larger settlement would have served as a defensive buffer.

Evidence of destruction in the citadel itself—tumbled walls, collapsed buildings, heavily charred timbers, and so on—is massive and unmistakable. For these and other reasons there was prolonged uncertainty as to which of the strata, that labeled Troy VI or the one called Troy VIIa, was the most plausible candidate for Priam's royal city. The latter was favored by Carl W. Blegen, director of the penultimate major excavations (Blegen 1963:164; Blegen et al. 1950–1958). Korfmann, his successor, believes the likeliest locus to be the upper part of that stratum (Latacz 2004:11, Figure 3). The accounts of that city and the war that became its leitmotif were doubtless inspired by *something* historical. But whatever that might have been was ineluctably metamorphosed in hundreds of retellings by Homer's balladeer predecessors and by the master himself before orality surrendered to writing some 17 generations after the event, according to John V. Luce's (1998: 12–13) calculations.

Homer's epic unmistakably exhibits the "formulaic" language (Foley 1990; Rubin 1995)—noun-epithet groups, repeated themes, metric patterns, "padding" by attention to what literate folk would regard as pointless trivia, and other devices—indicative of orality, albeit orality of a high sophistication. The essence of oral tradition, as a host of its students in many parts of the world have come to insist (e.g., Bahr 1998; Finnegan 1970:2–15; Lord 1960; Nagy 1996; Ong 1982; Parry et al. 1974; Vansina 1985), is *orality*. And orality has its raison d'être and most persuasive impact not only in the absence of writing but in the context of *performance*. As further pursued in the next chapter, each performance differs in greater or lesser degree from all other performances, depending on circumstances of place, occasion, audience and its reaction, inspiration and skill of the performer, and so on. Not only details may be altered, added, or deleted but whole episodes may be introduced or jettisoned. As emphasized before, views of the past are not fossilized in recitation, but they are adapted to the needs of the moment, presumably no less so in the ancient Aegean world than elsewhere and in other times.

In view of the foregoing, and taking nothing away from the power and artistic beauty of the *Iliad* and the *Odyssey*, calling their value as history into question is simply prudential. It is also unavoidable. Both G. S. Kirk (1976) and Gregory Nagy (1996), among others, believe the works attributed to Homer to have been composed out of many pieces of folklore, myth, poetry, song, and oral history and tradition, with parts probably dating to the Late Bronze Age, still others to the succeeding "Dark Age" or early Iron Age, and some even, in the form that has come down to us, redacted in post-Homeric times. The heroicized singularity known as the Trojan War could well, for all we know, have evolved from the conflation of multiple small-scale Mycenaean (Achaean) raids on the eastern coast of the Aegean (Wood 1985) or from the misidentification of the perpetrators of an indeed unusually disastrous assault, as proposed by Moses Finley (in Finley et al. 1964). Stripped of their patently fabulous attributes, the Homeric narratives are more likely revealing of metaphor and an Iron Age value system retrodicted to the Bronze Age Mycenaeans (the hero esteemed as a "sacker of cities," and so on) than history per se (e.g., Martin 2000:43–44). Homer, John Chadwick has insisted, was after all a great poet but a "pseudo-historian." "To look for historical fact in Homer," he says, "is as vain as to scan the Mycenaean tablets in search of poetry; they belong to different universes" (Chadwick 1976:186). No one really knows which, if any, of the events celebrated by Homer ever took place:

Even we [that is, modern historians of the ancient world], who have no shortage of concepts, and long experience of evaluation and interpretation, are in grave difficulties over those periods for which the evidence [other than archaeological] is largely derived from oral tradition, and for which the documents are extremely few and essentially unintelligible. Some of the supposed data are patently fictitious, the political unification of Attica by Theseus or the foundation of Rome by Aeneas, for example, but we quickly run out of such easily identified fictions. For the great bulk of the narrative we are faced with the "kernel of truth" *possibility*, and I am unaware of any stigmata that automatically distinguish fiction from fact [Finley 2000:18].

Granting the historical genuineness of the assaulted city, its identification with the archaeological site of Hissarlik is no longer in much doubt. But until just recently it was principally the lack of a convincing alternative that championed Schliemann's claim among skeptics. Pottery and other artifacts from more than one cultural level at that site included specimens of an age compatible with that usually assigned the Trojan War. The conjunction of results from modern excavation at Hissarlik and the recent discovery and decipherment of numerous clay tablets at the Hittite imperial capital of Hattusa in Anatolia now strongly affirms that identification. Hissarlik, it appears, was indeed the site of Troy, Homer's Ilios, the same place the Hittites referred to as "Wilusa." Troy/Ilios/Wilusa was not only familiar to the Hittites, it was a sometime ally and even component of their empire (Latacz 2004:75–119). The indispensability of the documents in dispelling much of the previous toponymic uncertainty does not, of course, bestow the raiments of history on the heroic tales in the *Iliad*. But quite apart from the epic itself, it is clear that catastrophe visited Troy/Hissarlik.

The cause of that catastrophe has been harder to isolate than the evidence of its reality. Destruction wrought by war or by domestic upheavals, earthquakes (Hissarlik lies in an active seismic zone), fires ignited by earthquakes or other natural forces, and destabilizing subsidence caused by overbuilding on the poorly consolidated rubble of former occupations—all or several in combination have been conjectured. The consensus today credits military action as perhaps the principal agent for the devastation manifested in the relevant stratum. Donald Easton (1985:190–191), however, has invoked subsidence as a major contributor even though "systematic destruction" by an enemy force was paramount. Others have suggested, as he points out, that the Achaeans (Mycenaeans)—assuming, after Homer, that they were the enemy—might have taken advantage of earthquake weakening of Troy's defenses to storm the city. To this plausible but unverifiable scenario he half-seriously appends as a nod to Homer Fritz Schachermeyr's idea that the victorious visitors then left a wooden horse as an offering of thanks to Poseidon (Easton 1985:189).

Years ago Moses Finley (Finley et al. 1964), in an exchange with J. L. Caskey, G. S. Kirk, and D. L. Page, had been willing to grant that archaeologists had indeed found a destroyed city, and he used the name Troy in referring to it. Accepting the identification of Carl Blegen that Troy was represented by the level denominated VIIa, he took the archaeological finds as more or less consonant with the probable age of the Mycenaean (Achaean) palace culture in Greece. But he insisted that archaeology had not thereby vindicated the *Iliad* or the *Odyssey* as historical documents. Given, he said, that everyone admits that those epics are "full of exaggerations, distortions, pure fictions and flagrant contradictions," he asked how it is possible to decide "that A is a fiction, B is not?" (Finley in Finley et al. 1964:1). Well, in many instances it is easy to at least make the "A" discrimination. To take just the first of these listed obstacles and not even bother with meddling gods or that face that Christopher Marlowe further immortalized as having "launched a thousand ships," innumerable examples immediately leap to mind. Readily commanding attention are the preternatural attributes of the heroes, the alleged scale and tenacity of a military coalition among what were probably little more than chiefdoms or petty kingdoms maintaining a decade-long overseas siege, the necessarily implied logistical system supplying both besieged and besiegers that would be the envy of a modern nation-state, and so on.

All we have to tell us about the Trojan War, Finley reminded his readers and interlocutors, is Homer. And that is not enough to stake a claim to historicity. He advocated that new and better informed understanding of the operation of oral traditions should make students of the Trojan War more circumspect than most of them had been in discerning history where it might not exist. He offered as cautionary examples of glaring misrepresentations of genuine historical events three great European epics that developed orally, *although in times when literacy subsisted.* Versions of those epics therefore soon found their way into written texts that can be compared with external evidence in the form of a body of historical records. The epic traditions Finley (in Finley et al. 1964:2–3) examined were the *Song of Roland,* in which an ignominious ambush at Roncevaux in 778 by Christian Basques, decimating the rear of Charlemagne's army on its retreat from Spain, is converted into a celebration of a noble defense of Christianity against a tidal wave of infidel Saracens; the *Nibelungenlied,* with its reversal of the Hun invasion of Burgundy in the fifth century and featuring personal interactions of historical figures who were not contemporaries; and the South Slav tradition about the 1389 Ottoman defeat of the Serbs at Kossovo, a humiliation attributed in the epic, rather like the Germans following World War I, to a "stab in the back." He states, "We must therefore reckon with three possibilities of fundamental distortion (apart from pure invention): (1) that a great heroic tradition *may* be built round an event which itself was of minor significance; (2) that the tradition *may* be picked up by regions and people to whom it was originally, as a matter of historic fact, utterly alien and unrelated; (3) that the tradition *may* in time distort (not just exaggerate) even the original kernel so that it is neither recognisable nor discoverable from internal evidence alone" (Finley in Finley et al. 1964:3).

In the absence of independent evidence, that is, criteria purely external to the traditions themselves, the stories the traditions tell, no matter how magnificent the telling, when told in the manner of histories, may well, for all we can know, be tales "told by an idiot, full of sound and fury, signifying nothing." Or perhaps the idiocy resides not in the teller but in the hearer who listens and hears histories not told.

While following the tourist route of signposts and souvenir shops at the present Turkish historical park at Hissarlik, the archaeologist Neil Silberman reflected sadly on the park's presentation and the public consumption of the *Iliad* as history. "I eventually came to discover," he wrote of that place, that "archaeology was not the handmaiden of history. It was the delivery boy of myth" (Silberman 1989:32). Ultimately, there is a public as well as scholarly price to be paid for historical naïveté, and the price is paid by debased standards of verification. Although more particularly concerned with a related problem in historical research, the historian William A. Chaney's admonition in his classic *The Cult of Kingship in Anglo-Saxon England* has a wider relevance: "If economists have been accused, like Oscar Wilde's cynic, of knowing the price of everything and the value of nothing, historians, on the other hand, often know the value of everything and the price of nothing" (Chaney 1970:221).

Moses Finley, knowing something about price as well as value, rejected the *Iliad* and the *Odyssey* as history because, particularly at the time he wrote, there was little in the archaeological record or anything else to credit them with more than a tenuous connection with Hissarlik (in Finley et al. 1964:3). Indeed, the archaeological chronology then developing of escalating warfare in the whole Aegean world, and in Anatolia and the Levant, mandated a more encompassing perspective than a focus on Hissarlik, let alone Homer's tales, especially if Blegen's suggested date for Troy's destruction might be brought down to be more in line with what seemed to be synchronous events elsewhere, a qualification since realized. Finley thought it incredible that the Mycenaeans in mainland Greece, faced themselves with the threat of immanent assault and possible destruction, would have sent off the main elements of their military capacity to attack a place with which they had long enjoyed peaceful trade. G. Ernest Wright (1983:71), similarly struck by the absence of any artifacts in any of the Hissarlik levels that might serve to identify the attackers, indicated that it might be wisest "to dissociate the whole archaeological discovery from myth and poetry, and even from the legend of Troy itself." Roland de Vaux, although striving for neutrality in the question of historicity in the matter, was impressed by J. Mellaart's conclusion, to wit: "I need hardly to point out that I find the traditional account of the Trojan War archaeologically and historically inacceptable" (quoted in de Vaux 1970:75). Wright, however, backed away from his essential agreement with Finley by appealing to the fact that in Homer "we do have actual texts." However, aside from his endorsing the need for careful literary analysis, he took no notice of their extended word-of-mouth transmission prior to their being written down in the redacted Hellenic texts that were the sole materials for such analysis (Wright 1983:71).

Finley's interlocutors in the exchange cited earlier, while yielding in various degrees to the force of his objections, still insisted on finding "kernels" of believability in the two texts. G. S. Kirk, for one, was impressed, if somewhat ambivalently, by what he took to be credible descriptions of Mycenaean society and values in the last heroic period of that civilization. He was thus inclined to believe that something of genuine historical value persists: "But can we believe that the interruption of the tradition [that celebrated in 'our' *Iliad*], whether poetical or non-poetical, caused by the upheavals at the end of the Bronze Age can have been so severe as to destroy not merely the details but the very outlines and whole substance of events belonging to the last heroic period of the Achaean civilization?" (Kirk in Finley et al. 1964:16).

D. L. Page was sympathetic to Kirk's view and argued further that nothing in the archaeology was incongruous with the Homeric account. He could discern no better alternative to a mainland Achaean expedition against Troy. Finley had rejected that entrenched view in favor of Troy's falling to "invaders from the north" whose ethnic identity or identities he could not really specify (Finley et al. 1964). Making the point that Troy (Hissarlik) was only one of many ancient cities giving evidence of destruction at the end of the Bronze Age, Finley called for a broader perspective, one embracing less parochial forces and causations than those that had been invoked to explain the single instance, however prominent that instance in Western mythology (Finley in Finley et al. 1964:4–8). Although Finley disliked the term "Sea Peoples" as a too-vague catch-all, those feared marauders as reported in Egyptian, Ugaritic, Hittite, and other documents were certainly contemporaries of Troy and may even have included Finley's "northern invaders." The "Sea Peoples" had even had the effrontery to attack Egypt in 1178 or 1179 B.C. They were repulsed, however, by Rameses III, as attested by texts and pictorial reliefs in that pharaoh's mortuary temple at Medinet Habu (Drews 1993:4–6). Whatever the identity of these raiders and pillagers, it is unlikely that they were Peloponnesian Achaeans, although that source may have contributed disaffected adventurers hoping to take advantage of a "good thing" in search of their fortunes. Finley's opponents in the Troy controversy found little to recommend in his proposal, claiming it merely substituted a hypothetical proxy for the invaders already supplied by Homer. Like Wright, they found the presence of a text scale-tipping, especially in the absence of in situ archaeological evidence that might speak to the issue. But Finley, I think, was on the right track.

Over the subsequent four decades more surveys and excavations have been undertaken in the eastern Mediterranean lands. More numerous and more precise regional chronologies have been among the benefits. These developments have prompted critical reexamination of many of the ideas previously and concurrently offered to explain the widespread destructions of cities and polities, Troy among them, that are such a salient attribute of the end of the Bronze Age. One of the more ambitious of such reexaminations, one that also proposes a resolution to many of the problems inadequately addressed by previous causal arguments, has been published by Robert Drews (1993). The proffered causes he examines and rejects as inadequate to the magnitude of the phenomenon they try to explain, although any one of them *might* seem compatible with archaeological evidence at this or that particular site, all fail to comport with that from many other sites, if not indeed the majority. Those would-be explanations include earthquakes and their aftereffects; migrations; droughts; the invention of ironworking, with its military implications for destabilization of preexisting "balance of power" relationships; increased piracy and the activity of raiders; and "systems collapse," this latter emphasizing breakdown of trading relations, social problems provoked by growing debt slavery, alienation of land, and other internal socioeconomic factors (Drews 1993:33–93). On the heels of his examination of these searches for unicausality, the rapid development of better paleoclimatic data and models may breathe new vigor into the perceptible influence of environmental change, if not as a sufficient universal cause, then at least as a contributing factor in certain instances (Weiss and Bradley 2001).

Even though warfare and destruction of communities occurred both earlier and later, of course, archaeologists and historians have shown them to be markedly clustered in the late thirteenth and early twelfth centuries B.C., that is, during the Bronze Age to Iron Age transition. This interval has appropriately been labeled the *Catastrophe* (Drews 1993). As summarized by Drews, the cities known to have been attacked, burned, and sacked within this little over a half century number 10 in Greece, 11 in central and eastern Anatolia, 1 or probably 2 each in western Anatolia and on Crete, 4 on Cyprus, 8 or possibly 9 in Syria, and another 9 in the southern Levant (Drews 1993:Figure 1). These include such famous cities, besides Troy, as Thebes, Tiryns, and Mycenae in Greece; Tarsus and even the Hittite imperial capital of Hattusas in Anatolia; Ugarit in Syria; and Hazor and Megiddo in the southern Levant. Even Egypt was attacked, although unsuccessfully, as we have seen. What was responsible for such devastation over so vast an area within so relatively short a time? After his disavowal of the previous theories, Drews came to the conclusion that it was the promise of sudden wealth made possible when "barbarians"—peasants, tribesmen, and petty chiefdoms in the interstices between and in the bordering lands beyond the rich urban centers and palaces—discovered they had acquired the means to overcome the ancien régimes, and they seized the opportunity: "the Catastrophe came about when men in 'barbarian' lands awoke to a truth that had been with them for some time: the chariot-based forces on which the Great Kingdoms relied could be overwhelmed by swarming infantries, the infantrymen being equipped with javelins, long swords, and a few essential pieces of defensive armor. The barbarians—in Libya, Palestine, Israel, Lycia, northern Greece, Italy, Sicily, Sardinia, and elsewhere—thus found it within their means to assault, plunder, and raze the richest palaces and cities on the horizon, and this they proceeded to do" (Drews 1993:104).

Instead of the Mycenaean Achaeans descending on Troy, Finley had posited "northern marauders" as that city's nemesis. It now seems well worth considering that they, like the Philistines in the Levant, were one of the regional manifestations of the widespread upheavals of the Catastrophe, whether or not they are to be subsumed in the category "Sea Peoples." I do not mean to imply thereby that the Trojan War controversy is finally resolved, nor do I intend to pursue the many pros and cons of Drews's hypothesis. What I do hope to have shown is how new information coupled with a change in perspective has opened additional possibilities for consideration. Whereas the Homeric location of Troy has been essentially vindicated by current research, the *Iliad* remains a magnificent historical fiction insofar as it can be assayed by the kinds of evidence archaeologists and documentary historians can muster. Drews's investigation of the Catastrophe, on the other hand, whatever its ultimate fate, promises more and better possibilities for testing unencumbered by compulsion to validate a venerated oral tradition. A change in the context of study does not eliminate the uniqueness of particulars so bounded, of course, but it is indispensable as protection against historical myopia. Nevertheless, and honoring the distinction between the fact of Troy and the legend of the Trojan War, one may still argue that, "while so many uncertainties of dating and political geography remain, there can be no grounds· for claiming that the historicity of the Trojan War has been proved. But for those who wish to believe—faith is once again possible. Faith is, of course, a theological virtue, not a historical one; but for faith to go in search of understanding is a perfectly respectable exercise" (Easton 1985:195).

Biblical Archaeology

I use the term *biblical archaeology* in this essay and not some other more geographically, chronologically, and culturally inclusive label like "Near Eastern archaeology" or "Syro-Palestinian archaeology" (Dever 1985, 1990). I do so because I am explicitly concerned here with the use by archaeologists of the Old Testament or Hebrew Bible as a historical reference. An important complication of such use is the danger of extrarational considerations unjustifiably conflating the meanings of the written texts and their oral antecedents. This emphasis on the Old Testament implies no diminution in historiographic challenges in the New Testament; it simply reflects the relatively fewer critical opportunities for archaeological involvement (but see Keller 1995:321–386). A superb examination of those latter historiographic controversies, accessible to secular and religiously minded readers alike, is to be found in Van Austin Harvey (1966). Its date of publication notwithstanding, Andrew White's 1895 classic exposition (White 1955) continues to reward reading. I am not concerned in the following pages with theological issues as such, of course, nor should any biblical archaeologist qua archaeologist, except where they threaten to compromise scientific or historiographic integrity.

Biblical archaeology has a strong claim to be primus inter pares in the world of scholarly acrimony. Passion sometimes seems as much engaged as rationality, to the point of confusing as much as enlightening visitors from other fields interested in learning something about it. Impinging on sensitive areas of Judeo-Christian personal identity as well as reverence for cultural patrimony, the fact of such touchiness is not unanticipated even if its intensity is. This is especially noteworthy when exhibited in circles not intimately engaged in the theater of Israeli biblical archaeology with that enterprise's additional agenda of nationalistic celebration and even justification.

At the risk of oversimplification, a risk not shunned by many of the antagonists themselves I hasten to add, the field of biblical archaeology has long been stretched between poles of alternating attraction. These endorse or discourage use of the Bible as a legitimate source of historical information. Today these polarities are often labeled "traditionalist" or "conservative" (not to say "reactionary") and "revisionist," with some important representatives of the latter lumped together under the rubric "Copenhagen school." To immediately smudge this neat polarity—remember my initial temerity regarding the risk of oversimplification—many scholars cannot in fairness be classified as adhering to one or the other. The real issue in contention, many would argue, is not whether the Bible is justifiably to be regarded as historically trustworthy but, rather, what parts of it may or may not properly be so considered and what the criteria are for deciding.

Accepting for purposes of discussion this smudging but probably more realistic trifurcation of opinion, and ignoring the distractions of searchers for a real Garden of Eden or Noah's ark, the following pages focus on one aspect of serious scholarship. This concerns historical questions arising from the undoubted orality of the stories that underlie much of the Old Testament. The examples chosen to illustrate these questions come from the early (pre-Monarchy) books only. This is not only because of space considerations, the sheer quantity of historical problems the Bible presents, and the fact of my limited knowledge of biblical and relevant extra-biblical ancient literature and Near Eastern archaeology, but also because if a selection has to be made, these first books are the most orally dependent and thus most pertinent to the subject of this volume. I briefly touch upon the first five books of the Old Testament (the Pentateuch) but pay particular attention to the problems of the Israelite "conquest" of Canaan as presented in the book of Joshua.

From its beginnings early in the eighteenth century, roughly contemporaneously with the birth of Egyptian and Mesopotamian archaeology, down to the present day, biblical archaeology has been overwhelmingly concerned with the Old Testament, or Hebrew Bible, and the early history of the Israelites. The discovery of historical ties connecting the ancient Holy Land with Egypt and Mesopotamia early became apparent with the decipherment of hieroglyphic documents and clay tablets impressed with cuneiform writing. These achievements made intelligible, if not always unambiguous, papyrus scrolls, inscribed stelae, temple and tomb walls bearing painted or chiseled texts, and potsherds exhibiting scribbled writing, scratched or in ink (ostraca). Some of these documents bore geographical, ethnic, deific, and personal names, as well as references to events previously known only in the Bible. Such revelations, riveting in themselves for the glimpses they provided into the ancient world, seemed for many people to offer even more: the prospect of confirming the Bible's historicity and with it the validating of faith in its religious message.

Whether committed or indifferent to theological matters, most scholars and members of the general public, particularly in Western Europe and the United States, quickly came to see archaeology as useful in illustrating, amplifying, and confirming the historical reliability of the Bible. Nevertheless, dissenters from assuming the latter mission have long been present, albeit in the minority, even before the current school of revisionists began to attract attention (e.g., S. Birch in 1872 and F. Brown in 1896, quoted in Moorey 1991:3 and 40–41, respectively). However, today, with the rise of a more secular archaeology in the Holy Land notwithstanding, one still reads that the task of biblical archaeology is "the clarification and illumination of the biblical text and content through archaeological investigation of the biblical world" (J. K. Eakins, quoted in Moorey 1991:175). But as interesting and long-standing as this dichotomy may be, the present essay is concerned with the altogether separate issues of the Bible's debt to oral tradition in its accounts of Israelite "history" and to what extent those accounts may justifiably be treated as historically reliable (e.g., the narratives of the Patriarchs, the Israelite enslavement in Egypt, the Exodus, the destruction of Jericho and the conquest of Canaan, the establishment of the Israelite monarchy).

One would think the orality of the foundational texts of at least the Pentateuch (Genesis through Deuteronomy) through Joshua and into Judges would be of equal interest whether one views contemporary biblically related archaeology in Israel and Palestine, and of course in pertinent parts of Egypt, Lebanon, Jordan, Syria, and Iraq, as essentially an adjunct of biblical studies or as an altogether separate and independent discipline happening to share some common interests with it. Curiously, only a minority of proponents of either archaeological persuasion seem to evince explicit and sustained interest in the profound implications of the oral conveyance of tradition over multiple generations. The essential orality of the greater part of the Old Testament is not in serious doubt (see Dundes 1999; Nielsen 1954; L. Thompson 1978:34–42; T. Thompson 1974, 1999). What is and long has been in doubt among many scholars is its historicity, questions of orality aside, and whether and how archaeologists are justified in using the Bible as a historical reference work (e.g., Dever 1990; Finkelstein and Silberman 2001; Hoppe 1984; Keller 1995; Laughlin 2000; Moorey 1991; T. Thompson 1999). Keller's interesting volume, just cited, requires patience with its author's ethnocentrism and his sometimes embracing premature conclusions.

In parallel fashion inadequate weight has been given to the fact that the earliest known *written* biblical texts grievously postdate the founding and early history of Israel that they purport to record. And they were supposedly copied, with unknown and unknowable degrees of fidelity, from older but now extinct documents, themselves presumably inspired by the latest renderings of the ancestral lineage of pertinent oral compositions. The books of the Old Testament are believed to have been initially composed as an integrated text *after* the Babylonian exile sometime in the sixth century B.C. (Laughlin 2000:153). Finkelstein and Silberman (2001:145) suggest the previous century. The oldest copies of Exodus are fragments of the Dead Sea Scrolls, probably written circa 250–100 B.C. (Millard 2000:55), and of Numbers by a few words inscribed on two small amulets from Jerusalem thought to date sometime between the late seventh and early sixth centuries B.C. (G. Barkay, cited in Laughlin 2000:168n35). This is sobering information to the historically minded, quite apart from whatever theological implications may be drawn from it. Some of the latter, of course, have played an important, even if explicitly unacknowledged, role in the highly disputaceous field of biblical archaeology down to the present (see the excellent bibliographies in the surveys by Keller [1995], Laughlin [2000], and Moorey [1991]).

As noted earlier, skepticism about the Bible as a source for historical knowledge had voices to speak for it long before the diffusion of its current prominence. The biblical scholar Philip Davies (1992, 2000), often identified with the so-called Copenhagen school of biblical revisionists, has commented on this fact and has added the conclusion he thinks should be drawn from it: "These narratives—as had been claimed earlier, before the obstructive interlude of Albrighteanism [!]—were literary constructions, serving the ideological interests of a period centuries later than the time in which they were set. It was therefore in their literary, philosophical, even theological character that their original purpose lay and their contemporary value should be primarily sought" (Davies 2000:27; brackets mine).

The author of the "interlude" to which Davies refers is of course the renowned William Foxwell Albright, commonly and rightly acclaimed as the most influential biblical archaeologist of the twentieth century. His students and associates included such luminaries as G. Ernest Wright, Nelson Glueck, and John Bright (for succinct assays of their impact on the field see Dever 1990:12–26, 39–51; Laughlin 2000:3–16; Moorey 1991:54–145). The "Albrightean synthesis," as their collective work has been called, exhibited impressive literary scholarship as well as fieldwork. It also at times betrayed, in company with many another charismatic movement, a capacity to overestimate its undoubted achievements and to dismissively treat antecedent or contemporary competing points of view. So dismissed are the "biblical historians" who believe that the Patriarchal narratives in Genesis:

were artificial creations of Israelite scribes of the Divided Monarchy [late tenth to early to mid sixth centuries B.C., or Iron Age IIb-c, Laughlin 2000:121] or tales told by imaginative rhapsodists around Israelite campfires during the centuries following their occupation of the country. Eminent names among scholars can be cited for regarding every item of Gen. 11–50 as reflecting late invention, or at least retrojection of events and conditions under the Monarchy into the remote past, about which nothing was thought to have been really known to the writers of later days.

Archaeological discoveries since 1925 have changed all this. Aside from a few die-hards among older scholars, there is scarcely a single biblical historian who has not been impressed by the rapid accumulation of data supporting the substantial historicity of patriarchal tradition" [Albright 1963:1–2].

In the same vein, Albright continues, "Numerous recent excavations . . . give us a remarkably precise idea of patriarchal Palestine, fitting well into the picture handed down in Genesis"; "historical skepticism is quite unwarranted"; and "our case for the substantial historicity of the tradition of the Patriarchs is clinched" (Albright 1963:3, 4, 5). He maintains that reliable knowledge of the age of the Patriarchs is based on writings, writings that date, he seems to believe, to the time of the Divided Monarchy, *but that those writings were themselves based on oral traditions* (Albright 1963:5). Pronouncing oral traditions to be in many ways superior to written records (he does not say in what ways they are superior), Albright nevertheless cautions that oral tradition "is peculiarly exposed to the phenomena of refraction and selection of elements suited for epic narrative, regardless of their chronological order." "We cannot," he says, "automatically accept as accurate the sequence of events in Genesis, nor the motivations ascribed to them, nor all of the details that make up those events" (Albright 1963:5). On a later page he adds the further liability that "gaps in the genealogies [in Genesis] is [*sic*] to be expected, since most oral tradition tends to skip over obscure or uninteresting periods" (Albright 1963:9) Nevertheless, "as a whole the picture in Genesis is historical, and there is no reason to doubt the general accuracy of the biographical details and the sketches of personality which make the Patriarchs come alive with a vividness unknown to a single extrabiblical character in the whole vast literature of the ancient Near East" (Albright 1963:9). And further, simply predicating his opinion on astonishing presuppositions about his own ability to discriminate between genuine and spurious historicity in oral traditions, rather than justifying that opinion with logic and appeals to evidence, Albright flatly declares that "that Abraham

(Abram) was an important figure in his day seems probable, since the traditions about him appear to have been handed down orally for many centuries *with little change*" (Albright 1963:7; italics mine).

Although some modern biblical history revisionists celebrate the eclipse of the Albrightean synthesis, that eclipse seems to be partial rather than complete. Alan Millard's recent and hardly unique essay *How Reliable Is Exodus?* (2000) demonstrates the veracity of that observation. His essay takes issue with the revisionists' dating of the presumed older manuscripts from which the Exodus version in the Dead Sea Scrolls is thought to have been copied and opts for a pre- rather than post-Babylonian exilic period for the copying.

But more to the point of the possible historicity of that Old Testament book, Millard argues that nothing in Exodus is incompatible with a Late Bronze Age ascription. Nevertheless, he does admit to the absence of a lot of critical data, including the name of the pharaoh who oppressed the Israelites. Previously, however, Albright (1983:39, 49) himself had implied, and Dever (1990:45) had argued, that that pharaoh had to have been Rameses II, circa 1279–1213 B.C. He was the predecessor of Merneptah, whose victory stela at Thebes, dating to about 1210 B.C., includes in its inscription the "earliest and most secure extra-Biblical textual reference to Israel" (Dever 2000:68). That name is listed among the enemy people in Canaan defeated by the Egyptians. This aside, Millard is curiously puzzled that anyone should find the miracles in the Exodus account of the flight from Egypt cause to be skeptical about claims for the latter document's historical reliability. The parting of the Red Sea, he says, fits well with the ubiquity of miracles in virtually all ancient narrations. He cites as examples Rameses II himself getting the god Seth to transform winter into summer in the Turkish and Syrian mountains so that his promised Hittite bride would be safe and comfortable on her journey to Egypt and how the Assyrian king Ashurbanipal had the gods send a thunderbolt that drove off would-be invaders. In a remarkable conclusion, he insists that "in neither of these examples is there any sign that the account is fiction or folklore." The parting and crossing of the Red Sea "is basically no different" (Millard 2000:57).

Returning to the "partial eclipse" of the Albrightean synthesis, the umbra of which some scholars find rather too close to totality (see Dever 2000 and Levy 2000 for energetic reactions), a fair representation of its extent is to be found in the view of the earlier cited Philip Davies (2000:72): "The gap between the Biblical Israel and the historical Israel as we derive it from archaeology is huge." Mincing no words, he concludes that "Biblical Israel is fiction. But like all good historical fiction, it has an often realistic and accurate setting [recall McGovern on *Greenlanders' Saga, Erik's Saga,* and *Gone With the Wind;* see also L. Thompson 1978:34]. This is also true of other parts of the Bible that modern critical scholars recognize as fiction: Ruth in Moab and Bethlehem, Jonah in Jaffa and Nineveh, Esther in the court of a known Persian king (or two), and Daniel in that of a Babylonian king" (Davies 2000:72). We might as well search archaeologically, says Davies, for "Merrie England" or the knights of King Arthur (Davies 2000: 72). Most contemporary biblical scholars, he says, simply do not credit as history the Patriarchal narratives in Genesis (Abraham, Isaac, Jacob). They also question the historicity of the Egyptian captivity, the Exodus, and the Israelite conquest of Canaan (Davies 2000:26–27).

While attending another calling in addition to serving honest scholarship, the cleric Leslie Hoppe, in his survey of biblical archaeology, essentially conforms to the revisionist persuasion when he writes:

> The historical reliability of the Book of Joshua is one thing; its theological affirmations are quite another. While Joshua reflects some historical data, its historical value is quite limited. The "facts" surrounding Israel's acquisition of her land serve as the backdrop for the drama of Israel's life with God.
>
> Like scenery these facts are meant to be suggestive rather than precise representations. *It is a mistake to focus on the scenery when the real action takes place at center stage—the interaction between God and Israel.* The simplicity and complexity of this relationship—not the communication of historical data—are what occupied the author of Joshua [Hoppe 1984:5–6; italics mine].

In thus removing the burdensome expectation, either self-assumed or externally imposed by sponsoring organizations or political pressures, that archaeologists should interpret their physical evidence in conformity with biblical narrative, Hoppe correspondingly relieves would-be believers of the Bible of having to confront potentially embarrassing incongruencies with the empirical record. Archaeology, he says, has nothing significant to say regarding the religious truth of the Bible: "The Bible's message is to be accepted by faith" (Hoppe 1984:6).

Thomas L. Thompson, perhaps the most prominent spokesman of the revisionists, forcefully argues the same point as Hoppe, although from a more secular perspective. Perusing and endorsing the mainly archaeologically and linguistically derived "new history of Palestine's peoples" that has increasingly replaced history written from the Bible, he asserts that the new history presents a picture so radically unfamiliar, and so very different from a biblical view as to be hardly recognizable to the writers of the Bible, so thoroughly has our understanding of the past been forced to change.

There is no Adam or Eve in this story, nor a Noah, Abraham and Sarah. And there is no place for them. Not even Moses and Joshua have roles in this history about the people who formed the Bible and its world. One good reason for leaving them out is that modern history is very limited in its ability to speak about the past. We can only write what we have evidence for. If we have no evidence, if we do not know anything about a period, we cannot write history about it. As a result, ancient history has many blank pages. There is another limitation. When the writers of the Bible wrote about the Israel of their traditions, where it came from, and what it was that God had created, they were doing something different than talking about the past or writing history. When present-day archaeologists and critical historians piece together the civilizations in which the biblical writers arose, they describe a world in which the authors of the Bible lived, but the best of them do so without using the Bible's own story. This is not because they disagree with it, but rather because they are doing something that the writers of the Bible never meant to do [T. Thompson 1999:103–104].

That "something that the writers of the Bible never meant to do," of course, was write a history book. Nevertheless, there is history in the Bible. That history, however, is incidental to the Bible's principal concerns, which are ultimately as Davies, Finkelstein and Silberman, Hoppe, Laughlin, Moorey, and the two Thompsons (and other revisionists) have characterized them—and, at least qualifiedly, as acknowledged by many of the traditionalists themselves.

The Near Eastern archaeologist William Dever is not alone when he claims to find credible history in sections of the Bible and is able to point to archaeological evidence that, when dispassionately considered, he feels to be more reasonably than not supportive of that history, even if it does not in an absolute sense "prove" it. In some instances he is doubtless right. The danger in this kind of argument, however, is that of circularity: one line of evidence lends credence to the other and that other then does reciprocal service. That is, one kind of data supplies the framework or context for interpreting the other; when that other is so interpreted, assuming some degree of compatibility, it then becomes confirmation of the first's correctness. Neither is thus independent of the other. However, inasmuch as it is the biblical account that is invariably known and intellectually digested before the archaeological record is worked out, it is the former that usually pre-determines the terms of the relationship. One or the other requires the introduction of an exogenous species of evidence to avoid the trap of circular reasoning. In seeking to properly calibrate biblical, that is, text-dependent, and archaeological chronologies, for example, the application of radiocarbon or some other independent chronometric method can be the critical third leg of the evidentiary stool on which conclusions may rest. Today this is, or should be, de rigueur.

Unfortunately, the sturdiness of the biblical textual "leg" that has to help support claims of historicity in the earlier Old Testament books is especially suspect. Those books not only purport to tell of people and events dating back into the Late Bronze and early Iron ages, but they are also the most dependent on faith in oral tradition, that is, on its variables of quantity, quality, tenure antecedent to collecting, and type and scale of almost certain redaction before and during successive commitments to writing. The Old Testament, *as we know it,* remember, dates only from the European Middle Ages and is itself based on incomplete, often ambiguous, and sometimes contradictory documents going back no earlier than the last few centuries B.C. But in those few centuries B.C., and indeed for hundreds of years earlier, certainly back into the times of the Divided Monarchy, substantial parts of the Bible are supported, as history, by extra-biblical texts and archaeological information.

The longer a story's preliterate genealogy, the greater the inherent likelihood of mutations great and small and with them the degeneration of whatever historical fidelity may once have existed. Something like this consideration seems to be reflected in Dever's (1990:3–11) attempted scaling of the degrees of historical reliability he would grant the earlier parts of the Old Testament. Genesis chapters 1–11 are thus classified as myths rather than history. Later chapters in Genesis and Exodus (the Patriarchal and Mosaic eras) he regards as having some historical "elements." But they are almost hopelessly mixed with legends, miracles, angels, unbelievably long-lived heroes, and stylistic anachronisms that testify to their having been written a long time after the "events" they presume to report. Dever finds somewhat more historical truth in the books of Joshua and Judges. Nevertheless, as he points out, these same books offer differing accounts of "the so-called conquest" and settlement of Canaan that can be reconciled neither with themselves nor with archaeology. Much more trustworthy history he feels is to be found in the books of Samuel, Kings, and Chronicles. These later books are concerned with the times of the United Monarchy (the reigns of Saul, David, Solomon) and the succeeding Divided Monarchy (the kingdoms of Israel and Judah). Now at last, on some points, Dever notes, these accounts can be checked against contemporary records from Egypt, Assyria, and Babylonia. But even here none of these biblical texts should be taken at face value as history. The Old Testament, he says, is a "curated artifact" (Dever 1990:9): "the narratives of Genesis [for example] are a composite of many layers of oral and written tradition, from many different time periods and social circumstances. It is thus impossible to isolate a *kernel of truth* [see Finley 2000 in the earlier discussion of Homer and Troy] and assign that to one specific period on the basis of historical 'fit'" (Dever 1990:24; italics mine).

And where is the "kernel of truth" in the later book of Joshua? Surely the historical reality of the generalissimo and his campaigns in destroying the citadels of the Canaanites and delivering their lands to the post-exilic Israelites left recoverable—and identifiable—confirmation in the rich archaeological record of the Holy Land. After all, the story of the "conquest" is second to none in its importance and sheer drama among all those told in the Hebrew Bible.

Since at least the 1950s and Kathleen Kenyon's excavations at the site of Jericho (Tell es-Sultan), scholars open to perhaps unsettling discoveries have had to conclude that the biblical accounts of Joshua's military campaigns have received little support from archaeology. In classic British understatement she says, "As regards the Jericho of the Book of Joshua, there are some chronological difficulties" (Kenyon 1993:674). Subsequent research, both in archaeology and literary criticism, has pointed in the same direction.

Although there are dissenters (B. Wood [1990], for example; but see also Bienkowski 1990), the contemporary consensus dates the conquest, Joshua's campaigns, and the arrival of the ancient Israelites in Canaan to around 1200 B.C., at the end of the *Late* Bronze Age and the beginning of the Iron Age. The celebrated walls of Jericho, however, date to the end of the *Middle* Bronze Age, circa 1560–1550 B.C. Not only were there no walls left standing at Jericho when Joshua supposedly arrived on the scene, there wasn't even a city. It was already a ruin, having been destroyed by fire long before, a destruction perhaps "ascribable to the disturbances that followed the expansion of the Hyksos from Egypt in about 1560 BCE" (Kenyon 1993:680). Furthermore, "according to the biblical account, Hiel the Bethelite was responsible for the first reoccupation of Jericho in the time of Ahab (early ninth century BCE)," but "no trace of an Iron Age occupation as early as this has so far been observed" (Kenyon 1993:680). Not until the seventh century B.C. was there renewed settlement at the site. In a poignant attempt to salvage something of the Joshua story, Kenyon, a believing Christian, seems to have wanted to pull her archaeological punch, so to speak, by suggesting "it is very possible that this destruction is truly remembered in the Book of Joshua, although archaeology cannot provide the proof" (Kenyon

1993:680). Not all scholars feel such compunction: "If the biblical list of cities destroyed by Joshua could be correlated site by site with massive destructions at the end of the Late Bronze Age, one could begin to find the probabilities persuasive. But no such correlation exists. To cite some destructions as being caused by Israelites while assuming alternative explanations for sites that do not fit the [biblical] pattern [the author mentions such alternative possibilities as the 'Sea Peoples,' especially the Philistines, and warfare among the Canaanite city-states] raises questions of methodological consistency" (Lance 1981:64).

The ethnologist Robert Lowie (1915:598), although dealing long ago with different material on another continent, had already made much the same methodological point with respect to shifting criteria. In yet another context the classicist Moses Finley has acknowledged as much (Finley et al. 1964:8n22). And so, I should add, have I (Mason 2000:245). Unfortunately, it seems to need repetition.

William Dever (1990:61) has pointed out that only 3 of the 16 cities the Bible says were destroyed by the Israelites in their invasion of their promised land show evidence of destruction at the appropriate time. Seven of the other sites were unoccupied at the time of the conquest or exhibit no trace of violence at any time. The remaining six places have either not been archaeologically identified or, if they have, they have not been excavated. Other sites do yield proof of destruction, but they are not among those the Israelites claimed to have laid waste. Dever concludes, "It may be stated confidently that the archaeological evidence today is overwhelmingly against the classic conquest model of Israelite origins, as envisioned in the book of Joshua and in much Biblical scholarship until recently" (Dever 1990:61).

Surveying the archaeological data pertinent to the conquest, Amihai Mazar (1990:328–334), on the other hand, believes them on balance insufficient to either support or refute it. For example, he thinks the Jericho evidence equivocal. Its defenders, he suggests, might have used the preexisting Middle Bronze Age walls when Joshua is alleged to have assaulted the place (Mazar 1990:331). But if pressed to seriously entertain this dodge, one needs to ask an immediately resulting question. Where is the occupational debris datable to the Late Bronze Age/initial Early Iron Age implicit in his scenario? However, it would be a search for a chimera in any case:

> The exodus from Egypt and the return from exile are two salvific acts of God which have been construed as parallels, with the liberation from Babylonian captivity considered a new exodus; yet there is no comparison between the narrative of *Exodus* and that of *Ezra*. The conquest of Jericho and that of Ai are episodes of a holy war in which

Yahweh delivers to Israel its Canaanite enemies; the destruction of Jerusalem is also a holy war in which Nebuchadnezzar is Yahweh's executor of judgment against his rebellious people, but one cannot treat in the same manner the narratives of *Joshua* and those of *Kings* and *Jeremiah*. These examples are extremes, but between them one is able to place many others. It is an illusion to attempt to force all these cases into the same "historical" category [de Vaux 1970:69].

While discrediting as history the "conquest model" of Canaan as presented in the Bible, Dever (1990:25) has no doubt that Israel did in fact emerge in that land in the Early Iron Age. Many biblical historians and archaeologists would doubtless agree. That Israel as a people and then as a nation-state coalesced in Palestine is widely accepted as historically true. Although ethnicity is notoriously difficult to identify archaeologically, as I have personal experience to know in another part of the world (Mason 1976, 1986:15–20, 210–219, 1993, 1997a), and most especially when it is in its formative stages, the attempt is not hopeless even if daunting. There are empirical clues pertinent to the "emergence" of Israel in Palestine that might be taken as more persuasive than those alleged to support the Egyptian captivity, the Exodus, the wandering in the wilderness, or Joshua's taking by storm the "promised land." Of course, the why and the how of Israel's genesis, the discredited invasion tale aside, remain wide open to debate.

Recent and ongoing surveys, subsurface testing, and excavations in the archaeologically long neglected central hill country of Canaan (in modern Israel and Palestine, i.e., the "West Bank") have yielded evidence suggesting the appearance of "new" people in that region in Iron Age I times. These people have been called "proto-Israelites," the "authentic progenitors of Biblical Israel," and they are present by the end of the thirteenth century B.C. (Dever 1990:75–81, 2000). Apart from the ethnic ascription of these people, the implication of the adjective "new" is unclear. Does it mean to suggest the arrival of foreigners? If so, are they immigrants to Palestine or to just the hills? Or are those people "new" in the sense of an indigenous population's having adopted some novel cultural equipment and perhaps possessed of an altered consciousness of their identity, a people who have become, so to speak, reborn? Although they exhibit innovations in certain of their paraphernalia, thus prompting their notice, they just as clearly betray strong continuities with earlier inhabitants, so much so that Philip Davies (2000:26) maintains they were descended from the native Canaanites themselves.

In his latest published statement in support of the "new people" thesis,

Dever (2000:33–34) cites (1) a population increase of a magnitude suggestive of an influx over a two-century period; (2) the location of settlements in previously sparsely inhabited terrain; (3) a novel, if simple, house plan and a village arrangement supposedly corresponding with descriptions of daily life in the books of Joshua, Judges, and Samuel; (4) features absent or at least less common in earlier times such as hillside terracing, plastered cisterns, sporadic appearance of iron tools, and consistent absence in middens of pig bones, presumably reflective of the proscription of pork as recorded in the Bible; and (5) a decrease in the incidence of identifiable religious shrines or structures.

Signs of cultural continuity with antecedent groups include a ceramic industry virtually unchanged except that vessels were now sometimes "partly handmade rather than fashioned on a fast wheel." Striking, if unique, continuities are shown by recovery of an abecedary (list of alphabetic letters) and a ceramic jar bearing a personal name known from the Bible but, like the abecedary, rendered in proto-Canaanite letters, and a bronze figurine of a bull. This last artifact, says Dever, "suggest[s] connections with the old Canaanite cult of the male deity El, whose principal epithet was 'Bull El'" (Dever 2000:34). El was also one of the two names of the early Israelite national god. Dever suggests that the new people were "still in the traditions of the older Canaanite fertility religions" (Dever 2000:34).

Persuaded or not as one might be to nominate the "new" people as Israelites or "proto-Israelites," the detritus they left is as properly subject to conventional analysis and incorporation into the regional cultural milieu as any archaeological assemblage anywhere else that is not required to conform to textual criteria of significance. There is extractable culture history in this material. The same is true of the archaeological sites that have been promoted as relics of the Joshua narratives, but they do not tell the same story when considered apart from them. Discount the extraordinary happenings, preternatural heroes, and paranormal agencies, and those sites are divorced from one world and resituated in quite another. It may be that such data as those just briefly reviewed respecting the identity of the "new" people, together with additional information, will prove sufficient to ratify the interpretation Dever (and others) has drawn from them. But whether it does or does not, Leonard L. Thompson's opening words in his book *Introducing Biblical Literature: A More Fantastic Country* may also appropriately serve to close this essay: "In introducing the Bible, our first obligation is to present the biblical world in all its fantasy and wonder. That world, rather than an expurgated reconstruction of it, contains the biblical legacy" (Thompson 1978:xv). And, "the world created in the Bible is not to be confused with the ancient world in which it arose. The Bible reports on a 'more fantastic country,' which has its own time and space and in which action is limited in different ways from our world: animals can speak, the sun stand still, and a god from afar can raise up nations and decide battles. It is that fantastic country, immediately accessible to any reader, which is of first concern to an interpreter of the Bible" (Thompson 1978:4).

5

On the Nature of Oral Tradition

The number of recorded oral traditions whereby the peoples of the world tell about their origins, let alone their subsequent histories, is daunting. Those that have never been recorded are of course incalculable, but their number must challenge infinity. Although it is dangerous to invoke such a quality as "human nature," as cultural anthropologists have reminded generations of students, people the world over do seem predisposed to tell stories. In addition to the flux of current rumors and gossip, every society known to history and ethnology has more venerable tales. These may tell of firsthand events important in the life of an individual and of sufficient significance to his or her community to have attracted its attention. For Potawatomi Indians of the late seventeenth century, an example might have been an eyewitness description of the arrival of the Frenchman La Salle aboard his fabulous sailing vessel *Griffon* at their island village at the mouth of Green Bay (in September 1679). For people today an even more dramatic example would be a verbal account of the first inkling of something seriously amiss in civil air operations on the morning of September 11, 2001. These kinds of stories are usually referred to as *oral histories,* whether or not they came to be written down, and I will use that term the same way here. Oral histories, then, are personal accounts of people, events, conditions, and so on observed or experienced in the lifetime of the individual telling about them. Although they vary in reliability, in the absence of reason to doubt, they are usually intended to be and are usually taken as truthful within the limitations of the narrator's abilities and circumstances.

More venerable still are the stories, including what had been in their own time oral histories, inherited from generations before that of the current receiving generation (e.g., "my great grandfather told my grandfather who told my father who told me"). These indirectly received hand-me-down stories are called *oral traditions.* And while they may include fairy tales, prayers, homilies, and so forth, they commonly also transmit stories about the creation of the world and the coming into being and subsequent adventures of the society that promulgates them. Of special interest here is that the latter stories are usually believed by both teller and listener to be true. As the Akimel O'Odham and Tohono O'Odham (Pima-Papago) people put it, "We think this story really happened" (Bahr et al. 1994:24). Oral traditions, as understood by their curators and their audience, have an antiquity, and sometimes also a prestige, greater than the personalized stories of more recent times that are properly classified as oral histories. Oral traditions are oral histories with tenure.

Oral histories are subject to change as their tellers age. That this is not a rare phenomenon may be attested by many an ethnographer who has returned to a field site after a lapse of some years or, more commonly, by family members hearing again the reminiscing of an aged senior. Elements in early renditions are altered or utterly disappear in subsequent retellings and novel details may emerge. Indeed, the latest version of an oral history may differ radically from its predecessors. Narrators, reflecting on their past experiences, inevitably forget some things, reinterpret in the light of later events what they remember, and perhaps unselfconsciously incorporate into those memories the recollections of others who witnessed the same events. As reviewed in Chapter 3, all of this is familiar ground to the psychologist of memory or the lawyer engaged in cross-examination. As stories leave the world that gave them birth, they typically expire within a generation or two. Those that survive and become the legacy of succeeding generations *as traditions* are susceptible to the selective forces of new circumstances. Differential amplification and dampening of parts of the message are inevitable and even more so are extinction and replacement. In all societies there are liars, of course. Some aboriginal people are known to have bragged about the lies they foisted on government officials, trusting anthropologists, or tourists (see Chapter 1 for a Paiute example recounted in Dansie 1999). More numerous are exaggerators and incompetents who knowingly or innocently make a muddle of traditional stories. It is also not uncommon for a collector of oral traditions to mistake a family or a lineage tradition for a clan, moiety, tribal, or even national tradition. As Ruth Finnegan (1970: 328–329), working with African material, and Ruth Benedict (1969 [1935]: 1:xiii), concerned with Zuni mythology, point out, it is all too easy to assume that a recorded tradition is *the* clan, tribal, or national tradition, unaware of the existence of unrecorded variants or even alternative traditions at odds with the one the researcher happens to know.

To one newly come to the subject it must seem that the numbers of books and articles devoted to the related and overlapping genres generally known as oral traditions, oral histories, folk histories, legends, mythologies, folklore and folktales, social memory, and cultural sagas and epics must rival those of the recorded instances of the phenomena themselves. Anthropologists, sociologists, folklorists, psychologists, classicists, historians, linguists and philologists, and literary and biblical scholars have all made contributions to this library, either because of primary interest or because of the myriad ways legends and myths and folklore are implicated in other matters such scholars study. It has become clear to all but the most refractory specialists that these disciplines benefit by interaction, for the phenomena themselves are multifaceted and interlinked, the boundaries between them more often than not indistinct and permeable. The recitation of, say, a single Nez Perce, Kwakiutl, or Wasco oral tradition may attract the attention of a social anthropologist because of allusions to sodality functions embedded in the story, whereas a linguist or a student of diffusion or acculturation might discern interesting signs of exogenous contacts. An archaeologist listening to or reading a record of the same recitation might detect a possible clue to a site's archaeoethnicity, a folklorist another instance of a myth type she is mapping, a psychologist an insight into a hitherto unfamiliar facet of stress accommodation, a student of epithet formation in classical epics a suggestive parallel sufficient to shake his ethnocentrism, or a literary scholar not previously exposed to the subtle power of such an oral narration a glimpse of a precursor of some part of that with which he is professionally engaged. A given origin myth or hero tale does not intrinsically and exhaustively reveal its message to the practitioners of but one field of study. It retains the potential to speak to others as well, if, in the sometimes alleged words of the Iroquois culture hero Deganawida, they will but "close their mouths and open their ears." Listening, however, as respect for such stories demands, cannot be passive. It must be critical if unfamiliar decibels are to be perceived as something more than noise. This is not easy. It requires work.

Although I am concerned in this study with North American Indian oral traditions and their implications for archaeological reconstructions of the histories of their societies, I quickly became aware that much of what I needed to know about oral traditions rested on knowledge garnered in a wider world, one comprising researchers with diverse disciplinary allegiances working in every part of the globe. In fact, most of the pioneering work was done in that wider world. And while there is no substitute for indigenous North American oral traditions in all their singularities—an observation equally true of African, Polynesian, Siberian, Australian, and other analogs, of course—so also is it true that none of them can be properly understood in geographical or single disciplinary isolation. They are all variable instances of a universal phenomenon. Documented revisions of Oceanian verbal genealogies throw light on the extrahistorical purposes of Amazonian genealogy keeping, twentieth-century Serbo-Croatian epic ballads inform students of the orality of ancient Homeric epics, and knowing what kinds of things counted as historically worth remembering by nineteenth-century Arapahoes prepares the student of, say, early twentieth-century Tiv or Dinka for a better understanding of theirs. Comprehending the nature, evolution, structure, multiple functions, and unanticipated consequences of oral traditions is a challenge best met by knowing something of the work that has been done and the insights that have been gained in the culturally varied cross-disciplinary studies beyond as well as within a researcher's immediate focus of interest. Although exceptions are noted in these pages, there are many North American archaeologists, as well as Native American advocates of science and tradition coequality, who seem unfamiliar with that wider world. A lot of what I criticize in the following pages is a consequence of that unhappy fact.

The Orality of Oral Traditions

That oral traditions, like oral histories, are verbally communicated should not require stating except that in fact their majority are known to most of their would-be consumers today through reading rather than listening. Almost inevitably, when archaeologists and other students cite an oral tradition in connection with their work, they are actually referring to a written version of the genre and not the thing itself. Ethnographies and compilations of myths, legends, and other folklore record, or purport to record, what were in their original form sequences of somatic and not just verbal acts generated in a context distinct from that of the reader. The consequences of this translation of what existed in a transient but dynamic state into a permanent but static—and necessarily simplified—representation have been explored by many students (e.g., Finnegan 1970; Henige 1982:76–79; Leach 1954:7; Lord 1960; Nagy 1996; Ong 1982:66–68, 146–147; Swann 1992, 2004; Stith Thompson 1951:455; Vansina 1985).

In trying to do justice to the stories told by Oregon Indians that he brought together and published in *Coyote Was Going There: Indian Literature of the Oregon Country,* Jarold Ramsey (1977:xxv) poignantly expresses this dilemma:

Reading these stories off the printed page, we are inclined to forget that they have been utterly transformed for us—taken down from a wholly oral/traditional mode of existence in an unthought-of mode, print, and translated out of the original languages into an alien language, English. More seriously, seeing them unfold in orderly rows of type across uniform pages we may fall into the habit of reading them simply as stories in our terms, as prose narratives. To experience them in this way is to lose imaginative contact with the artistic and social conditions that govern them. When Archie Phinney, a Nez Perce trained by Franz Boas, returned to his tribe and began transcribing their myths, he became so distressed by what he was losing in the process that he wrote to Boas: "A sad thing in recording these animal stories is the loss of spirit—the fascination furnished by the peculiar Indian vocal tradition for humor. Indians are better story-tellers than whites. When I read my story mechanically I find only the cold corpse."

David Henige (1982:76) goes further and feels justified in referring to most, especially the most respected, tellers of traditional stories in any society as artists. He writes, for instance, "The historian treats the ethnographic interview largely as an intellectual experience—the opportunity to consult informants about the past. However, this idea of the interview will be fully shared by the informant only rarely. As members of a society in which the spoken word plays a prominent social role, informants are likely to regard orality as a performing art" and

> In predominantly oral societies . . . the essence of oral art is the complementary relationship between the artist and his listeners and there is rarely any desire to allow a text to constrain this relationship. Whether the audience is only one person—say, the historian—or whether it happens to consist of many members of the informant's group, the informant will always feel a need to treat what he is doing, among other things, as a living art. It is important, indeed essential, that the historian understands the role of his informants as performing artists and considers the effects of this when dealing with their testimony. He would be quite wrong to isolate the telling from its social setting [Henige 1982:76].

The last warning is usually ignored by archaeologists who seek to use oral traditions in their reconstructions of the past. Indeed, they typically have little opportunity to take advantage of the varieties of what may be essential information that the details of context and performance typically offer members of an audience hearing, seeing, and interacting with a speaker, singer, or chanter as he or she "renews the life" of a tale. Again, this is because their usual sources are written ones that preserve little of the life setting of the original. That context, the when and where and in what circumstances, and the performance nuances of the storyteller—facial expressions, gestures, subtle body language, tonal alteration, variation in pace, and so on—can be critical factors in communicating with listeners the essential meaning of a story and how literally it is intended to be taken. And the speaker is as likely as not to be an advocate as well as a teller of stories. The interests of the storyteller's own family, faction, or clan are apt to be engaged as much as fidelity to the tale (Henige 1982:76–79). One does not have to be a member of an oral society to appreciate the potential magnitude of information loss when only words, usually translated, are preserved. Precisely because the archaeologist is usually at a disadvantage because of reliance on written versions of what were once verbal utterances in an active setting, there should be a recognition of the need to be familiar enough with the work of students of orality to be sensitive to the likelihood that information of uncertain salience to the raconteur and his or her audience is missing. The appropriate response to this enigma should be to proceed with due caution. Not many archaeologists know enough to be properly diffident.

Henige and numerous other students of storytelling in oral societies (see especially Finnegan 1970; Lord 1960; Parry 1971; and Parry et al. 1974) rightly stress the influence of social settings. A ceremonial milieu, with or without masks and other regalia, whether or not in a kiva or analogous sacrosanct precinct, with the participation of a priest, shaman, or other raconteur supported by or bereft of assistants, prompters, or dancers, is a different dynamic altogether from those prevailing on more mundane occasions. The latter may include scheduled or spontaneous performances, sober or lighthearted situations, and purposes ranging from instruction to entertainment. As critical can be the manner of interaction between individual actor and particular audience. Even on the simplest level, the "text" is only partly the medium. In translating orality to literacy, that compound component of seeing, hearing, feeling, and participating in a social event is inescapably forfeited. It is instructive to note that some recitations of Osage oral traditions, for example, were "chanted" rather than simply spoken (Dorsey 1888). On the other hand, owners of painted bison hide calendars among the Kiowas invited men at the winter camps to come and sit around their tipi fires, there to smoke and talk about the calendar, to reminisce, and recite in ordinary speech "some mythic or historic tradition, or some noted deed on the warpath, which is then discussed by the circle. Thus the history of the tribe is formulated and handed down" (Mooney 1898:144–145). There is much "recitative chanting" in Ojibwa Midewiwin and Menomini Mita'wit society ceremonies (Hoffman 1896:66–137). Menomini chanting is accompanied by the use of a drum and rattles as well as by dancing and smoking. It employs duplication of phrases and "interjected meaningless notes, to give emphasis and to fill up the measure of drum beats," to prolong it and impress observers "not members of the society" (Hoffman 1896:79). For the Central Eskimos (Inuit), Franz Boas (1888:648) wrote, "All these tales [myths, legends, traditions] must be considered recitatives, many of them beginning with a musical phrase and continuing as a rhythmic recitation, others being recited in rhythmic phrases throughout. Other traditions are told in a more detailed and prosaic manner, songs or recitations, however, being sometimes included."

Context and way of speaking can intentionally elicit effects a naive reader of an oral tradition might fail to discern. During the period of lengthy Arctic nights, Greenlandic Eskimo storytellers, so John Bierhorst (1985:58) relates, used their talents to help pass time by inducing slumber in their listeners. As prelude to performing their verbal art, the boast was often "no one has ever heard this story to the end."

The Shape of Oral Traditions

Ruth Benedict wrote in the introduction to her massive compendium *Zuni Mythology,* "No folktale is generic. It is always the tale of one particular people with one particular livelihood and social organization and religion" (Benedict 1969 [1935]:xiii). One may substitute "culture" for "folktale" and "tale" in this statement and still do justice to her theoretical commitment to the so-called American anthropological school of historical particularism. Yet, just as Benedict was simultaneously perceiving some contrasting sets of similarities among North American Indian cultures sufficient to persuade her to divide them into opposing types in her classic *Patterns of Culture* (Benedict 1955 [1934]), so did she recognize the sharing of many mythic themes, plots, and character types among different Indian cultures. Examined in sufficiently painstaking detail, every folktale and every culture is unique, however many attributes they may share in common. No two have experienced identical vicissitudes, attending as they are on time, place, and accident. But uniqueness so considered is ultimately a function of scale. Shared attributes must also command attention. And studies by anthropologists, folklorists, historians, and other students of folklore have identified and classified those in imposing numbers in local, regional, continental, and even global perspectives (e.g., S. Thompson's multivolume *Motif-Index of Folk-Literature,* 1955–1958).

Focusing on oral traditions purporting to describe or explain cultural origins and histories draws notice to commonalities of structure and content that are easily masked by too engrossing a fascination with unique details, however important the latter may be for certain purposes. Among these commonalities are recurring kinds of stories, or building blocks of stories, whose distributions call for explanation. Attempted explanations variously have invoked migrations of people; diffusion among neighbors; correlations with cultural evolutionary stages; independent invention among societies faced with similar problems in comparable environments, however widely separated they are; deep impulses innate in the human brain; and so on. Whatever the proper explanation may be in any given case, the multiple instances of the same or similar stories have stimulated the development of several taxonomies to facilitate their grouping into various categories based on particular attributes. Thus, in his *Tales of the North American Indians,* Stith Thompson discerned certain "fundamental types" and numbers of their well-represented varieties. Some examples are *creation myths,* stories that "show the preparation for the present order of affairs" and that may or may not include *migration legends* entailing emergence from beneath the surface of the earth (Thompson 1967 [1929]:xvii). Other examples are *trickster tales* of coyotes, rabbits, ravens, or other animals that have many human qualities and unpredictably engage in wise and benevolent or stupid and malevolent behaviors affecting people—tales in which it is usually "quite impossible to tell whether animal or person is in the mind of the narrator" (Thompson 1967 [1929]:xviii). In the words of an Apache storyteller, "They say that all the animals were people in those days" (Bierhorst 1985:12).

Thompson suggests how it is possible to assimilate aboriginal North American material into the "motifs" and their variants that he and colleagues around the world had been assembling for their global *Motif-Index of Folk-Literature* (S. Thompson 1955–1958). In his previously cited 1967 (1929) publication, Thompson, as a first step, had cataloged the North American stories under 17 of the world survey's major motif headings. For North America specifically, each of these broad groupings includes as many as seven more precisely drawn subsidiary categories. These latter, in turn, each comprise up to 25 smaller categories of story varieties, and most of these, of course, have numerous variants. While there is no need to examine all of these distinctions here, it is useful to be reminded of the abundance and multifariousness of North American Indian oral creations by looking at just one of the major motif headings and its divisions and subdivisions. The letters, numbers, headings, and descriptive labels are those of the *Motif-Index of Folk-Literature,* and the following example (Thompson 1967 [1929]:361) is but the commencement of the classification listing for the indigenous North American stories.

A. Mythological Motifs

Gods and culture heroes

A21.1. The woman who fell from the sky

A31. Creator's grandmother

A226. Sun father-in-law

A284.2. Thunderbird

A315. Mistress of the under world

A531. Culture hero pacifies monsters

A540. Divinity teaches arts and crafts

A561. Divinity's departure for west

A565. Dying culture hero

A575. Departed deity grants requests to visitors

A580. Divinity's expected return

Other classifications are possible, of course, depending on the researcher's needs. Some students make a distinction between mythology ("the important tales") and "folktales in general, which would include stories of romance, adventure tales, and humorous anecdotes," a distinction not always easy to maintain (Bierhorst 1985:5). This same writer believes many North American Indian myths fall into one of the following categories (Bierhorst 1985:7–20):

Earth Diver—Water creatures (duck, loon, muskrat, otter) dive beneath the primal global ocean for a piece of dirt from which dry land may be created. After several failed attempts, one succeeds. A widespread Old World myth, in North America Bierhorst finds it everywhere except in the Southwest and the Arctic.

World Flood—Even more widespread than the Earth Diver myth. Because it is incorporated in many different myths, Bierhorst sometimes regards it as a "motif," not a story or myth in itself.

The Theft of Fire—An actor steals fire from a (usually forbidden) source through stealth or trickery and brings it home (like Prometheus). Analogous tales involve stealing the sun itself or heat or daylight.

The "Orpheus" Tale—A husband searches for his wife in the land of the dead. He is allowed to retrieve her if he will not look at or touch her or break some other prohibition. He breaks the conditions of her release and loses her. In some versions this is the origin of permanent death. The story in one form or another, says Bierhorst, is universal in North America except the far north.

The Bird Nester—A father and son desire the same woman. The father tricks his son into climbing to a high nest from which he cannot escape.

The father then takes the woman. Rescued by a supernatural helper, the son takes revenge on his father. Versions of this story are widespread in North and South America.

Bierhorst discusses other types of myths as well, including that of a dying god, as in some renditions of the Piman character Elder Brother. Several forms of this idea occur in the Midwest and Great Basin as well as in the Southwest. All or at least a great many of these stories have animals as the actors. Each of these, as Bierhorst says, "is in some sense a person, as are all animal protagonists in world folklore." They belong in the "myth age . . . [which] ends when the [animal] 'people' are changed into the animals of today" (Bierhorst 1985:12). Another myth classifier, Sam Gill (1987), identifies many of the types listed by Bierhorst but adds to them, or in some cases substitutes for them, groupings he labels "Emergence"; "Two Creators"; "World Parent," perhaps a variant of the former; "Plant and Animal Origins," as in Corn Woman and the Eskimo Sedna myths; "Trickster"; and "Speech," the latter as a creator itself and perpetuator of things already created.

The phenomenal number and diversity of oral traditions in native North America, and not just those variably defined as myths, as well as other possible ways of classifying them, are readily sampled by perusing any of numerous published collections in addition to those previously cited (e.g., Alexander 1916; Bierhorst 1976; Bonnefoy 1991:1159–1160; Erdoes and Ortiz 1984; Ford 1985; Gill 1983; Lankford 1987; Marriott and Rachlin 1968; Swann 2004). Most ethnographies, of course, pay some attention to oral traditions either under that label or such others as "oral literature," "myths," "legends," "folklore," "traditional history," and "traditional cosmology" (or "cosmogony") or as subdivisions of "religious beliefs" or "cultural (or social) memory." Collectively, their number is huge even if their variety is something less and their quality uneven. A few examples among the widely available, more awesome members of this literature are, for just the Kwakiutl Indians, Boas 1910 and 1969 [1935–1943] and Boas and Hunt 1975a [1902–1905] and 1975b [1906]; for the Yuroks, Kroeber 1976; for the Bella Coolas, McIlwraith 1992 [1948]; for the Haidas, J. R. Swanton via Bringhurst 1999; and for the Pimas, Bahr et al. 1994. Anyone dipping into just these must quail at the thought of the totality they foreshadow.

The Work of Oral Traditions

Oral traditions do work for the societies that produce and perpetuate them. They do not pop into and out of people's attention like an afterthought or a burp. They serve the needs of their proprietors in ways that are often obvious and acknowledged by them. Sometimes they operate more subtly. The oral traditions to which North American archaeologists sometimes turn in their attempts to understand the past are the products of preliterate societies mainly lacking the panoply of socioeconomic stratification, central political control, and developed labor specialization typical of nation states. These societies are of the kinds anthropologists variously call bands, tribes, "bigman" and village communities, or, more rarely, as in some parts of the Southeast, Southwest, and Northwest Coast, chiefdoms and even, arguably, kingdoms (in the Southeast). And invariably, the traditions, *as known,* are of just recent vintage, having been harvested by amateur as well as professional ethnographers from informants indebted in turn to their parents or grandparents. Much less commonly, it may be possible to suggest continuity with something similar told to a missionary or explorer one, two, or even three centuries earlier preserved in documentary form. A pertinent example of the latter, for archaeologists working in the eastern United States and Canada, is the invaluable 73-volume *Jesuit Relations and Allied Documents: Travels and Explorations of the Jesuit Missionaries in New France, 1610–1791* (Thwaites 1896–1901). But notwithstanding the short histories typical of oral traditions as received, many archaeologists, and even more Indians, government functionaries, and politicians, are not hesitant about extrapolating from them to interpret cultural or human skeletal remains hundreds, thousands, or even circa 9 or 10 thousand years older—as in the previously discussed Kennewick Man case—and of debatable, if not impossible, ethnic affiliation with those traditions.

The problems associated with such extrapolations are weighty and not always amenable to solution. First among them is the necessity to avoid the ethnocentric fallacy of ascribing the same assumptions and logic—the same Weltanschauung or worldview—of the investigator to the curators of oral traditions. The latter are (were) speaking from, for, and to a way of thinking distinct from that of the scientist or systematic historiographer. They were not trying to say the same thing and simply bungled the job. Oral traditions are not "to be understood as fragmentary and corrupted remains of stories that once existed in the same conceptual framework as recent European narrative history, or at least chronicle" (Cowgill 1993:561). David Henige (1982:5) amplifies this important point when he notes that "even greater than the differences between written and oral sources are the disparities in understanding and conceiving the past by societies that rely on writing and those that must depend only on the spoken word to carry an ever-growing past continually into an ever-changing present." Although using terms succeeded today by the circumlocutions sensitive people feel more comfortable with, the prolific ethnographer J. N. B. Hewitt, himself of Iroquois ancestry, essentially made the same point a century ago. In his pioneering *Iroquoian Cosmology* he wrote, "It is no ready task to embody in the language of enlightenment the thought of barbarism. The viewpoint of the one plane of thought differs much from that of the other" (Hewitt 1903:137).

In one of the chapters of her *The Social Life of Stories: Narrative and Knowledge in the Yukon Territory,* Julie Cruikshank (1998:45–70) has described coming face-to-face with something like this disparity of understood meanings in the contemporary world. At various meetings in the Yukon Territory, scientists and local Indians have been brought together to talk about such things of mutual interest as the human history of the land, environmental knowledge, and the desirability of cooperative efforts to manage wildlife resources. At one of these meetings an elderly Tutchone lady rose to offer her views about early caribou migration routes and other topics being discussed. She prefaced her comments with these words: "Where do these people come from, outside? You tell different stories from us people. You people talk from paper—Me, I want to talk from Grandpa" (Cruikshank 1998:45). This anecdote is also preface to Cruikshank's superb critique of well-meaning but naive attempts to co-opt the traditional knowledge of primarily oral societies into the more rigid categories and systematized (and bureaucratic) thought patterns of modern science and administrative requirements. She is able to show how the world and its workings as conceived and transmitted through purely verbal channels are so embedded in local area and personal time that when they are removed from that environment they lose much of their intelligibility. What in essence was provincial and immediate may readily become nonsense when outsiders try to fit it into the universalizing aims of national integration or public policy as, for instance, in educational development or programs for ecosystem protection. These have limited capacity to meaningfully digest such phenomena as men who become and talk to caribou. Or fish who, having willingly offered themselves to be taken, feel insulted when thrown back because they are judged to be undersized; they and their kin may not be so cooperative in the future, whatever wildlife managers say. Cruikshank's observations will be familiar to many ethnologists, but they have rarely been so cogently and empathetically expressed. And they speak to archaeologists who would put the "history" in oral traditions into the conceptual vocabulary of modern science and historiography.

As Cruikshank (1998), Cowgill (1993), Henige (1974, 1982), Goody (1987, 2000), Goody and Watt (1968), Ong (1982), Vansina (1985), Bahr (1998), Bahr et al. (1994), and many others have shown, it is not simply the fact of writing versus its absence that is the key issue, important as that is, but rather the way the two forms of communication influence the way people think and the things they think about and, indeed, are enabled to think about. That present assertions about the past might independently be compared with portrayals of that past when it was the present is the sorcerer's stone, the possession of which elevates literacy above orality.

The existence of literacy, of course, does not in itself confer lasting tenability on everything thereby reported. Within the relatively brief span of a few centuries in the history of literate Western civilization notions of credibility varied radically across social strata, national frontiers, and through time. What had once seemed believable, later did not (e.g., an earth-centered solar system). And "very few historians [today] . . . would hesitate to apply the category 'legend' to the story of the saint who, after being beheaded, walked a few hundred yards to a cathedral with his head under his arm, entered the sanctuary and there sang the *Te Deum*" (Harvey 1966:116).

S. H. Hooke (1963) has emphasized the role of the orally constructed past in his observations regarding the social functions of Near Eastern mythology. The following has equal relevance to aboriginal North America as well:

The historical truth of the story contained in the myth was irrelevant [although usually believed]. The function of history is to find out and to record as accurately as possible the behavior of communities in the past, i.e., to discover and impart a certain kind of knowledge. The function of the myth was not knowledge but action, action essential for the very existence of the community. Mankind has in the past existed for vast periods of time without feeling any need for history [in the above sense]; but, long before the appearance of the earliest forms of historical records, the myth had a vital function in the life of the community; as an essential part of ritual it helped to secure those conditions upon which the life of the community depended [Hooke 1963:12–13].

Jack Goody and Ian Watt (1968) do not deny preliterate, or mainly oral people, a "felt need" for history, as does Hooke. But they are in essential agreement with his characterization of the nature of that history. Oral traditions ("histories" in their sense) "act as 'charters' of present social institutions rather than as faithful historical records of times past" (Goody and Watt 1968:33; the authors follow this by citing Malinowski [1926:23, 43] on myth). Goody and Watt then go on to credit oral societies with more immediate flexibility than literate ones in adapting their "histories" to chang-

ing circumstances because of the absence of a more or less permanent record subject to independent check:

> Deities and other supernatural agencies which have served their pur-
> pose can be quietly dropped from the contemporary pantheon; and as
> the society changes, myths too are forgotten, attributed to other per-
> sonages, or transformed in their meaning.
>
> One of the most important results of this homeostatic tendency is
> that the individual has little perception of the past except in terms of
> the present; whereas the annals of a literate society cannot but enforce
> a more objective recognition of the distinction between what was and
> what is. . . . Myth and history [in oral societies] merge into one: the
> elements in the cultural heritage which cease to have a contemporary
> relevance tend to be soon forgotten or transformed; and as the indi-
> viduals of each generation acquire their vocabulary, their genealogies,
> and their myths, they are unaware that various words, proper names
> and stories have dropped out, or that others have changed their mean-
> ing or been replaced.
>
> . . . The pastness of the past, then, depends upon a historical sensi-
> bility which can hardly begin to operate without permanent written
> records; and writing introduces similar changes in the transmission of
> other items of the cultural repertoire [Goody and Watt 1968:33–34].

And similarly, in the words of David Henige (1982:4–5):

> One of the historian's most difficult problems is that oral evidence
> [traditions and histories] changes imperceptibly as time passes. As for
> the human species, a principle of natural selection tends to operate, by
> which those traditions that are best able to outlive changing circum-
> stances are those that exist today. But, as with plants and animals, sur-
> viving requires that they adapt to whatever changes they encounter.
> However reluctantly, we must assume that many contemporary ver-
> sions of traditions are to some extent the debris of an obliterated past,
> the result of its mental landscape being repeatedly exposed to weath-
> ering, its shapes deposited in secondary patterns and shifting with the
> wind. Inevitably, many traditions cannot be regarded as historical fact.
> Accepting this will be hardest when there is nowhere else to turn, but
> this is a pity rather than an argument.

These quotations from some of the deservedly most influential students
of oral traditions and histories should not be misconstrued as representing

commitment to a doctrine of radical historical presentism either on their part or mine. Goody, Watt, Henige, and the others are aware of instances of genuine agreement subsisting between some of the beliefs people have about their society's past and what actually or probably occurred. The problem for the scientific historiographer, of course, is how to establish isomorphism and not simply assume it. To an extent not readily stipulated in most instances, traditional stories are thought to serve present social needs even as they offer what are commonly understood to be belief-worthy accounts about the past. If they did not do these things, they would not survive. When societies change, stresses are placed on those stories and they are replaced with new ones. As Eric Hobsbawm (Hobsbawm and Ranger 1983:8) puts it, "Where the old ways are alive, traditions need be neither revived nor invented." The old stories survive as long as they do their work of offering the sense of legitimacy that adheres to continuity with the past, of safeguarding ancestral roots, of facilitating identification with a place—and of having a tenured affiliation with its associated if no longer resident powers, sacred and profane.

Even though concerned with literate nineteenth- and twentieth-century America, specifically with "collective memory" and the changing image in that memory of Abraham Lincoln, the sociologist Barry Schwartz (2000) speaks to the dual role of tradition in a way that is relevant to nonliterate societies as well. As he cogently observes, "if, independently of historical evidence, our changing understanding of the past uniquely parallels changes in our society, then the only relevant reality would be the present, and the very concept of collective memory [or tradition] would be meaningless" (Schwartz 2000:7). I believe it is this realization, whether it is given voice or not, that explains much of the tenaciousness with which many cultural historians cling to oral traditions as clues to the past. Surely, it would seem, there must be a kernel of historical veracity in some of the stories told by tribal and other nonliterate people. That such people have survived is itself testimony to their self-conceived pasts being something more than delusions. The idea of at least a kernel of historicity does not entail acceptance of everything in myth and legend, notwithstanding Robert Lowie's (1915:598, 1917:162) warnings, not lightly to be dismissed, against accepting as history what we find plausible in our own terms while ignoring what we do not.

Ruth Benedict, however, working from the huge collections of Zuni folklore resulting from her two years of fieldwork and the earlier investigations of Frank Hamilton Cushing and Mathilda Cox Stevenson and those of her contemporaries Elsie Clews Parsons, E. L. Handy, and Ruth Bunzel, found a convenient theoretical fence and sat on it. She developed an awareness of "presentism" in her analysis of that mythology even as she detected what she took to be vestigial history. Benedict wrote, for example, that "a living folklore, such as that of Zuni, reflects the contemporary interests and judgments of its tellers, and adapts incidents to its own cultural usages" (Benedict 1969 [1935]:xiv). *But,*

> Like any cultural trait, folklore tends, of course, to perpetuate tradi-
> tional forms, and there is a certain lag in folklore as there is in con-
> temporary statecraft or in morals. But the scope of this conservatism
> is limited in folklore as in other traits. It is never sufficient to give us
> license to reconstruct the items of a racial memory; and contemporary
> attitudes are always to be reckoned with, rather than those that have
> been superseded in that culture. In the present collection [of Zuni
> folklore] the cultural lag is apparent in many details of overt behavior.
> In the folktales, for example, except in those recognized by the tellers
> as Mexican, entrance to the house is by means of a ladder to the roof
> and down another ladder from the hatchway, yet doors have been
> common in Zuni since 1888 and are today [1922–1923] universal ex-
> cept in the kivas. Old conditions, therefore, have been equally retained
> in the ceremonial house and in the folktale. The same may be said of
> the use of stone knives. Stone knives are still laid upon altars and used
> in ceremonies; and in folktales also heroes use stone knives instead of
> the omnipresent contemporary store knife. More elaborate modern
> innovations are also unrecognized in folklore. At present sheep herd-
> ing occupies much of the life of Zuni men, and hunting is in abey-
> ance. In the tales, however, all heroes are hunters, and there is no men-
> tion of sheep herding except in tales recognized as Mexican. In like
> manner men do not now come courting with a bundle of gifts for the
> girl, but in folklore this is a convention usually observed [Benedict
> 1969 (1935):xiv–xv].

Zuni oral traditions, says Benedict, contain stories and story elements that are either difficult to reconcile with the notion of functional compatibility with current societal interests and needs or that are best understood as ves-tiges surviving from an earlier time. The Zuni taboo on polygamy is be-lieved by Benedict and the Zunis themselves to be of long standing, even though it contrasts with what was common in most other North American Indian societies *and in Zuni mythology itself.* If, Benedict (1969 [1935]:xvi) points out, the latter occurrences are to be explained by appeal to sur-vival from ancient practices, "we should still have to explain why the mar-riage with eight wives or with two husbands is prominent in Zuni mythology and not generally over North America." Marriage with two or more wives (simultaneously, that is), while unexceptional among other people over much of the continent, "does not figure in their tales as [much as] it does in pueblo folklore" (Benedict 1969 [1935]:xvi). Alas, Benedict's (1969 [1935]:xvi) solution to this conundrum as being "a grandiose folkloristic convention partaking on the one hand of usual mythological exaggeration and on the other of a compensatory daydream" also fails to satisfy. It is, after all, the opposition of monogamy in historical Zuni society and polygyny and even polyandry in Zuni oral traditions, and particularly the specification of eight wives and two husbands, that she advances as requiring explanation. This was a reasonable attitude for her to take. Likewise incompatible with preoccupation with contemporary needs and values or with a doctrine of cultural survivals are the Zuni folklore themes of child abandonment and "Death sought by summoning the Apache." Analogous problems are rife in the oral traditions of many societies around the world, of course, and historical (both indigenously evolved and diffusional), functional, structural, psychoanalytical, "compensatory" (in Benedict's terminology), and other would-be explanations have risen to the challenge.

The problem of possible historicity in Zuni oral traditions is regarded by Benedict as of minor importance. Of their accuracy as history she is plainly skeptical. Early optimistic attempts, by investigators like Jesse Walter Fewkes and Frank Hamilton Cushing, to reconstruct the histories of people like the Hopi and the Zuni were based on too literal an interpretation of those people's folklore (see Bernardini 2005 and Lyons 2003 for the most recent extended attempts to do better). The Zuni migration incident known as the "Choice of eggs," for instance, is filled with the same just-so or "that's why" stories as occur in courtship, witch, and other tales: "they certainly give no basis for reconstruction of history" (Benedict 1969 [1935]:xliii). She gives the example of the tale "Tupe kills the Apaches" as offered in explanation of the origin of the scalp dance just two generations before the account was given her. There being six or so other stories purporting to recount the origin of that ceremony—and the ceremony "obviously" having a longer tenure than her informant allowed—Benedict relegates the tale told her to "literary flourish." In the same way, she also tells of "a true story of treachery against Navaho visitors which happened two generations ago . . . as told by the grandson of the chief actor as an origin of albinos in Zuni . . . yet immediately after telling the tale he named albinos who had been born considerably before the date of the incident. I did not point out to him the inconsistency and he saw none. The tale did not even represent history according to his personal knowledge" (Benedict 1969 [1935]:xliii).

Zuni oral traditions, like those of other people, do work for their societies. They serve present needs, if often in an opaque manner, and they some-times preserve, usually also in the same manner, historical information. Extracting the latter is the task of critical historiography. It is not a clearly labeled component to be freely plucked from its matrix. And in all likeli-hood, for the reasons explored in this study and in the work of such students of oral traditions as already cited, the historiographical analyst's understand-ing of its meaning will not and can not be that of its authors. Further, when those traditions pertain to times increasingly remote from that of their tell-ers, their burden of historical accuracy is progressively lightened. Something else must not be overlooked. It seems some stories are just stories. Some of these ignore linguistic and cultural frontiers and may be borrowed sim-ply for amusement. In 1886 the pioneer ethnographer of the Zunis, Frank Hamilton Cushing, told three of his Zuni friends an Italian folktale called "The Cock and the Mouse." This type of story, called a cumulation story, is widely represented in Europe; in these stories, a person, or animal in this case, petitions another for a needed or much desired service or commodity. This other character, however, requires something the petitioner lacks as payment for supplying the want. In search of whatever that payment calls for, the first character appeals to a third who can supply it. The third agrees if the first will provide what he or she wants. Lacking that also, the first character must then go to a fourth in hopes of satisfying the third. And so it goes, potentially ad infinitum. Just a year or so later, Cushing was taken by surprise to hear this tale retold by one of his friends, only this time substantially recast as a Zuni story. The cock, for example, had become a turkeylike creature ("turkey's younger brother"), the indigenous emphasis on the number four emerged repeatedly, and several "that's why" explana-tions had been added (e.g., why doctors only cure when they are paid, how it came to be that tom turkeys have red fleshy crests on their heads). Both the original Italian and the derived Zuni stories, originally published by Cushing in 1901, were reprinted by Alan Dundes (1965:269–276), who rightly credited Cushing as having produced, however unintentionally, one of the first experiments in the cross-cultural transmission of folktales in the history of folklore studies.

The Origins of Oral Traditions

Barring the relatively infrequent instances of attested parenthood, searching for the progenitors of so incorporeal a thing as an oral tradition can be like trying to track a chimera to its lair. Nevertheless, legions of students have searched for historical bases for verbal traditions. Others have posited the psychic unity of humankind or something in the physical environment as instrumental in their origin. Some have suggested that their ultimate source may be discovered by appeal to Freudian or another branch of psychoanalysis. Still others believe myths and legends to have been initially generated out of religious or some other form of ritual. Whether the light that has been generated in arguments over these alternatives is commensurate with the heat is questionable. See, for example, the historical versus ritual origins debate in the *Journal of American Folklore* among William Bascom (1957, 1958), Stanley Hyman (1955, 1958), and Lord Raglan (1957).

Inasmuch as questions of possible historical content in oral traditions and of how to test for them, particularly but not exclusively by archaeological means, are the raison d'être of the present work, it is important to present for consideration what is probably the most recurrent argument of the historicists when faced with what they themselves acknowledge as ambiguous, inconsistent, contradictory, or even nonexistent evidence. While many other specimens of this argument could be given (see, for example, the section "On Preliterate Historical Memory Among the Dogrib Indians of the Canadian Subarctic" in Chapter 6), Bascom's statement of it in one of his just cited papers is especially succinct. In that paper he says,

> A major weakness in this argument [that myths and many other oral traditions have no historical basis and thus cannot be their cause] is that the mass of evidence of historical inaccuracies in folklore, which could easily be extended [beyond the examples Bascom accepts from Raglan's *The Hero* (1949)], does not disprove the possibility of historical origins. If some myths and tales can have their origins in human social situations or other historical events [this last equation is close to a rhetorical sleight-of-hand, as one of his foregoing adversaries charges], however inaccurately they may be reported, it is not necessary to look for their origins in ritual any more than in natural phenomena.
>
> Even the fact that one tale is completely contradicted by historical records does not prove that it, or any other tale, has no basis in historical events [Bascom 1957:103].

Frustration with the problematical results of most of these avenues of inquiry has provoked not a few scholars to abandon asking after origins on the grounds that such questions are for all intents and purposes answerless. Nevertheless, on the working assumption of a historical basis for a particular myth, what sustains hope is not the previously invoked chimera but the wishful anticipation of recovering an as yet unrecognized corroboratory clue—an archaeological or historiographical afterbirth, so to speak. This requires knowledge, imagination, persistence, and luck. Such a search is apt to turn up many an ambiguity, each difficult to distinguish in the compost of centuries or millennia from the remnants of a long expelled placenta. Even if a specimen of the latter can be recognized, however, does it uniquely signal the thing whose genesis is sought? This is where "bridging arguments," as archaeologists like to label potentially testable connections between thought-to-be related phenomena, as cause and effect, call for critical examination. They are too commonly fragilely, even if enthusiastically, constructed; failed and simply uncorroborated examples litter the archaeological landscape. Nonetheless, without endorsing the squandering of time and resources, a laissez-faire approach to research inspiration has its virtues. If caution is jettisoned in such an approach, however, its tosser should be prepared for the chance that something irretrievable might accompany the toss. With respect to would-be couplings of archaeology and oral traditions, however arrived at, there is good but not inviolable sense in E. J. Forsdyke's (1956:166) contention that "archaeological discovery may throw light upon the legends [of pre-Homeric Greece in this case], but the use of legendary statements for historical interpretation of material records is a reversal of proper procedure." Still, some ideas are good whatever their source. But if other investigators are to be persuaded of their viability for research purposes, accompanying bridging arguments must be as explicit, necessary, and sufficient as possible, however Sisyphean the effort proves to be.

The Italian-Zuni cumulation story in the last paragraph of the preceding section illustrates how one story, if not technically a tradition, came into being in a particular society: it was borrowed from another one, then modified to comport with its new home. Ethnology, folklore studies, and world history provide inexhaustible proofs of this phenomenon even in the simultaneous presence of innumerable other stories of uncertain and probably unknowable genesis. Where there is a more or less continuous geographical distribution of a particular kind of oral tradition, the most parsimonious provisional explanation for that distribution, all other options being equal, is to posit a single place and time of origin (monogenesis) and then diffusion to the limits of the tradition's occurrences. On the old diffusionist principle that very simple notions (e.g., that animals can talk) are more apt to arise independently than more complicated ones (e.g., Grandmother Spider made a clay bowl in which she placed a piece of the sun and thus brought daylight to the people, ever after which pottery making became the responsibility of women), the greater the number of shared details in the story's form and content the more persuasive is the argument for historical linkage. So stated, the problem, of course, revolves around stipulating the limits of simplicity and how many and what kinds of attributes constitute complexity. Also, stories as they diffuse tend to change. And how far is it, one needs to ask, before the variation that almost inevitably piggybacks on diffusion metamorphoses into what in effect is a new story. Debates over these issues are legion in the annals of anthropology and folklore studies. And in countless cases exhaustion rather than resolution has ended them, temporarily anyway. Richard M. Dorson's "Current Folklore Theories" (1963) and "The Search for Origins" section of Dundes's book *The Study of Folklore* (1965:53–125; see also 475–481) provide succinct surveys. A classic example of the diffusion model confined to aboriginal North America is Stith Thompson's study of "The Star Husband Tale" (1953; reprinted in Dundes 1965:414–474).

Matters, unfortunately, are not always so clear-cut as the dichotomy diffusion versus multiple independent origins implies. Sometimes, possibly very often, the presence of the same or a suspiciously similar story (or story theme or structure or plot or set of characters) in two or more societies, especially neighboring societies, is not so much the result of fortuitous independent invention or of borrowing and local reconfiguring of a singular prototype but, rather, a cooperatively, if not fully consciously, generated byproduct of societies in interaction. Donald Bahr (1998:25–26) has likened this to something like a kind of intersocietal conversation. In a comparison of sets of myths, each set recorded in about 1930 for the Pimas, Yavapais, and Maricopas, Bahr has analyzed their three *mythologies.* This latter term, in his usage, comprises "all of the myths that one narrator tells in the order that he or she tells them" that are concerned with "ancient times" and that are believed to be true by the narrator who, of course, does not call them "myths" (Bahr 1998:59n1). In his comparison, he points out that the three tribes were not only contiguous, but that they

affected one another spiritually and mythologically as well. They did so but subtly. They hardly mention one another in their [verbal] texts. Each states at some point that the others were created, and each may mention a battle with a neighbor near the end of the time of ancientness, but for the most part the mythologists and mythologies are silent about one another. This is merely a polite silence, however. Behind it there are squeaks of mutual adjustment, as if each tribe had formed its history in clear awareness of what the others had said. The adjustment was not for consensus nor for open debate, but for the sake of maintaining a proper difference; that is, a non-contradicting, oblique, and I will say "echoing" difference on topics of mutual, and I think deep, interest. . . . we do not have three independent mythologies here, but three dependent ones [Bahr 1998:25–26].

Put another way in another publication, this time with reference to North American Indian mythologies generally, not just those of the three southwestern tribes previously discussed, Bahr (2001:606) maintains that "there is no question of nor interest in a provable historical truth in a mythology. Mythologies were formed and continually reformed in reaction to each other, not in the memory of some real, recoverable, evidence-leaving event [what I have earlier referred to as an 'afterbirth']."

Although neither Bahr nor I would presume to jettison all claims of genuine history in oral traditions, the foregoing, albeit qualified, affirmation to the contrary in Bahr's mythological studies is a serious "slow down" sign in the path of impatient pursuers of cultural histories. While many traditions purport to tell of things that happened in the past, they provide no ethnocentrically free safe-conduct passes to that past. As shown below, this is true of literate as well as oral societies. It is the absence in the latter of the proverbial "paper trail," however, that especially invites skepticism. Regardless of that caution, the temptation to override it is understandable where there may be nothing else to appeal to. Indeed, the siren call to grasp an otherwise unobtainable "kernel of truth" can be an intoxicating promise, David Henige's (1982:76) previously quoted warning notwithstanding. This temptation is an old one.

It is probably at least as old as the fourth century B.C., when Euhemerus sought to link the gods of the ancients through the process of deification to historical personages who were thought to have been real. It persists in various guises today in searches for Noah's ark or the most likely route of Moses and the ancient Israelites in fleeing Egypt and, more seriously, in attempts to desanctify Quetzalcoatl, Deganawida, or the Pima-Papago, allegedly Hohokam, Elder Brother. How did any of these characters originate? What is real—if anything—in their initiation? Where is *history* in any of this?

Richard Dorson (1972:200), paraphrasing Lord Raglan's jaundiced view of anything put forward as history in oral traditions, distills the latter's dissatisfaction in two questions: "How can the historicists winnow out fabulous monsters and dragons and call the residue fact?" and "If part of the narrative is fiction, why not the whole?" Robert Lowie, in a couple of famous essays dealing largely with American Indian traditions (1915, 1917, and previously cited in Chapter 2), anticipated by two decades the thrust of Raglan's (1949) independent objections to oral traditional history qua history. Raglan, it should be noted, was unaware of Lowie's work until after he had published his classic study *The Hero: A Study in Tradition, Myth, and Drama*. The problems these two men confronted have not gone away, although there now exist new tools for dealing with some of them. Much of this book is necessarily concerned with those same problems plus others intrinsic to attempted articulations with archaeological evidence and reasoning.

As explored at some length in the next section of this chapter, the best evidence relating to the majority of oral traditions seems to indicate time depths that are relatively shallow—*shallow, that is, as measured from the dates, where knowable or inferable, of their recorded verbal deliveries,* whether or not those traditions deal with world beginnings or other "ancient" matters. Linked to this fact is a preoccupation in those narratives with what literate people would regard as trivia. That phenomenon exists for good mnemonic reasons: for padding or filler, as in the form of easily remembered epithets, repetitive phrasing, and commonplace odds and ends conveniently juggled to take up time and mimic novelty.

A related phenomenon, more often inferred than demonstrated, that bears more directly on the question of historical tradition genesis as opposed to repetition, is the "snowball" type of story. A fine example of the type has been sketched by the aforementioned Fitzroy Richard Somerset, Fourth Baron Raglan himself (Raglan 1949:30–31). If a celebrated Blackfoot warrior or a powerful Choctaw shaman, let us say, is substituted for Queen Elizabeth I in the following scenario, and the type of domicile suitably altered, the pertinence of the Baron's example will be apparent. The snowball type of story, says Raglan, "grows as it goes," in a process somewhat like this:

Stage I.—"This house dates from Elizabethan times, and since it lies close to the road which the Virgin Queen must have taken when travelling from X to Y, it may well have been visited by her."

Stage II.—"This house is said to have been visited by Queen Elizabeth on her way from X to Y."

Stage III.—"The state bedroom is over the entrance. It is this room which Queen Elizabeth probably occupied when she broke her journey here on her way from X to Y."

Stage IV.—"According to a local tradition, the truth of which there is no reason to doubt, the bed in the room over the entrance is that in which Queen Elizabeth slept, when she broke her journey here on her way from X to Y." A man whom I [Lord Raglan] asked how he knew that Queen Elizabeth had slept in his house, asked in return, in a surprised and indignant tone, "Why shouldn't she have?" The idea that it might be desirable, or even possible, to verify the statement had obviously never occurred to him [Raglan 1949:30–31].

In some cases, traditions may arise with astonishing alacrity. They can be invented. In some sense, of course, all traditions, their not being biologically inherited, are invented. Only rarely, as far as can be known, do they spring out of a "eureka!" moment. But in the right circumstances they can arise in a single generation and come to command wide acceptance as venerable, as possessing a tenure they have not in fact accrued. Because of recency and the existence of written records, modern Europe has provided well-documented instances of the phenomenon. The invention of traditions, Eric Hobsbawm avers (in Hobsbawm and Ranger 1983:4–5), may be expected "to occur more frequently when a rapid transformation of society weakens or destroys the social patterns for which 'old' traditions had been designed . . . or when such old traditions and their institutional carriers and promulgators no longer prove sufficiently adaptable and flexible, or are otherwise eliminated."

Chapter 9 presents at length the case for invented traditions, in the Hobsbawm sense, by Central Siouan–speaking Indians in the nineteenth century. Instances of such inventions by the Catawbas and Teton Sioux have already been touched upon at the end of Chapter 2. This present section concludes with an arresting British specimen of the genre and the tenacity of belief it can generate even in the face of clearly contradictory historical evidence. It is taken from the work of the historian Hugh Trevor-Roper in England and Scotland. He writes, "Today, whenever Scotchmen gather together to celebrate their national identity, they assert it openly by certain distinctive national apparatus. They wear the kilt, woven in a tartan whose colour and pattern indicates their 'clan'; and if they indulge in music, their instrument is the bagpipe. This apparatus, to which they ascribe great antiquity, is in fact largely modern. It was developed after, sometime long after, the Union with England [in 1707] against which it is in a sense, a protest" (Trevor-Roper 1983:15). The kilt, "now regarded as one of the ancient traditions of Scotland," did not exist until a few years after 1726, when an English Quaker in Lancashire by the name of Thomas Rawlinson invented it (Trevor-Roper 1983:21).

Colonel David Stewart of Garth, who had joined the original 42nd Highlanders at the age of sixteen, had spent his entire adult life in the army, most of it abroad. As a half-pay officer after 1815, he devoted himself to the study first of the Highland regiments, then of Highland life and traditions: traditions which he discovered more often, perhaps, in the officers' mess than in the straths and glens of Scotland. These traditions by now included the kilt and the clan tartans, both of which were accepted without question by the colonel. The notion that the kilt had been invented by an Englishman had indeed come to his ears, but he declined to entertain it for a minute: *it was, he said, refuted by "the universal belief of the people that the philibeg [kilt] had been part of their garb as far back as tradition reaches"* [Trevor-Roper 1983:28–29; my italics].

The Nature of Time in Oral Traditions

As the concept is typically employed in Native American and other oral societies, "ancientness" is the time beyond the witness or attested recollection of the oldest living members of society. In that time there may or may not have existed mortal people like those of the present world, but there certainly were humanlike beings, albeit with extraordinary or godlike attributes. There were also animals having such human qualities as articulate speech ("in those days animals were people"). Characteristic of stories about the time of ancientness is the absence not only of chronometry, of course, but also of respect for inviolability of sequence. Unless such narratives can be correlated with independently datable extraneous evidence, of the kind written records or archaeology can sometimes provide, they essentially float in timelessness. It is an error to assume that aboriginal or any other people wholly or mainly reliant on the verbal transmission of their histories share with scholars the same preoccupations with chronology, temporal linearity, sequentiality, causality, or narrative consistency. "Achronicity," says David Henige (1974:14), "is one of the concomitants of an oral non-calendrical society." As Jan Vansina (1985:174) observes, "Each culture has its own notions of time, and calendars [as we measure time] do not exist in oral society." Even the order of succeeding major events may be violated, as the availability of information extrinsic to traditions can sometimes reveal. Vansina (1985:177), following Lowie (1917), thus notes how "the Assiniboine ascribe the introduction of the horse to the era of creation and not to the eighteenth century." Lacking reliable sources of pertinent information external to the traditions themselves, there is no way of placing the persons, things, and events they relate in calendrical or chronometric time. What is related might never have happened at all.

Attempting to correlate quite differently conceived notions of temporality, one stemming from a critically unreflexive folk legacy, the other being its literary and professionalized opposite, while concurrently respecting the fact of their independent integrities, is not to be undertaken naively. Particularly is this so when one of them tries to co-opt the other in its autonomous efforts to plumb the past, measure it, and make sense of it.

Although concerned primarily with marginally literate as well as wholly illiterate nineteenth- and twentieth-century Euroamerican and Afro-American regional communities, Barbara Allen and William Lynwood Montell (1981) provide valuable insights pertinent to this discussion. Writing on the "characteristics of orally communicated history" (and only infrequently distinguishing between oral history and oral tradition, strictly defined), they identify two of its several hallmarks as a "disregard for standard chronology" and a marked tendency for "telescoping historical time" (Allen and Montell 1981:26–29, 35–36). The first points up the time of an event by reference to other events rather than by reference to a fixed time scale; at best, to use an analogy with a common archaeological contrast, orally communicated history relies on a *relative* rather than an *absolute* time scale ("it happened before the river bottom was cleared," "before my time," "before the Gold Rush"). Allen and Montell generalize their discussion to assert that "persons, places, and events are important in the human perception of history; time is not" and "the chronological order of events being recounted is usually scrambled" (Allen and Montell 1981:27–28). People, particularly in the kinds of societies they have devoted their lives to studying, tend to focus on an event or topic and talk around it. Calendrically organized recollection is distinctly exceptional. The second temporal characteristic of verbal history, that of "telescoping," refers to the loss of intervening events between important or otherwise remembered happenings so that "key events or elements in the past are brought into direct association with each other" (Allen and Montell 1981:35). This happens frequently in genealogies.

During his fieldwork in the early 1930s with the Berens River Saulteaux, a division of the Ojibwa people residing east of Lake Winnipeg in Manitoba and western Ontario, A. Irving Hallowell (1937) recorded their incomprehension of the kind of temporal ordering Western historians find essential for making sense of the past. While they sometimes spoke of things that had happened "long ago," that is, before the birth of their grandparents, that remote time was as frequently collapsed into the present as it was distanced from it. Happenings said to have occurred "long ago," Hallowell discovered, seemed to lack a consistent or coherent manner of relationship among themselves: there was no "well-defined temporal schema." There were "discrete happenings" related in Saulteaux traditions, but these were "often unconnected and sometimes contradictory." Furthermore, "the past and the present are part of a whole because they are bound together by the persistence and contemporary reality of mythological characters *not even now grown old*" (Hallowell 1937:668; my emphasis). Hallowell stated, "One hundred and fifty years is the outside limit of any genuine historic past. . . . Events attributed to so distant a past that they cannot be connected with any known generation of human individuals are simply described as having taken place 'long ago.' Consequently we are plunged into a bottomless mythological epoch that lacks temporal guide posts of any conventional sort. As a matter of fact, it would be more accurate to assert that once we enter the mythological world of Saulteaux belief, temporal concepts actually lose most, if not all, chronological significance" (Hallowell 1937:666–667).

There was a "far distant past," Hallowell learned. This was the time when the earth was "new." In that time winter lasted all year long. There were giant forms of snakes, mosquitoes, beaver, trout, and presumably other animals as well. The kingfisher was not then as pretty as he is now, the muskrat had a longer tail, and weasels lacked white winter coats. All humans in that far-off time were covered with hair and women had toothed vaginas. Probably following a great flood, the anthropomorphic heroes of mythology made their appearance (Hallowell 1937:667–668).

Like Hallowell and many other ethnographers elsewhere, Catharine McClellan (1970) has discovered that among the people with whom she has worked, in this case the Tlingit and northwestern Athapaskan tribes, conceptions and uses of time rarely converge with those of Western historians. Unconcerned with historical, if not to say logical, incompatibilities, they are quite comfortable with what she refers to as "myth-time," the time of beginnings and of the origin of things, simultaneously existing before, yet coexisting with, the recent past (that of the proximate generation) and even the present. What McClellan calls "the quality of myth-time" appears to override any constraints—if there are such—to temporal ordering (McClellan 1970:116–118). These Indians are fully aware that time passes, of course. They recognize that today, the right here and now, is not yesterday when they were someplace else and doing something different. But myth-time, while very old, is essentially ageless; it weaves in and out of all of recency, like a ghost with powers of intervention. It is so integral a part of today that it is for all intents and purposes omnipresent.

Although different in details, the fundamental structure of history as conveyed to ethnographers by the Dogrib Indians of Canada's Northwest Territories (Helm and Gillespie 1981) is consonant with the two foregoing examples as well as innumerable others that might be cited. Briefly, the Dogribs distinguish between time before and time after the intrusion of Europeans. The latter, in the sense of face-to-face contact, historians know occurred in the 1780s. Rumors of new people coming into their land, and doubtless also the introduction of a few examples of their manufactures, came to them through neighboring tribes a few years earlier. Helm and Gillespie call the first division of Dogrib time "the era of Floating Time." This era is essentially "time-less" because of the absence of a calendar or any other means of calibrating its beginnings and duration, and stories about it lack the discipline of a coherent sense of sequence. Its end, of course, is extrinsically imposed. The principal exception to this character-ization seems to lie in occasional distinctions between a long-ago age when things happened that no longer occur and a later time that was still be-fore knowledge of the existence of Europeans, when the world became as it is today. The time inaugurated by the coming of Europeans Helm and Gillespie call "the era of Linear Time," or the time of "folk history." Now, sequential organization of history recollection and absolute dating of parts of genealogies become possible in principle, if not inevitable in practice. Because of these possibilities, this latter division of Dogrib temporality is examined in greater detail in Chapter 6.

Far to the south in New Mexico and Arizona the Zuni people hold a number of similar beliefs about the nature of time and the age of the events they relate in their traditions. The first people, the ancestors of the Zunis, sometimes called "moss people," lived in the "fourth underworld." This was in "the time of the beginning" when people did not look like they do now and when animals could speak: "This time of the beginning had no begin-ning; it simply *was,* before the time of the emergence [when people arrived on the earth's surface]" (Young 1988:116). But,

> Although they [the Zunis] may introduce a myth [which they regard as history] as having occurred "a long time ago" or "in the begin-ning," they do not envision the events of the myth as over and done with, situated at a single point in a linear flow of time; instead, they perceive them as ever-present, informing the here and now. It is this perspective that accounts for the "presentness" of the beings of myth and folktale in Zuni life.
>
> For the Zunis, time is *cyclical,* apparent in the orderly and regular motions and "returns" of the sun, moon, and stars, and both time and space are *organic,* continuous entities. One may say that time for them is reversible; past, present, and future are coexistent. . . . The kachina dancers in the plaza do not *represent* the gods, they become the gods, and the time of the myth is one with the present. The efficacy of ritual activity is the result of the merging of the here and now with the myth time and space [Young 1988:117].

Trying with only partial success to make sense of this in Western terms, Young retreats from this relatively straightforward assertion of equivalences of "here" and "there" and "then" and "now." Again, in her own words: "Al-though I have discussed Zuni spatial and temporal perceptions in terms such as the 'merging,' 'collapsing,' and 'coalescing' of boundaries between the here and now and myth time and space, I do not mean to imply that this results in a permanent condition so that the two states (time and space; myth and 'here and now') are unified in every aspect from that moment on. Rather, the relationship between the two is best expressed as a dialectic interaction made possible by the fluid boundary that exists between the two [she includes a diagram in which she tries to schematize this relationship]" (Young 1988:117–119).

Among others, the Gitksan, a subgroup of the Tsimshian, and the inter-marrying Wet'suwet'en, a Carrier (Athapaskan-speaking) group, both in western British Columbia, claim ancient histories are carried and preserved in their oral traditions, which in turn exist in "dream time" (Mills 1994). Parallel beliefs among the Mohaves in California and Arizona have previously been mentioned (Chapter 2). According to the ethnohistorian Jay Miller (1998), who endorses their accounts as credible, the oral traditions transmitted in the Tsimshian ceremonies/recitations known as *adawx* are believed to preserve genuine historical information covering significant events over a 10,000-year span—as Western scientists reckon time. There are also Northwest Coast Indians who, in conversation with me, stoutly maintained that their people *actually*, not figuratively, *remember* their ancestors crossing the Bering Straits. Probably many more, however, maintain that they have always lived in their present land; that they were created there. The veridicality of their traditions is honestly held by a great many native people, not only in opposition to sometimes incongruous evidence derived from archaeological or documentary history but also even when confronted by incompatible interpretations thought to be supported by those same or other traditions, many of which are exclusively "owned" and restricted in their recitation to certain lineages or households. Notwithstanding such challenges, for many of their adherents the traditions are regarded as being as factual as the lived-in world of their familiar mountains, forests, and fjords.

As recounted by Julie Cruikshank (2002:24), in 1991, in *Delgamuukw v. British Columbia,* the British Columbia Supreme Court rejected Gitksan and Wet'suwet'en land claims on the grounds that oral traditions are "beliefs" only, not legally factual evidence. But this ruling was overturned in 1997 by the Supreme Court of Canada because of constitutionally protected aboriginal rights the court interpreted as requiring suspension of ordinary evidentiary standards so that oral traditions might be treated more like written historical records rather than "hearsay" opinion. It seems certain that this decision will generate interesting unintended ramifications. In fact, some of these were anticipated in a volume edited by Owen Lippert (2000).

Alexander von Gernet's (2000:110–116) contribution to that volume is especially relevant to my own views in the present work.

Across the continent, in New York, northern Pennsylvania, and the Ontario peninsula between Lakes Erie and Ontario and Lake Huron's Georgian Bay, the cluster of Iroquoian-speaking tribes shared significant parts of what, in their totality, the great Iroquoianist William N. Fenton has characterized as probably the most extensive and detailed creation myth in aboriginal North America (Fenton 1962, 1998:34–50 [the latter is a somewhat revised version of the former]). "One continuous mythological tradition confronts us," he says, and "it has three hundred years of recorded history, and . . . it extends into pre-Columbian times" (Fenton 1962:285). The creation or cosmological origin myth of the Iroquois League tribes (Mohawk, Oneida, Onondaga, Cayuga, Seneca, and also some of the late-joining Tuscaroras) is the first of the three grand divisions of time by means of which Iroquois annalists see their own culture history. This first division is usually referred to as the myth of the "Woman Who Fell from the Sky" or the "Earth Grasper." Fenton has found traces of 25 versions of it, the earliest fragment recorded in 1623, a Huron variant. The greatest collection of the stories was recorded by the Tuscarora anthropologist/folklorist J. N. B. Hewitt in the late nineteenth century (1903 and 1928). With the addition of twentieth-century renditions, the Oneida tribal historian Anthony Wonderley (2000) estimates that some 40 written versions now exist, almost all in an incomplete or highly abbreviated state. The second grand division of Iroquois time is the epic of Deganawida, the period of the formation of the League of the Iroquois, as discussed below. The third and final division is that of the *Kai'wi:yo:,* "the good message," when the historically known prophet Handsome Lake preached the new religion (1799–1815), and on down to the present-day Longhouse culture. Some Iroquois, however, conflate much of the content of the preceding two temporal divisions with this one, even attributing the founding of the League itself to Handsome Lake.

The creation or "Woman Who Fell from the Sky" myth comprises a sequence of three episodes, each of which is variously rendered in the numerous recorded versions. There being no need to go into detail here, a brief glimpse of the character of these episodes may serve to invite the interested reader to consult the cited references. The initial episode describes a world above the sky in which godlike anthropomorphic beings live very much like the Iroquois who later told the story. There was no sun, however, but a tree from whose flowers light radiated throughout that upper world. Beneath the sky world was only a boundless primeval ocean unrelieved by any illumination, an ocean nevertheless inhabited by animals having the ability to speak. An adult female (Sky-woman) fell or was pushed by her husband or brother through a hole in the sky into the black abyss below. Either she was already pregnant or she became so later. She may or may not have been carrying corn, dried meat, and firewood when she fell from the sky world.

In the second episode, while Sky-woman is falling, one of the creatures below spots her and calls a council of aquatic animals to prepare for her safe arrival. Turtle, either immediately or after tests of other animals' buoyancy, volunteers himself as a platform while others try to dive to the bottom of the ocean to bring up mud to put on his back. After several failures, Muskrat (usually) brings some up, even though drowning in the attempt. Sky-woman lands safely on the little patch of mud, which quickly expands to become an island with trees and meadows. She now becomes Earth Mother or Old Woman or Wicked Grandmother. In the Huron story she is called Aataentsic, the mother of mankind (Trigger 1976:77–78).

The third episode is called the World of Sapling or Sky-holder. It tells the story of the character who was formerly Sky-woman, who is now living on earth where she gives birth either to twin boys, one good, the other bad, or a daughter who, after rejecting several animal suitors who appear in human form, marries Turtle and becomes the mother of the twins. The boys quarreled while in the womb. One boy is born naturally; the evil boy burrows through his mother's side and emerges from her armpit, killing her. In both the Iroquois and Huron renditions, the evil twin is associated with flint, the raw material of weapons. The good twin creates rivers that flow in both directions. The evil twin frustrates this boon to canoeists in the obvious way and also creates waterfalls and other obstructions. The former causes corn to grow, brings good weather, and releases game animals from a cave where they had been confined. The latter boy (or his grandmother) introduces disease and death, and so the stage is set for the depiction of early human life.

Until recently, archaeology has had little to offer debates about the age and origins of the League of the Iroquois. That debate has depended upon the opinion of various tribal members queried about the matter; a few scanty references in French, English, and Dutch records; and what ethnologists have tried to squeeze out of Iroquois folklore. The existence of the league in colonial and later times is of course a historical fact and a good deal about its structure and operation reasonably well known. It was in 1851 that Lewis Henry Morgan published his landmark *League of the Ho-de-no-sau-nee or Iroquois* (Morgan 1962 [1851]). However, the age of the League, that is, the time when it came into being, is more speculative. Morgan's estimate of approximately 1459 falls within the range 1450–1550 that William N. Fenton (1998:69, Table 1, 129), in his comprehensive synthesis of the history and historiography of the Iroquois confederation, has come to regard as most probable. Later and much earlier times have also been proposed by others, of course (e.g., Engelbrecht 2003:129–131). But as Fenton (1998:130) has argued, it is misleading to look for a specific date for the founding of the League; it likely was not a single event but a development that must have taken some time. There is general agreement, for instance, that the Senecas were the last of the original five tribes or nations to join the confederacy. Probably to be understood in the same way is Bruce Trigger's (1976:163) endorsement of circa 1440 for the birth of the Huron confederation. This is based on the understanding Jesuit missionaries had of what those people told them, as well as on the not unreasonable assumption that those northern Iroquoian-speakers may have been concurrently responding to the same or similar pressures fostering intertribal alliances across Lake Ontario.

In contrast to the uncertainties about the *age* of the League and whether it began before or only after European contact, its earliest *mention* by Europeans—Dutch in this instance—is in 1634 or 1635 (Fenton 1998:52; Kuhn and Sempowski 2001:303 [citing Gehring and Starna 1988]). The earliest record of the *legend* of the founding of the League is no earlier than 1743 (Fenton 1998:51). Thereafter appear additional versions of the oral tradition in written form. With respect to these latter, Fenton (1998:65) mentions William M. Beauchamp's conclusion that "the most famous name in Iroquois [League] annals—Hiawatha—was almost unknown until the middle of the nineteenth century." Comparing the nine major versions of the League origin (Deganawida) myth, it is clear that the more modern versions "are much more detailed and longer than earlier ones, as if the legend gained content in later times" (Fenton 1998:98).

The late-twentieth-century archaeological demonstration of the evolution of the Iroquoian tribes known to historical record out of local prehistoric forebears and the clear evidence of village consolidations in late prehistoric-protohistoric time have given rise to the hope of an archaeological answer to the question of the League's genesis. Assuming the historicity of generally consistent Iroquois oral traditions that the formation of the League commenced in the eastern half of their territory and that the Senecas were the latest of the Five Nations to join, and working with the idea that increased social and ceremonial linkages resulting from political and (sometimes) military cooperation might find a reflection in the archaeological record, a corollary that has occurred to others, two researchers devised a new way of testing that hypothetical consequence (Kuhn and Sempowski 2001).

While simple in conception, their test put heavy demands on a critically limited available sample of archaeological evidence, that of aboriginal clay smoking pipes. It also required careful statistical handling of physico-chemical analyses of the composition of those pipes as well as of temporally and culturally associated potsherds, data derived from two different kinds of x-ray studies linked to spectrometric analysis. Assuming that domestic ceramics were normally made using nearby sources of clay, it was possible for the archaeologists to physico-chemically "fingerprint" them and thus help in the determination that any given sample of clay pots or pipes probably derived from that source rather than some other. In this way it proved possible to identify those clay attributes characteristic of Mohawk products on the one hand and their Seneca counterparts on the other.

Because the Mohawks and the Senecas were respectively the easternmost and westernmost tribes to join the League, the former being believed among the earliest, an increased visibility of articles native to the one might theoretically be expected to turn up in the other beginning about the time of Seneca consolidation into the confederacy. That smoking pipes are historically known to have played an important role in political and ceremonial gatherings, the two not always easily distinguishable, and to have been sometimes exchanged as gifts, archaeological examples seemed to offer an opportunity to confirm the aforementioned visibility hypothesis. This might then be taken as an independent sign of the date when the League finally coalesced into its "classic Five Nations form." William Engelbrecht (2003:131–133), citing research by Dean R. Snow, James W. Bradley, and others, has pointed to the relatively sudden and broad diffusion of marine shell artifacts in the late fifteenth to early sixteenth centuries as perhaps another material consequence of that development.

No pipes identifiable as Mohawk have been found on Seneca sites dated earlier than 1590–1605. Contra the authors' citing of atypically late oral traditions possibly alluding to Iroquois confederation, this 15-year period falls half a century to one and a half centuries later than the majority of traditional and ethnohistoric estimates as summarized by Fenton and noted previously. The date put forward on the pipe evidence as approximating the time of the League's final coalescence is that 15-year period when the first Mohawk pipes make their appearance in the Seneca archaeological sequence (Kuhn and Sempowski 2001:312). The authors of this innovating study probably enjoy the assent of most Iroquoianists in asserting the compatibility of their archaeological data with traditional accounts of the westerly expansion of the Iroquois League. Their crediting agreement between those two sources with respect to dating the Five Nation's "final coalescence," however, is something of an exaggeration. Nevertheless, if their suggested date range is approximately correct, it would tend to support claims of post-European contact for that "coalescence" and indirectly bear on its inception as precursor of its "revitalization movement" attributes (Wallace 1958). According to James W. Bradley (1987:104), the League was up and running in at least its internal mission of fostering cooperation among its members when European manufactures intruded on the scene. He claims that trade goods appear as early on Seneca as on Mohawk sites.

This exercise in conjoining archaeology and oral traditions is praiseworthy in its intent whether or not future investigations ratify its conclusions. Its authors acknowledge its shortcomings, shortcomings they hope will be rectified by continuing research along lines to some of which they draw attention. Difficult but critical in this regard will be efforts to recover additional pipe samples—only five Mohawk specimens are known from the study's three Seneca sites—expand the inventory of both earlier and later site assemblages, continue to retest and refine the Seneca site sequence, encourage replication studies using Mohawk assemblages, and pursue the search for other possible types of independent information. Barring the discovery, hardly to be hoped for, of a now unknown early document recording native testimony, it is unlikely that oral traditions will be able to add anything to what they have already afforded. Alone, or more typically in combination with documentary and ethnographic evidence, oral traditions have been a source of clues in this and in other cases: for example, asserted eastern beginnings of League formation; Seneca tardiness in joining; importance of pipe smoking and exchange; information on League ideology, structure, and function; community organization; the False Face sodality. Thus archaeologists have been prompted to grope for means of identifying physical consequences that may be implied by those clues. More often than not, such attempts to drape mute artifacts and earthen features with sociological or symbolic meaning necessarily involve a degree of willingness to suspend disbelief. This should be preliminary and a spur to further testing, as it clearly is in the present case. Not infrequently in other cases juxtaposing oral traditions and archaeology, hypothesis too readily leaps into dogma, plausibility into alleged certainty—both propelled more by enthusiasm than credible bridging argument. This is all the more to be regretted in an enterprise in which knowledge claims in both domains so often outweigh their justification and in which their combination invites permanent disbelief.

The Pimas (Akimel O'Odham), Papagos (Tohono O'Odham), Yavapais, and Maricopas of Arizona appear to share, along with many other indigenous peoples in America and in other parts of the world, the trifurcated segmentation of past time that Jan Vansina (1985) found to be so recurring a configuration of traditions in nonliterate societies as to suggest something approaching universality. This configuration has informed, and has been amplified by, Donald Bahr's detailed studies of the oral traditions and histories of the aforementioned Arizona tribes (e.g., Bahr 1971, 1998, 2001; Bahr et al. 1994). Those people do not themselves think of their tellings of past time in the same conceptual framework as that employed by Vansina and Bahr, of course. And the same is true of the Nunamiut Eskimos, Dogribs, and other oral societies mentioned in this book. If they did, they would not be what they are. In each case a storyteller's view is that of the cultural "insider" speaking on indigenously meaningful ground, giving what anthropologists call the "emic" perspective (see Chapter 2). The "outsider's" point of view, the so-called "etic" perspective, represents the investigator's best effort at translating the former's semantic idiom into terms that make sense in the analytical language of systematic inquiry. The latter, it is important to remember, does not replace or substitute itself for the former. It seeks to understand it and make it comprehensible in the cross-cultural comparative investigations of the folkloric and anthropological disciplines. In his attempt to thus understand Pima, Maricopa, and other oral traditions on their own grounds as well as his, Bahr makes an additional important observation. The native tellers whose stories he has heard, and those whose earlier accounts he has read about, did not, so far as he could judge, make up their stories; rather, "they thought they had had them from time immemorial" (Bahr 1998:31). This, as well as their ingenuous assumption of the historical credibility of their historical traditions, is also, I am sure, equally true of the other people whose stories about the past I have just reviewed.

The past-telling stories told by the people Bahr has studied, as well as those told by most other people known to students of oral traditions, are concerned on the one hand with vaguely long-ago affairs and on the other with much more recently circumscribed ones, the memory of which is more detailed, consistent, and compatible with tests of verisimilitude. The first of these sets of stories comprises the tribal mythologies. These are Eden-like tales of long ago, or ancientness. They tell of the origins of the world, of humans and animals—these are frequently hard to distinguish, each having powers of which they are now bereft—of tribal institutions, and of the stars, the sun, and gods and other fabulous beings who do incredible things. Although many Indian mythologies, in Bahr's sense, also relate the creation of white people, those mythologies otherwise seem to end before the latter's arrival or return and settlement in the Indian world. According to some of the stories, white people are the resurrected dead of Indian societies. Bahr (1998:31) states, "The narrated ancient world was large but the actors were scattered and few. Few of the events told in mythologies are of a nature to leave lasting physical traces [although some prominent landscape features came to be rationalized in mythological terms], and the storytellers usually did not know where the events happened or precisely when. Years are not counted in the tales, dates are not assigned, and the places are often just 'somewhere around here.'" Post-mythological stories, those of "recentness," begin with "dated (usually by genealogy, not year) history" (Bahr 1998:31). Probably the greater part of this last division of time corresponds with what I have previously called oral history (as opposed to oral tradition). Bahr writes:

> After Eden, what is there in native American accounts of the past? There is the present, or rather, the recent past that leads up to the present: recentness as opposed to ancientness. As the student of oral traditions Jan Vansina (1985:23–32, 116–8, 167–9, 182–5) has stated, this time of recentness generally goes back no further than 100 or 125 years. Between this time and ancientness, there is what Vansina calls a "floating gap," a disconnect, a chasm, a void of unknown and unknowable duration. The void is not made palpable by the native tradition. No moment, hour, or day of silence is observed between the end of the telling of a mythology (ancientness, Eden) and the onset of the telling of the recent past. It is just that the two tellings do not connect. The typical native statement is "and sometime after *that* [the last event included in the mythology], *this* happened [the earliest event of recentness]."
>
> . . . Native recentness reaches back about a hundred years from the "today" of the narrator. For narrators of 1930, the date of the texts we have been discussing, ancientness—Eden—ended and recentness began in 1830. Indeed, this seems accurate. The earliest "actual" skirmishes between tribes and the oldest "real" ancestors identified in genealogies cluster around 1830. Narrated ancientness, however, seems to end on the day before the first whites came, which for the region I studied would be around 1550. Thus, a gap of about three hundred "real" years separates the two zones of the past. This gap is not recognized by native narrators [Bahr 2001:596].

Neither the ages of their boundaries nor mutually exclusive characters of their contents unambiguously or invariably divide the intervening "floating gap" from "ancientness" or from "recentness." Only the calendrical age of the border zone between the last two can sometimes be approximated without reliance on external sources of information. This assertion holds generally and not only for the Pimas, Papagos, Maricopas, and Yavapais. The latter, incidentally, are unusual in lacking stories of their own origins (Bahr 1998:30). In the absence of independent checks foreign to the traditions oral people recite, everything before recentness floats in time. And undated and undatable things and events related to ancientness may migrate in and out of any particular sequence as demonstrated, for example, by the previously reviewed non-Indian stories studied by Allen and Montell, the Nunamiut Inuit studied by Gubser and discussed by Hudson (see Chapter 2), the Berens River Saulteaux (Ojibwa) studied by Hallowell, the Dogribs as reported by Helm and Gillespie, and the Iroquois creation myth Fenton has analyzed. Furthermore, ancientness not infrequently crosses the floating gap to infiltrate and thus "inform" sectors of recentness. Invaluable, indeed necessary, as they are to would-be analyst-users standing outside these traditions, the boundaries of the latter's etic categories, even though logical and having empirical justification, are themselves sometimes permeable due to refraction from the native concepts they are intended to subsume. Native storytellers have never been under any compunction to craft their productions to fit conceptual and structural constraints other than their own. Their traditions are sovereign on their home grounds. On those grounds, neither ancientness nor recentness, oral tradition nor oral history, is a virginal realm immaculately untouched by the other. It is often the case, in Hallowell's (1937:668) earlier quoted words, that "the persistence and contemporary reality of mythological characters [are] not even now grown old."

6

Mixing Apples and Oranges, or
Looking for Kernels of Truth

The suitability of the first metaphor in the chapter title will quickly become obvious. That of the "kernels of truth" alludes to Moses I. Finley's (2000) caution to students of antiquity when placing reliance on oral tradition relating to the civilizations of the ancient Mediterranean (see the section "The Search for Homer's Troy" in Chapter 4). I see no reason for that caution's inapplicability in the following instances.

Midewiwin Scrolls, Ojibwa Origins, and a Famous Victory

In his comprehensive 1992 volume on the history and culture of Michigan Indians, archaeologist and ethnohistorian Charles E. Cleland argues that the oral traditions of the Ojibwa people deserve serious consideration *as history* in its modern Western sense. However, because historical "facts" seen from an Indian perspective differ in significant ways from those of non-Indian people, he maintains that they reflect different *realities*—an undefined term by which he seems to mean views or conceptions of truth. "Where possible," he says, "these other [Ojibwa] realities have been incorporated" in his consideration of Indian history (Cleland 1992:vii–viii).

Two different kinds of truth, says Cleland (1992:4), are clearly recognized by the Ojibwa Indians. These are *daebaudjimowin,* "a chronicle known from personal experience" (e.g., oral history), and *auwaetchigum,* "truths that transcend history, that is, truths of parable and allegory" (presumably including oral tradition?). Observing this distinction and using one version of migration legends as discussed below, "we see the process of historic truth being transformed into mythological truth" (Cleland 1992:10). This process appears to credit oral traditions generally, apparently not just those associated with the migration charts, as having once been personally experienced or witnessed (*daebaudjimowin*) but over time having evolved into the more venerable collective entity *auwaetchigum*. Although unstated, it seems to be with reference to this kind of transformation that the author invokes "the truths of mythology," an expression otherwise having no clear referent.

Two demonstrations incorporating Ojibwa oral traditions into Western historical writing are offered as models. One of these, here examined first, is more implicitly than explicitly endorsed as *credible* in the sense archaeologists and historians use that term. Its implicit status as credible history is conferred by virtue of its being offered in support of the author's thesis. This is the claim by some Ojibwas that certain of the so-called migration scrolls or charts of the Midewiwin, or Grand Medicine, Society—or, rather, one of the oral traditions purporting to interpret their meaning—locate the place of origin of both the Ojibwa people and the Midewiwin Society on the Atlantic coast (Cleland 1992:8–10). The native documents at issue are groups of pictographs painted or scratched on rolled or folded sheets of bark.

Cleland's principal source on the Midewiwin, or Mide, migration charts is Selwyn Dewdney's 1975 study *The Sacred Scrolls of the Southern Ojibway.* He also cites earlier students of Mide traditions, specifically Walter J. Hoffman (1891) and William W. Warren (1984 [1885]), as sources attesting to the migration charts as locating the homeland of the ancestral Ojibwa people on the Atlantic coast and as tracing their subsequent movements westward to Lake Superior and beyond (Cleland 1992:4–10, 35n6–8). But in fact, Hoffman basically reiterates Warren's testimony on this particular issue and adds little to it beyond mention of one scroll he thinks shows the Mide Otter, a prominent supernatural agent, emerging from the "great salt sea" before (the creation of?) the first people (see Hoffman 1891:183–184, 282; also cited in Vennum 1978:785n79). It is Warren, himself part Ojibwa, who attests to Mide priests promulgating this belief, having overheard some of their ceremonies and having had the benefit of an interview with an old *We-kaun* (master, priest) from whose lips he had first learned of the tradition (Warren 1984 [1885]:76–81). Warren's invaluable manuscript was completed in 1853 and first published in 1885.

Dewdney (1975), like his just cited predecessors, is careful to make clear the mnemonic nature of these birchbark scrolls of the Midewiwin Society. In discussing their religious/mythological character, he stresses their equivocal genealogies and the fact of their recopying, the Ojibwa propensity to indulge in indirection and allegory in their thinking about such matters, and the freedom of the Mide priests to alter, exclude, or introduce new elements in their recitations of associated traditions. Although one of the roles of a Mide priest (*We-kaun*) was to serve as a *kanawencikewiwini,* "preserve-man," and thus the priests were "expected to retain knowledge of the Ojibwa past" (Vennum 1978:760), such retention was of variable quality.

Vennum, for example, cites one Mide priest's difficulties in interpreting the meanings of another priest's pictographs and, indeed, in his mistaking a song scroll for a migration chart (Vennum 1978:761n24). He also points out that charts purporting to record migrations are rarely alike and that Mide priests often terminated the western end point of such records at their own settlement, thus enhancing its, and their own, importance (Vennum 1978:761–762). These considerations make interpretations of the scrolls and the commentaries they evoke something well short of trans-tribal dogma.

Dewdney identifies six types of scrolls or charts. It is his second type, the *migration charts,* as they are commonly called, that are germane here. Thoroughly familiar with the work of earlier investigators, and being himself the honored recipient of one of the last scroll owner's explications of his scrolls' meanings, Dewdney (1975:10) reluctantly finds himself, in contrast to Cleland's equivocation, forced to conclude "my attempt to support the Mide oral tradition of a salt water origin [of the Ojibwa people] was from the beginning doomed to fail." Perhaps the coup de grâce to that attempt— or certainly a major contributor to it—was the stubborn fact that "a Mide master was free to make selections from the total lore at his command, producing simple condensed accounts for one purpose or relating in detail one or more variations on the same theme, some of which, taken literally, contradict each other" (Dewdney 1975:24). The same warning applies to depictions of alleged places on the pictographic scrolls. Compare, for example, the different versions of what passes for Leech Lake on the Mide priest Red Sky's own "creation," "migration," and "end" scrolls (Dewdney 1975:26–27, Figure 25). And the identification of Leech Lake (in interior Minnesota just a bit north of the latitude of the western end of Lake Superior) vies with the greatest of the Great Lakes itself as least problematical of the geographical features said to be depicted. The oldest known migration charts, according to Dewdney (1975:75), show nothing east or west of Lake Superior. As Vennum (1978) understands the pertinent scrolls, the geography of the Ojibwa world, at least before eighteenth- and nineteenth-century population dispersions north, south, and west of Lake Superior, was pretty largely encompassed by that lake and its drainage basin.

An important conclusion of Dewdney's study is that the so-called migration scrolls or charts depict the spread of conversions to the Midewiwin faith rather than migrations of people. In his own words, those scrolls, "as authoritatively interpreted" by the Mide master Red Sky himself, show "the journeys of the [Mide] Council's agent . . . *not a movement of Ojibway bands*" (Dewdney 1975:175; my italics). The "Council" referred to seems to have been the occasion at which the Midewiwin religion was inaugurated (the "Council's agent" was Otter, Bear, or the sacred cowrie shells called *megis*—alternative bearers of the Mide "gospel"). One version of Red Sky's account, revealingly enough, locates that momentous event in Palestine (Dewdney 1975:31). "A distinction must be made," says Dewdney, "between the migrations of ancestral groups and the dissemination of the Mide religion. The following charts [the bark pictographic migration scrolls], although they are clearly intended to indicate where bands of Ojibway had established communities to which the Mide message could be brought, give no indication of population movements. *It is the message that moves* [my emphasis]. The only known interpretation of this group of scrolls is Red Sky's, which is solely concerned with the agent's mission to bring the Midewiwin to the people, *wherever they may be found*" (Dewdney 1975:59).

"None of the Migration charts reveals any real knowledge of the geography east of the Sault," Dewdney (1975:69) notes. Using a little imagination, however, and making allowance for the rudimentary state of cartography among mid-nineteenth-century Ojibwas, one may grant Red Sky's (and Dewdney's) identifications of various pictographs on his and several other migration scrolls (there are eight or nine)—and on one or more of seven additional "possible migration charts"—as plausibly representing Lake Superior and some landmarks westward to Leech Lake. The latter was an important center of Midewiwin activities in that century. Although the Mide cult and, in some versions of its oral traditions, the Ojibway people themselves are said by Red Sky and certain of his Mide priest predecessors to have originated on the Atlantic coast, the depictions of the country east of Lake Superior are, as previously pointed out by Dewdney, devoid of "any real knowledge."

The mentions in Mide thought of an Atlantic coastal origin probably had more to do with the direction from which early Christian missionaries came than with aboriginal genesis. There is no doubting the heavy infusion of Bible stories into a matrix of indigenous belief (Dewdney 1975:24, 28–30; Warren 1984 [1885]:71, 76–81). Warren provides a delightful anecdote about the astonishment of Mide priests to find so many parallels between their own beliefs and the Old Testament stories he translated and read to them. They could only conclude thereby that the Bible must also be true (Warren 1984 [1885]:71). Warren himself was inclined to endorse the widespread belief of his time in the Hebrew ancestry of the Ojibwa, Blackfoot, and other "Algic" peoples, if not all American Indians (Warren 1984 [1885]:61–72).

Although it may be that elements of the Midewiwin had a precontact birth, the larger parts of that organization and its body of doctrine, as known in the ethnohistorical and ethnographic literature, are probably of postcontact derivation, as Harold Hickerson (1962) long argued. Christopher

Vecsey (1983) places its emergence no earlier than the end of the eighteenth century. A radiocarbon assay on a supposed Midewiwin bark scroll from archaeological contexts in Ontario has an uncalibrated range of A.D. 1490 to 1630 (Kidd 1981). That the "scroll" had anything to do with the Midewiwin Society specifically is purely conjectural. Although well preserved, its surface bears no trace of scribing or painting (Kidd 1965).

The presentation in Cleland's book of Ojibwa beliefs relating to an original Atlantic coast homeland is an inadequate gloss of a complex and ambiguous collection of traditions. It does not take into consideration numerous and obstinate uncertainties as well as flat contradictions in those traditions. It is also hard to square with the recorded testimony of the Mide scroll owner Red Sky and the critique of Selwyn Dewdney, the scroll analyst on whose work Cleland nevertheless principally relies.

In the absence of express engagement with the discrepancy between intention and execution in combining Ojibwa traditional narratives and Western science and historiography, the author's best intentions to foster a dialogue are frustrated. The two ways of presenting the past remain monologues—unintegrated presentations. The oral tradition with which he introduces his book is nowhere resolved with the relevant archaeology the author so ably reviews. That archaeological evidence, he maintains, reveals strong cultural continuity in the regional sequences of the Upper Great Lakes from prehistoric Late Woodland cultures to those of the historic period: "To the west, in southern Wisconsin, the Oneota [archaeological] tradition (often linked historically with Siouan-speaking groups) developed. To the east of Lake Huron and in the Lakes Erie and Ontario basins were the Owasco-Glen Meyer and Pickering groups that led to the historic Iroquoian-speaking tribes such as the Five Nations Iroquois, Neutral, and Huron. In the middle, from southern Michigan through the Upper Peninsula and in Ontario north of the Lakes, we find the Late Woodland cultures that seem to be the predecessors of Algonquian-speaking groups such as the Ojibwa, Ottawa, Potawatomi, and Miami" (Cleland 1992:25).

The barriers to marrying the two disparate kinds of history are made clear in Cleland's own discussion, and he does not offer pragmatic means of reconciliation. Archaeologists, in contrast to Indians who put their faith in traditions, he points out, differ "radically" in how they try to understand the past (Cleland 1992:10), and the differences lead to sharply contrasting results (Cleland 1992:29). Archaeology is "based upon objective observation and the formulation and testing of hypotheses through the use of newly acquired information" and "is very distinct from mythology; it is not constructed on faith and belief, but upon healthy skepticism" (Cleland 1992:10). These are serious barriers to fulfilling his recommendation that native oral traditions receive equal treatment with written historical documents and archaeological evidence in investigating what happened in past centuries (Cleland 1992:4–5, 8–10, 32–34). What is left is the hope that "with time an intermediate view will develop that is based upon mutual respect for the different contexts of history" (Cleland 1992:34). This, however, is not the same as reducing the difference to a failure of "people with written traditions" having "great difficulty applying democratic principles to oral traditions" (Cleland 1992:33).

The second of the two examples Cleland advances "as a testimony to the accuracy of oral history [*tradition,* as usually defined and as I use it here]" (Cleland 1992:125n44), also would seem to be the kind of truth Ojibwas know as *auwaetchigum* (see above) except that it is regarded as *historically* true and, in that sense, does not "transcend history." This is a story about a celebrated Ojibwa triumph over an invading Iroquois war party in 1662. The version (there is more than one) of the oral tradition Cleland cites is that of an Ojibwa named Charles Kawbawgam, as related in the late nineteenth century to one Homer H. Kidder. After Cleland had studied a microfilm of the Kidder typescript in the archives of the American Philosophical Society in Philadelphia, this interesting text was at last published and thus made available to a wider audience (Bourgeois 1994). Before examining Kawbawgam's account, it will be useful to see what the extant historical documents have to say regarding the Ojibwa-Iroquois clash his narration allegedly recounted.

The first written account of this affair is in *The Jesuit Relations and Allied Documents* (Thwaites 1896–1901:48:75–77). This short notice simply recorded that 100 *Agnieronnons* (Mohawks) and *Onneiochronnons* (Oneidas), "the haughtiest of the five Iroquois nations," set out in the spring of 1662 to find and attack the *Outaouax* (Ottawas, "our *upper Algonquins*"). While following the shores of Lake Huron ("the Lake of the Hurons") the invaders were themselves surprised by a band of *Sauteurs* (Saulteaurs). By this name, the report indicates, "we designate the Savages living near the sault of Lake Superior." The Saulteaurs, having surrounded their enemies, assaulted them at daybreak. Only a few were said to have escaped. Contrary to what later versions of the story assert, such geographical information as is provided in this brief account would appear to locate the action *east* of Sault Ste. Marie either in the North Channel beyond Georgian Bay (both parts of Lake Huron) or at the northwestern end of Lake Huron proper.

Rather than this earliest and more sketchy mention of the Ojibwa-Iroquois battle, Cleland has selected the next and far more detailed published account to compare with Kawbawgam's narrative. This is in Nicholas Perrot's *Memoir on the Manners, Customs, and Religion of the Savages of North*

America, as translated into English by Emma Helen Blair (1911–1912:1:25–272) from its earlier publication in French, edited by Jules Tailhan, S. J. (1864). Perrot's invaluable *Memoir* is believed to have been composed sometime between 1680 and 1718 (Blair 1911–1912:1:13). Perrot provided no date for the battle. But *assuming it was the same engagement* as that recounted in the *Jesuit Relations,* thus dating to 1662 as Blair (1911–1912:1:178) stipulates, Perrot's reporting of it was any time between 18 and 56 years after the event.

In this later description (Blair 1911–1912:1:178–181), a war party of 100 Iroquois ascended the Sault and secretly encamped in a dense wood "five leagues or thereabout from the rapids." Calculating that the standard French league of that time equaled 2.42 English miles and the "common" league 2.76 miles (Thwaites 1902:2), and bearing in mind that the distance is only an estimate and could hardly have been measured, this would be very roughly 12 or 14 miles west of Sault Ste. Marie. Presumably, it is upon this approximation as well as a local coastline not discordant with that described in the memoir that the pertinent location is believed to be at modern Iroquois Point, near Brimley in Chippewa County, Michigan (Cleland 1992:95–96).

According to Perrot, one of the Saulteaurs, Ottawas, Nipissings, or Amikwas fishing and hunting elk in the area spotted smoke and raised suspicions. A hundred men were collected under the leadership of a Saulteaur, who sent scouts to investigate. These were able to locate the encamped Iroquois without alerting them, count their number, note the presence of women with them, and return with their report. The Saulteaurs, as they are now collectively called, set out immediately and, traveling all night and passing the Iroquois camp undetected in a dense fog, made their way into a cove in its rear. During the following night they silently surrounded and infiltrated the rising ground overlooking the still unalerted, now sleeping camp. The enemy's dogs were kept from barking by throwing them meat. At first light of dawn the Saulteaurs attacked. After loosing a volley of arrows, they fell on the survivors with clubs. At this point, says Perrot, the youths among the attackers lost their nerve and fled to their canoes. But they rallied at the sounds of their seniors' victory cries and killed the remnants of the assaulted force fleeing in their direction. None of the Iroquois escaped death except a few scouts away at the time of the Saulteaur onslaught. When they returned, they found only the beheaded (and in some instances partially eaten) corpses of their former companions. They then "made diligent haste to carry back to their own country this dismal news." The Saulteaurs "and their companions" went home in the triumph their enemies had expected to claim.

The foregoing is the gist of Perrot's description of the 1662 Iroquois disaster, that for which the Ojibwa narrator Charles Kawbawgam in 1893 is represented as giving "a nearly identical account" in one of his tellings of Ojibwa oral traditions, an account that must be credited, says Cleland (1992:125n44), to orality from generation to generation because the story-teller was illiterate in English. What about French? Tailhan's edition had been published in 1864. Were all of Kawbawgam's friends and relations, white as well as Indian, illiterate? However that may be, the "nearly identical" agreement subsisting between the two accounts is hardly an accurate characterization.

Even ignoring discrepancies in what modern literate people might consider inconsequential details—but which, because of cultural differences, Indians of Kawbawgam's generation might not—there are as many disparities as agreements between the Perrot and Kawbawgam narratives. The similarities shared by these two accounts boil down to (1) a memorable battle occurred, (2) information regarding its location appears to be in essential agreement within a matter of a few miles, (3) the antagonists were Iroquois and Algonquians (specifically some of the forerunners of the nascent Ojibwas), (4) both sides sent out scouts, (5) the Algonquians located the Iroquois camp but waited a day or two in order to reconnoiter and prepare a plan of attack, (6) the Iroquois remained unaware of their discovery, (7) their camp was surrounded under cover of darkness, (8) the attack was launched at dawn on the sleeping camp, (9) a complete Algonquian victory ensued, and (10) few of the Iroquois escaped. Six of these parallels suggest that the two narratives may indeed refer to the same historical event. Points 4, 7, and 8, however, while in agreement, are hardly persuasive, being ever repeated features of Indian warfare generally. Point 1 is of dubious diagnostic value inasmuch as any battle from the victor's point of view is a memorable one. Even point 2, especially given Kawbawgam's references to modern place names (he made mention of "Iroquois Point," "Whiskey Bay," and "Point aux Pins"), may not signal an independent concordance in the two stories. Given all the other considerations (above and below), Kawbawgam's geographical identifications, impressive at first sight, could simply reflect his desire to retroactively put currently familiar names on Perrot's *unnamed* points and inlets.

Both the Perrot and Kawbawgam renditions of the famous battle differ from that in the *Jesuit Relations,* not least in the matter of its location. The latter places it east of the Sault in northern Lake Huron or the North Channel, whereas the former two elect the shore of Lake Superior just west of the Sault. Again discounting variances in many small details, such as are inevitable even in modern military after-action reports of the same engagement, and the *Jesuit Relations* version aside, the dissimilarities between the Perrot and Kawbawgam descriptions should be noted: (1) Ojibwa scouts, while reconnoitering, transformed themselves into a beaver and an otter—this and the next two assertions are uniquely Kawbawgam's; (2) Iroquois scouts passed the camp of the Ojibwas without seeing them; (3) as the Iroquois paddled along the coast of Lake Superior they sang war songs and, upon landing and establishing their encampment, they began a war dance that lasted, as a helpful spirit informed the Ojibwas would be the case, for four days and nights (this hardly accords with Perrot's depiction of raiders making a secret encampment in order to avoid discovery before setting out on mayhem and plunder of the unsuspecting local inhabitants); (4) there was but one woman in the Iroquois party according to Kawbawgam, whereas there were several in Perrot's reckoning (what makes this noteworthy is that the solitary woman is said to have dreamed every night of impending doom for the Iroquois, but their leader ignored her warnings—a reaction out of keeping with a people as preoccupied with dreams as portents of the future as the Iroquois); and (5) unlike the earlier rendition of this story, Kawbawgam's has all of the Iroquois killed except two the Ojibwas intended as messengers (these had their ears, noses, fingers, and toes cut off before they were sent home with a taunting invitation to their kinsmen and friends to come visiting again). The heads of the slain, we are told, were lined up along the shore of Lake Superior for half a mile.

Kawbawgam's recital of the Ojibwa's victory over the Iroquois falls well short of being "nearly identical" to Perrot's. It is a different story, albeit probably inspired by traditions, helped along or not by the preexistence of more than one published report of one or more genuine historical occurrences. Generated from a venerable and cross-culturally recurrent theme of triumphs over ancient enemies, it is replete with deletions, substitutions, and additions of elements. And like most such tales, it has "improved" with the telling. Furthermore, as the editor of the volume containing Kawbawgam's story notes, there are at least six different accounts of the affair antedating the latter's version of it. In one of these, 300 Chippewas (Ojibwas) defeated a thousand Iroquois while suffering but one casualty (Alexander Henry's 1776 report cited in Bourgeois 1994:114n). In another, the engagement took place around 1750, not 1662 (Warren 1984 [1885]:147). Neither Kawbawgam nor Perrot himself gives a date for what they each relate. Warren wrote his depiction of the Iroquois defeat sometime between 1851 and 1853; it was not published until 1885, eight years before Kawbawgam's rendition was recorded. Having personally obtained his details from the headman of the La Pointe Ojibwas, Warren has the Ojibwas, organized as a war expedition, headed east in hopes of finding and attacking *Naud-o-ways* (Iroquois). While still just west of Sault Ste. Marie, the Ojibwas found the camp (at Iroquois Point) of a large war party of the very people they themselves were planning on attacking (Warren 1984 [1885]:147–148). They found the Iroquois carousing and drunken. They surrounded them, waited until their enemies had drunk themselves into insensibility, and then launched their assault. Few of the Iroquois escaped.

With several narratives supposed to tell the same tale, but with each different from the others in significant as well as trivial ways, assaying historical fidelity among the competing versions requires access to external independent information or, failing that, a willingness to accept as most plausible a composite version that melds the commonalities among all, or most, or just those versions that seem most compatible among themselves. This second-best, and necessarily tentative, solution rests on the principle that, in the absence of anything better, less than total consistency among the accounts is better than consigning the whole genre to the wastebasket. This is a common dilemma in the study of written history, of course, and not just in that of oral traditions. But the dilemma is compounded in the latter by the virtual certainty of concurrent filtering out of original narrative elements and their modification or replacement by new ones in secondary, tertiary, quaternary, and more retellings as oral history is transmuted into oral tradition. How original, that is, how close to a firsthand account of an event is the oldest known version? It is easy to overlook the fact that many historical documents are not wholly independent sources of information but may be themselves records of oral histories and oral traditions.

With their publication dates and the alleged date of the Ojibwa-Iroquois battle, the records in the *Jesuit Relations* and in Perrot's *Memoir* would seem to have the best claims to original oral history status. No Jesuit or any other European, as far as is known, was witness to this affair. They could only have heard about it via who knows how many Indian and French intermediaries. Transmission across space as well as time of word-of-mouth communication affords many opportunities for mutation. Making the unsafe assumption that orality was the sole means of passing the story along from generation to generation, it is reasonable to appeal to the earliest renditions of what is thought to be the same story to support a claim of serious historicity in Kawbawgam's version. But an examination of the several other extant candidates for historical status should alert students of oral traditions to the dangers of relying on just one of them. Furthermore, the assumption of an essentially unvarying verbal recitation across the generations from 1662 to 1893, as Cleland (1992:125n44) stresses, ignores the pre-1893 existence of four or five published sources, some copies of which were potentially available to missionaries, government agents, traders, literate Indians, Metis, and white neighbors to nudge along the tales that Ojibwa people told. That fact alone is sufficient to compromise this proffered claim of oral historical autochthony.

On Preliterate Historical Memory Among the Dogrib Indians of the Canadian Subarctic

Although archaeology is not directly involved, there are nevertheless implications for it (see end of chapter) in an interesting study by ethnographers June Helm and Beryl C. Gillespie (1981) in which they conclude that bona fide history from the early eighteenth century, and possibly earlier, is preserved in modern oral traditions of the Dogrib Indians in the Mackenzie District of Canada's Northwest Territories. At the least, if we accept their arguments, the case they make would seem to push the lower limits of the upper chamber of Vansina's hourglass metaphor farther back by another half century than elsewhere has seemed warranted (Vansina 1985:23–24, 168–169; Bahr 1998:32; Mason 2000:258–259 and this volume, Chapter 9).

The authors introduce their study by taking Robert Lowie (1917) to task for demanding impossible standards before oral traditions may be acceptable as historical evidence. Among those standards they would disallow are Lowie's requirements (1) that cited traditions "record accurately" events and (2) that the events so recorded are "historically significant" (Helm and Gillespie 1981:8). The latter requirement is especially nettlesome for those who have difficulty accepting that there is a difference in kind between an unreflective recitation of a received narrative and the investigated, critically evaluated product of systematic historiography. Combining the two without due recognition of their inherent incompatibilities threatens the integrity of each (e.g., note the events regarded as historically significant in Plains Indian winter counts; see Chapter 2 for a few examples). Lowie's objection that oral traditions are usually full of "origin myths, monsters, and all" is itself regarded as objectionable by the authors when offered as reason to ignore claims of historicity in those traditions (Helm and Gillespie 1981:8). But they neglect to address his logic in laying out his scruple: namely, on what grounds does one choose to accept as factual one item in an oral tradition but reject another without falling into the trap of arbitrary selectivity? (See Finley 2000:1; Leach 1954:265–268; Price 1980:161–164, 175–178.)

At any rate, Helm and Gillespie maintain that there are instances of North American Indian oral traditions that do in fact "record happenings, *usually occurring within one hundred and fifty years or so prior to the taking of native testimony*" [my emphasis], and that those happenings are of a kind that "Euroamerican history and Lowie (1917:165) deem 'significant'"

(Helm and Gillespie 1981:8). As examples, they cite G. T. Emmons (1911) and C. McClellan (1970) on first encounters of Europeans and certain northwestern North American Indian groups. The critical factor, Helm and Gillespie urge, is not accuracy "but to what extent . . . [is an oral tradition] in accord with the European record, and in what respects (and in terms of what native cultural perceptions) does it depart" (Helm and Gillespie 1981:8). Fair enough—assuming, that is, *nondependence of either source on the other for the information at issue.*

With the use of interpreters, oral traditions were collected in interviews with middle-aged and elderly Dogrib informants over a decade from the early 1960s to the mid-1970s. Before midcentury, the ethnographers point out, few Dogribs spoke English and fewer still could read. Some of the stories they recorded included allusions to events and conditions possibly as remote as the late eighteenth century. These appeared to be "congruent with the published Euroamerican historical record" with respect to certain "circumstances, events, and persons" (Helm and Gillespie 1981:8). On occasion, possible correspondences between the stories they heard and unpublished written accounts came to light in subsequent examination of archival resources of the Hudson's Bay Company. The traditions Helm and Gillespie collected, and a couple of other relevant ones independently recorded by Nancy O. Lurie in the same period, are, of course, "free texts, and individual variations in choice, elaboration, and emphasis of episodes and details are to be expected" (Helm and Gillespie 1981:17). Nevertheless, they believe that, stimulated by increasing interaction with European traders, missionaries, and government agents following the initial years of contact, "Dogribs [came to] evince a firm comprehension of both historical actualities and their temporal succession" (Helm and Gillespie 1981:9). But they also caution: "We leave as an open question whether in truly aboriginal times generations experienced changes sufficiently fast-paced and emergent one from the other to permit a developmental perspective in their folk history" (Helm and Gillespie 1981:9).

As Helm and Gillespie came to understand, the Dogribs of today divide their past into what might be called "an era of Floating Time" and "an era of evolutionary or Linear Time." The first of these seems devoid of any idea of temporal succession *except that* it itself hints at a division into (a) a fathomless mythic world long antedating the advent of Europeans and (b) a successor world, one still "remote beyond temporal reckoning" but that "treat[s] of a world much as it is today," albeit still innocent of Europeans. The era or "domain" of Linear Time constitutes "folk history" with "recognized temporal succession related to European records and dates" (Helm and Gillespie 1981:9).

The authors trifurcate the era of Linear Time into Proto-Contact, Early

Contact, and Stabilized Contact periods. In the first of these, the Dogribs had only indirect awareness of new people in the world through rumors from intermediaries and the rare infiltration of alien products. Face-to-face Dogrib-European encounters commencing in the 1780s initiated the second period. The third, or Stabilized Contact, period (ca. 1840 forward) was marked by more or less regular interaction with Europeans and the establishment of missions (Helm and Gillespie 1981:11–13, Table 1).

During the Proto-Contact period, to judge from their traditions, the Dogribs, not yet possessing firearms, suffered grievously from attacks by Crees and Yellowknives and/or other Chipewyans who earlier had become so armed. Helm and Gillespie (1981:11, Table 1) note that the famous Scottish explorer Alexander Mackenzie confirms in his journals one such attack in the late eighteenth century. For later time, that is, during the Early Contact period, there are more documents recording events, some of which definitely, or more often problematically, find corresponding incidents mentioned in recitations of Dogrib traditions. Several of these have been found in the 1823 and 1828 published accounts of Sir John Franklin and in unpublished traders' notes preserved in the Hudson's Bay Company archives. A couple of these parallels may be mentioned as relevant to the following events.

Historical written records cited by Helm and Gillespie acknowledge the rescue from starvation of the survivors of Franklin's first expedition at Fort Enterprise (just north of the headwaters of the Yellowknife River that flows into Great Slave Lake) by a band of Yellowknife Indians led by a man called Akaitcho. These same people are recorded as periodically harassing the Dogribs between 1812 and 1823. Documentary reports of retribution by the latter mention their slaughtering in 1823 of the women and girls in a band of Yellowknives led by a headman named Long Leg. Dogrib tradition, according to several of the ethnographers' informants, preserves the tale of Akaitcho's band saving starving white men at Fort Enterprise as well as the Yellowknife custom of trading at Old Fort Providence, located on the north shore of Great Slave Lake until its abandonment in 1823 with the absorption of the North West Company by the Hudson's Bay Company. Ethnographic information credits the modern Dogribs with correctly identifying the sites of these two places. Finally, a tale of magically attracting a group of Yellowknives to be slaughtered may allude to the disaster the Dogribs visited on Long Leg's band. However, the details in that oral tradition fail to match the account of the Dogrib (a possible participant?) who reported the affair to the post traders (Helm and Gillespie 1981:14–15).

The most detailed "historical" Dogrib tradition, at least as published in this study, deals with a confrontation between a Dogrib leader named Edzo and the Yellowknife Akaitcho and his men ("Akaitcho's bunch"), a confrontation resulting in the intimidation of the latter and the establishment of permanent peace (Helm and Gillespie 1981:14–23). The story has eight episodes, each with many variations in particulars. The ethnographers June Helm and Nancy O. Lurie independently recorded this story from four informants between them. These informants had years of baptism from 1877 to 1904; their years of testimony were between 1967 and 1969. Seven other informants, each interviewed by Helm, Lurie, or Gillespie, proffered additional information relevant to the time when the Edzo-Akaitcho drama supposedly took place (Helm and Gillespie 1981:15, Table 2). Part of the especially detailed testimony of one Joseph Naedzo (1887–1973), "The Bear Lake Prophet," is given at some length. Except for Akaitcho, none of the named characters—there are five major and a variable number of minor ones—in the several versions of the story can positively be identified in the historical record. But through an assiduous combing of published and unpublished documents, especially the latter in the Hudson's Bay Company archives, attempted reconstructions of genealogies, and comparisons of personal and place name variants in the Dogrib, Yellowknife/Chipewyan, and Cree languages, Helm and Gillespie nominate some other historically known individuals as possible candidates for the unrecognized figures in the Edzo-Akaitcho story. While none of these suggestions can be considered as indubitable, of course, some appear to be at least plausible.

As support for the credibility of the story line itself, the authors cite a passage in the Fort Simpson (on the Mackenzie River some 250 miles west of the other mentioned establishments) post journal of November 26, 1829. This journal also is preserved in the Hudson's Bay Company archives. The pertinent passage reports news of a Chipewyan-mediated confrontation between Yellowknives under Akaitcho and a group of "Martin Lake Slaves," as the Dogribs were called by the traders at that post. Although the establishment of peace that is so prominently the denouement of the Edzo-Akaitcho encounter fails to accord with the post journal's report that the contending parties "separated with mutual reproaches for the past—and strong languidge [sic] implying another attack," the ethnographers propose this account as plausible vindication of the oral tradition as history. They offer as explanation for the discrepancy in the alleged outcomes the somewhat tortuous means by which the version in the post journal came to be:

> After all, that account as received into the documentary record involved at least five links in a chain of testimonies: from (1) Dogribs who may or may not have been eyewitnesses to some of the events to Beaulieu [a Metis outpost trader who took the trouble to see that the

news was passed on]; from (2) Beaulieu to the two youths who carried his message to Fort Simpson; from (3) those youths, who doubtless communicated through (4) an interpreter, to the trader Edward Smith; and from (5) Edward Smith's written version to us. Whatever the actual events, each link in the chain of transmission of the "news" offered opportunity for interpretation, distortion, and omission [Helm and Gillespie 1981:23].

This sensible note of caution needs also to be heeded when considering the existence of another written source: this one from a trader at Fort Resolution, recorded some four months later than the one at Fort Simpson, that makes note of a "Red Knife" (Yellowknife) and "Slaves of Mackenzie's River District" (Dogribs) peace settlement (Helm and Gillespie 1981:23). And certainly no more immune from these cautions are the multiple oral chains of transmission of the traditions themselves, even though the authors fail to make that point explicitly.

Also warranting critical attention when assaying possible historical content in Dogrib oral traditions is the question of their independence vis-à-vis European records. Helm and Gillespie touch one aspect of this problem in their "open question" earlier quoted. After all, the two peoples had been in increasingly familiar interaction following the Proto-Contact period. They talked to each other regarding matters of mutual interest. That one party to the growing dialog produced written accounts of certain of those matters and could buttress their recollections accordingly in discussions with the other must throw into question the idea of autochthony of the oral traditions. The authors have done a creditable job in seeking independent verification of the stories their informants told. Their work exhibits rigor as well as imagination. But the problem of determining autochthony remains. And so does another.

In a 1970 prize-winning graduate student paper, "Yellowknives: *Quo Iverunt?*," published by the American Ethnological Society and based on Helm's and her own Helm-directed fieldwork, Beryl Gillespie reports a state of affairs that must give pause to anyone concerned with questions of historicity in oral traditions. This account was written just 11 years before her joint paper with Helm but only one to two years after her interviews with five of the Dogrib informants listed in that collaborative effort as having provided information on the era relevant to the Edzo-Akaitcho drama (Helm and Gillespie 1981:Table 2). It is unfortunate that the earlier paper received no notice in the joint Helm-Gillespie contribution. For in that paper, Gillespie wrote, "of special interest in the disappearance of the Yellowknives as a viable group *is the total absence of their existence in the memory culture of other contiguous Dene groups*" (Gillespie 1970:61; my emphasis).

Today the Yellowknife "tribe" is extinct. According to Gillespie, it gradually disappeared as a self- and other-identified social and political entity between about 1830 and the end of the first quarter of the twentieth century. As a recognized group having its own territory, "in 1900 the Yellowknives signed an adhesion to a treaty originally signed by certain Cree, Beaver and Chipewyans the previous year. There were nearly 200 Yellowknives who attended the adhesion. They were led by a chief and two headmen who signed on their behalf. The formal adhesion document clearly distinguishes these 'Yellow Knives' from the 'Dog Ribs,' 'Slaves' and 'Chipewyans' of Great Slave Lake who signed the same adhesion on the same day" (Alexander von Gernet, personal communication, 2004).

As noted by J. Alden Mason (1946) in his ethnographic and linguistic work in the western Subarctic, the Yellowknives were rapidly losing their separate identity at Great Slave Lake in 1913. However, it was still possible to discern slight dialect differences from the people usually identified as Chipewyan, and other Indian groups retained separate names for them. Gillespie was able to show that "European observers not only had French and English terms to distinguish Yellowknives from Chipewyans but were aware of different native terms for the two tribes" (Gillespie 1970:63). By 1928, she says, the Yellowknives as a distinct people ceased to exist because of assimilation with Dogribs and Chipewyans in addition to a devastating influenza epidemic in that year. She points out that in 1928 (presumably before the epidemic) Cornelius Osgood (1936:33) still gave them separate nomenclatorial status. Although today extinct, written records, published and unpublished, affirm the historical existence of the Yellowknives from late in the third decade of the twentieth century well back into the Early Contact period. Nevertheless, says Gillespie,

> Helm's fieldwork during the 1960's [unpublished field notes] with the Dogribs, the Dene peoples west of the Yellowknives between Great Slave and Great Bear Lakes, encouraged further inquiry into the vague and obscure disappearance of the Yellowknife Indians not only as a people but as a memory. No Dogrib informant was able to identify the English terms "Yellowknife," "Red Knife" or "Copper Indians" [all terms for the same people]. Nor would they admit that in translation into Athapaskan could it be applied to any past or contemporary Indian group. The inability to identify or remember any Yellowknife Indians has not been just a Dogrib loss of memory. No Dene group of

the Great Slave Lake area investigated is familiar with this group [Gillespie 1970:61–62].

In addition, "not one informant could explain why people had written about Yellowknife Indians having lived in this area [where those people are historically known to have lived] before 1900. Dogribs could easily give detailed accounts of the past but the events, peoples and places were associated with Dogribs and Chipewyans, never Yellowknives" (Gillespie 1970:62).

Whereas Helm and Gillespie find multiple references to Yellowknives in Dogrib oral traditions, as they report in their 1981 paper, Dogrib knowledge of any such people having ever existed is flatly denied in Gillespie's 1970 paper. Their historical presence, however, is unequivocal. There is even a portrait of the Yellowknife leader Akaitcho, who becomes a Chipewyan in the 1970 published traditions, surviving in a lithograph of an 1821 watercolor by Lt. Robert Hood of the Franklin expedition (Gillespie 1981:286, Figure 3).

The dissolution of the Yellowknives as a people distinguishable from Dogribs, Crees, Slaveys, and even other Chipewyan-speaking Indians is an understandable phenomenon, given the historical events reviewed by Gillespie. There is little reason to doubt the dilution and then extinguishing of their identity among their surviving neighbors. Just as, in another and later situation, the ethnographer James W. Van Stone (1965) found no cultural reason to posit a surviving Dogrib component in the Chipewyan community of Snowdrift at the eastern end of Great Slave Lake, even though some of its inhabitants claimed their presence (according to unpublished field notes of David M. Smith cited in Gillespie 1970:69n11), so Wendell H. Oswalt in his popular textbook *This Land Was Theirs* (2002) submerges the Yellowknives in his description of the Chipewyans.

There is grist for the tradition-as-history skeptic's mill here. Living Dogribs, the ethnographers report, do indeed make no distinction between Yellowknives and Chipewyans. Both are referred to by the single name *tedzot'i* (Helm and Gillespie 1981:10) or, in a later rendition, *Tédzont'in* (Helm 2000:221–222). When speaking of the enemy Yellowknives of the early nineteenth century specifically, the Dogribs refer to them as "Akaitcho's bunch" (*Ekeco weceke,* Akaitcho/his followers) (Helm 2000:222; Helm and Gillespie 1981:14). Where the latter designation is not employed in the recitation of a tradition, the ethnographers maintain that it is usually clear from context when Yellowknives are the referent. So the Yellowknives of Dogrib traditions are thus identified by the ethnographers themselves. They have done this not on the basis of independent information unique to those narratives but on the basis of historical documents written by Europeans that tell of Akaitcho himself or of places and events those original writers associated, for whatever reasons, with the people contemporaneously known to them as Yellowknives—associations that seem to parallel story lines or elements the ethnographers found in the tales the Dogribs tell. If those records had been destroyed or had never been written, the sobering truncation of "historical memory" exhibited by this specimen of Dogrib, indeed Dene, oral tradition would have expelled the Yellowknife people even from the possibility of speculative reconstitution. By how frail a thread do oral societies hang suspended over oblivion!

And, similarly, components of their praxis. Analogous to Gillespie's ethnographic report of Yellowknife extinction in Dene cultural memory is the issue of possible Monacan burial mounds in faraway Virginia—a recent example of the archaeological implications mentioned in this section's opening sentence. Lack of references "in current Monacan oral history of a connection between Monacans and the mounds of central Virginia" has been taken by C. Clifford Boyd, Jr. (2004:362) as one of several reasons for believing there was in fact no such connection with the Monacans' Late Woodland ancestors. Here the absence of oral traditional references to mound building is used to buttress a negative historical argument. Although Boyd may be correct in his conclusion, this particular species of support for it, like the missing Yellowknives in Dogrib and other Dene traditions, is of unreliable value.

7

Mammoth Remembrances

With few exceptions (e.g., Hanks 1997; Harris 1997; Miller 1998), archaeologists today reject Indian claims that their oral traditions preserve knowledge—often described as "memories"—of extinct animals and geological events that date back to late Pleistocene times some 10,000 years ago. Of course, there are many more members of the general public, including Indians, still subscribing to such beliefs. A few antiscience irreconcilables even insist on the coexistence of Indians and dinosaurs (Deloria 1997a:220–225). But it is archaeologists, ethnologists, and folklorists who are the focus of attention here.

Before the development of modern archaeology, geology, and paleontology, there was no reliable way of knowing the age of fossil animal remains dug out of the ground or eroded out of a riverbank. This ignorance was exacerbated in just recently discovered lands by limited familiarity with the modern fauna. One could not be sure that some of those bones did not represent exotic creatures still living beyond the present frontier. Certain animal tales told by Indians or, perhaps more often, heard third- or fourth-hand from Europeans acquainted with those people, who passed them along to fascinated listeners, piqued many an imagination, among them Thomas Jefferson's. Like Hebrew-speaking Indian tribes, giant creatures never encountered by white people in America might still exist just beyond that next bend in the river or over that next mountain range. Who dared discount in advance what an as yet unexplored land, or the unplumbed recent past of the pre-Columbian world, might harbor? Before the middle of the nineteenth century, claims had been made of stone tools in apparent association with mammoth or mastodon skeletons in the central and lower Mississippi Valley (see references in Williams 1957). While these claims fell short of convincing, they were certainly tantalizing. Perhaps some of the numerous Indian stories of fabulous beasts had something genuine behind them after all.

The lure of possible actuality behind these stories may have helped mislead some mid-nineteenth-century investigators of pre-Columbian Mesoamerican ruins in their discernment of elephants in highly stylized Mayan stone carvings (Wauchope 1962:24–25). Coetaneously, it also inspired fakers of ancient artifacts to hoodwink people with antiquarian interests by planting some of their wares in genuine archaeological sites. Although eventually found out, such vandalism did cause needless distraction to serious researchers. Notorious among these forgeries were "Hopewellian" effigy platform smoking pipes with bowls carved to represent elephants or mammoths "discovered" at a mound site in Davenport, Iowa (McKusick 1970) and the Holly Oak pendant, a marine shell bearing an engraved image of a mammoth from a multicomponent site in Delaware (Griffin et al. 1988; Meltzer and Sturtevant 1983).

Until the advent of radiocarbon dating and the resulting initiation of an absolute pre–tree ring datable chronology for prehistoric American cultures, effectively a late-twentieth-century development, the absolute time depth underlying the native peoples when contacted by Europeans was largely unknown and unfathomable. It might be only a couple of thousand years or many times that number. Most archaeologists inclined in the conservative direction of just a few millennia. There was similar uncertainty about the duration of the Holocene or Recent geological epoch and the end of the last ice age. It would seem that the startling discovery at Folsom, New Mexico, in 1926–1927 of distinctive fluted projectile points in unmistakable association with the butchered remains of an extinct species of Pleistocene bison would have ended uncertainty and tilted opinion on the antiquity of humans in America in the direction of much greater age than previously assumed. But there were obstacles to such an extension. These included uncertainties about just when the Pleistocene epoch ended and the lurking possibility that relict populations of certain of its characteristic mammals, like the Folsom bison, and perhaps also mammoths, mastodons, ground sloths, giant beavers, horses, American camels, and other members of what is called the Rancholabrean fauna, may have lingered on into considerably more recent times rather than all expiring together 10, 20, or however many thousand years ago. A number of archaeologists and anthropologists found this possibility attractive, not least because it seemed to make sense of yet another possibility: that of a kernel of historical truth in certain otherwise puzzling American Indian oral traditions about strange large animals.

In 1934, eight years after the first Folsom discoveries but still a good decade and a half before the advent of radiocarbon dating, William Duncan Strong published a highly influential paper predicated on that pair of possibilities. Aware of numerous references in Eskimo and eastern and south-central North American Indian traditions regarding monsters unlike known modern animals, Strong argued for their careful consideration before dismissal as strictly fictional. Given the innumerable gaps in contemporary archaeological knowledge, this was received by many of his colleagues as sensible advice. There seemed two likely ways of explaining the native traditions. The first Strong called "myths of observation." These were "mythical rationalization[s] based on the observation of fossil bones" (Strong 1934:81). Although interesting, he thought such myths unlikely evidence that people had ever actually seen such creatures in the flesh. They were simply fanciful attempts to accommodate exotic phenomena in an imaginary bestiary. The second type of explanation warranted closer attention. This embraced those stories he labeled "historical traditions." These, he claimed, "seem to embody a former knowledge of the living animals in question, perhaps grown hazy through long oral transmission" (Strong 1934:81). If such stories were "specific enough and numerous enough [they] may have definite historical value." Nevertheless, Strong (1934:81–82) said, "that conclusive proof of such suggested associations will generally rest with the palaeontologist and archaeologist goes without saying." It was, of course, no easy matter to consistently distinguish the two groups of tales.

Examples of Strong's "historical traditions" from New England and Labrador tribes include what he took to be references to human encounters, usually of a fabulous nature, with what might have been mammoths or mastodons. He cited a 1744 Abenaki account quoted from Pierre Francois-Xavier de Charlevoix in which reference is made to a large "moose" with a fifth "arm" growing out of its shoulders. Strong then drew attention to a Naskapi tradition that he himself had collected a short time before publishing his 1934 article, a tradition in which a man-eating monster is described as having an enormous head with huge ears and a long nose. A Penobscot yarn earlier recorded by Frank Speck was likewise called upon as pertinent. This one told of herds of huge long-toothed beasts that drank the rivers dry and had to sleep leaning against trees because they could not get up if they once lay down. In the Naskapi case a man who had once seen pictures of elephants identified the man-eating monster as such an animal. This should immediately have raised a warning flag in Strong's mind. It did. Nevertheless, he persuaded himself that the concurrence of older informants, who claimed their memories of the monster and the first man's description of it were similar, reinforced the plausibility of that informant's identification. Even though the identifications may have been prejudiced by previous exposure to external information, Strong still felt that that complication was insufficient in itself to reject the sincere testimony of his informants.

Strong noted other references to possible proboscidean "memories" among the Micmacs and, far to the south along the Gulf coast, among the Atakapas, Alabamas, Koasatis, and Chitimachas. Other accounts, as related by the Iroquois, seemed to refer to giant "buffalos" that trampled down trees in their passage through the forest. Vaguely depicted monsters of unknown affiliation similarly bulldozed the forests in Ojibwa and other tribal territories. Strong did not endorse any of these oral traditions as truly historical. His point was that they—or, rather, some of them—should be considered candidates for such status until they could be subjected to confirming or disconfirming scientific tests. Obviously, the stories were filled with fabulously impossible characters and situations. Even so, Strong wanted to be sure a baby (or kernel of historical truth) would not be thrown out with the bathwater of skepticism. He cautiously suspected there might be one.

Frank Speck (1935), responding in part to Strong's citing his Penobscot folktale as relevant to his own thesis published the previous year, offered additional information that cast a quite different light on the whole matter. Tales of a great man-eating monster occur in the oral traditions of a number of northeastern Algonquian-speaking tribes, Speck pointed out, and they manifest themselves in variable ways, usually as an episode in the adventures of a primal culture hero-creator-trickster-transformer named Gluskap or a cognate. While the creature in question is often referred to in terms simply understood as "Great Beast," a more specific name translates as "Stiff-legged Bear." This is the case even with the Mistassini band of the Naskapis with whom Speck had worked. Although some Montagnais living near white communities who had seen pictures of elephants and one who claimed actually to have seen a live elephant himself gave the same name for *that* animal, most of Speck's informants thought it referred to "a carnivorous monster of the bear kind living in a former age" when one of the heroes of their mythology could splinter great trees and shatter boulders with an arrow shot from his bow (Speck 1935:160). The support Strong thought he could muster from Speck's Penobscot reporting was thus undercut by the latter's additional information and broader experience with the native sources. The kernel of truth Strong sought in the oral traditions, while still a tantalizing possibility, was not to be found in Frank Speck's ethnographic fruit.

In 1937 F. T. Siebert, Jr., suggested that, rather than Indian tales of monster beasts being taken as possibly "reminiscent of the mammoth or mastodon" or, presumably, any other extinct Pleistocene animal, they should be evaluated purely in terms of the native belief systems taken on their own terms and not made to conform to modern Western paleontological taxa. In that same year, and in the same journal, A. Irving Hallowell, independently of

Siebert's recommendation, did exactly that. Informed by his own ethnographic work among the Saulteaux in Manitoba and western Ontario, he wrote:

> In many of the mythological narratives, the form of the name given to familiar animals contains the augmentative prefix. There are references to the Great Snake, the Great Mosquito, the Great Beaver, the Great Trout, etc. This has a temporal significance. Formerly the earth was inhabited by many of these monster species now only represented by smaller varieties of their kind. In the myths there are likewise accounts of how certain of these great animals became extinct (the Great Mosquito) or how the familiar variety of the species came into being (as, e.g., small snakes). It was explained to me that the mythological characters [i.e., culture heroes] had power enough to overcome the monster fauna but that ordinary human beings would be constantly harassed if they had to live on the earth with such creatures today. Nevertheless, a few such species still survive according to the firm conviction of the Indians. There are Indians now living, in fact, who have seen them. But the events in the myths which involve the monster animals are conceptualized as occurring in the distant past. They took place "long ago" in a period when the earth was "new." Consequently a temporal distinction is recognized between those days and the present [Hallowell 1937:668].

Loren C. Eiseley (1943), eight years after Speck's (1935) sobering check on any enthusiasm for seeing evidence of memories of mammoths in northeastern Algonquian legends, addressed the critical question of postglacial large mammal extinctions in the (still pre–radiocarbon dating) archaeological chronology of the time. The immediate catalyst for his examination of this topic was an essay by Alfred L. Kroeber, in one part of which archaeologists were cautioned not to uncritically endorse such an antiquity for the Folsom finds as would seem to require, by reason of the relatively short estimated age span of the more recent prehistoric cultures as then known, a major hiatus separating the two (Kroeber 1940:474–476). The earliest of these post-Folsom cultures were generally held to be no more than a few thousand years old. At the time Kroeber wrote, geologists thought the Pleistocene epoch, toward the end of which the bison species associated with the Folsom cultural material (then named *Bison taylori*, now *Bison bison antiquus*) became extinct, had itself ended sometime between 10 and 25 thousand years ago. Instead of embracing the resulting enigma of some 100 or more centuries empty of any trace of human presence, but nevertheless accepting the faunal-cultural associations as valid, Kroeber thought a more reasonable solution was to investigate the possibility that some populations of Pleistocene animals had survived the end of that epoch, finally becoming extinct as recently as, say, 3,000 years ago. At the time he wrote, he and Strong were by no means alone in wanting to consider such an alternative. After all, maybe the geologists and paleontologists were excessive in their age estimates. Although it was not Kroeber's purpose in writing his article to grind other people's axes, it likely did encourage further entertaining of the idea that there was more than aboriginal fancy in tales of encounters with monsters no longer met in the here and now.

Eiseley thought there were fewer difficulties with the geologically estimated time depth of the Folsom–terminal Pleistocene faunal association than was the case with Kroeber's penchant for a short chronology. He pointed out the consistent coexistence with each other of the extinct late Pleistocene species wherever they were found and the equally consistent absence of associated Recent or Holocene species. Where bison remains were found in context with later archaeological cultures, for example, they were not the extinct species linked to Folsom. By the time Eiseley wrote, other "Folsom-like" cultures (now called Clovis) had been discovered to be unambiguously contemporaneous with such other large ice age species as mammoth, mastodon, native American horse, American camel, and ground sloth. The megafauna thus represented was largely a cold-adapted one. None of the fluted projectile points found with such a fauna resembled those of later periods. Eiseley countered Kroeber's self-confessed inability to conceive of any geological or climatic changes as causally linked to large-scale extinctions at the end of Pleistocene time. Among other arguments, he invited his illustrious colleague's attention to the by then well-developed data of European late Pleistocene and postglacial paleontology and its independent support by pollen chronology and the archaeological record itself. He pointed out "that [ice age] fauna, let it be emphasized, does not hesitate in its departure. It does not linger on in isolated valleys. Mammoth and woolly rhino have shot their bolt. They go" (Eiseley 1943:211). According to those mutually compatible records, there were no survivals of that ice age fauna postdating the earliest Mesolithic sites. It seems unlikely, Eiseley reasoned, that the course of events in the New World was any different. For these and other reasons he felt the idea of even local populations of Pleistocene animals surviving in America for thousands of years after the terminal Pleistocene an untenable one. And although Eiseley did not make a point of it, well before he wrote his essay the archaeological gap that Kroeber found so persuasive in his own thinking was starting to close as still early, but post-Clovis and Folsom, cultures (e.g., Cody, née Scottsbluff) were coming to light, even though it would be a little while yet before they could be securely dated.

Ignoring or simply ignorant of Speck's skepticism regarding Strong's hypothesis or of Eiseley's review of relevant issues, and grossly misrepresenting the views of a distinguished paleontologist—it is clear from context that George Gaylord Simpson was the referent, even though no citation was offered—M. F. Ashley Montagu (1944) declared his belief that Strong's hypothesis had come into general acceptance. Furthermore, he suggested that mammoths may have locally survived "as recently as five hundred years ago." In support of this notion he footnoted "several conversations" with another paleontologist, this time named, who ventured his opinion that had the first Spanish explorers made it into the interior (presumably of North America) they might have been able to have seen that animal for themselves. Without naming him, nor identifying his source, Ashley Montagu again erroneously attributed to the still unidentified "distinguished American paleontologist (whose special interest is the horse)" the belief that the native American horse never became extinct and that the historical Indians' herds were primarily drawn from that stock rather than that introduced by the Spaniards (Montagu 1944:568–569n1).

As another prop in support of Strong's suggestions of "historical traditions" as genuine memories of late-surviving ice age mammals, Ashley Montagu offered Robert Koch's 1840 or 1841 rendition of certain Osage traditions he had collected while hunting in Missouri for fossils of extinct animals (see Williams 1957 for a critical examination of Koch's claims of sometime artifact associations with some of his fossils, claims Ashley Montagu did not question). The traditions Koch related tell of epic "battles" between native animals and "large and monstrous animals" invading from the east. So furious were these animal wars that the Indians, fearful for their own lives, were no longer able to hunt and were in danger of starvation. After great slaughter on both sides, the "huge monsters" departed westward. The Indians themselves and the "Great Spirit" then buried the carcasses, the former thereafter returning to the places of burial to hold ceremonies. Sometime later, a white emigrant family settled at one of these pieces of "sacred ground." After a couple of removals at Osage insistence, a permanent white settlement was made and digging at a spring for water power to drive a mill for grinding grain turned up what proved to be mastodon bones. Ashley Montagu leaped to the inference of "historical tradition." Luckily for archaeology and paleontology, the bones were not those of dinosaurs.

Both distressingly hardy and popular is the species of fallacious reasoning by means of which the presence of a geographical or other physical feature compatible with something in a tradition regarding a long-ago event is taken as confirmation of the tradition's historical factualness. Thus, in the foregoing instance, a mid-nineteenth-century Osage tradition makes vivid mention of now extinguished monsters; cleaning up their remains, people helped the "Great Spirit" bury them; since then, Osages are said to hold ceremonies where those interments were made; and subsequent erosion or digging at one such place turned up large extinct animal bones. Therefore, the tradition must be true, at least in fundamentals if not all details. The Osages must have seen Pleistocene animals. Either nineteenth-century Osages retained 10,000-year-old memories or the monsters of their tradition survived into recent times, as Ashley Montagu was prepared to believe.

This kind of simple, evidentially deficient reification of traditions into history still flourishes, replete with crossings of absent *t*'s and dottings of missing *i*'s. It recurs in a couple of recently published interpretations of a myth relating to Crater Lake in south-central Oregon. A mid-eighteenth-century Klamath oral tradition describes in dramatic terms an explosive eruption and shattering of a mountain and its subsequent replacement by a lake. On the western edge of the seismically active historical Klamath territory lies beautiful Crater Lake. It occupies the depression where a volcanic mountain once stood, a peak posthumously christened by geologists Mount Mazama, the collapse of which they have dated at close to 7,700 years ago. Notwithstanding the region's seismic history and the rather impressive temporal hiatus, the Klamath tradition is claimed by certain mythologists to be a genuine memory of that specific geological event (Barber and Barber 2004:6–8; Deloria 1997a:194–198). That very claim is endorsed as "straightforward" in a short review article on the "budding [and disputatious] discipline called geomythology" (Krajick 2005:764).

In 1945 Loren Eiseley revisited the debate over Indian oral traditions and the possibility of late survivals of Pleistocene fossil vertebrates. The focus of his attention this time was more in the nature of an intellectual history: an examination of European and Euroamerican currents of thought conducive to acceptance of authenticity of claimed encounters of Indians and otherwise unobserved exotic beasts. He prefaced his observations by reminding his readers not to overlook the sensible cautions William Duncan Strong had taken pains to include in his seminal article on the subject, cautions some later writers would fail to heed.

Many American Indian traditions that might seem to preserve knowledge of late-surviving large ancient animals that either became extinct just shortly before the arrival in America of Europeans, or that perhaps still existed just beyond the peripheries of exploration, Eiseley proposed were less than culturally virginal. Rather, they were a product of European suggestion operating upon Native American mythological creations. "We have, in short," he said, "occupied ourselves with so-called aboriginal tradition" (Eiseley 1945:85). Americans of European descent with an interest in such matters, such as Thomas Jefferson in his exchanges with the great French naturalist Georges Louis Leclerc de Buffon, felt it incumbent on themselves to defend the American fauna against Old World charges of inferiority (particularly in the matter of size). But there was another agency at work as well.

Eiseley drew attention to the great emotional as well as intellectual ferment in the Western world in the late eighteenth and nineteenth centuries over religion and such questions as the age of the earth and the immutability and, indeed, permanence of animal species then beginning to be seriously investigated by the developing sciences of geology, biology, and paleontology. Clergymen were not alone in maintaining that God's perfection necessarily precluded the extinction of any of His creations. Widely accepted was the idea that, while certain kinds of animals could be locally extirpated, none could totally disappear from the face of the earth. Some representatives must still exist, even if in out-of-the-way places. Holders of such a view, being predisposed to hear what they wanted to hear, could readily leap from myths about giant beasts told by Indians to vindication of their own convictions. And many of their native informants, as ignorant of Western zoological taxonomy as the whites were of their mythological ones, were anxious to reconcile the two in ways that both would find acceptable (to paraphrase Eiseley's point: "Oh, what you call . . . must be what we call . . . "). Jefferson himself, so Eiseley reported, was thus informed by a Delaware chief that mammoths still existed. Other Indians obligingly confirmed Jefferson's misidentification of fossil ground sloth bones as those of a huge lionlike carnivore (Eiseley 1945:86). One is reminded, the writer pointed out, of the experience of other Europeans in their quests for gold.

There were other important considerations often overlooked by those who were impressed by aboriginal tales of giant creatures, some of which might be thought to refer to, say, mammoths or mastodons. Among these was the fact that most such tales were heard or, in the case of most scholars, *read* in letters or published accounts, after they had been filtered through the variable and ethnocentrically slanted reporting of one or more intermediaries. Eiseley also drew attention to the importation of African slaves, numbers of whom escaped to marry or be adopted into Indian tribes, bringing with them stories or even personal knowledge of elephants, alive as well as dead. While their influence might be expected to have affected mainly southeastern tribes as, for example, reported by John R. Swanton (1911:355, 363), more northerly groups may have rationalized some of their mythological creations in line with fabulous tales of monsters whose remains in north-western America were the object of Russian exploration for mammoth ivory. These suggestions struck Eiseley as worthy of serious consideration, being less far-fetched than prodigal invoking of tenacious memories.

Nevertheless, the appeal to tenacious memories has itself proven tenacious. In the penultimate example to be looked at here, the revivified monster is not the usually favored mammoth or mastodon but the Pleistocene giant beaver *Castoroides ohioensis.* In a very interesting and carefully (if mistakenly, in my opinion) argued paper, the folklorist Jane C. Beck (1972) proposed that that creature has been preserved as a "prehistoric memory," or at least a "vestigial remnant of a memory," in the oral traditions of a number of northeastern Algonquian tribes. The recorded traditions in which that "memory" lingers are Malecite, where the most detailed account was found, Montagnais, Micmac, and Passamoquoddy. In some of the Micmac stories about beavers there seemed to be a "forgetting" of what Beck believed was the "original tale" in which the beaver was of the giant variety. Although the giant beaver is not known in Penobscot stories, she thought it once was but had been "forgotten" (Beck 1972:116).

Beck did not argue for the late survival of the Pleistocene giant beaver. Rather, she urged her readers to consider as more likely that among the Algonquian inhabitants of northern New England, the maritime provinces, and portions of Quebec and Labrador there were some who retained the "fossilized memory" of that animal from the time when it actually had existed, whenever that was. She suggested that those memories had lasted for some 6,000 to 9,000 years, basing that estimate on the then held opinion of the paleontologist Claude W. Hibbard that mammoths may have survived that late in Michigan (letter to Beck). This opinion had later to be abandoned in the face of accumulating data indicating time of extinction at around 11,000 B.P. (see Kurten and Anderson 1980:352–354). Because the giant beaver was a contemporary of the mammoth, it, too, Beck assumed (in company with most paleontologists), probably expired at about the same time. "Thus," she wrote, "it seems more credible than ever that the tales the Indians tell of the great beast that cannot lie down but must sleep leaning against trees are fossilized memories of the mammoth. Likewise, it seems plausible that the monster beaver tales might stem from early times and be a memory of the giant beaver that once roamed the face of this continent" (Beck 1972:117).

In support of her willingness to grant such lengthy tenures to tribal "memories," she cited the credence granted them in other instances by Ashley Montagu (1944), Pendergast and Meighan (1959), and Speck (1935). Although the first and last publications have already been discussed, it must be added that Beck's appeal to Speck is predicated on a total misunderstanding of what he had written. The Pendergast and Meighan article has been critically evaluated elsewhere (Mason 2000; Sturtevant 1966). Both of Strong's classes of traditions, Beck concluded, were manifested in the giant beaver stories. While some of those of the Micmac people were "myths of observation," simply rationalizations evoked by finding unusually big bones—presumably having some morphological similarity to those of the modern beaver—those of the Malecites she proffered as "historical traditions," bona fide memories of the real thing. In the latter case, she thought, finding big bones would have served those people as confirmation of their memories.

Asserting, however, the presence of authentic recollections of the Pleistocene giant beaver was embarrassed by Beck's understanding that humans had not migrated into northeastern North America at an early enough time to have there seen those creatures. She cited James B. Griffin (1952:23) as her authority. That reference, however, is actually to the chapter by Georg K. Neumann in the Griffin-edited *Archeology of Eastern United States.* Beck drew from that chapter that the proto-northeastern Algonquians had probably originated somewhere to the west or northwest. Therefore, their memories of the giant beaver must be relics of encounters their ancestors had had with such creatures in their place of departure. Evidently unaware of publications describing already discovered Paleoindian artifacts in the Northeast similar to those of the western Clovis and Folsom cultures, as at the Bull Brook site in Massachusetts, Beck was obliged to seek elsewhere for a sufficiently ancient culture coexisting with giant beavers from which place she might derive her folkloric origins. The only people other than her northeastern Algonquians for whom she could find evidence of giant beavers in oral traditions were, fittingly, the Beaver Indians in British Columbia. They, however, did not appeal as the source of those ancient memories. Rather, arguing from the diffusionist assumption, which she referred to as a "tested theory," that "the periphery is the best place to go for remnants of an archaic culture," she thought the giant beaver–"remembering" Beaver and northeastern Algonquian peoples had provided her with the solution to her dilemma (Beck 1972:119–120). "Thus," she said, "wouldn't we expect that if a memory of the monster beaver survived, it would be at the very edges of where the giant beaver was once known?" (Beck 1972:119–120). Talk about having your cake (beaver in this case) and eating it, too!

The last example of references to fabulous monsters and/or Pleistocene animals surviving in recorded oral "histories" (traditions) comes from the Southern Ponca reservation in Oklahoma. It is to be found in James H. Howard's 1965 Ponca monograph published by the Bureau of American

Ethnology. The tradition Howard published was written in 1947 by one Peter Le Claire, a Ponca Indian himself. Le Claire based his typewritten account on notes he had taken in 1928 on what he had been told by an elderly Southern Ponca chief, Mi-jin-ha-the or John Bull, a one-time Sun Dance participant and an "expert on tribal history and customs." This gentleman passed on to Le Claire "the traditional history" of the Ponca tribe as he had received it when being raised by two of his grandfathers (Le Claire in Howard 1965:16–23). There are, however, as is evident from Howard's discussion, and as is commonly the case with other people's verbally transmitted legends as well, other "traditional histories" of the Poncas, no two of which agree in all particulars and some not at all in significant matters. Howard believed that Le Claire had incorporated some elements from such other traditions in his rendition of John Bull's recollections of what his grandfathers had told him in the previous century.

Le Claire's rendering of Bull's narrative begins with the Poncas leaving their *Hu-tho-gah,* or circular camp, and migrating down the Ohio River to escape abuse by "people of light complexion." They crossed the Mississippi. Reference is made to a man whose brief description Howard plausibly takes to reflect the Poncas's having seen depictions of the Crucifixion. At the catlinite quarries at Pipestone in southwestern Minnesota God gave the Poncas the "pipe"—probably a reference to the calumet or "peace pipe." This seeming acquisition of the calumet in post-European contact times is immediately contradicted, however, by the assertion of its having been handed down to sons and grandsons for "thousands of years" from a named ancient chief. The people moved on westward and crossed the Missouri, repeatedly going on buffalo hunts as far as the Rocky Mountains and circling back to the Niobrara River in northern Nebraska.

According to Donald N. Brown and Lee Irwin (2001:416–417, Figure 1), Ponca territory in the late eighteenth century variably extended between the White River in South Dakota and the Niobrara in northern Nebraska and from the Missouri River west to the Black Hills—sometimes as far as the eastern border of Wyoming. Those authors give the date 1785 for the first appearance in history of the Poncas as a distinct tribe. Howard (1965: 15) believes they were already separated by about 1715 from the Omaha tribe, to which they probably originally belonged as a named division.

Apparently after the aforementioned pattern of cross-country bison hunting had been established, the Poncas—or some of them—while traveling from Santee in northeastern Nebraska to the Niobrara River, which joins the Missouri River just a few miles to the west, found a dead *Pa-snu-tah* or elephant—indeed, a "hairy elephant," according to Le Claire, and a *living prehistoric* animal (my emphasis) known as *Wah-kon-da-gee.* The latter is described as being about 8 feet high and 40 feet long with yellow hair and forked feet. Near Verdel, just a few miles farther west of the dead elephant and the initial sighting of *Wah-kon-da-gee,* the Indians saw that monstrous creature go into its "hole," as was its wont on the coldest winter days. At the confluence of the Keya Paha and Niobrara rivers at a place called Twin Buttes, some 45 or 50 miles west of the *Wah-kon-da-gee's* hole, a second "hairy elephant" was seen in or near a cave. Le Claire maintained that this one, unlike the first, was alive (Howard 1965:18n15). In their far western travels into the Big Horn Mountains in Wyoming where John Bull claimed they constructed a great rock trail marker (or medicine wheel?) in the form of a wagon wheel, the Poncas came to know of the existence of still more strange creatures, in this case a race of dwarfs.

In support of the veracity of his grandfathers' account of Ponca history, Bull, or conceivably Le Claire, either editorialized or reported as the grandfathers' assertion that "the Ponca is [*sic*] very strict with the history. Anyone making a mistake is corrected by groups of old men" (Howard 1965:20). It would be interesting to know the now unknowable: did Bull or his grandfathers share his or their rendition of Ponca history with "groups of old men"? If they did, is the result of such exposure incorporated in those parts of the narrative just surveyed? Such knowledge would be an invaluable contribution to Ponca historiography and our own philosophy of historiography quite apart from its irrelevance for paleontology and archaeological culture history.

8

On the Historicity of Symbols and Symbolic Praxis

No more daunting challenge confronts archaeologists than the search for the beliefs reflected in physical manifestations of human activities in now defunct cultures. No more so is this true than when those manifestations, through their forms and/or contexts, seem to hint at something additional to or other than mundane or strictly utilitarian ends. Inferring the primary function of, say, a flint projectile point found embedded in a deer bone in a midden is of a different order of magnitude than comprehending what a similar artifact signified when placed in a clay pot on the floor of a grave. The latter presents a less tractable and therefore more interesting problem. How to come to grips with the meaning embedded in such a situation is a simultaneously alluring and repelling challenge. Alluring, because of the irresistible questions "Why?" and "What did it mean?" Repelling, because the means to be used and the route to discernment and confirmation in addressing those questions are rarely obvious, intrinsically contentious, and more usually than not, especially in preliterate contexts, apt to end in ambiguity. Archaeological objects and other evidence of actions suggestive of ritual and ceremony tantalize their discoverers and tease the imagination of anyone with a sense of wonder. And that indicts just about everybody.

But archaeologists having any training in ethnology or ethnography may be fortunate in the availability of suggestive parallels recorded in still extant or just recently extinguished cultural practices. Yet these must be employed cautiously. Analogical reasoning can provide valuable inspiration, although it cannot "prove" anything. It can, however, spur the search for independent support that may prove decisive. Unfortunately, the latter is usually hard to come by. Independent evidence is apt to be more coy than the claims made for it. And therein lies the endemic dilemma of extracting from archaeological vestiges of symbolic actions—or more correctly, reading into them—what their now silent practitioners thought they were doing. Those original practices themselves may incorporate booby traps: ambiguous, confused, disguised, or multiple meanings qualifying, diluting, or even corrupting the messages supposedly conveyed by outwardly similar signs and actions. Politics, history, and the literature of ethnology, ethnography, sociology, and psychology are filled with examples inviting heed. Even though archaeologists should not assume that the thoughts and actions of people in other times and places are any easier to "read" than they are in the here and now, they sometimes conduct themselves as though they do. On the other hand, the dilemma facing archaeologists is not absolute. There is no warrant for the presumption that those "thoughts and actions of people in other times and places" are irrevocably beyond the comprehension of people in our time and place. Common humanity and the consequent sharing of some filaments of cultural evolution argue otherwise. That that possibility of comprehension is limited rather than unconditional does not vitiate its value. In the words of Van Austin Harvey (1966:17) in discussing Christian theological history: "In what sense does the historian necessarily assume the principle of analogy, the similarity of the past to the present? If he does, what does this do to traditional belief? If he does not, in what sense can we talk about probability and improbability at all?"

As an archaeologist, I can appreciate the commonly self-imposed pressure to "make sense" of the symbolic world of past societies. Few people can look at a rock painting, a mound group, an excavated site feature containing exotic artifacts, or a set of human bones rearticulated out of anatomical order and not wonder what it means. What was going on here? What were these people doing? What did it mean to them—and why? How can one ever know?

Maybe it is not possible to know in any given instance. If not, then perhaps a reasoned guess will do as a start and be better than nothing, psychologically anyway. And even a guess may lead serendipitously to something more tangible. There are many paths to the worthwhile, although it is always wisest to test the ground before selecting one to the exclusion of the others. Unfortunately, there is often little choice, and what is available is "chosen" if immobility is to be avoided. As just indicated, there are sources that may supply hints, if not answers. Should there be grounds for positing some continuity between certain archaeological remains and later people represented in explorers', missionaries', or ethnographers' accounts, the information contained in those sources may throw light into archaeological corners. Maybe "elders" or other "traditional people" still living retain oral traditions that can do just that. Archaeologists, after all, can use all the help they can get, particularly when dealing with the symbolic realm. But just how to assay success in attaining reliable information in so elusive and potentially deceptive a field of investigation is itself difficult to pin down. It does not infrequently seem that observers as well as participants in research conducted in this field are inclined to hold more flexible standards of credibility than is generally the case in other types of archaeological research. Few hold its practitioners to the same degree of rigor expected of colleagues in, say, stratigraphic, seriational, or associational analysis, faunal identification and paleoenvironmental reconstruction, or even ceramic or lithic typology. Doubtless, many would declare comparable stringency unlikely if not impossible of realization because the subject matter is so inherently evasive. Nevertheless, interest in "symbolic archaeology" is understandably lively. Unlike some of the procedures by which it is pursued, the subject itself is a legitimate branch of scholarly inquiry, hence the concerns expressed in the following pages. The focus here, of course, is with serious scholarship, not the impressionistic rationalizations of dilettantes or charlatans of the popular press.

As was characteristic of another enthusiasm, that of the hyperdiffusionists of the late nineteenth and early twentieth centuries, too much of this genre treats analogies as proofs and similarities, "correspondences" and "parallels," as evidence establishing genetic, that is, historical, connections between the here and now and the there and then. Such conclusions, while doubtless valid in many cases, are prudentially best considered tentative or potentially spurious, no matter how attractive they may be, until subjected to confirmatory independent tests. The diverse cultural elements marshaled in many such studies are usually reliably reported, I believe, even if taken out of context. What is often wanting in positing "connections" among such data, however, is explicit justification or due consideration of the adequacy of linking arguments. This want is perhaps most glaring when ethnographic data are enlisted to decipher the "hidden meanings" (metaphoric, figurative, allegorical) that may be asserted to inhere in otherwise symbolically intractable archaeological artifacts. Such decipherments resemble gossamer threads flung across geographical, linguistic, or sociocultural chasms, sometimes with breathtaking indifference to temporal hiatus. It often happens, of course, that what is intended thereby is simply suggestion, something to stir up useful conjecture in the hope of learning something more tangible. Unfortunately, contributors to this enterprise frequently fail to make their intentions clear. But in any case, it is as incumbent on symbolic researchers as on any others to explicitly assist their audience in distinguishing between conclusions put forward as believed to be genuinely consequent on available evidence as opposed to those merely entertained as possibilities. Ultimately, of course, the onus lies with the reader. But in so potentially treacherous a field of investigation as inquiring into the meaning and historicity of symbols and symbolic praxis, the unknowns, unknowables, and uncertainties are pervasive enough to tax the most fair-minded without also requiring them to have to guess what the writer means to say. Is he or she serious or simply throwing out hunches in the hope that maybe one of them will eventually be snagged by an as yet unrecognized fact? While either intention is warrantable, of course, it is just that the reader is entitled to know exactly what is on offer.

A Hopi "Magician" and a "Ho-Chunk" Culture Hero

In an earlier work (Mason 2000), I critically examined the claims of two experienced archaeologists to having discovered the probable symbolic import of certain finds they had made (McGregor 1943; Salzer 1987, 1993, 1997). Omitting most of the details presented in that previous publication, suffice it to say that upon inspection the two claims enjoyed unequal support from autonomous sources of information. In McGregor's case, one commonly cited by proponents of historical veracity in oral traditions, several Hopi Indians, not previously familiar with what they were about to see, seemed able to identify the ceremony responsible for the accouterments accompanying an approximately 800-year-old burial that archaeologist had excavated at the Ridge Ruin site near Flagstaff, Arizona. At the time of their identification, the Hopis said that particular ceremony had been abandoned for half a century. What bestowed credibility on their seeming recognition of what they were shown was their detailed description of certain other artifacts they had not yet been shown but which, they maintained, would have been expectable in such a burial. These artifacts were not so simple or common as to be readily guessed at. When McGregor then produced them for their inspection, they were essentially as predicted. Barring unacknowledged prior information by the Hopis of all that the archaeological field crew had found, and McGregor was convinced otherwise, the Ridge Ruin episode provided impressive evidence of continuity of symbolic meaning in an oral cultural tradition sufficient to spark recognition over a span of eight centuries.

In the second case alluded to, the almost surgical excavation of a rock-shelter in the Driftless Area of southwestern Wisconsin made it possible to date rock paintings at that place to about a thousand years ago (Salzer 1987, 1993, 1997; Salzer and Rajnovich 2001). The pictographs were interpreted by their excavator and by Robert L. Hall, an independent anthropological student of native legends, as depictions of characters and actions in a Winnebago (Ho-Chunk, Hochungara) oral tradition concerning one Red Horn, or He Who Wears Human Heads As Earrings. On that basis the claim was made that "at least some of the stories of the modern Winnebago people were being told a thousand years ago" (Salzer 1993:95) and that "both [archaeological discoveries and ethnographic data] agree that some of these [Winnebago] oral traditions were handed down in recognizable form over a period of at least a thousand years" (Salzer and Rajnovich 2001:69). This is a strong claim, and it needs strong support. If the symbols painted on the walls of the Gottschall rockshelter really do tell in recognizable fashion the same story first recorded by the ethnographer Paul Radin (1948) in the early twentieth century, then why not accept as equally valid similarly ancient "historical" traditions of the alleged ancestors of the Winnebagoes or any other people (see next chapter)? Of course, one would first have to disentangle the fabulous from the plausible, Robert Lowie's earlier reviewed misgivings about futility notwithstanding, and the metaphorical from the merely opaque—intimidating challenges in themselves (see Mason 2000: 257; Radin 1923:79–85). But in this case, at least at first glance, one need not be too demanding. After all, the Red Horn myth is not overtly touted as a piece of ancient history. However, its interpreters believe they have discerned authentic historical implications in it—as in their identifying the "ideological ancestors" (Salzer and Rajnovich 2001:69) of the modern Winnebagoes in the prehistoric Effigy Mound culture. Salzer and Rajnovich, along with some other archaeologists, consider it likely that that culture was at least partly ancestral to the (still prehistoric) Oneota culture that *itself* is thought to have given rise to the historical Winnebago tribe (see Hall 1993, but also R. Mason 1993). Perhaps they are right. But even if they are not, and the historical allusions they perceive in the Red Horn mythology are simply projections of their own imaginations, the identification of that story with the pictographs in the Gottschall rockshelter, *if it comes to be accepted as justified by other researchers,* would then be seen as providing ancillary support to those willing to grant historical veracity to comparably old oral traditions anywhere else.

But the alleged correspondence of the pictographs with the Red Horn story is undemonstrated. And the antiquity of that story is not independently known. Maybe there is such a correspondence and such alleged antiquity and maybe there is not. With present information it is impossible to know. What has been shown is an intriguing possibility that eludes ratification. But possibility should not be conflated with anything more than plausibility. After all, the figures in the paintings would be compatible with many other recorded legends and doubtless with many more extinct ones as well. The presence of overpaintings indicates at least two periods of pictographic activity. Were all of the figures thought to be relevant to the Red Horn mythology painted concurrently as an intentional composition or were they simply sporadic creations of individuals? The cave's excavators strongly incline to the former interpretation, although they admit some uncertainty (Salzer and Rajnovich 2001:17–18). It is important to stress in this connection that the rockshelter has yielded artifacts and other features, including specially prepared artificial soils, that have led to its being called a "shrine." However that may be, the supposition that the Gottschall site records the Red Horn mythology appears to be in the process of reification, increasing numbers of writers referring to it as if it were a settled matter (e.g., Benn 1995:121; Birmingham and Eisenberg 2000:67, 119, 121, 149). Perhaps some day it will be. In the meantime, it is evident that the Red Horn "identification" of the pictographs has driven the interpretation of the archaeological evidence rather than the other way around.

The Long-Nosed God

A number of archaeologists believe that the Red Horn mythology has historical ties with a class of small copper, bone, or shell masklike objects from Mississippian and closely related cultures along a broad north-south axis in the central United States. In the form of a miniature stylized anthropomorphic head, these "Long-Nosed God maskettes," as they are usually called, typically feature cleft foreheads and exaggerated noses. That they were worn as ear ornaments is evident from their position in graves and depictions of their placement on human heads inscribed on shell gorgets, done in repoussé on copper plates, and painted on rockshelter or cave walls. A challenging study by James R. Duncan and Carol Diaz-Granados (2000) has attempted to transfuse meaning into these remnants of prehistoric ideology from oral traditions garnered in the ethnographic literature, notwithstanding a centuries-long hiatus between them. In justifying their laudable aim, the authors note that "to suggest that specific artifact types can be linked to an oral tradition, to infer completeness to a group of objects which heretofore have largely been viewed as isolated, amenable only to description, is an approach that is gaining acceptance by scholars" (Duncan and Diaz-Granados 2000:1).

Quite apart from whatever relevance the Red Horn stories may have (Hall 1997:145–154), the larger issue of searching out ideological connotations of a specific class of strictly prehistoric artifacts is a challenging pursuit onto treacherous ground. As implied earlier in this chapter, it is difficult to know whether to admire or pity those who attempt it. Both verbs find support in the present study, and they tend to keep intimate company.

Duncan and Diaz-Granados display admirable familiarity with ethnographic studies, drawing as they do on Osage, Hidatsa, Crow, Caddo, Pawnee, Kansa, Ponca, Quapaw, and some other oral traditions about twins. They also command the relevant archaeological data. Their study is an exercise of lively and informed imagination, as exhibited, for example, in their proposed equating of the symbolism—by which is meant "the meaning"—of Long-Nosed God ear ornaments with that of the "Thunderers" in certain oral traditions. These virtues, however, are not built upon by laying out linking arguments that lead in a step-by-step logical progression to the authors' conclusions. The latter are thus no more than tantalizing plausibilities rather than probabilities. They lack sufficient or necessary connections between ethnographic and archaeological data to warrant confidence. Operationally, if not explicitly, the assumption is simply made of isomorphism between certain recorded versions of an *ethnographically known* oral tradition and the beliefs of an *archaeological* population. For example, with no bridging argument, the same beliefs of a single modern Osage clansman are retroactively attributed to the prehistoric makers of the Long-Nosed God maskettes (Duncan and Diaz-Granados 2000:9). Similarly, the maskettes are declared to "represent a specific set of beings found in oral traditions recorded in numerous ethnographic accounts" (Duncan and Diaz-Granados 2000:3). This declaration, while it may be true, is also undemonstrated.

An accompanying handicap of this kind of symbolic speculation is that it leads too facilely to a belief that one knows more than one does—or, perhaps more regrettably, that its consumers will think they have learned something. Thus are variations in size and shape of maskette noses said to be statements about the social status, the state of adoption or nonadoption, or the death and even "resurrection" of persons thought to be signified by them (Duncan and Diaz-Granados 2000:10–11). Leaps of faith like this invite skepticism rather than approbation, even while acknowledging good intentions.

Reading Effigy Mounds, Hopewell Earthworks, and Finding Mesoamerica

Among the most alluring subjects for symbolic interpretation are the earth sculptures of the Effigy Mound culture of Wisconsin and adjacent portions of Iowa and Illinois. In their excellent review of the history of mound studies in Wisconsin, Robert A. Birmingham and Leslie E. Eisenberg (2000:3) estimate the former existence of some 15,000 to 20,000 mounds in more than 3,000 locations. Most of them have been partly or even totally eradicated by development since the early nineteenth century. Relatively few have survived intact. Although collectively representing perhaps two millennia of construction activity, the great majority of these mounds, including many of the round and linear-shaped ones believed to be associated with those formed as silhouettes of animals or mythological beings, are assignable to the Late Woodland Effigy Mound culture of circa A.D. 500–700 to 1100–1200.

Assuming the correctness of the latter date range, some four or five centuries separate the cessation of effigy mound building and the first meetings of Indians and Europeans in the upper Midwest. But because, aside from fragments of hearsay, it was not until the late nineteenth century and well into the twentieth century that the first upper Midwest tribal ethnographies were written and most of their oral traditions collected, that hiatus between historically known and prehistoric aboriginal societies effectively expands to about seven centuries. Notwithstanding that lacuna, the archaeological literature contains such asseverations as, for one example, "the Ho-Chunk (among others, perhaps even the Menominee) retained major aspects of an ancient belief system and social structure that *can be traced back to the mound builders*" (Birmingham and Eisenberg 2000:141; my italics). This conviction is difficult to reconcile with its proponents' depiction of the results of the European arrival:

> Of any time in the eventful and dramatic history of Native Americans, contact with Europeans was the most catastrophic. Within a comparatively brief period, as much as 80 percent of the indigenous population of North America died from infectious diseases [for a refutation of population losses anywhere approaching such a figure see Henige 1990]. Whole tribes probably disappeared, and entirely new tribes were created by the survivors. . . . So much cultural disruption occurred during the early part of the historic period that it is frequently difficult to connect known tribes to their prehistoric ancestors. Archaeologist Carol Mason [1976:335] characterized this break in the record as an "archaeological Grand Canyon, more easily looked across than spanned or jumped" [Birmingham and Eisenberg 2000:173].

Despite the testimony of sixteenth-century Spanish explorer-adventurers in the southeastern United States that some of its inhabitants built earthen mounds, a majority of later European colonists and their descendants were puzzled by the numbers and varieties of such structures they encountered in their expansion into the midcontinent. Of course, the Spanish accounts, let alone translated published versions of them, were rare and generally unknown to the majority of those colonists, French, English, Dutch, and so on. The colonists not only did not themselves observe Indians constructing such earthworks, but they were also inclined to regard those people as insufficiently organized, skilled, or motivated to have been their builders.

Furthermore, the natives themselves commonly denied knowledge of their authorship, or they attributed them to unknown, usually ancient, or even alien people. These hints of a possibly earlier population dispossessed of its domain by the forebears of the present Indians were not unwelcome to these new claimants of the lands beyond the Appalachian Mountains. The latter could comfort themselves that the tracts they were taking from the Indians had previously been taken from still others now unknown. Out of such circumstances were fantasies generated about the mounds and other earthworks having been the products of a lost non-Indian race. Candidates for that romantic status were not wanting. Included among them were ancient Israelites, Canaanites, Phoenicians, Irish monks, royal Welsh expatriates, and Vikings (Feder 1990:95–114; Silverberg 1968). Extraterrestrials and other contenders would be nominated later.

Although not all speculation about the identity of the "Mound Builders" dismissed Native Americans from the list of possibilities, it was not until the last quarter of the nineteenth century that the latter prevailed over their competitors. A number of factors contributed to this outcome, principally among them systematic archaeological investigation. Culminating this achievement was the publication of Cyrus Thomas's monumental "Report on the Mound Explorations of the Bureau of Ethnology." This made its appearance as the *Twelfth Annual Report of the Bureau of American Ethnology for 1890–91* (Thomas 1894).

In fact, J. W. Powell, the director of the Smithsonian Institution's Bureau of Ethnology, later the Bureau of American Ethnology, under whose auspices Cyrus Thomas was engaged, had been persuaded before Thomas himself that none other than American Indians had been the Mound Builders: "With regard to the mounds so widely scattered between the two oceans, it may also be said that mound-building tribes were known in the early history of discovery of this continent, and that the vestiges of art discovered do not excel in any respect the arts of the Indian tribes known to history. There is, therefore, no reason for us to search for an extra-limital origin through lost tribes for the arts discovered in the mounds of North America" (Powell 1881:74).

It is one of the chief ironies of the lengthy controversy over the identification of the builders of the ancient earthworks that most Indians contributed as much as non-Indians to confusing the issue Thomas was trying to clarify and, if possible, answer. The Indians themselves, as already indicated, either exhibited little interest and less knowledge about them or consigned them to unknown ancients or to "remembered" fictitious and even preternatural agents. Some Cherokees in the early 1800s, for example, while denying knowing who had built the mounds in their domains in

Tennessee and the Carolinas, credited their own ancestors with having constructed those in the Ohio Valley (John Haywood cited in Silverberg 1968:56–57). This accreditation kept even Cyrus Thomas confused. Archaeology has since dated the Ohio Valley mounds to several centuries before and after the time of Christ and to the activities of the Adena and Hopewell cultures. According to Delaware Indian oral traditions recorded in the 1770s by the missionary-scholar John Heckewelder, those people's eastward-migrating ancestors had once waged a bloody war with the Ohio mound builders, a race of giants, who then fled down the Mississippi River never to be seen or heard of again (Silverberg 1968:54–56).

Well before his definitive 1894 mound research conclusions were published, Thomas had repeatedly made note of the confused nature of Indian opinions regarding the mounds and their makers. In addition to his own witnessing of this state of affairs, he drew on those of his eminent scholarly predecessors, not least among them the eighteenth-century traveling naturalist from Philadelphia William Bartram and the nineteenth-century professional land surveyor and pioneer antiquarian Increase Lapham (Thomas 1887:22, 82, 87). In the words of the latter, based on his own repeated observations, "They [the present Indians in Wisconsin] extended their cultivation over the mounds with as little feeling of respect as is manifested by men of the race who are now fast destroying them" (Lapham 1855:89–90). Furthermore, he wrote, "If the present tribes have no traditions running back as far as the times of Allouez [1622–1689] and Marquette [1637–1675], or even to the more recent time of Jonathan Carver [1710–1780], it is not strange that none should exist in regard to the mounds, which must be of much earlier date" (Lapham 1855:89–90). Regardless of reported Indian indifference and evident ignorance, Lapham maintained that it had been "the ancestors of the present tribes of Indians" who had constructed the effigy and other mounds he had measured and mapped in Wisconsin. The only possible exception to this insightful generalization he would allow was the great Aztalan site near Madison whose earthen pyramids he thought might represent the work of "a colony of Mexicans" (Lapham 1855:50).

A further irony in all of this is that a mere half century after Lapham published his landmark work, the ethnographer Paul Radin credited the historic Winnebago (Ho-Chunk) tribe with "unquestionably" having constructed the famous effigy mounds, the age of which is now known through radiocarbon dating and other archaeological evidence to be strictly prehistoric. Not only did Radin attribute to Winnebago informants the basis for his assertion that those people had made the mounds—most of them in the eighteenth century—he even reported having been told by some of "the older people" that they had "distinct recollections of the erection of some of them" (Radin 1923:79–80). James B. Griffin, who was always suspicious of these assertions, was told by his fellow archaeologist W. C. McKern, one-time director of the Milwaukee Public Museum, that when he had "asked the people with whom Radin had worked how they knew their ancestors had built the Effigy Mounds they replied that Radin told them that was the case" (Griffin 1995:15–16).

And in perhaps the greatest irony of all, as the following paragraphs will suggest, descendants and contemporaries of the Winnebagoes who, according to Radin, attributed the effigy and many other mounds to their ancestors, also began to interpret their symbolic meanings to antiquarians and archaeologists who inquired about them. The denial by their earliest historic period ancestors that they knew anything about the mounds has itself come to be denied by their own descendants. This is not only an irony; it is a quandary for archaeologists:

> In the case of Radin and the Winnebago, his stature as an ethnographer casts a long shadow and throws the cloak of authority over whatever else he was doing besides his own ethnographic business. Archaeologists lean on the bits and pieces of possibly pertinent information, using them to support one or another interpretation of their archaeological data. . . . Radin's collection of 20th-century memories may or may not represent earlier Winnebago culture at all. To agree with those recollections when they are useful and ignore them when they are not gives archaeologists a convenient authority to appeal to but no way of demonstrating that their analogies are correct: connections between modern ethnography and even 18th century Winnebago life have not been established [C. Mason 1985:100].

The effigy mounds, in addition to sometimes enclosing burials, have been variously diagnosed as defensive earthworks by numerous observers, including many of Paul Radin's own Winnebago informants (Radin 1923:82). They have also been nominated as astronomical alignments; territorial boundary markers of lineages, bands, or some other unit of society; clan or phratry identifiers; ceremonial centers fostering social cohesion; symbolic representations of cosmology; attempts to ensure or restore balance and harmony in the world, that is, to function as "world-renewal" structures; or as combining several of these and conceivably still other purposes concurrently or alternately. Running the gamut from the absurd to the reasonable, even the most ethnographically plausible of these extra-inhumation functions should not be accepted as anything more than provisional interpretations, notwithstanding the enthusiasm with which they are often promulgated.

Numbers of researchers have made serious systematic attempts to decipher the symbolism of the several recurring shapes of effigy mounds (see the numerous references to the influential work of people like Charles E. Brown, Robert L. Hall, R. Clark Mallam, Paul Radin, and Chandler W. Rowe, among others, in Birmingham and Eisenberg 2000:109–136). In many of the earlier studies "identifications" of the mounds were based on how they looked to modern observers: for example, "bird" mounds, "bear" mounds, "catfish" mounds, "panther" mounds, and so on. The subjectivity of the resulting classifications inevitably led to a search for help from a presumed authoritative source: American Indians themselves as the generic if not direct descendants of the mound builders. Their knowledge and opinions, not always equivalent, while they had long been noted, came to be more consistently sought after on the grounds that *their* way of looking at things could be beneficial in correcting ethnocentric misperceptions of the symbolism embodied in the mound shapes. Indians have thus been consulted in the flesh or via their oral histories and traditions. Archaeologists have also sought clues to mound and artifact symbolism by searching for parallels in designs found on beadwork, painted on shields, woven in mats or baskets, carved on masks, and so on in museum ethnographic collections where the meanings of such designs may be included in the cataloguing documentation. All of these endeavors have their uses. They do not, however, abolish the barriers standing between the times represented by written history and ethnography on the one hand and prehistoric archaeology on the other.

Calling upon his impressive command of much of the pertinent ethnographic and ethnohistorical literature and on the opinions of a few "well-informed" Indians as reported by such early students of effigy mounds as Charles E. Brown and Arlow B. Stout, Robert L. Hall (1993:42–44) feels able to identify many of the tumuli of the Effigy Mound culture as corresponding to certain named clans of the Winnebago Indians some 7 to 14 centuries later. I have calculated this interval as bracketed by the best current estimates of the tenure of the Effigy Mound culture and the time for which the historical Winnebagoes supposedly spoke for themselves at the dawn of the twentieth century in interviews with the above-cited interlocutors and the ethnographer Paul Radin. Although a regional facies of the Oneota culture fills a good part of that lengthy interval, and many archaeologists, Hall sporadically among them, believe that latter culture to be the proximate prehistoric ancestor of the Winnebago Indians, there are no effigy mounds known for the span of time thus occupied. These considerations notwithstanding, Hall argues for a genetic (historical) correlation between bird-shaped effigy mounds and the Winnebago Warrior clan because an alternate name for the latter was Hawk; some of the bird-shaped mounds may have been meant to represent those raptors. On the other hand, Hall also suggests that bird-shaped effigy mounds might signal the ancient presence of a Thunder clan on the grounds that such clans were present in a number of historically known midwestern tribes that "associated" them with thunderbirds. Moreover, many of the non-effigy-shaped mounds, including simple round and oval ones, are asserted to also be thunderbird representations, though simplified by the omission of diagnostic features. The Winnebagoes also had a Water Spirit clan. This totem "was a medicine animal with antlers and a very long tail" (Hall 1993:42). Neighboring tribes envisioned the Water Spirit as a horned panther. Notwithstanding the absence of anything that might be construed as horns or antlers, Hall believes the Winnebago Water Spirit clan "could justifiably be compared both to the 'panther' and the 'turtle' forms of long-tailed effigies" (Hall 1993:42). More than that, he says, it is a "rather obvious fact that many linear mounds were only highly stylized panther mounds in which the long tail came to dominate the outline" (Hall 1993:44).

Another specimen of the same genre is by the same author, certainly one of the most influential thinkers in this difficult field (Hall 1997). But again, historically minded critical readers must deal with simultaneously ingenious and stochastic reasoning. This example concerns the use of symbolic interpretation as a means to construct an empathic superstructure atop what Hall has sometimes construed the product of archaeological research to be: "the soulless artifact of a dehumanized science" (Hall 1976:363). A small part of a tour de force volume of essays appropriately titled *An Archaeology of the Soul*, the example I have selected is typical of the author's search for integration among discrete bits of information painstakingly garnered from archaeological and ethnological sources. But judging his success in the enterprise unfortunately requires the reader's trust in the author's often called upon faculty to recognize and correctly decipher metaphors in the conceptual systems of defunct societies as presumably reflected in their archaeological debris. Dealing among other things with certain pre–Effigy Mound culture earthworks in Ohio attributed to the Middle Woodland Hopewell culture, the pertinent essay, "The Sweat Bath and Related Female Metaphors" (Hall 1997:124–131), is briefly summarized here because it helps in assaying the speculative logic that led to some of the problematic conclusions in the previous case. How much of historical verisimilitude is to be granted is dependent on that assay.

Hall introduces his chapter with a brief discourse on the distribution and functions of the sweat bath or lodge. The primacy of heat in such structures is analogous to cooking and thus to physical transformations that, Hall argues, following Claude Lévi-Strauss in the latter's *The Raw and the Cooked* (1969), a text he cites, prompted mental associations that became metaphorically transferred to social relations. Thus the boy who is called Scarface in a Blackfoot myth is transformed when he joins Morning Star and the Sun (the latter's father) in a sweat lodge. Scarface there loses his scar and becomes indistinguishable from Morning Star. This story is "paralleled," says Hall, in two Mesoamerican myths about the birth of the sun. In the first, a Huichol story, a physically handicapped son of the moon is consumed in an oven, revives, and becomes the sun. The second myth is Aztec. In this one, a disfigured man jumps into a hearth, reidentified by Hall as a sweat bath, at Teotihuacán, is consumed, but revives as the sun. A version of this story completes the metamorphosis after the protagonist, revived in the fire, jumps into a pool of cold water. This last action, being a Blackfoot practice as well, is offered as a relevant piece of ethnographic information. Similarly, the reader is informed that some authorities at the Maya site of Palenque in Chiapas have suggested that three temple-associated rooms at that place "probably" were meant to represent the sweat baths in which were born the gods of the Palenque Triad. While it seems clear that these "parallels" are thought to have genetic, in the sense of historical, implications, the question of analogies or homologies is never directly confronted. That is, the reader is never presented with a coherent argument dismissing autochthonous origins in favor of diffusion from an assumed common source. The latter is always implied. But then Hall goes on to draw attention to sun origin myths among the Australian aborigines, among the ancient Egyptians, and in the Finnish *Kalevala* epic. With the possible exception of the last (see below), it seems unlikely that even so committed a diffusionist as Hall means to posit a single genesis for all. But maybe he does.

Reading certain Lakota and Ojibwa myths as supporting evidence, Hall interprets the North American sweat bath lodge to be a "uterine metaphor," a "portal" giving access to a different world or state of being. He reintroduces the currently unfashionable theory of trans–North Atlantic diffusion, in this instance with respect to the sweat bath specifically. Without endorsing either alternative, he suggests a west-to-east transmission is as much a possibility as the older preference for its opposite. This matter aside, a veritable web of ostensibly relevant ethnographic and archaeological cultural traits is then woven to make hand and paw depictions, or their alleged simplified surrogates—and not only sweat bath structures—into female metaphors. Among these traits are certain designs, themes, and other elements drawn from Omaha facial painting, Adena stone tablets, Hopewellian ceramic vessels, Hopewell copper tubes and bone artifacts, Plains Sun Dance structures, the widespread Earth Diver mythology, the motif of the toothed vagina, stories from the Maya *Popol Vuh,* Winnebago Medicine Society ritual language, body painting associated with the Mandan Okipa Society, fire drilling both among the Pawnees and as depicted in the Maya Dresden Codex, and the Ollin glyph on the famous Aztec Calendar Stone. These and much else, or the metaphors they are asserted to represent, are interpreted as demonstrating "a continuity of thought and belief for more than two thousand years" (Hall 1997:129). Either deducing from or using as another confirmatory instance of this type of reasoning—it is impossible to tell which is intended—Hall feels confident in identifying a section of a Hopewell earthwork in Butler County, Ohio, as representing a vulva and, thus, a symbol for a portal (Hall 1997:129). Similarly, because, as he says, a bear paw can serve, like the human hand, by analogy, as "a natural female metaphor," Hall partakes of what he claims to be the Hopewellian "perception" of a bear paw as a female metaphor in a stone enclosure on Black Run in Ross County, Ohio (Hall 1997:128). This is an awesome assertion. But is it credible? After all, even Sigmund Freud is alleged to have observed that sometimes a cigar is simply a cigar.

Earlier, I quoted part of Robert Hall's melancholy objection to archaeology as "soulless," as simply "a dehumanized science." I did this to show an important component of the motivating energy behind his and many others' endeavors to access the time-obscured meanings underlying archaeological remains: the understandable desire to get closer to the humanity responsible for those remains. But I had another object or two in mind as well. I have, as mentioned elsewhere in this book, both read and heard innumerable complaints of other critics of archaeology about its "cold" and "impersonal" scientific nature; its "clinical detachment" from, "objectification" of, and "insensitive" and even "exploitative" handling of ancient human remains and artifacts; and its ethnocentric agenda in the "colonizing appropriation" of other people's pasts by the "disrespectful" subordination of Native American "ways of knowing" to Western epistemology. Here I wish simply to suggest that many of those critics mistake intellectual commitment for elitist insensitivity, excavation for mining, and critical questioning of beliefs for scoffing. While cloddish individuals are to be found everywhere, they do not deserve confusing with the generality of archaeologists. Those accusing archaeologists of dehumanizing the subject of their discipline should reflect on the possibility that the very enterprise of scientific investigations into the human past is a form of homage to that past and the people time has consigned to it. The effort that it requires, the striving to minimize error, and the perpetual burden of doubt about the very possibility of ever getting it right are in themselves testimony to the seriousness of that homage. Archaeologists may not always give voice to such matters, but I think their efforts to wrest knowledge from the speechless informants constituting the prehistoric record in the form of sediments, bones, artifacts, and ruins testify to the authenticity of the commitment.

Nevertheless, Hall has touched a sensitive nerve. The study of symbolism in archaeology, and particularly in the pursuit of culture history, is no less important because of its difficulty. Regardless of its shortcomings on which I have been harping, doubtless to the irritation of many of my colleagues, archaeologists cannot in conscience ignore its enlightening potential. They are obliged to persevere in their efforts to supplement—perhaps someday even to replace—informed conjectures and inspired hunches with arguments that are severe upon leaps of faith or demands for repeated suspensions of disbelief. That obligation to persevere is mandated by the ethnographically and historically attested fact that human beings perceive symbols to be as imperative to their survival as food. Symbols permeate human life. And like human life itself, they are subject to change over the course of their "lifetimes." Their signification is likewise mutable, especially when communicated orally across generations. It would be an unwarranted assumption to presume that a silhouette of, say, a fish etched or painted on a cliff face was meant solely as a representation of the taxon *Pisces* and not something more—or that that something more is the same wherever and whenever it appears. Fishes and swastikas and circles and tridents and equal-armed crosses and wavy lines can be made to mean anything, even the sign of a dream or a vision; and their modern would-be "readers" can likewise read anything into them if they are handicapped, as they usually are, by ignorance of the generative context. Intimate familiarity, however, with the ceremonies and symbolism of peoples known ethnographically or through historical accounts, especially when there are grounds for postulating some continuity with particular prehistoric cultures, offers potential for insights into some of the more incorporeal aspects of those cultures than would otherwise be feasible. This commonplace of archaeological textbooks is not to be gainsaid. What needs to be added to it, as I have been implying if not insisting in foregoing paragraphs, is the requirement that, ideally, step-by-step argumentation, supported by empirical data wherever possible, should link the historical/ethnographic information with the prehistoric/archaeological data through as detailed a chain of temporal intermediaries—protohistoric sites, for example—as can be traced. Of course, the ideal will only rarely be approached, let alone attained. But the ideal should be the goal. And if it remains beyond reach, proffered historical connections between known ethnographic/historical facts and targeted prehistoric/archaeological phenomena in need of explanation should be labeled for what they are: guesses or hunches, working hypotheses, tentative conclusions, or probabilities, depending on the nature of the evidence and the logical necessity of the linking arguments. I realize that enthusiasm for one's own conclusions, or those of others that are most compatible with one's own view of things, will usually, and perhaps quite unconsciously, bypass such stringency. The penalty that must ultimately be paid—the inability of those not intimately familiar with the subject to discriminate between inspired conjecture and justified conclusions—will be exacted on the prestige of the whole endeavor.

As just intimated, there is nothing wrong and much that is right in speculative thinking about the past, provided it is offered for what it is and nothing more. Common experience in many fields has repeatedly shown how informed intellectual playing with odds and ends of information not yet fitted into a coherent body of knowledge may on occasion yield results that do so fit. In the absence of specific items of information bearing on the necessary implications of an explicit test-inviting hypothesis, simply playing around with whatever is available is a justifiable, if sloppy, potential way out of impasse, one that will perhaps lead to something capable of more demanding examination. Even a house of cards may prove useful as a model. Fortunately, more substantial stuff than that is often at hand if one knows how and where to look.

Detecting the Immaterial in Thule Eskimo Technology

Sites of the prehistoric culture archaeologists call Thule have a pan-Arctic distribution from Alaska to Greenland. The earliest date from about a thousand years ago, whereas the latest represent the proximal ancestors of the historical Eskimo people—Inuit certainly, if not the far westerly Yuit. Material and temporal evidence for this continuity is sufficient enough to endorse the assumption of language commonality as well, that is, dialects of Inupik Eskimo. And, likewise, the sharing of some symbolic content seems reasonable to suggest. Robert McGhee (1977) employed this idea to help understand the differential use of ivory and sea mammal bone versus antler in the production and use of Thule artifacts. Through an understanding of ethnographically recorded Inuit symbolism and oral traditions, McGhee was able to show that much more than availability of raw materials and what outsiders would regard as pragmatically functional considerations must have been equally salient in Thule as in historical Inuit culture and that those other determining factors were likely symbolic in nature.

Examination of Thule artifacts from a small winter village site on remote

Bathurst Island, far above the Arctic Circle in the Queen Elizabeth Islands in the central Canadian Arctic Archipelago, drew McGhee's attention to an intriguing dichotomy. Those weapons in the site assemblage used to hunt sea mammals (harpoon heads) were made exclusively from either sea mammal bone or ivory, whereas arrowheads, a terrestrial weapon for hunting caribou, were made only from antler. Because the artifact sample was small, it was necessary to check much larger collections from geographically and temporally separated Thule sites to determine whether the dichotomy held up. In relative terms, it did. At those richer Thule sites, the styles of arrowheads similar and even identical to those used by the historic Inuits to hunt caribou were both numerous and consistently manufactured of antler. Less clear-cut was the association of harpoon components with ivory and sea mammal bone. Although in a majority of cases that linkage was confirmed, confidence in it was tempered by the much smaller survival rate of such artifacts in the archaeological record due to losses on sea ice and attrition in sea mammal hunting. Very limited samples of other kinds of manufactures utilizing those three materials, however, did sort out in such a way as to lend inferential support, once ethnographic and oral tradition information suggested their relevance to McGhee's original insight. For example, components of sewing kits (needle cases, thimble holders), pendants, and combs identical to those known to be women's in Inuit society and tiny figurines combining bird and human female attributes were all made of ivory.

By and large, the particular combinations of raw materials and functional classes of artifacts in Thule assemblages were compatible with what would be expected if the symbolic code of the Inuit Eskimos regarding men and women, land and sea, summer and winter, and similar dualities, as revealed in their traditional beliefs and practices, had been those of their Thule forebears as well. Although McGhee noted that few ethnographers of the Inuit people recorded their raw material preferences in making their ornaments, weapons, and other tools, he was able to cite a couple of exceptions. Those observations seemed compatible with the distributional patterns he had detected among the Thule sites. Perhaps more important was the agreement among students of the Inuit that the most pervasive dichotomy in their perception of their environment was that of sea versus land. This was reflected in such proscriptions as making caribou skin clothing while living on sea ice, wearing items of clothing made from walrus hide when hunting on the land, and cooking caribou and seal or other sea mammal flesh in the same pot or consuming them on the same day. Among some Inuit groups at least, steatite could not be carved into oil lamps or other things while people were living on the ice, moss (also a land resource) had to be substituted for by bits of ivory to serve as walrus oil lamp wicks in the winter camps on the sea ice, and wood could not be worked during the whaling season. McGhee also saw binary oppositions in Inuit mythology whereby men or maleness was mystically associated with land and the moon while women had symbolic links to the sea: a female deity created whales and certain seals and presided on the sea floor over one of the lands of the dead. Even the seasons harbored male-female dualism. As McGhee (1977:147) suggested, Inuit cosmology might be summarized this way: "land:sea :: summer:winter :: man:woman, and perhaps :: antler:ivory (where : can be read 'is to', :: can be read 'as')."

Whether or not continuing research validates any part of McGhee's retrodiction of the symbolic content of prehistoric Thule artifacts from knowledge of historical Inuit beliefs, his strategy is to be commended for its testability. Using ethnographic data and oral traditions, he was able to identify Inuit cosmological tenets that could reasonably be expected to have consequences in the physical world. Taking advantage of credible evidence of cultural continuity with Thule material culture and being able to show how the simple availability of certain kinds of raw materials so often failed to mirror those of the artifacts whose differential distributions initially puzzled him, a failure not easily attributable to chance alone, he focused his attention on the possible physical consequences of an ancient belief system consonant with that of the descendant Inuits. The result was a more persuasive insight into a realm of culture history in that part of the world than had previously seemed feasible. There is no proof that the conclusions reached are unimpeachable of course, but they are highly tenable.

Teasing Numerological Codes Out of Prehistoric Huron Ceramics

Among the more recent attempts to "read" the symbolism in prehistoric artifacts is that of Joyce M. Wright (1999). Inspired by mystical associations with numbers among early seventeenth-century Huron Indians as alluded to by Jesuit missionaries and other French observers, Wright has proposed that the strong continuity in much of historic-period Huron material culture with that of their likely ancestors in the fourteenth-century Uren and Middleport cultures was paralleled in their nonmaterial culture as well. An important component of this orally transmitted culture that might have left a recoverable material record was their numerology, even if only tangentially expressed. Wright believes she has found such a record in the incised or trailed horizontal lines embellishing the rims on the clay cooking pots and smoking pipes of those prehistoric cultures. Instead of the variable numbers of those lines having been arbitrary, she suggests that they might have been physical expressions of conventionalized associations of certain numbers and ideas transmitted from generation to generation. The numbers of lines on Uren and Middleport ceramics are empirical archaeological facts, of course. Huron numerological symbolism is inferred from various remarks extracted from surviving historical documents. That there is a decipherable connection between the two is an inviting possibility.

Sensible of the pitfalls awaiting those who would discover the identity of symbolic intentions in prehistoric ancestors by assuming essential conformity with those of their historical descendants, Wright nevertheless builds a respectable argument in defense of this method. That it falls somewhat short of persuasive is owing to her failure to establish probable, as opposed to simply possible, linkages between Huron number symbolism and markings on Middle Ontario Iroquois stage ceramics. The numerology of the historic period Hurons, that is, their ascribing occult freight to numbers, usually has to be surmised from the not always unambiguous French references to the social and other situations in which numbers were used to convey extranumeric meanings. It is here that Wright has expended enormous effort in careful page-by-page searching through many of the volumes of *The Jesuit Relations and Allied Documents* and the index-less reports of Samuel de Champlain and Fr. Gabriel Sagard, not to mention her consulting numerous later works on the postdiaspora Hurons and on the League Iroquois in New York. Out of this effort, Wright felt able to discern clues of contextual differences in Huron number use from which she inferred their likely, or at least suggestively possible, occult associations. These proposed associations of numbers and symbolic functions totaled eight. The numerals she classified according to her associational functions are 2, 3, 4, 5, 6, 9, 10, and 12 (Wright 1999:Chapter 4 and Table 13). Other numbers defied classification because of rarity or lack of clarity or consistency regarding their use. A few specimens of these proposed linkages follow. These are presented here with Wright's functionally descriptive designations and one example (the first she listed) of the quoted French historical references that supplied the clues upon which she made her suggested associations.

2—*The Number of Creation and Ceremony.* Original reference: "Before Aataentsic fell from the Sky, there were no men on earth. However that may be, she brought forth two boys, Tawiscaron and Iouskeha" (Wright 1999:87).

3—*The Number of Balance* (this has the title "Restoration and Maintenance of Balance" in Wright's Table 13). Original reference: "Presents speak, as I have already stated. They all have their meaning. Those who deliver a prisoner of war, give him three gifts; such, for instance, as

three collars of Porcelain beads, to break the bonds that tied him,—
one by the Legs, another by the arms, and the third by the middle of
the body" (Wright 1999:94).

4—*The Number of Social Relations, Including Foreign Interaction.* Original reference: "When our lodge was erected in the Algonquin fashion
each of us chose his place in it, the four chief men in the four corners,
and the others after them, arranged side by side, rather crowded together" (Wright 1999:106).

There is a lot of potential overlapping among Wright's associational categories, as among "Restoration and Maintenance of Balance," "Restoration
and Maintenance of Balance Magnified," and "Social Restoration." This
potential also holds between "Creation and Ceremony" and almost any of
the others. Doubtless, as she suggests, the same number might have serviced
more than one associational category, depending on time, place, circumstance, and the sophistication of the enumerator (see below).

However reasonable the attempt to tease out suggested occult meanings
in number usage among the Hurons and the segregating of those meanings
into numeric classes, retroactively crediting them to the Uren and Middleport people of the Middle Ontario Iroquois stage calls for ingenuity in testing. As just mentioned, Wright has tackled this challenge by postulating
nonrandomness in the numbers of horizontal lines pot makers, believed to
have been women, and clay smoking pipe makers, thought to have been
men, incised or trailed on their respective products. With relatively few exceptions, the percentage frequencies of numbers of lines on ceramic vessels were similar from site to site, thus indicating widely shared customary
behavior among their makers. But it is, of course, a big step to derive a
message-bearing code from such behavior. The variable numbers of horizontal lines were selected for study because of their presence on rimsherds
large enough to preserve complete rim designs in sufficient quantities to
allow counts of original whole vessels and pipes. When garnered from her
sample of culturally relevant sites, they were numerous enough to satisfy her
demanding statistical standards. In an important caution, Wright suggested
that the same number of horizontal lines—or their absence altogether—may
not have carried the same message on cooking vessels as on smoking pipes.

A few examples will serve to illustrate some of the problems intrinsic to
extrapolating from uncertainly grasped historic Huron numerological beliefs to those of their prehistoric forerunners in the Middle Ontario Iroquois cultural stage. Wright concluded from her search of the early documents that six is the number the Hurons seemed to associate with health
and sustenance. There is no known comparable association of food or cook-

ing and a specific number. She suggests, in a hedging qualification, that the presence of six horizontal lines on the neck of a ceramic vessel might indirectly appertain to food, food in either its sustenance or curative role, because the presence of food is implied by "health and sustenance." It should be noted, however, that some shamanistic practices also relate to curing (the restoration of health) but that such activities appear to be linked with the number five ("sorcerous communication" in her taxonomy of number symbolism). Instead of or in addition to the foregoing, a case might be made for associating the number four, said to be concerned with social and foreign relations, with feasts, an important part of those relations, and thus again betokening food. In this last possible connection Wright observed that the Hurons had *four* types of feasts and that their linguistic and cultural relatives, the Iroquois, celebrated the Green Corn Festival and the Harvest Festival, each lasting *four* days (Wright 1999:153–154).

Although clay pots were the common cooking vessel during the Middle Ontario Iroquois stage, and those with three horizontal lines were the most popular variety (except at the Nodwell site), "the early historic data provided no indication of a particular relationship between the number three and food" (Wright 1999:157). This curious discrepancy is therefore rationalized to comport with the "restoration and maintenance of balance" ascribed to number three on the grounds that food "restores and maintains human well-being" (Wright 1999:157). In a similar manner, because vessels inscribed with four lines are the most common alternative to three-lined vessels, even though the number four is supposed to be connected with both intratribal and intertribal social relations, a symbolic association with food can be suggested, as was done in the preceding paragraph (Wright 1999: 164). And while three- and four-lined vessels, especially when their frequencies are combined, were by far the most popular vessels, among smoking pipes that preeminence was occupied by plain undecorated ones. The latter fact is explained by "the speculation that they represent those times when the men just wanted to smoke without sending any symbolic 'messages'" (Wright 1999:164–165). And those other times? Is it to be supposed that men kept sets of variously lined pipes to smoke at those other, presumably message-signaling, times? One is also prompted to ask why women seemed always concerned to send symbolic messages when engaged in the everyday chore of cooking. And for whom were the messages intended?

There are other enigmas in this semiological exercise that are not diminished by suppositions that rest on ambiguous evidence or that fail to comport with contradictory empirical fact, as in the case of the number 10, the number supposedly signifying death. The famous Huron Feast of the Dead, for instance, is cited as probably having occurred every 10 years in accordance with Wright's mustering of early historical references that she credits with linking the two phenomena (Wright 1999:120–121). But almost half of her enlisted relevant citations do not concern death but healing illness, dream fulfillment associated with illness, and a man's misfortunes after having escaped from captivity. Furthermore, as she mentions, no less authoritative witnesses or contemporary commentators than Samuel de Champlain and Jean de Brebeuf thought the lapses between Feasts of the Dead were 8, 9, 10, 11, or 12 years. Possibly they varied between those extremes. Gabriel Sagard, as Wright notes, gave the intervals as approximately 10 years (Wright 1999:120–121). Even if the latter were correct, given what is known about the Feast of the Dead, it would be no warrant for interpreting the significance of the number 10 as distinctively or even primarily concerned with death itself, even though the feast lasted 10 days. It might equally, or even predominantly in Huron thinking, have had an association with time for village removal, an event sometimes coinciding with the Feast of the Dead. Other possibilities include allusions to reaffirmation of life, celebrating the indissolubility of kinship bonds, redistributions of goods, or solidarity with traditional trading partners and allies—all matters linked to that occasion (Trigger 1976:85–90, 426–429).

Unique among the 215 ceramic vessels at the Nodwell site was one from House 9 embellished with 10 horizontal lines. No human remains were found in this longhouse. Indeed, although some were present in Houses 4 and 7, they were rare throughout the site (J. V. Wright 1974:87–88). Perhaps, it was suggested, there had once been burials in House 9 but they had been removed (J. M. Wright 1999:155). Lending greater credence to the pot's alleged semantic signal for death would have been its discovery in one of the two houses where human remains were found rather than in a house where they were absent.

As just reviewed, it was the piecing together of early French hints of Huron numerology that suggested potential access to a prehistoric symbolic code. This access depends on the assumption of continuity between the two. Explicitly, the Hurons observed by the French presumably had inherited their numerology from their remembered forebears, those forebears from their own forebears, and so on in a chain of oral histories metamorphosing into a tradition—an oral and material tradition. This eminently defensible assumption of intergenerational transmittal of symbolic, not just numerological, signification is of course the basis for most interpretations of the "original meanings" of much American Indian pictography. It is intuitively appealing. Its vulnerability, apart from the obvious ones of sampling problems and accuracy in the reporting of the data initiating the retrodiction, is the assumption of sufficient fidelity in intergenerational transmission to warrant attributing to remote generations beliefs held by their recent progeny. Still requiring stronger support in the present instance, however, is the motivating presumption of intentional "message" content residing in numbers of rim-embellishing lines as opposed to unselfconscious routine in executing limited options. Even with mixed success, Wright's achievement has been to go beyond intuition and to inaugurate a means for testing at least some of the results of her hypothesis.

Hearing Echoes of a Prehistoric Puebloan Litany

Certainly one of the most self-confident recent attempts to enlist oral traditions in reconstructions of the prehistoric past, in this case through the medium of Hopi designs painted on pottery and murals and as interpreted via sacred song texts, is by Emory Sekaquaptewa, a Hopi, and Dorothy Washburn, a specialist in metaphoric thinking and visual display (2004). Given their regard for oral traditions as reliable independent sources for such purposes, notwithstanding certain inherent difficulties that they take pains to explicate, the authors appeal to those traditions in order to procure a fuller picture of the Hopi past than the archaeological record alone can provide. The past on which oral traditions are alleged to throw light, however, is not one of cultural changes or sequences of events. Rather, it is the retrojection of the Hopi people's historically documented "lifeway" and its underlying "cosmological principles" into pre-European-contact times. If the authors' analytical model should prove as trustworthy as their enthusiasm, not only Hopi archaeology will be the richer for it. According to their lengthy essay, that model is to be expanded upon in a future book.

Sekaquaptewa and Washburn (2004:483–484) emphatically reject the term *prehistoric,* employing it only when difficult to avoid and then always quarantining it in quotation marks. They do this because the prehistoric Hopis did not, "from their perspective," consider themselves prehistoric! Another reason is the authors' confidence in their own ability to "decode" the meanings of precontact Hopi painted designs with sufficient precision to permit those designs to "take their place in the infinitely varied store of human creative expression as yet another mode of recording that has been developed by 'nonliterate' peoples" (Sekaquaptewa and Washburn 2004:483–484). For the same reasons, the term *nonliterate* is also anathematized unless insulated by quotation marks, as in their foregoing statement. "Western analysts," Sekaquaptewa and Washburn (2004:484) proclaim, "persist at their own peril in the interpretation of these and other peoples throughout the world as peoples who lived before 'written' history." Thus the authors use circumlocutions and quotation marks and ignore the English dictionary, overlooking in the process that it is the present generation, not extinct ones, that has need of these terms. If useful, well-defined words are to be proscribed because they would have been incomprehensible to extinct generations, or a particular faction sees pejorative connotations that are not there, the substitution of other expressions to convey the same meanings opens the writers to their own objections. Complying with the authors' logic, people in England who died in or before the reign of William IV should not be called pre-Victorians nor Frenchmen deceased in the decades before the Revolution of 1789 be said to have lived in the last days of the ancien régime. But according to the authors, Hopis who painted a design on a pot or figures on a kiva wall were engaged in an activity tantamount to writing even if they did not know it.

"In this article," Sekaquaptewa and Washburn (2004:483) write, "we have focused on the Hopi as our example of a small puebloan group dependant on dry farming corn agriculture in order to study how oral tradition, specifically ritual song, encompasses the cosmological knowledge of a culture." Further,

> We argue that because ritual song texts embody the whole complex of cosmological ideas that frames the lifeway of puebloan agricultural peoples, they can be used as guides to reconstruct the past, for we have found the same metaphors consistently exhibited in 14th- to 16th-century kiva mural images and ceramic designs from the sites of Awatovi and Kawaika'a in the immediate area of the present Hopi villages. The same concepts are imaged in generally contemporaneous murals at the sites of Pottery Mound and Kuaua along the Rio Grande and on other ceramic designs of these centuries just prior to Western contact [Sekaquaptewa and Washburn forthcoming].

The authors explain that "our working principles are simple and stem, in fact, from those in constant use by archaeologists. Without complicated models or theories we are able to *postulate the 'prehistoric' cosmology underpinning the early agricultural communities of the Southwest* based on our understanding of the cosmological principles voiced in ritual song" (Sekaquaptewa and Washburn 2004:483–484; my italics).

The authors may have done without "complicated models or theories," but they did not spurn breathtaking leaps of faith: "We argue that consistent complexes of cosmological ideas passed down orally and visually are valid evidence for reconstructing past ideational systems of thought and action." And they argue "that the cosmological information that is *metaphorically* embedded in ritual song is also *metaphorically* reiterated in various kinds of image formats, such as precontact kiva murals and pottery design, that allow us to push our understanding of the past well beyond the beginning of tape recording of Hopi songs expressing oral traditions" (Sekaquaptewa and Washburn 2004:457; my italics). And just how is this feat accomplished?

The authors maintain that the same "cosmological information" is shared by the 125 Hopi katsina song texts or, rather, certain words and phrases in those song texts that they have analyzed. All are from the twentieth century. Those song texts, they point out, are but a fraction of what once existed: "The vast majority of Hopi ritual songs are unrecorded, and of those that are, most have not been transcribed from tape into written Hopi; nor have they been translated into English" (Sekaquaptewa and Washburn 2004:462–463). Furthermore, *each song text must also be understood as the creative expression of one individual* expressing his or her shared communal experiences *in compound song words and phrases of his or her own invention*" (Sekaquaptewa and Washburn 2004:459; my emphases). Understanding the underlying meaning of these recorded twentieth-century song words and phrases is asserted to reveal the otherwise subterranean meaning of designs and images painted on pots and walls four to six centuries earlier, that is, by people some 16 to 24 generations since removed. What makes the connection possible, Sekaquaptewa and Washburn insist, is the unchanging character of Hopi "cosmological principles" and metaphors.

Their reasoning, as distilled from many pages of not always consistent phraseology and logic, is dependent on acceptance of seven premises. These are as follows. First, "all" twentieth-century Hopis share the same "cosmological information," apparently a synonym for what others call "worldview"; second, that information is orally "embedded" in ritual song texts and visually in dance, ceremonial paraphernalia, and painted designs and images; third, the foregoing embeddedness takes the form of "symbolic meanings" that, in turn, fourth, have metaphoric functions that "promote" the guidance of Hopi life (the "basic metaphors of Hopi life"); and, fifth, the "content" of those metaphors reveals strong consistency throughout the twentieth century. Therefore, the addition of two other even more sweeping premises converts Hopi "prehistory" into recorded *history*—in the Western sense of the term. These two premises are:

> [Sixth,] well-integrated cultural systems with finely tuned universes of cultural principles and practices are always found to be guided by vibrant cosmological systems. These cosmological systems will be characterized by constancy in the metaphors that support the social institutions and ritual practices that permeate every cultural activity and

knit the culture together. Thus, we expect to find the same metaphors in other media.

. . . Our [seventh] premise is, simply, not only that *all* modes will carry and transmit these cosmological principles of life but also that they will all carry the same messages. That is, what is transmitted verbally in song will also be transmitted visually in mural image and ceramic design, as well as in other related performance means and media. Further [an eighth premise?], these cosmological systems will have time depth. Constancy in meaning and continuity in their use will thus be evident in the ethnographic present, the *historic* period, and the *prehistoric* past [Sekaquaptewa and Washburn 2004:460; my emphases of the authors' violations of their own terminological strictures].

Each song and image, it should be remembered, "embodies ideas" and is the "creation" of a different individual. Therefore, those songs, images, and embodied ideas manifest themselves "in an almost endless number of ways" (Sekaquaptewa and Washburn 2004:474–475). While "images" and "songs" appear from the way they are used to be semantically different from "ideas," it is unclear whether "idea" is a synonym for "symbol" and/or "metaphor." If the latter, a good part of the writers' asseveration of "constancy in meaning and continuity in their use" is undercut. Even if that synonymy is denied, claims that each song text and visual image is one individual's "creative" expression "of his or her own invention" and, further, that "some [individuals] are more proficient at certain of these expressive activities—song, ceramic design, mural imagery—than others" (Sekaquaptewa and Washburn 2004:462) must raise serious doubts about many of the analysts' attributions of twentieth-century Hopi metaphors to their prehistoric forebears.

It is obvious to even nonspecialists that continuities as well as changes have marked Hopi material culture through centuries. Some of those continuities may be seen in certain design elements in pottery decoration and in wall painting conventions, as the authors illustrate. However, the authors' opening argument and guiding contention "that consistent complexes of cosmological ideas passed down orally and visually [as sampled, it needs stressing, in twentieth-century renderings only] are valid evidence for reconstructing past [at least four to six centuries past] ideational systems of thought and action" (Sekaquaptewa and Washburn 2004:457) is an assertion of belief and not a "demonstration." Symbols may persist while their meanings shift, even in societies possessing securer means than the Hopis had for monitoring fidelity. The ceremonial regalia of British royalty exhibit many continuities over multiple reigns but do not thereby signify the same ideational content for Queen Elizabeth II and her subjects as subsisted in the days of the first Elizabeth. The wearing or depiction of a brimless, conical stocking cap in modern France or the United States is not the symbolic statement it was in their respective revolutions. Even at approximately the same time, assuming the correctness of Sekaquaptewa and Washburn's "decoding," Hopi paintings of identical or similar objects could have quite disparate meanings. In their "metaphorical readings," for instance, what is interpreted as a depiction of a "netted gourd" in the hand of a mural figure at Awatovi is said to be a symbol signifying water (Sekaquaptewa and Washburn 2004:460, Figure 1, and 475). But in the hand of a figure in a polychrome Sikyatki bowl the "netted gourd" represents "the proffering of prayers" (Sekaquaptewa and Washburn 2004:479, Figure 7). Of course, identical symbols may carry different semantic freight in varied contexts, as the authors point out in their discussion of the nature of metaphor (Sekaquaptewa and Washburn 2004:467). But without contextual information beyond that of ritual versus mundane settings—if even that much can be determined—and exempting, as they do, time as a consequential variable, how is one to know *the* intended meaning of an alleged visual metaphor? That this is a difficulty for the authors themselves is indicated by their frequent recourse to such qualifying phrases as "almost certainly represents," "may represent," "appears to be," "may be," and "who appears to be."

The authors employ an outmoded conception of cultures as closed systems, as boxes containing people all of whom, notwithstanding their alleged expressive creativity, come across in the authors' presentation as ideological automatons. Twentieth-century Hopi modes of thought and expressive conventions are represented as essentially identical to those prevailing centuries prior to Spanish contact. This assertion is hard to reconcile with detailed studies of Hopi archaeology, ethnohistory, and ethnography as described or referenced, for example, in Volume 9 of the Smithsonian Institution's *Handbook of North American Indians* (Ortiz 1979). Thus, in a chapter on twentieth-century Hopi history—the very century Sekaquaptewa and Washburn take as their source model from which to reconstruct Hopi cosmological and metaphoric thinking in prehistory—a quite different picture emerges. Ethnographic and historical records indicate that before the middle of that century the Hopis had seen "their whole world view undergo new and irreversible alterations" (Dockstader 1979:531). Additional cautions have earlier been addressed in the present book with reference to issues that can now be seen as relevant to Sekaquaptewa and Washburn's model of Hopi ideographic tenacity and inflexibility. Not least among these are Peter Whiteley's observations regarding Hopi resentment of outsiders' "appropriation" of knowledge "property rights" without compensation, not to mention their guardianship of lore they regard as closed to outsiders, even to certain Hopis (Whiteley 1998:37). Equally pertinent is Peter Nabokov's report on the multiplicity of Hopi versions of their tribal past (Nabokov 1996:38). Ruth Benedict's and M. Jane Young's studies of Zuni myths and conceptions of time are likewise instructive in this context (Benedict 1969 [1935]:121–123; Young 1988:136), the Hopis having in the past taken lengthy refuge with those people.

However, an important caution against blanket dismissal of modern informants' "readings" of prehistoric Hopi or other Puebloan symbolic representations has also been presented at the start of this chapter (in the section discussing "A Hopi 'Magician'"). But impressive as the latter case is, assuming the correctness of the investigator's crediting no foreknowledge of his finds to his informants, it is difficult to affirmatively generalize from it against the more numerous and weightier negative factors previously examined. And to the latter must be added what Sekaquaptewa and Washburn never even considered: the serious demographic consequences for the Hopi people, and, indeed, most of the aboriginal Southwest in general, of the introduction of virulent Old World diseases resulting from the Spanish conquest of Mexico and the Southwest. For example, Steadman Upham (1992:229–230) estimates that while the Hopi population on the eve of Spanish contact was about 29,300, it was probably at least halved within the first century thereafter. Indeed, given the experiences of other better documented groups, he concludes that an 80-percent loss during the first 50 years of contact is quite possible. Daniel Reff (1992:269) takes note of a great disease-induced reduction in Hopi population prior to 1629: "The [total] Pueblo population [an estimated 100,000 at the time of conquest] . . . declined by over 80 percent between 1608 and 1680, much as populations did in northwestern Mexico" (Reff 1992:270). In such a prolonged catastrophe, even if the numbers are inflated beyond probability (Henige 1990), with its presumably heavy culling of the elders—the relayers of traditional knowledge—how much stability of worldview ("cosmological system") and metaphoric content of symbolic representation could have been sustained over the following hundreds of years, even into the twentieth century?

The known and likely consequences of severe depopulation on continuity in the transmission of traditional knowledge has previously been briefly examined in the case of the southeastern Catawbas (Chapter 2). Those consequences will be encountered again in more detail in the discussion of the Central Siouans in the following chapter.

And a Few Other Attempts to Grasp the Nettle

Of particular interest to archaeologists because of their wide distribution and greater endurance relative to symbols imposed on more perishable canvases are pictographs and petroglyphs executed on rock surfaces, especially when minimally exposed to weathering. The study of this global phenomenon is complex and the research strategies addressing it multifaceted, ranging as they do from ingenious to imbecilic (see Whitley 2001 for a sampling of the former). My purpose here is modest in scope and aim: to briefly consider one North American geographical and cultural corpus of such indigenous work with respect to the sometime claim that it represents, albeit obliquely, a sort of historical record that can be deciphered by extrapolation from oral traditions. Together with other examples of North American rock art, still in places surviving in astonishing numbers, such "messages from the past" exhibit an almost pancontinental representation. Reference has previously been made to the parietal paintings in the Gottschall rockshelter. While the latter is a recent discovery, European mention of Indian rock art is everywhere almost as old as the first explorations. Among the earliest to be noted, and a continuing subject of interest, are the "picture writings" painted on the rock surfaces of the Canadian Shield in Saskatchewan, Manitoba, Ontario, and parts of Quebec, Minnesota, the Upper Peninsula of Michigan, and Wisconsin (Dewdney and Kidd 1967; Rajnovich 1994). Making up these paintings in various combinations are red sticklike to solid-body figures of humans, bears, dogs or wolves, birds, turtles, snakes, ungulates, boats, shelters—including some that have been "identified" as Midewiwin lodges—circles with and without radii, crosses, "tally" marks, bows and arrows, anthropomorphs and zoomorphs that may be depictions of spirits or manitous, drums, smoking pipes, amorphous smudges, and even unmistakable renditions of horses, their riders, and guns.

It is apparent that a considerable time span is collectively reflected in these paintings. Some may be ascribable to the Laurel culture in the first millennium A.D., according to Grace Rajnovich's survey of the correspondences in the geographic boundaries of that Initial Shield Woodland culture and certain concentrations of the rock paintings. Other examples are as late as the early twentieth century. Probably most archaeologists working in this region believe such Late Woodland cultures as Blackduck and Selkirk were at least partly derived from Laurel and that they, in turn, were ancestral to such Algonquian-speaking peoples as the Ojibwas and Crees, who appear to have been well-established residents over most of the boreal forest country of the Canadian Shield when first encountered by Europeans in the seventeenth and eighteenth centuries. A case may thus be made for centuries-old regional developmental continuity, possibly even on the order of two millennia (Cleland and Peske 1968:56; Cleland et al. 1984:244; Meyer and Smailes 1975:51–52; Rajnovich 1994:45–46, 50–51). Many identical figures occur on Midewiwin bark scrolls made in the nineteenth and early twentieth centuries. Although Kenneth Kidd reported the discovery of a possible late prehistoric Midewiwin scroll from Burntside Lake, Ontario (cited by Rajnovich 1994:54–55), I have already questioned that identification in Chapter 6. And, of course, the fact that similar devices were painted on scrolls and rock faces over some period of time and some considerable stretch of territory constitutes no guarantee that the meanings originally connected with those devices remained the same or were even coevally consonant. The possibility that they did (or were) should be considered no more than a working hypothesis in search of verification. Rajnovich's balanced evaluation of evidence provides innumerable instances in support of alternative positions on this question. For instance, according to verbal testimony, the duration of a journey is supposedly indicated in one painting by a crescent moon (Rajnovich 1994:92) but that of a battle is not necessarily implied by a sun symbol, as some informants claimed (Rajnovich 1994:54–55). The latter, a circle with seven radii, which might analogously be taken as a day sign, is instead interpreted to be a depiction of the turtle manitou *in his guise as the sun.* The symbolism may therefore be that of power, because the turtle was regarded as powerful in war. Sometimes a circle with radii is claimed to represent a turtle, the turtle manitou, the sun, power, medicine, a vision, a metaphor of something else, or several or all of these things to different people. Depictions of people—or perhaps the apparent people are actually manitous—in canoes are common in this rock art. These have been said to represent actual physical journeys, spiritual journeys in search of healing powers or other "medicine," or something in a personal dream. While most of the designs are conventional, their meanings in any given instance embraced a strong personal component and were in that sense idiosyncratic. That some of the conventionalizations enjoyed a lengthy tenure has archaeological support, as just seen. Given the semantic freedoms accorded their historical manifestations, however, a similar longevity cannot be assumed for their message contents.

Garrick Mallery (1886), in one of his great pioneering studies of American Indian pictographs, suggested three possible ways by which he thought their meaning might be discovered. The first way—and the only direct and least equivocal way—is to procure explanations from the individuals who had made them in the first place or who had had their meanings related to them by their authors. This was a feasible option in the case of Mallery's investigations in the late nineteenth century when, for example, he was able to talk with some of the pictographers who had painted Lakota calendars ("winter counts") or autobiographical records on bison robes. Examples of this approach have been given in Chapter 2 in "And Whence Came the Lakota Sioux?" Many years before, in the early 1800s, the ethnographic artist George Catlin (1913 [1841]:1:166–174) had used this approach with the Mandan chief Mah-to-toh-pa, who had so recorded his own war exploits. The second of Mallery's suggested methods was to look for similarities in the pictographs and in the conventional "ideographic gesture-signs" in an understood sign language known or thought to have been employed by the same people. The arms-up configuration in both pictographs and sign language, for instance, or the painting of a wavy line and its suggestion in gesture, might be taken as signifying the same concepts, barring evidence to the contrary. His third method was contextual: unknown pictographs might yield their meaning by virtue of their ideally repeated associations with others of known meaning (Mallery 1886:233).

Of course, one had better have good reasons to trust one's informants. Mallery (1886:251) drew attention to an 1852 news report of a Mormon official who confidently "translated" what others took to be an unremarkable group of aboriginal ("Shoshoni") petroglyphs on a cliff face in Sam Pete Valley, Utah, as having been made in commemoration of "the second King of the Lamanites twelve hundred years after their departure from Jerusalem." But even if the bona fides of an informant are beyond question, it is a dangerous procedure to grant them infallibility. Even experts may disagree. Thus William Warren, one of the native authorities on nineteenth-century Ojibwa life, sided with certain tribal elders who disputed the majority opinion of their peers regarding the "meaning" of the name Ojibwa or Ojibway (Warren 1984 [1885]:35–36). Whereas the minority believed that *ojib* ("puckered up"), when added to *ubway* ("to roast"), referred to the shriveling of the flesh of war captives being tortured by fire, the majority held that *Ojibwa* derived from an old style of moccasin having a puckered or drawn-up seam on top. Although Ojibwas, and perhaps especially Mide priests, talked a lot about words and signs and their various meanings, it is critical not to attribute to them the procedures of modern semantic analysis or the institutionalized rigidities of something like the Académie Française. Rajnovich (1994) supplies many instances of multiple meanings for the same signs, not excluding "readings" by a single informant. Obviously, however, when the intended significance of, say, a particular winter count or autobiographical robe painting is supplied by its creator, it must be accepted as authoritative in each instance. Generalizing from such authority, however, is another matter entirely. Projecting into antecedent, particularly prehistoric, times symbolic interpretations informed by a given historical example from a system so accommodating of idiosyncrasies is not lightly to be recommended, even if one is unwilling to take so stringent a position as that staked out by Michael Shanks and Christopher Tilley (1992:132). It is critical to keep in mind that a visual symbol, having been transferred from someone's mind to a rock wall or a piece of bark, has become an artifact or a component of an artifact. It has entered the sphere of material culture. It exists today as part of the archaeological record, but the thought that put it there does not. To get at *that* is the challenge. If the reader is willing to overlook in the following quotation the challengeable condemnation of the comparative method, one can understand the discomfort many archaeologists feel when certain of their colleagues claim insights into prehistoric semiotics before which an ethnographer or linguist or psychologist would quail.

> Any determinate social totality is characterized by distinctive practices, strategies and structures which are temporally, spatially and socially situated and articulated. Material culture is part of this articulation. This means that material culture can only be realistically interpreted once it is contextually situated in a double moment. First, explanations must be related to the field of internal relations of individual social totalities, and this invalidates cross-cultural approaches. Secondly, they must be contextually situated in the spatio-temporal moments of the totality. There is no point in attempting to formulate a highly specific general model of the significance of particular aspects of material culture-patterning such as types of burial practices, good for all time and all places. Material culture only has significance within the context of a particular social totality and the structures, structuring principles, conditions for social action and the nature of social practices which will differ from one particular case to another [Shanks and Tilley 1992:132].

If not for precisely the same reasons, Philip Phillips and James A. Brown (1978:1:145) have expressed their reservations about interpreting the meanings of the motifs in the iconography of the shell engravings from the Craig Mound at Spiro, Oklahoma, a symbolic system vastly more sophisticated than that (or those) of the Canadian Shield far to the north:

> It seems to have been inevitable that our treatment of motifs takes the form of a glossary. We have been unable to find any workable system of categories, which is hardly surprising since the essential virtue of a motif is its conventional meaning of which, ninety-nine times

out of a hundred, we haven't a clue. There is not much sense in putting groups of non-meanings into an arrangement that itself can have no meaning. One example should suffice.

In his study of peyotism, Weston La Barre points out that Huichol ritual paraphernalia is heavily symbolized. With his eagle and hawk plumes the singing shaman can see and hear anything anywhere, cure the sick, transform the dead, even call down the sun. The plumes symbolize the antlers of deer, which in turn symbolize peyote and the chair of "Grandfather Fire," the greatest shaman of them all, whose flames are his plumes. Deer antlers also symbolize arrows, the arrow being *par excellence* the symbol of prayer . . . and so on (paraphrased by Firth [1973, p. 200]). Suppose, in a brilliant flash of analogic intuition, we were to bring together depictions of eagle and hawk plumes, deer antlers, and arrows under the same heading, it might be thought rather strange. And it would not greatly add intelligibility if we called it "Grandfather's chair." No reflection on Weston La Barre, of course, but there are some who seem to know as much about symbolization in the Southern Cult as La Barre knows about the Huicholi.

In closing this limited perusal of the problems involved in attributing usable historical information to signs and symbols preserved archaeologically, an attribution heavily dependent on oral testimony, histories, and traditions, I feel obliged to direct the reader's attention to additional, and not always compatible, perspectives on extracting information from sources I am loath to trust. Good recent sources for such perspectives include Brown (1997 [focused on religious themes in the Eastern Woodlands]), Ian Hodder's edited collections of essays (1982, 1987a, and 1987b; see the especially engaging argument by von Gernet and Timmins [1987] in the latter volume), and Robb (1998). I would also advise a look at M. Alison Wylie's essay in the first of the Hodder-edited volumes, particularly with respect to her strictures regarding assumptions of radical discontinuity between ethnographic or historical present and archaeological past (Wylie 1982:43). And, lest enthusiasm for some of these other perspectives threatens sober skepticism, I recommend Shepard Krech (1999), the essays in James A. Clifton's edited volume of 1990, and, for a bit of tragicomic relief, Alan Leveillee's (2002) brief essay.

9

On the Central Siouans Before
J. Owen Dorsey

As seen in previous examples, where there is an absence or paucity of written records, appeals to oral traditions are an especially common accompaniment of archaeological and ethnographic investigations of a society's history. Although such prominent figures as Robert Lowie (1915, 1917) and Lord Raglan (1949) held verbal traditions about ancient origins, homelands, and migrations as worthless, or at best historically superfluous, and many later scholars have voiced more nuanced cautions, the hope for a usable "kernel" of genuine historicity persists. Indeed, current multicultural ideology is giving that hope renewed appeal in the academic as well as the wider world. In its more level-headed manifestations, traditional tales of tribal migrations and ancient homelands are treated as potential historical data to be evaluated in the light of independent sources of information. If sustained by those other sources, the traditions in question are elevated to higher ontological status than initially held. Ironically, however, they thus also become superfluous in the Lowiean scale of historical utility that accords veracious primacy to archaeological, ethnographic, linguistic, and documentary information. If evidence from any of the latter sources is clearly incompatible with a given tradition, the tradition must be disallowed legitimacy *as history.*

Certitude, however, is more often sought than found in reconstructing the past. In this endeavor scientific and documentary evidence more often provide no more than degrees of possibilities, plausibilities, and probabilities. Because of this, most students of the past attempt to bring to bear on any and all historical problems as many independent kinds of information as they can muster. Neglecting this sensible procedure is an invitation to error. Normally, there will be cause to give greater weight to some kinds of information than to others, as in the following instances. Unfortunately, in some cases paucity of information directly bearing on a question at issue will elevate indirect varieties to otherwise unearned cogency.

An example of the foregoing phenomenon is illustrated in my own largely frustrated search for data supportive of the beliefs of the native people themselves, as well as of a majority of anthropologists and historians, that the Menomini Indians' residence at or near the mouth of the Menominee River between Wisconsin and the Upper Peninsula of Michigan extended back into prehistoric time (see Beck 2002:1–2 for that belief's latest uncritical iteration). Notwithstanding a plethora of archaeological sites, several site surveys, and cultural resource management projects in the relevant area, and despite a recorded Menomini historical tenure, archaeologists have yet to find early European trade goods in contexts old enough to also yield aboriginal pottery and stone tools that might then be compared with those known in regional prehistoric sites (Mason 1997a). The minimum criteria I had earlier set for assigning ethnic labels to archaeological assemblages (Mason 1976) remain to be met in this case. The archaeological identity of the Menominis is still unknown. Conjectures, some more reasonable than others, have had to stand in for demonstration (see examples cited in Mason 1997a). A highly knowledgeable colleague, in trying to be helpful, could only offer the information that the Menominis lack migration traditions (or any that have survived, that is) and that this might be taken as support for their claim of local prehistoric roots. Ironically, the Foxes or Mesquakies (Behm 1992; Wittry 1963), amalgamating segments of Hurons, Petuns, and Ottawas (aborning Wyandots), and Potawatomis (Mason 1986), all known early historic period visitors and immigrants to Wisconsin, have there been identified by archaeological as well as documentary means. As will be apparent in the next section, however, the puzzle of the archaeologically missing Menominis has recently taken a new twist.

The Winnebago (Ho-Chunk) Indians
at First European Contact

More directly pertinent to the historically known tribes considered in this chapter, especially considering some of *their* traditions, are the Siouan-speaking Winnebagoes (today often called Ho-Chunks), "neighbors" of the Algonquian-speaking Menominis—wherever *they* may have been when they first entered historical notice. Many years ago it appeared that a good case could be made for a Lake Winnebago phase (a subdivision or "focus" in the then current terminology) of the Oneota archaeological culture as being the prehistoric ancestor of the historic Winnebago tribe (Griffin 1937, 1960; McKern 1945). The phase name reflected the concentration of ceramically distinctive sites in the environs dominated by Lake Winnebago and its proximate tributaries in east-central and northeastern Wisconsin.

Much of this region and the southern end of Green Bay were also believed to encompass the homeland of the Winnebago Indians when first visited by a European, Jean Nicolet, in 1634. Although that proposed connection between the archaeological entity and the historical tribe became widely accepted, partly because it was compatible with a dawning perception of a likely correlation elsewhere in the Midwest of different Siouan-speaking peoples (e.g., the Iowas) and other Oneota phases (the Orr phase, in that instance [Mott 1938; M. M. Wedel 1959]), it was never buttressed by evidence in the ground. And that remains true to this day. There are still no known protohistoric or prehistoric site assemblages unequivocally deserving the tribal appellation "Winnebago." Like the Menominis, the Winnebagoes remain floating on the surface of a shallow history with no anchors gripping the underlying bed of prehistory (C. Mason 1976, 1993; R. Mason 1993; but see Overstreet 1993 and Richards 1993 for firm and more cautious dissents, respectively).

However, a recent reinterpretation has been put forward by Robert L. Hall (2003) of the sketchy earliest and most important historical record bearing on the western end of the route taken by Nicolet in his journey from Quebec to the land of the Winnebagoes. Hall argues that that record and the imprecision of the earliest French maps pertinent to following Nicolet's route need to be reconsidered, not least for the failure of archaeological evidence to support the conventional deciphering. While the strengths and weaknesses of all of Hall's arguments are tangential to the immediate focus of this chapter, his conclusions are not. Howsoever they are evaluated, the latter are potentially critical to the search for an archaeological identification of both the Winnebagoes and the Menominis. They offer—but do not cement—a solution to those two enigmas. And they involve a third native group in the effort: the Iliniweks, Illinis, or Illinois.

As students of the Indian tribes of the midwestern United States have long been aware, the Iliniweks first came into written notice in the 1640 volume of *The Jesuit Relations and Allied Documents: Travels and Explorations of the Jesuit Missionaries in New France, 1610–1791* (Thwaites 1896–1901, hereafter referred to as *Jesuit Relations*). The author of the relevant passages, the missionary Paul Le Jeune, based his account on his recollection of what Nicolet had told him six years previously. The latter unfortunately had died on his way back from visiting the Winnebagoes, such journals as he may have kept also being lost. By Le Jeune's transmission of Nicolet's understanding (*Jesuit Relations* 18:231–233), the *Eriniouai* (Illinois) were neighbors of the *Ouinipigou* (Winnebagoes). Locate the Winnebagoes of 1634 on a map and the Illinois of that same period must thereby be not far away—or so it would seem. However, the *Pouutouatami* (Potawatomis) were also included as neighbors of the Winnebagoes according to the Nicolet–Le Jeune record. But the Potawatomis at that time were probably still residents of the Lower Peninsula of Michigan, a land they subsequently vacated for fear of "endless wars" with their enemies. Their relocation to the north and west was well along by 1641 (Clifton 1977:36–37). The Jesuit missionary Jerome Lalemont, relating the events of that year, was an eyewitness to the migration (*Jesuit Relations* 23:225). From his account, the Potawatomis first sought refuge in the vicinity of the Sault between Lakes Huron and Superior before moving southwest into Wisconsin.

Further complicating matters in locating the 1634 Illinois is the inclusion of the *Maroumine* (Menominis), *Naduesiu* (Sioux), *Assinipour* (Assiniboines), and *Rasaouakoueton* (either Mascoutens or a band of the Ottawas, depending on how certain authorities have "corrected" what they have taken to be a misspelling in the original document [Mason 1986:15]) on the list of peoples being "in the neighborhood of this nation [the Winnebagoes]" (*Jesuit Relations* 18:231–233). To my knowledge, no one can document where the possibly named band of the Ottawas was in 1634. The same is true of the Mascoutens, although in their case the most likely environs before approximately 1650–1670 were somewhere around the western end of Lake Erie (Brose 2001:61; Stothers 2000). Le Jeune's recounting of the Winnebago tribal neighborhood as understood by Nicolet included the observation that "these [the aforementioned tribes] are the names of a part of the nations which are beyond the shores of the great river saint Lawrence and of the great lakes of the Hurons on the North" (*Jesuit Relations* 18:231–233). Evidently, "neighborhood" must be interpreted in a pretty generous way.

Robert L. Hall, as indicated above, has suggested in his rethinking of the western route taken by Nicolet that the Illinois are more critical in locating the Winnebagoes of the 1634 era than the other way around (Hall 2003). That is, the Illinois Indians should cease being considered the variable dependent on where the Winnebagoes are to be located at the dawn of history. Instead, attention should focus on the independent achievements of archaeologists in identifying through ethnohistorical research and excavation early historic period Illinois (Iliniwek) village sites in Illinois and Missouri.

In brief, Hall's suggested revision of the conventional view is to expel the Winnebagoes from their assumed eastern Wisconsin territory no later than circa 1450, previous to which time their residence there, he and most other archaeologists presume, is represented by the Lake Winnebago phase of the Oneota culture (Hall 2003; C. Mason 1993; R. Mason 1993). While the reasons for this exodus are not explored, the failure of archaeologists to find good evidence of their presence thereafter for the next couple of centuries, when coupled with Hall's tenable reinterpretation of the ambiguous pertinent written and cartographic evidence, invites consideration of alternative possibilities. One of these, he suggests, is that Nicolet was referring to the west coast of Lake Michigan, not Green Bay, when he reported coming ashore to meet the Winnebagoes. If this took place near the southwestern end of that lake, then those people are candidates for identification as the carriers of the Huber phase of Oneota, which archaeological culture left numerous late prehistoric and protohistoric sites otherwise bereft of a plausible tie to a known historical people—to an "archaeoethnicity" (Mason 1997a). As Hall explains, not many years after Nicolet's visit, the Winnebago tribe was practically destroyed in wars with the Illinois. There are good reasons for believing that these latter were descendants of people who had just recently intruded themselves, together with their distinctive and prehistorically foreign Danner series pottery, into northern Illinois and northeastern Missouri from somewhere around the western end of Lake Erie. Hall maintains, and I concur, that the Illinois and Missouri archaeologists who have convincingly identified the material remains of the Illinois (Iliniwek) Indians in their respective states are correct in ascribing to them but short antecedent tenures (perhaps only two or three generations) in the now historically and archaeologically identified places where and when they were first (1673) met by French explorers.

Whereas the archaeological signature of the Illinois has now been recognized, that of the Winnebagoes still awaits confirmation. Hall's hypothesis that it should spell Huber phase Oneota is worth considering for a number of reasons. Chief among them are (1) the plausibility of his revisionist reading of the documentary evidence, (2) the offering of a reasonable solution to the late eastern Wisconsin archaeoethnic blank, (3) the intellectual satisfaction of linking the otherwise post-1450-orphaned Winnebagoes with a contemporary archaeological assemblage otherwise stranded without known historical progeny, (4) the compatibility of the mid-seventeenth-century destruction of Winnebago tribal structure and the likely extinction by that time of Huber Oneota culture, and (5) as a bonus, the preservation of the Oneota-Siouan link. This is an attractive if shaky conjectural structure, one that is well worth testing. And that testing will have to deal with still unanswered questions and complicating implications. For example, a strictly archaeological objection is raised by evidence of in-place continuity of material culture that suggests derivation of Huber from the antecedent Fisher phase. That culture made its appearance on the local scene perhaps as early as the twelfth century A.D. (Emerson and Brown 1992:82). Huber thus is difficult to see as an intrusion. Furthermore, Charles H. Faulkner's (1972) suggested link between Huber and the Miami Indians remains a still viable one notwithstanding lingering problems in linking pottery types to specific ethnicities (Brown 1990; Emerson and Brown 1992:110). Also, what could have precipitated the apparently numerous Lake Winnebago phase Oneota people into a seemingly abrupt and wholesale abandonment in the fifteenth century of an expansive territory they had occupied for many centuries previously, only to migrate some 200 miles south to there continue their horticultural-forager way of life? The question of departure, of course, can be posed independently of the hypothesized move to northern Illinois, except that they are linked in Hall's model. The Menominis are also implicated in this scenario. Le Jeune recorded Nicolet as saying (*Jesuit Relations* 18:231), after he had entered the "second fresh-water sea" (Lake Huron was the first), he had had to pass those people before he could reach the Winnebagoes who dwelt on the same shore ("banks"). If Hall is correct in identifying that sea as Lake Michigan itself, rather than its much smaller northwestern appendage Green Bay, then the Menominis must abandon their claim that they were living at or near the mouth of the Menominee River when they were first seen by a European. Perhaps this explains the prolonged failure to locate protohistoric or early historic Menominis in their self-proclaimed "homeland" as reviewed earlier. A further departure from orthodoxy requires the Winnebagoes to have had three different Oneota phase pottery traditions in succession: Lake Winnebago, Huber, and Orr or Orr-like (this last to accommodate late and western-looking minority ceramics in the Green Bay region where Hall thinks remnants of the Winnebagoes reconstituted themselves as a tribe sometime before the 1660s or 1670s, perhaps ca. 1650).

May not Winnebago oral traditions regarding their tribal history be called on to throw light on all or some of the foregoing? Hall, who once suggested to me that the lack of a migration legend among the Menominis might qualify as evidence in support of their claim to having resided in their traditional homeland since prehistoric times, is unwilling to grant comparable consideration to the Winnebago (Ho-Chunk) traditions that locate the place of their early tribal origin as Red Banks (on Green Bay, near the modern city). Instead, he thinks those traditions really refer to the post–Huber phase reinvestment of that part of Wisconsin by tribal remnants in the middle or slightly later seventeenth century (Hall 2003:240). He is similarly unaccepting of the historicity of other traditions (of which more below) that locate the original homeland of the Winnebago ancestors, together with those of certain other tribes, as north of the Great Lakes. He relegates those traditions instead to a "historicalization [*sic*] of a mythical origin in the northern night sky that is implicit in the social organization of many of the Siouan groups of the Missouri and Mississippi valleys, a social organization that relates in some way to seven stars (Hall 1993,

28–30)" (Hall 2003:239). Quite apart from the astronomical allusion, he is doubtless correct in suggesting a mythical rationalization for such a tribal genesis.

Winnebago Congeners South and West

In 1883 in Washington, D.C., visiting headmen of the Iowa tribe met the pioneer ethnographer J. Owen Dorsey and there told him about their tribal origin. The story they told involved the Winnebago people and some others as well as their own. As Raymond J. DeMallie and Douglas R. Parks (2001:1067) have pointed out, Dorsey integrated what the Iowas told him with what he had learned about Plains Siouan migration traditions he and others had collected from late-nineteenth-century reservation Indians. He also added to this what he had garnered from earlier travelers', missionaries', and explorers' reports, most of whose renderings of Indian traditions provided but impoverished glimpses of what must originally have been richer canvases. The resulting collation of these oral traditions was his seminal article "Migrations of Siouan Tribes" (Dorsey 1886).

Dorsey opened his essay with a brief mention of the artist–pioneer ethnographer George Catlin. In 1841 Catlin had published speculations about Mandan tribal beginnings on the banks of the Ohio and Muskingum rivers, speculations alleging a Mandan tradition he had obtained from those people but did not publish (Catlin 1913 [1841]:1:92, 231–232, and 1913 [1841]:2:appendix A and preceding map). Dorsey's citing these speculations was clearly equivocal. Catlin had also suggested that those people, whom he knew had been residing on the Missouri River in modern North Dakota since before Lewis and Clark, were partly descended from the fabled Welsh colony of Prince Madoc. Dorsey betrayed hesitancy in accrediting Catlin's account, quite apart from the Prince Madoc story, reference to which he omitted in his text and cartographic editing (compare Catlin's original with Dorsey's rendition of it). But because the Mandans spoke a Siouan language, Dorsey nonetheless used Catlin's report in support of other Siouan-speakers' traditions of a general Siouan western migration that had been initiated unknown centuries ago. In one recent taxonomy, that published by Parks and Rankin (2001), Mandan is the sole representative of one of the four subgroups of the Siouan language family. It is similarly represented in the earlier "Consensus Classification of the Native Languages of North America" (Goddard 1996:4–8 [Table 3]).

In his Washington meeting with the Iowas, Dorsey was informed of their belief that at one time the Chiwere Siouan–speaking Iowas, Otos, and Missouris, together with the Dhegihan Siouan–speaking Omahas and Poncas, had been one "nation" with the Winnebagoes. The latter's language is some-times classified as Chiwere Siouan—or Winnebago–Chiwere Siouan in rec-ognition of its greater distinctiveness than that exhibited by the other three Chiwere Siouan tongues vis-à-vis one another. Dorsey cited a parallel ac-count by Albert Gallatin, pioneer linguist and Thomas Jefferson's secretary of the treasury, who had earlier reported that those people had all migrated from the north in "a distant epoch" (Gallatin 1836:127).

Adding to this information, Dorsey (1886:213) referenced Edwin James's account of Major S. H. Long's 1819–1820 expedition from Pittsburgh to the Rocky Mountains. That document recorded that the Otos, then residing in an earth lodge village on the Platte River in east-central Nebraska, believed that their ancestors and those of the Winnebagoes, Iowas, and Missouris (note the absence of the Omahas and Poncas, contra the Iowa chiefs' recita-tion of the tribes to Dorsey) had once been a single people living north of the Great Lakes (Thwaites 1904–1907:15:131). The members of that same "nation," according to a different informant reported by Prince Maximil-ian of Wied in 1832–1834 (Thwaites 1904–1907:24:313–314), called them-selves Hoton-ga (Fish-eaters). Absent again are the Omahas and Poncas. In this second account the nation, being "discontented," decided to migrate southwesterly to take up buffalo hunting. After "performing a considerable journey" the first fission of the nation occurred when the Winnebagoes se-ceded and settled on the shore of a lake (Lake Michigan, claimed Dorsey, referring to the parallel earlier Oto testimony by Major Long).

Drawing on additional and probably much later sources of informa-tion, Dorsey tried to piece together what transpired following the great trek from north of the Great Lakes and the separation of the proto-Winnebagoes from the other Chiwere Sioux, as well as the possible involvement of the Dhegiha-speaking Omahas and Poncas. Until definitively identified, such tribal names as the foregoing are best preceded by the modifier "proto." In order to avoid awkward repetition, however, that prefix is intended to be implicit where it is not explicit. The post-Winnebago-secession trekkers, by one account, continued their southerly and westerly movement. Eventually they encountered and crossed the Mississippi River and separated into the several areas where they later were first met by Europeans. Complicating matters, Dorsey also reported:

Ages ago the ancestors of the Omahas, Ponkas, Osages, Kansas, Kwapas [Quapaws—who, with the previous four tribes, were also Dhegihan Siouans], Pawnee Loups (Skidi) and Rees [Arikaras—who, with the Pawnees, were Caddoan speakers], dwelt east of the Mississippi. They were not all in one region, but they were allies, and their general course was westward. They drove other tribes before them. *Five of these peoples, the Omahas, Ponkas, Osages, Kansas and Kwapas, were then together as one nation.* They were called Arkansa or Alkansa by the Illinois tribes, and they dwelt near the Ohio river. At the mouth of the Ohio a separation occurred. Some went down the Mississippi, hence arose their name, "U-ga'-qpa (Oo-ga-khpa)" or Kwapa (Quapaw), meaning "the down-stream people." This was prior to 1540, when De Soto met the Kwapas, who were then a distinct tribe [Dorsey 1886:215; my italics].

Dorsey then related that the rest of the Dhegihan Siouans, or "Arkansas," became known as Omahas, "those going against the wind or current." It is *historically* puzzling that the Omahas and Poncas—presumably their ancestors, that is—were claimed to have been a part of two original "nations": one with Chiwere-Winnebago brethren, the other, more linguistically plausible, with other Dhegihans only. The two "nations," of course, might be taken as a "social memory" of the realignment of constituent groups accompanying the migration and fragmentation of the initial "great nation." Allowing for purpose of argument the possibility of a bilingual original "nation," that is, one constituted of Proto-Chiwere and Proto-Dhegiha speakers, even the temporally shallowest linguistic estimate for their emergence as separate language groups of Siouan, as seen below, is probably too remote to retrospectively endow "social memory," with trustworthy historical content. More likely, the exclusively Dhegihan "nation" was a later ex post facto rationalization of then current arrangements vis-à-vis those thought to have existed in a bygone era. Association with the Pawnees and Arikaras betrays later times (see Henning and Thiessen 2004: 383, 392, 395–397) if not historical invention.

In a recent study, Robert L. Rankin's dating of divergence times among Siouan languages places the separation of Dhegiha from Winnebago-Chiwere sometime around 1,500 years ago, whereas Winnebago and Chiwere began drifting apart a bit less than a millennium ago (see chart in Alex 2000:215). An earlier study by James W. Springer and Stanley R. Witkowski (1982:Figure 3) had estimated these two bifurcations commencing at about 500 years later in each case. Whichever approximations are closest to the truth, both divergences, in the overall purview of North American culture history, were relatively recent. That being so, the archaeological records of corresponding age in the Ohio region should offer candidates supportive of the traditions, if their allusions to past residence therein are dependable. Such candidates, should any reside there, have been shy about offering themselves. Nor has anything tangible turned up north of the Great Lakes that might put bones inside the tradition of a southward-yearning parent "nation." But, as Hall (2003:239) points out, no linguist doubts that the ancestors of the historically known Chiwere-speaking and Dhegiha-speaking tribes had in each case once constituted a single people. Except for the later careers of some of their offspring, their traditional derivations remain undiscovered.

Another important source of oral traditions relating legends of Dhegiha and Chiwere migrations and fissions is contained in Alice C. Fletcher and Francis La Flesche's great *The Omaha Tribe* (1911). An important finding in that study, information for which was collected during the last two decades of the nineteenth century and the first half decade of the twentieth, was the great variability of many of the stories to which they became privy (it was helpful in this regard that La Flesche was an Omaha himself). And this variability was not unique to the Omahas. They give as one example the version of "the" Ponca creation story as told to one Standing Buffalo by his mother (Fletcher and La Flesche 1911:49). For another, they relate how, among the Osages, "each of the five groups [the bands making up the tribe] had its own traditions, *and one did not interfere with another*" (Fletcher and La Flesche 1911:62; my italics).

And here are two versions of how accidental fissioning of original unity among the ancient precursors of the Omahas and their kith and kin took place. I have inserted the second rendering of the legend into the first, using italics to indicate where it differs from the first:

> The people were moving down the Uha'i ke river [the Ohio]. When they came to a wide river [the Mississippi] they made skin boats in which to cross the river. [*When the river was reached the people made a rope of grape vines. They fastened one end on the eastern bank and the other end was taken by strong swimmers and carried across the river and fastened to the western bank. The people crossed the river by clinging to the grapevine.*]
>
> As they were crossing, a storm came up. The Omaha and Iowa got safely across, but the Quapaw drifted down the stream and were never seen again within the last century. [*When about half their number were across, including the Iowa and Omaha, the rope broke, leaving the rest of the people behind. Those who were left were the Quapaw. This crossing was made on a foggy morning, and those left behind, believing that their companions who had crossed had followed the river downward on the western side, themselves turned down-stream on the eastern side, and so the two groups lost sight of each other.*]
>
> When the Iowa made their landing they camped in a sandy place. The strong wind blew the sand over the people and gave them a grayish appearance. From this circumstance they called themselves Pa'xude,

"gray head," and the Omaha have known them by that name ever since. The Iowa accompanied the Omaha up the Mississippi to a stream spoken of as "Raccoon river"—probably the Des Moines, and the people followed this river to its headwaters, which brought them into the region of the Pipestone quarry [Fletcher and La Flesche 1911:36].

As previously seen in Dorsey's recounting of the Siouan migration stories, with the separation of the Quapaws at the mouth of the Ohio River, the remainder of the "Arkansa," "Alkansa," or "Arkansas" (still all Dhegihan Siouans) became known as Omahas. That appellation would later survive, or be revived, as the name of the historically known tribe following the fissioning off of the groups of people who came to be called Osages, Kansas, and Poncas. Because the Omahas and Poncas, or the Omahas alone, were sometimes portrayed as part of the ancient "nation" after it had vacated the country north of the Great Lakes, one or both of those names—Omaha particularly—may have served as a sometime covering term, at least retrospectively, for all of the pre-Mississippi-crossing Dhegiha speakers. This would have paralleled its known analogous usage following the crossing and the defection of the Quapaws, as previously reviewed. There is evidence that the Poncas were a distinct division of the Omahas until their separation as an independent tribe in the eighteenth century (Brown and Irwin 2001: 416; Howard 1965:15). WJ McGee's (1897:191–194) often-cited account of early Dhegiha tribal migration legends was simply, as he himself acknowledged, a restatement of Dorsey's.

As given in other readings of the relevant traditions (Liberty et al. 2001), following the departure of the Quapaws at the mouth of the Ohio, the rest of the Dhegihans ascended the Mississippi to the Missouri, thence went up to the debouchure of the Osage River in central Missouri, where a three-way division took place. The now separating Osages went up the Osage River. The emergent Kansa tribe resumed ascending the Missouri to the Kansas River in northeastern Kansas. Meanwhile, the proto-Omahas and Poncas, still one people, crossed to the east bank of the Missouri where, after being joined by the Iowas, they traveled "northwest" (presumably more north than west) to the tributaries of the Des Moines and the catlinite quarries in southwestern Minnesota (Liberty et al. 2001:399). Liberty, Wood, and Irwin (2001) also offer another possible interpretation of the migrations following arrival at the mouth of the Ohio River.

Returning to Dorsey's narrative, following the secession of the nascent Winnebagoes, the rest of the first described original nation continued its southerly and westerly movement. Eventually, the Mississippi was crossed and the now rapidly fissioning remainder went on to the locales where they were later first met by Europeans. Revisiting the events initiated by the arrival of the now Winnebago-less "parent nation" at the Mississippi, Dorsey (1886:213), mainly following information supplied by the previously cited Long expedition, has the nascent Iowas detach themselves from the main body of migrants. The proto-Missouris then split from the rest and settled at the mouth of the Missouri River. The people who would become the Otos withdrew by themselves either at the same place or elsewhere on the Mississippi. Subsequently, they ascended the Missouri or they went cross-country to where it was joined by the "Great Nemaha" (the Big Nemaha River in southeastern Nebraska). Thereafter they seem to have made several moves up and back down the Missouri and Platte rivers. Meanwhile, the Iowas must have split themselves, because one group of them that had lived "for a long time" on the lower Missouri was "rejoined by the band above mentioned." The latter would seem to refer either to those who had separated from the rest of the migrants upon first reaching the Mississippi or those who at one time had established a village near Council Bluffs, Iowa, but on the opposite bank of the Missouri. The two now rejoined Iowa bands returned to the Mississippi, ascended it, and ensconced themselves on the Des Moines River. Dorsey (1886:213–214) dates this movement no earlier than 1740–1750. Of course, employing migration traditions only, it would be impossible to convert relative sequences of events assumed to have been real into calendrical ones.

Mildred Mott Wedel (1986:14–15), using historical records, has been able to establish that the first definite meeting of Iowas and a European was in 1676 when the Jesuit Louis Andre met some who were visiting a Winnebago village somewhere in northeastern Wisconsin. At that time the Iowas were estimated to reside some 200 leagues to the west (roughly between 480 and 550 miles, with the then standard French league equal to about 2.42 English miles and the "common" league 2.76 miles [Thwaites 1902:2]) or 12 days' journey beyond the Mississippi. Wedel (2001:432) interprets the traditions as related by Dorsey (1886:213) as indicating an ancestral group, from which the proto-Iowas split off in the distant past, residing between the Mississippi River and Lake Michigan, most likely somewhere around Green Bay. Those remaining behind were the Winnebagoes. Regardless of where this took place, the linguistic estimates previously reviewed suggest a time on the order of A.D. 1100–1200 at the earliest to A.D. 1600–1700 at the latest. Archaeological implications follow on the linked assumptions that linguistic divergence would have mirrored declining social intercourse as the two speech communities grew apart and that *some* differentiation in material products, such as ceramic styles, would have reflected that lessening interaction. With the good evidence that certain "proto- and early historic village sites on the Upper Iowa River are identified as the Orr focus" and the linking of those same sites with the Iowas (Wedel 2001:432), somewhat earlier than the upper limits of the time range is more likely than much greater age. Orr, Lake Winnebago, and Huber phase Oneota potteries, when sampled in representative collections, are not easily to be confused. Perhaps also relevant here, as Wedel herself seemed to think, was Alanson B. Skinner's finding that some Iowa oral traditions had been "borrowed" from the Santee Sioux (Wedel 2001:432). Surely time and not just propinquity would seem to be implicated. And that probably weighs in at the early end of the scale. Although there is ethnohistoric and archaeological evidence to connect all the Chiwere-speaking tribes, Winnebagoes provisionally aside, with various phases of Oneota cultural remains, the Iowas, as just indicated, and the Missouris also (Bray 1991; Chapman 1946, 1959; O'Brien and Wood 1998:349–356) provide some of the strongest demonstrations of such connections (Henning 2001).

In the case of the Dhegiha people, Dale R. Henning (1993) and Thomas D. Thiessen (Henning and Thiessen 2004:392–398) accept, although with unequal conviction, an Oneota archaeological connection for the Osages, Kansas, and Omahas. Unfortunately, most of the Osage sites having reliable ethnohistoric tribal identification have yielded a lot of European trade goods and few examples of the native manufactures they replaced. Sites attributed to the Kansas (Kansa) typically have little in the way of culturally diagnostic native-made pottery, a critical criterion for establishing Oneota affiliation. Notwithstanding this limitation, Michael J. O'Brien and W. Raymond Wood (1998:356), in agreement with Henning (1993), recognize some Oneota-like, although parochially distinctive, ceramics in the pertinent assemblages. This impression has led them, again in concert with Henning, to infer that perhaps Oneota cultural influence *had been diffused* to the inhabitants of the sites attributed to the Kansa and Osage Indians, thus implying an acculturation situation. It should be noted that the earliest so-called Kansa sites in particular lack unambiguous historical credentials, whatever their artifactual attributes. But those three authorities are themselves unambiguous in their asserting "there are no known antecedents for the Osage or Kansa *in the area where they lived historically,* despite the great amount of work that has been done in the several federal reservoirs investigated in the historic Osage homeland" (O'Brien and Wood 1998:356; original emphasis). Their conclusion incorporates a quotation from Henning (1993): "The most plausible hypothesis at the moment is that 'the Dhegiha-speaking peoples were late arrivals in the western prairies . . . who adopted to regional traditions [of style and technology] where they settled'" (O'Brien and Wood 1998:356). The Kansa sites in question are located in eastern Kansas and western Missouri, the Osage (as early as the late 1600s) along the Osage River and its tributaries in central to western Missouri. Assuming reliability of (1) the tribal ascriptions of the pertinent archaeological site assemblages and (2) the Oneota-like attributes identified in some of the pottery, the foregoing argument ends in a contradiction. Oneota derivation is an archaeological diagnosis that can only be made on the basis of material culture, mainly ceramic culture in this case. Such a derivation of the Osage and Kansa peoples requires the retention of something of Oneota identity when and where they arrived at their historical habitats as well as its possession while on their trek from wherever they started out. But the attribution of locally reconfigured Oneota trappings to the result of diffusion to already resident native communities would seem to preclude the original posited identity of those communities as original participants in Oneota culture. A reader of this conundrum might be tempted to argue that the people's speaking a Dhegiha tongue may stand in lieu of insufficiently diagnostic material attributes in these two cases and thus come down on the side of Oneota ancestry. But that would assume what needs to be shown. Garrick A. Bailey (2001:476), taking due note of widely shared Dhegiha legends about eastern origins, concluded that such a migration of the Osages, at least, still lacks archaeological verification because of lack of identifiable prehistoric and protohistoric Osage sites.

Indeed, Alfred E. Johnson (1991) has argued that Oneota sites in northeastern Kansas attributed to the Kansa may well represent Oto occupations instead. He has suggested that the Kansa were not an Oneota derivative. Rather than having migrated to their historically known territory as other Dhegiha speakers are thought to have done, the Kansa people developed their tribal identity in eastern Kansas from local prehistoric forebears identifiable in the Pomona variant of the Central Plains tradition. This dissenting view, while defensible, is a minority one (e.g., Thiessen's Tables 2.2 and 2.3 and the conclusions drawn therefrom in Henning and Thiessen 2004: 370–380). Difficulties in unraveling individual constituents in multicomponent sites contribute to the problem and make understandable the equivocation so often met with in the relevant publications.

On a time level sufficiently early to cement a developmental link between a historically known tribe and a still surviving indigenous material culture, the Omaha and Iowa evidence appears to be among the most persuasive. Until just recently, however, it could be said that the Omahas "have no satisfactory prehistoric archaeological expression" and that they "are archaeologically detectable only in the late eighteenth century" (O'Shea and Ludwickson 1992:16). Now the culmination of years of work and hard thinking at the huge, multicomponent Oneota Blood Run site astride the

Big Sioux River in northwestern Iowa and adjacent South Dakota has materially changed that picture (Henning and Thiessen 2004). To archaeological evidence of Oneota occupations running from about 1500 to a bit after 1700 at that locality, historical information, mainly derived from the travel notes of Pierre-Charles Le Sueur (ca. 1657–1704), adds clues about the likely ethnic identifications of the inhabitants responsible for the archaeological remains. These clues point to the Omahas/Poncas, probably still one tribal entity, as the original and major Oneota occupants of Blood Run. Toward the end of the site's occupational history, visits and/or residence by Iowas and Otos are also suggested by early French maps based in large part on Le Sueur's notes (Thiessen in Henning and Thiessen 2004:369–380).

Because of his conditional acceptance of an Oneota origin for the Osage, Kansa, and Omaha tribes, the latter now least conditionally, Henning in his 1993 publication felt that "it seemed only logical that the Quapaw and Ponca should have shared in that [Oneota] tradition, given their comparable migration legends and close linguistic ties, both of which point to recent separation" (Henning 1993:254). The Poncas, at least before their detachment from the Omahas, seem on the Blood Run information to have conformed with Henning's surmise. While the Ponca were not definitely recognized as a separate tribe before 1786 (Henning 1993:259), James H. Howard (1965:15) thinks Ponca separation from the Omahas probably occurred circa 1715. Even though the Quapaws can be absolutely identified well before this latter date, a host of other thorny issues must be confronted.

The Quapaws—Indigenes or Immigrants?

The Quapaw Indians of the southern part of the central Mississippi Valley pose a number of still unanswered questions for archaeologists and other historically minded anthropologists. Although the Ofo Indians in northern Mississippi and the Biloxis in southern Alabama were also Siouan speakers, but of the Eastern subgroup of that linguistic family, the Dhegiha-speaking Quapaws were the sole representatives of the Central Siouan subgroup in the central and lower Mississippi Valley (Springer and Witkowski 1982:71–73). The historical territory of their closest linguistic relatives, the Osages, was well to the north and west in central and western Missouri. It is not that Quapaw geographical-linguistic isolation was unique. The Iroquoian-speaking Cherokees in western North Carolina, eastern Tennessee, and northwestern Georgia are another famous example, but such isolation does raise questions in need of answers. Currently, language historians like Springer and Witkowski (1982) believe the pattern of Siouan language distribution and the kinds and degrees of lexical, phonological, and grammatical attributes bearing on questions of genetic affiliations suggest that the original homeland of the hypothetical mother tongue of all the Siouan languages, Proto-Siouan, lies somewhere in the vicinity of the central Mississippi Valley. In this model, probably sometime in the first millennium B.C. "daughter" languages of the original began developing and spreading out from that homeland. The proliferating progeny that strayed from it the least and survived to receive scholarly notice constitute the Central Siouan subgroup that embraces the several languages classified as Dhegiha, Chiwere or Chiwere-Winnebago, and Dakota. Other taxonomies of the Siouan languages overlap with the foregoing scheme even as they propose different subgroupings. Parks and Rankin (2001), for example, combine all of the foregoing Siouan languages, minus Ofo and Biloxi, but plus Assiniboine and a few others, in their "Mississippi Valley subgroup." But in both of these classifications, Quapaw reposes decidedly in Dhegiha. The importance of this fact will become apparent in the following discussion.

In their major synthesis of the archaeology of the central Mississippi Valley, Dan F. Morse and Phyllis A. Morse (1983) maintain that the Quapaw Indians had long been indigenous to eastern Arkansas. They claim that the weight of available evidence does not sustain the Quapaw migration tradition as credible (Morse and Morse 1983:321). Credible or not, that tradition (see Nuttall's 1821 report in Lottinville 1980 [1821]:93) is compatible with those of the other Dhegiha speakers as previously surveyed. According to those traditions, the ancestors of the Quapaws had migrated to the lands their descendants occupied at the time of initial French contact in 1673. Morse and Morse (1983:321) conclude instead that "the Quapaw are probably derived from the Middle and Late Mississippian cultures of eastern Arkansas and southeast Missouri rather than being recent migrants either from the Ohio Valley or the Plains." They muster nonarchaeological as well as archaeological reasons in support of their contention. The Mississippian cultures they posit as the penultimate and ultimate forebears of the Quapaws are the Nodena and "Quapaw" phases. This view is reiterated in a 1990 essay by Dan Morse.

For most people, a persuasive argument for a relatively recent intrusion into the central Mississippi Valley by the Quapaw progenitors is the Dhegiha character of Quapaw speech. Although Quapaw is no longer a living language, there is enough documentation of its salient features in historical sources and from word lists collected by the linguist Robert Rankin from modern Quapaws who still remember something of the vocabulary to remove any doubt about its affinities (see Hoffman 1990:211–212). Thus, one of the Morses' original reasons for urging caution in accepting the migration legend as historically trustworthy, namely that the Quapaw language was not well enough known to warrant confident assignment to the Dhegiha taxon of the Siouan family, an opinion earlier advanced by James B. Griffin (1960:813), must now be deleted from their list of relevant considerations.

That the historical Quapaw are known to have had a patrilineal descent system in a culture area predominantly matrilineal would seem to favor the tradition-supported thesis of a recent migration from someplace well up the Mississippi Valley where patrilineality was common among the historically known tribes (Driver 1961:Map 32). Countering that line of reasoning is a sociological inference connected with the Morses' hypothesis that the Quapaws were the descendants of a people, a "chiefdom," called "Pacaha," that had been visited by Hernando de Soto in 1541, 132 years before the next European, this time French, contact with the natives of the same region (Morse and Morse 1983:305–315). Mention is made in one of the de Soto expedition narratives about the paramount chief of Pacaha giving one of his wives, a sister, and another high-ranking woman to the Spanish leader. The sociological inference drawn from this incident is that it "may be interpreted as supporting a theory of patrilineal descent for the Pacaha" (Morse 1990:87). This is slender evidence for such a dubious conclusion, especially given ethnographic records of similar practices in matrilineal societies elsewhere (e.g., as in the textbook example of the Trobriand Islanders). But even if taken as justified, its relevance to Quapaw origins is contingent on acceptance of two more propositions: that part if not all of the Late Mississippian archaeological culture called Nodena represents the physical remains of the societal entity the Spaniards labeled Pacaha and that archaeological evidence ties the Quapaws to Nodena and thus Pacaha.

The suggested tie between the Quapaw tribe and the Nodena phase is, however, not direct. Between the two is the "Quapaw phase." This archaeological entity is thought to have developed wholly or in part out of Nodena and to represent the historical Quapaws and their proximate ancestors. But evidently there is not a one-to-one equivalence between the Quapaw tribe and the Quapaw phase, for "Quapaw Indians constituted a very small portion and then the latest period of the Quapaw phase" (Morse and Morse 1983:284). The Nodena phase is dated circa A.D. 1400–1650 (Morse 1990: 69). "The Quapaw phase," state the Morses, "begins within the protohistoric [period] and extends into the seventeenth and eighteenth centuries as the historic Quapaw tribe" (Morse and Morse 1983:300).

While sites of the Nodena phase are concentrated in northeastern Arkansas and the southeastern corner of the Missouri "boot heel," those of the Quapaw phase are found far to the south along the Arkansas River from its mouth northwesterly to the vicinity of Little Rock and along the lower stretch of the Little Red River near where it joins the White (Hoffman

1990:223; Morse and Morse 1983:318–320 and Figure 12.1). Stephen Williams (2001:197, Figures 14.5 and 14.6) also implicates the Oliver phase across from the mouth of the Arkansas River in the Yazoo Delta of Mississippi in Quapaw archaeological identity, even though he grants the Quapaw people a longer tenure in the neighborhood than that accorded that phase.

In theory, physical evidence, such as projectile point styles, pottery types, and traces of house forms and their arrangements—the "meat and potatoes" of archaeological culture history building—should provide good grounds for tracing continuity between the Nodena and Quapaw phases. On such grounds, as the Morses point out, "the Quapaw phase is as Mississippian as the Parkin and Nodena phases" (Morse and Morse 1983:300). Unfortunately, "we do not yet have a definite seventeenth-century Quapaw assemblage to compare to the sixteenth-seventeenth-century Nodena phase" (Morse 1990:97; my emphasis).

Michael P. Hoffman (1990:225) wishes for the discovery of a mid-eighteenth- to early nineteenth-century Quapaw village in order to test the Quapaw phase = Quapaw ethnicity equation (or, to be closer to the Morses' stipulation, part of the Quapaw phase = Quapaw ethnicity equation). George Sabo III (2000:187) reiterates that wish. Lacking such crucial knowledge, without which it is impossible to know whether the Quapaws were or were not indigenous to eastern Arkansas where they were met by Jolliet and Marquette in 1673, it is virtually impossible at present to flatly accept or reject the veracity of the Quapaw migration traditions. Under these circumstances, and assuming for argument's sake the possibility of somehow being able to assert the correctness of those traditions, we would still be in a bind, because, as Hoffman (1990:224) laments, we would not know what in the way of an archaeological assemblage we would be looking for. In retrospect, as most scholars today recognize, it was a mistake to have extended the tribal designation Quapaw to an inadequately defined archaeological phase, even if the Menard (Menard-Hodges) site originally was and "remains our best candidate for the historic site of [the Quapaw village called] Osotuoy" (Sabo 2000:186). According to this same author, renaming the Quapaw phase "Menard complex" is a growing trend (Sabo 2000:186). One can only hope it continues. This is especially so inasmuch as some writers have proposed the Tunicas as more likely than the Quapaws to have been responsible for the Menard ("Quapaw") phase as well as to have peopled the Pacaha polity of de Soto's time (Swanton 1952:215; Young and Hoffman 2001:497).

The problem of Quapaw tribal origins, what Hoffman (1990:219) has called "the Quapaw Paradox," is unresolved. The archaeology that suggests to some scholars prolonged residence and deep roots in Late Mississippian cultures in eastern Arkansas fails to counter, let alone overcome, what others perceive as evidence of relatively recent intrusion from elsewhere. As summarized by Hoffman (1990) and Sabo (2000), that evidence consists of regionally atypical descent reckoning among the Quapaws, the absence of any clues that the Quapaws shared in the widespread Southeast ancestor cult and maintenance of sacred fires, the lack of a match between the French descriptions of bark-covered houses and the archaeological findings of wattle-and-daub structures at the critical Menard-Hodges site, the fact that the Quapaw tongue belongs to the Dhegiha branch of Central Siouan, and, of course, the legends of an Ohio Valley homeland and subsequent descent of the Mississippi Valley.

It is of course possible to argue that the Dhegiha division of Siouan evolved in the central Mississippi Valley in or near the area where Proto-Siouan is thought by some linguists to have originated much earlier. Perhaps the Quapaws thus represent a relict community of predispersal Dhegihans who never left home. Such a scenario has as a corollary all of the other Dhegiha-speaking tribes launching migrations from the same place. From what is known of their historical movements well to the north and west, such a thesis stretches credulity. Given the absence of Siouan place names in the central valley and the invisibility of signs of linguistic influence from surrounding non-Siouans (Springer and Witkowski 1982), it seems more parsimonious to deny the Quapaws such a lengthy tenure in their historical home. And if they are denied that tenure, from where are they to be derived?

Although tightly constrained by paucity of firm information, Hoffman addresses the foregoing question by posing what seem to be the likely consequences of such a denial. *If,* he stipulates, the Quapaws came from the Ohio Valley in the archaeologically relatively recent past, as their traditions attest and their language does not disallow, and *if* the identification of the Menard ("Quapaw") phase with that tribe is in fact correct, "then the Quapaw must have been very adaptable people" (Hoffman 1990:220). Adaptability in this context would be manifested by their having taken over "the ceramic and general life-style of the preexisting or contemporary cultures in the area" of their new home (Hoffman 1990:220). Hoffman is clearly skeptical about such a proposition. As the reader will recollect, however, Henning (1993) as well as O'Brien and Wood (1998), following his lead, adopted a similar model to reconcile Osage and Kansa discrepancies with theoretical archaeological expectations (see above). But in the present case, acceptance of Hoffman's two stipulations requires the presence of an archaeological culture ancestral to the Menard ("Quapaw") phase in the Ohio Valley. A nominee for that hypothetical ancestor, Hoffman (1990:221) mentions, is the somewhat loosely defined protohistoric Caborn–Welborn phase around the confluence of the Ohio and Wabash rivers in a small area of southwestern Indiana and neighboring Kentucky (Green and Munson 1978; Muller 1986:255–258). Hoffman (1990:221) notes the presence of some "northeastern Arkansas and southeastern Missouri pottery in the Caborn–Welborn collections, but [that] nothing looks very similar to the Quapaw phase ceramic complex." Early European trade goods in some of those same collections, he suggests, may just as well indicate contemporaneity with, rather than ancestry for, the Quapaw phase (Hoffman 1990:221). Questioning the integrity of the Caborn–Welborn phase, Dale Henning is also cautious in entertaining a possible genetic connection with Dhegihan peoples generally. That archaeological phase is "very different from the traditional remains on known Dhegihan sites" (Henning 1993:255–256).

To digress but a moment before considering Caborn–Welborn further, it is curious how attractive the confluence of the Ohio and Wabash rivers specifically has been for many would-be reconstructors of Indian history. The Caborn–Welborn sites, so far peculiar to that junction, are but the latest stimulus for that continuing enthusiasm. For example, J. Owen Dorsey and Cyrus Thomas (1910:119), citing unreferenced work by Dorsey himself and Horatio Hale that dealt with language and traditions, had the "seat" of the Dhegihans, including the Quapaws, on the Ohio and Wabash rivers before the migration of all those people to the mouth of the Ohio. While Thomas (1910) credited Pacaha identity as Quapaw, he was also sympathetic to a Quapaw homeland on the Wabash and lower Ohio rivers. He noted that the missionary Gravier reported in 1700 that those contiguous stretches of water were called the "river of the Akansea" by the Illinois (Iliniwek) and Miami Indians, after the name by which the Quapaws, who "formerly dwelt on their banks," were sometimes known. John R. Swanton had the Quapaws living on the Ohio above its junction with the Wabash sometime before 1673. He rejected any relationship with the Pacaha or Capaha (Swanton 1952:213–214). A much earlier example of the lure of the Ohio–Wabash confluence is provided by Albert S. Gatschet in his 1884 compendium of Creek migration legends. In that work he included the fantastic legend recounted by one Milfort, "great war-chief" of the Creeks in the late eighteenth century, evidently recorded by Col. Benjamin Hawkins. According to that chief, the Creeks, then known as "Moskoquis," migrated from their homeland in northwestern Mexico following the Spanish defeat of the Aztecs. Among their later adventures was a prodigious pursuit of the "Alibamu" tribe from the Red River to the Mississippi and then to *the confluence of the Ohio and Wabash rivers* before both tribes turned south, eventually to occupy more conventional territories. With the help of the French, all ended happily (Gatschet 1884:224–228, 233–235). Gatschet recognized fantasy when he saw it. Fortunately, in this instance he published it anyway and made note of his reservations.

The age range of Caborn-Welborn sites is not well established. It is not certain that all of the sites have associated European trade goods. A significant part of the ceramic complex duplicates a large part of that of the generally older, more geographically expansive, and more structurally complex Angel Middle Mississippian phase. Other attributes of the pottery, like ticked-line incised triangles and chevrons and notched appliqué strips, suggest Oneota and Fort Ancient affiliations to the northwest and to the east, respectively (Green and Munson 1978:300–302). If Caborn-Welborn is as late as the loss of platform mounds and other indicators of Middle Mississippian status and the introduction of European manufactures suggest, it is probably too late to have been involved in the so-called Vacant Quarter phenomenon (Williams 1990, 2001), although not necessarily in Quapaw ethnogenesis. Williams's Vacant Quarter hypothesis attempts to lay out and explain the evidence for late prehistoric abandonment of large permanent Mississippian temple-towns and perhaps even a general depopulation over a great riverine network roughly centered where the Ohio joins the Mississippi—the dispersal point that figures so prominently in the legends reviewed earlier in this chapter. The possibility of general depopulation in Williams's hypothesis appears to be receiving support from more recent site surveys and excavations in back-country upland areas in southern Illinois (Cobb and Butler 2002). The Morses, it will be remembered, derive the Quapaw (Menard) phase from the Nodena phase. In their view, after circa A.D. 1400 there was no longer a substantial permanent population in the Cairo Lowlands around the Ohio-Mississippi confluence. This area was a part of the Vacant Quarter that extends eastward to include the territory of the Angel and Caborn-Welborn phases. Much of that population, they maintain, had shifted southward to the southern part of the Missouri "boot heel" and adjacent northeastern Arkansas "to help form the Nodena phase" (Morse and Morse 1983:283). Assuming the approximate correctness of the relevant chronologies, if the Quapaws had any connection with Caborn-Welborn, it would have been too late to support the hypothesis of indirect derivation via Nodena. It would not have been too late, however, for a more direct one. But the latter possibility must await testing until the procurement of an adequate unmixed artifact sample from a well-documented seventeenth-century Quapaw Indian site in the central Mississippi Valley, as well as further clarification of the cultural attributes and temporal placement of the Caborn-Welborn phase in the lower Ohio Valley.

On to the Prairies and the Plains

Enormously complicating research in aboriginal historic period archaeology is the all too frequent paucity of sites containing reliable samples of indigenous material culture, that is, artifacts—pottery particularly—that retain the diagnostic characteristics of their late prehistoric linear forerunners. Henning (1993) has argued that whereas the Dhegihans were very conservative in retaining their language, traditional social customs, religious beliefs, and legends, they were quick to jettison their traditional technologies and subsistence practices in favor of those of new peoples they came to associate with in the course of their migrations. The Quapaw Indians, he suggests, are an example of this and provide a caution to "the analyst depending entirely upon archaeological remains and the historic record of Quapaw occupancy [who] could make the error of assigning the Quapaw to a long regional Mississippian tradition" (Henning 1993:260). As the previously reviewed laments of the Morses, Hoffman, and Sabo emphasize, the great lacuna in that particular case has been the failure of researchers to find an archaeological assemblage most plausibly identifiable with those people. Until that can be achieved, the "Quapaw Paradox" can be used neither in confirmation nor refutation of Henning's thesis of the Dhegihans as materialistic chameleons. That broader generalization states that "the shared prehistoric technological traditions of the Dhegihan speaking tribes is, at the present state of the discipline of anthropology, lost" (Henning 1993:261). "Archaeologically, they [the Dhegihans] quickly became 'lost,' leaving no trace of their past material culture in their new homeland," Henning (1993:262) states. Henning's circumvention of this inconvenience is to make a virtue of scarcity by eschewing archaeological reliance on the "direct historical approach" with its assumption of "technological tenacity" or "material culture retention" (Henning 1993:253, 262). Nevertheless, some of the migratory Dhegihan Siouans did leave traces of their material cultural legacy in their new homes, as Henning himself points out. Employing mainly ceramic and other indications of Oneota ancestry, he specifically documents the retention of some Dhegihan traditional material culture at four sites in the eastern prairies (Henning 1993:257–259). These are the already discussed Blood Run site attributed to the Omahas/Poncas, the Doniphan site in Kansas attributed to the Kansa tribe, and two additional sites (King Hill in northwestern Missouri and Fanning in northeastern Kansas) that he thinks were probably

Kansa villages. This is a short list. As lamented before, it is the case that the majority of sites that can be shown through historical records to have been occupied by named tribal peoples who are believed to have earlier lived elsewhere—and not just Dhegihan speakers—by the very fact of such documentary identifiability, usually date to a time late enough for their traditional technologies to have already been largely replaced by European or Euroamerican manufactures.

Because of such a depleted native material culture record, many scholars are willing to shift a heavier evidential load onto one or more of the backs of ethnohistory, linguistics, ethnological theory, or oral tradition, as Henning has argued. The argument for greater reliance on the latter, where the archaeology of the Dhegihans is poorly developed or simply ambiguous, has been championed most recently by Susan C. Vehik (1993). After summarizing the usually cited migration traditions of the Osages, Poncas, and their other Dhegihan brethren, she finds them on balance more historically persuasive than some of the alternatives archaeologists have proffered. As coda to her willingness to consider those legends as possessing historical value, Vehik is explicit that they are, in the form we know them, European interpretations of what they were told by the Indians. Most archaeological interpretations of Dhegihan origins, she claims, conflict with their oral traditions and necessitate either their substantial reinterpretation or outright dismissal. Specifically cited for proposing at one time or another that certain or all of the Dhegihan-speaking historical tribes originated somewhere in the contiguous corners of Kansas, Missouri, Arkansas, and Oklahoma are David A. Baerreis, Carl H. Chapman, Joan E. Freeman, Alfred E. Johnson, and Robert P. Wiegers (see Vehik's bibliography for the pertinent references). Historians and cultural anthropologists, on the other hand (W. David Baird, James H. Howard, and William E. Unrau are given as examples), she finds more accepting of the migration stories (Vehik 1993:231). O'Brien and Wood (1998:345–357) have published an interesting account of some of the controversies.

The presence of Osage sites historically documented to the late 1600s and early 1700s in a part of the contiguous four corners also occupied by, or very near to, contemporaneous Wichita and perhaps other Plains Caddoan tribes suggests intrusion of the former but not the latter (Vehik 1993:237). Whereas the latter, and also the Caddoan-speaking Pawnees farther north in northern Kansas and Nebraska, exhibit sufficient continuity in their cultural traits with prehistoric phases in the same areas to support theses of essentially in situ evolution, such physical vestiges of Osage patrimony as have come to light do not (Vehik 1993:241). O'Brien and Wood (1998:348), although they are not by their own admission Oneota experts, are convinced enough of the Oneota character of some of the pottery thought to be associated with certain western Missouri Osage occupations to add that tribe to Henning's listing of the Omaha and Kansa as Dhegihan tribes yielding occasional evidence of their ancestral material culture. Notwithstanding the extreme rarity of candidates for pre-European-contact Oneota sites in the historic Osage tribal territory, it is nevertheless possible that some Osages were prehistoric residents there. But that possibility is incompatible, as Vehik (1993:246) points out, with the dearth of evidence that Dhegihan and Caddoan societies had ever been in close contact for any appreciable time. "Had," she says, "Dhegihan societies [and not Osage only] developed on the Plains in the study area, their sociocultural and material culture inventories should exhibit greater similarities to Caddoan societies" (Vehik 1993:246). This observation is also not especially supportive of Henning's attribution of chameleon-like alacrity to Dhegihan technological change. Concluding that "the greater similarity of Dhegihans to Mississippi Valley Siouans and Algonkins [sic], in spite of a historic residence near Caddoan and other Plains societies, is indicative of a comparatively late Dhegihan arrival on the Plains, probably during the seventeenth century," Vehik (1993:246) finds greater credibility in the Dhegihan migration legends than in the archaeological reconstructions of western genesis.

A curiously ambiguous support she proffers for this opinion concerns place names. She is specifically impressed that the Omaha, Osage, and other Dhegihan-speaking peoples have their own names for certain localities whose English designations they recognize. In the absence of heftier countervailing evidence, this is taken as corroboration of the migration legends (Vehik 1993:231–232). Such an argument, even granting the proviso, is open to other interpretations: for example, the assumed or asserted geographical congruity of certain places named in the two languages may reflect no more than one-time sharing of contemporary usage by speakers of those tongues with no implications for earlier times, let alone migrations. This does not negate her proposition, merely the weight that should be given it.

Vehik, as just seen, suggests a seventeenth-century arrival on the Plains by the Dhegiha Sioux. In company with a majority of other archaeologists, she derives them from the east. Just when this movement, or, more probably, movements, took place is open to debate. Complicating resolution of that problem is determining the place or places from which the alleged migration or migrations began. Parts of the recorded migration stories concern the treks, stays, and deflections of the individual tribes after their separations from their "parent nation" and, later, from each other. Segments of the more recent relocations, having taken place in historical time, have been verified by written sources. As previously reviewed, four loci are suggested in traditional accounts for the original and subsequent dispersal areas. Sequentially, these are (1) "north" of the Great Lakes, (2) the point of the parting of the ways when the Winnebagoes separated themselves from their still restless travel companions ("progeny" in the metaphor of the latters' retrospections), (3) the Ohio Valley, and (4) the jumping-off place at the confluence of the Ohio and Mississippi rivers. While I know of no archaeologists willing to stake their professional reputations on endorsing historical veracity for point 1, there are many willing to concede to one or another of the later "episodes" something of potential historical merit. Robert T. Bray's (1991:7) statement "the migration legend [of all the Chiwere Sioux leaving the southwestern Great Lakes for the west] may have some basis in fact" is a fair, though not the most enthusiastic, example of the concession.

According to Henning (2001:229), "the earliest Oneota sites may be those in central Wisconsin, dating [A.D.] 900–1000." This qualified assessment can be arguably extended to eastern Wisconsin as well (Boszhardt 2004; Hall 2004; Overstreet 2001). "Oneota groups," Henning (2001:229) adds, "were probably attracted to the Eastern Plains periphery as early as 1100 by the bison herds, and by no later than 1300 they established large villages in western Iowa." Robert F. Sasso (1993) also adds the importance of increasing availability of bison to his list of reasons for the expansion of Oneota settlements west of the Mississippi. Even farther afield, as Henning maintains, a small group of Oneota sites at or near the juncture of the Chariton and Missouri rivers is especially relevant to the dating of Oneota (and Dhegiha speakers') western movements. "The Chariton River *group continuity* of north-central Missouri began about 1350 and evolved rapidly, culminating in the occupations at the Utz site, home of the Missouria tribe" (Henning 2001:230; citations deleted, emphasis mine; see also Bray 1991). Manifestations of Oneota phases, Henning explains, "are frequently grouped culturally and spatially, forming 'group continuities' that suggest technological and probable biological relationships through time within geographically defined areas" (Henning 2001:229; citations deleted). At present, it is difficult to credit any age estimates for more westerly Oneota sites much earlier than the late fourteenth century (see Henning 2001 for such possibilities). As O'Brien and Wood (1998:345–357) point out with respect to the earliest likely Kansa and Osage occupations in western Missouri, their middens testify to their already having acquired European trade goods.

Linguistic estimates of times of divergence among the various offsprings of the Proto-Dhegiha-Chiwere-Winnebago Central Siouan language group are anything but precise. But they do provide rough orders of magnitude to compare with the sometimes tighter chronological control of archaeological remains thought to be affiliated. To those linguistic age ranges previously introduced, namely those of Rankin (in Alex 2000:215) and Springer and Witkowski (1982), three of Robert C. Hollow, Jr.'s explicitly glottochronological calculations (in Hollow and Parks 1980; see also Parks and Rankin 2001:Table 4) are now integrated. All of these scholars warn against acceptance of their calendrical appraisals as immune to future modification. Nevertheless, combining these estimates, it appears that Proto-Dhegiha-Chiwere-Winnebago separated from Proto-Dakota, the other main division of Central Siouan, sometime in the six-century span between A.D. 200 and 800. Proto-Dhegiha split from Proto-Chiwere no earlier than A.D. 550 and no later than 1000 (Hollow calculates A.D. 800 for the Osage-Dhegiha cleavage from Winnebago specifically). Winnebago and the Chiwere Iowas, Otos, and Missouris parted linguistic company circa 1200–1500.

Testing the Siouan Traditions as Reliable Autochthonous History

It can be seen from the foregoing that the respective chronological assays based on archaeological and on language information, given the broad parameters of the latter especially, are roughly compatible. While it may appear that comparing the two radically different types of data sources is like comparing apples and oranges, it is well to keep in mind that what is being compared are best likened to baskets that contain different quantities of those fruits. But there are still other things in those baskets: migration traditions *and* when those traditions surrendered their orality to writing. There were, of course, innumerable traditions both shared among and unique to each of the Central Siouan societies. As Marjorie M. Schweitzer (2001:450) writes of the nineteenth-century Otos and Missouris, for example, their mythologies were highly diverse, and each clan had its peculiar origin narratives that no outsiders were permitted to hear; each narrative was owned by a particular family. Louis F. Burns (2004:12–14) records the same for the Osages. The oral traditions that survived to be recorded were a mere fraction of what once existed. Nevertheless, those recounting the prehistoric migrations reviewed earlier in this chapter are similar enough to suggest a common inspiration. But their commitment to literary preservation was late in the tenures of each of those Siouan tribes: except for rare fragments, they were recorded in the nineteenth and early twentieth centuries. Among the earliest of the latter are excerpts published in the accounts of the 1819–1820 Long expedition (Thwaites 1904–1907:15:131), Nuttall's 1821 report (in Lottinville 1980 [1821]:93), Prince Maximilian of Wied's 1832–1834 *Travels* (Thwaites 1904–1907:24:313–314), and Gallatin's 1836 American

Antiquarian Society's *Transactions and Collections* paper. Included in Prince Maximilian's account of his travels is a recounting by an Indian agent named Major Bean of a tradition told to him by an "old chief" of how "before the arrival of the Whites in America" the Winnebagoes, Iowas, Otos, and Missouris belonged to one "large band." It seems reasonable to assume that the old chief was referring to a time antedating European intrusion into the Midwest rather than that his words should be taken literally. Such an assumption suggests sometime in the middle to late seventeenth century if the tradition as related, then repeated by the intermediary, and finally recorded in writing is to be taken as historical rather than mythical.

However, as just emphasized, the major sources on the Siouan migration myths are much later still, as previously cited in the syntheses of people like J. O. Dorsey, G. A. Dorsey, McGee, Mooney, and Fletcher and La Flesche. Those writers sought to meld what they regarded as the most trustworthy older accounts of migrations with more focused information they had collected firsthand and via reliable associates. It is to these later syntheses that appeals are usually made for information about the traditions.

As an experiment, the following exercise attempts to ascertain the feasibility of an autonomous folkloric calendar for the initiation of the mouth-of-the-Ohio exodus that is so prominent a benchmark in the Central Siouan migration traditions. The result of this attempt can then be compared with independent insights from archaeology and linguistics relevant to dating that storied scattering of the tribes. If any of the just cited migration episodes are to be experimentally adopted at their face value, this latter—and latest in the two, three, or four foundational migrations referred to in the legends—would seem to enjoy the most popular as well as plausible claim. The experiment is predicated on the probity of the model of oral tradition historicity developed by Africanist historian Jan Vansina (1985), using a worldwide sample of nonliterate societies. Prerequisite to its adoption, however, is settling on a calculation date that most closely approximates the earliest possible time when the most coherent renderings of the Central Siouan migration stories were recorded. Somewhat arbitrarily, 1820, the last year of the Long expedition, seems the earliest defensible candidate for that datum. It should be stressed at this point that both my suggested calibration year from which to retrodict a generic Central Siouan "commencement of recency" quantum and the duration estimates Vansina and others about to be mentioned have used to gauge the retentiveness of nonliterate historical memories are best approximations only. While open to challenge, of course, I believe them both to be defensible. Similarly, the Vansina model should be considered a guide to research, not a formula to be applied mechanically. Although also briefly treated in another connection in Chapter 5 of the present book, this model calls for a short digression here before its implications for the Siouan traditions can be pursued and juxtaposed with other data.

In *Oral Tradition as History* (1985), Vansina described what he had found to be a recurring trifurcation of orally transmitted histories in his extensive sampling of tribal societies around the world. Those tripartite histories he likened to an imaginary hourglass. In the upper chamber is "recent time," the relatively brief period in which real people and events are remembered even as they retrogress from the present (that is, the moment the oral narrative was told and committed to permanent record) to the limits of the oldest society member's recollections of them. The major part, if not all, of that knowledge qualifies as "oral history" as previously defined. A three- to five-generational span appears to be the maximal duration of the upper chamber's authentic temporality. Vansina does not set fixed year limits on the duration of recency so described but rather the range within which variation seems typically confined. The shallowest time depth he has recorded for any society is but 80 years (for the Tio people of the Congo [Vansina 1985:24]). A perusal of his other ethnographic and ethnohistoric examples suggests a more common tenure of 100 to, at the outside, 150 years from any given "now"—the time of the history recitation—to the beginning of recency. In special circumstances, apparently in more hierarchically structured societies, the upper chamber of the hourglass may sometimes be more elongate still. In Donald Bahr's (2001:596) findings with the Pimas, Maricopas, and other Arizona tribes, "recentness" typically is no more than a century in length. Well before Vansina's work, Harold Hickerson (1988:32–33) had noted that among the Ojibwas and related peoples historical accuracy in oral traditions "normally" did not go back "more than two or three generations ago, perhaps at most 70–100 years." Irving Hallowell (1937:666–667), as quoted in Chapter 5 of the present book, was a bit more generous than Hickerson. But even he was not willing to extend any true historicity beyond 150 years from the present. Sven Liljeblad (1986:651) has reported similar limits for Great Basin tribes: "most historical legends recorded by 1900," he writes, "would therefore refer to early postcontact time."

The lower chamber of Vansina's hourglass houses the time/place of cosmology; of god-doings; of the comings and goings of spirit beings; of creations and origins of mountains, rivers, and monsters; of human and tribal origins; of talking animals and other preternaturals; of fantastic happenings. It is the abode of conventional beliefs about times no living or remembered person has ever witnessed. It is "ancientness," the time/place that Bahr (2001) has likened to Eden. It is atemporal, timeless.

The hourglass neck between the two chambers is Vansina's "floating gap." It expands and contracts and probably varies in length from society to society. As long as a society remains an oral one, with the passage of sidereal time the floating gap and ever-trailing ancientness continue drifting just beneath the ascending surface of recentness. Within the floating gap, distinctions between the upper and lower chambers are blurred and apt to be confused. Tribal peoples themselves usually seem unaware of the gap's existence (Vansina 1985:23), and analysts cannot always be sure of its boundaries. Rarely, when there exists an extraneous source of reliable information, something in the usually "unknown and unknowable duration" of the gap (Bahr 2001:596) may be identifiable in real (sidereal) time and thereby a bit of the gap's temporal reach revealed. Thus Bahr (2001:596), using the date of the Spanish arrival in the Southwest and his calendrical assaying of the limits of "recentness" among the people whose traditions he has studied, has shown that the floating gap in their verbal accounts is about 300 years in length. Before the sixteenth-century Spanish *entrada* was Eden, ancientness.

Splitting Vansina's average maximum tenure estimate of 100 to 150 years from any given "now" to the upper end of the floating gap seems a reasonable compromise where multiple societies are involved and certainty is elusive. And by provisionally adopting the year 1820 for the collective "now" of the earliest consistent tellings of migration stories resembling anything like those later synthesized by the Dorseys, Fletcher and La Flesche, and the others, it appears that the resulting probable *earliest* date for the Mississippi crossings themselves is circa 1695. This estimate is strictly contingent on the traditions as given *and* on adoption of the Vansina model with its cross-culturally derived chronometric estimates. Employing 25 years as the measure of a generation (Buettner-Janusch 1973:346), that 125 years from 1820 back to 1695 spans five generations. Such seeming precision, of course, is simply an artifact of the quantitative estimates just adopted and should be taken with a grain of salt. But it strongly suggests that the mass exodus of the Central Siouans from the mouth of the Ohio, if historically genuine and not retrospectively invented, took place sometime in that five-generation century and a quarter quantum following the final decade of the seventeenth century.

The earlier limit of this range falls a couple of decades *after* the time, the 1670s, in which all but the Kansa and Ponca tribes—and also the Quapaw, if their problematical identification with the Pacaha entity of the de Soto era is accepted—first came to European notice. The Kansa and Ponca peoples appeared in the historical record somewhat later; the former in the 1680s according to Bailey and Young (2001:462). The latter, however, may not have separated from the Omahas until the early 1700s or possibly as late as 1785 (Brown and Irwin 2001:416), notwithstanding some Poncas' insistence on much earlier autonomy. In 1880, for instance, J. Owen Dorsey learned of a Ponca belief that *since their birth as an independent tribe* they had had a succession of seven "old men" (head chiefs). Invoking a Dakota usage, assumed to be equivalent, of "old man" to signify a period of 70 years, Dorsey (1886:221–222), crediting for speculation's sake the Ponca count of the "old men," thereby calculated their tribal origin at about A.D. 1380–1390. Whatever may be thought of such a reckoning, at the time of first European notice most of the Central Siouans were already well away from their alleged eastern homeland. As has been seen, the Missouris or proto-Missouris had been ensconced in their place of first historical record by circa 1350—if their connection to the aforementioned archaeological Chariton River group continuity withstands critical examination.

Continuing for argument's sake to accept my initiating calculation date and the temporal parameters of the Vansina hourglass model of oral traditions, if credence is granted the mouth of the Ohio as the staging area for the dispersal of the post-north-of-the-Great Lakes, post-Winnebago-separation, and post-Ohio Valley-residence Siouans, then those people had fissioned and relocated with breathtaking alacrity. By 1670, on the testimony of the earliest documentary reports, they were far removed from where their traditions derive them. In round numbers and as the crow flies, the Quapaws were already established some 250 miles south of the Ohio's mouth in southeastern Arkansas, the Omahas/Poncas were 550 miles northwest of it in southwestern Minnesota and/or northwestern Iowa, the Missouris 250 miles northwest in north-central Missouri, the Osages 250 miles west in southwestern Missouri, and so on. Clearly, the attainment of such a far-flung diaspora by that date puts severe strain on the foregoing experiment at calibrating the migration traditions with the calendar. The gist of the traditions, if not their details, might still be correct, of course, and the suggested chronometry wrong despite its compatibility with duration-of-recency assays as worked out in oral tradition studies elsewhere. As earlier reviewed, independent evidence of greater antiquity for the spread of the Central Siouans is indicated by historical linguistics. There is also some support for this conclusion from archaeology, as in the trans-Mississippi Oneota sequence and the Chariton River group continuity. These disparities with the experimental results would be only marginally slighter had Vansina's 150-year maximum for recency been adopted. Selecting a later calculation date, which might have been taken to favor an a priori bias against genuine historicity in the traditions, would of course have increased the disparities with the independent chronological indicators.

There seems little doubt, chronometry aside, that the Central Siouans did spread over a lot of territory and much of it in protohistoric and early historic time. Moreover, they were not alone. The upper Mississippi Valley during this epoch seems to have been in turmoil, with the commencement of the westerly and southerly movements of the Teton, Yanktonai, and Yankton Dakota contributing pressure on neighboring Central Siouan groups as well as on the Cheyennes (Hyde 1937:9–42; Secoy 1953:65–73; White 2000). To what degree this phenomenon influenced surviving migration stories is an open and interesting question. Certainly some Central Siouan peoples had already shifted their distributions well before these later pressures were applied.

Despite the apparent disparities with the probable survival limitations of credible historicity intrinsic in oral traditions as previously reviewed, evidence independent of the traditions themselves concurs that significant trans-Mississippi movements had indeed occurred, whether or not they commenced at the mouth of the Ohio. The repeated suggestions and sometimes even demonstrations of an association of at least a hefty minority of those people with Oneota assemblages at multiple sites, and the evidence of a longer tenure of that archaeological culture east of the Mississippi River than west of it, establish both a relative time line and the direction of movement. But as seen from the foregoing exercise, the initiation of those movements, either at the mouth of the Ohio or elsewhere, took place at a time or times antedating oral traditional "recency." That being the case, how then could the Iowas, Omahas, Osages, and others have "retained" knowledge of the migrations as detailed in their oral traditions? Is this case persuasive enough to override this discrepancy?

A possible escape from the dilemma beckons from the floating gap. But that transient niche is potentially deceptive. To relegate these mouth-of-the-Ohio and antecedent migrations to the "gap," if indeed not to ancientness (remember the preternatural swimmers stretching the hawserlike vine from bank to bank across the Mississippi, a strong hint in itself), is to surrender claim in this instance on oral traditions *as credibly autonomous* history. Any correspondence they might exhibit with truly sovereign evidence could be explained as simply coincidental, no more to be believed, say, than the swimming incident or the Romeo and Juliet story attending the separation of the Otos and Missouris (in Thwaites 1904–1907:15:131, 24:313). But, then, Vansina's upper chamber and the compatible tenures of verifiable history elsewhere assayed by Bahr, Hickerson, and others also appear out of *chronometric agreement* with germane archaeological and historical linguistic evidence. Yet the traditions' repeated talk of migrations, evidentially innocuous taken by themselves, do invite further consideration when coupled with such scientific criteria as are available.

And, Finally, Who Were the Rememberers and Just What Were They Remembering?

For purposes of this experiment, I somewhat liberally selected the year 1820 as the provisional *collective* "now" of the earliest and, unfortunately, sketchiest migration stories anticipating those much more numerous and detailed narratives subsequently published by the Dorseys, Fletcher and La Flesche, and others. It is important to remember, however, that these succeeding accounts were in fact collected not only much later in the century but even into the first decades of the following. Before most of the former and all of the latter had been recorded, their bearers' societies had suffered frightful losses of life owing to forced dislocations, chronic warfare, and, most of all, repeated visitations of virulent European-introduced diseases. However exaggerated some of the post-Columbian depopulation estimates (David Henige 1986 and 1990, contra Henry F. Dobyns 1983 and other authors), there is little doubt of the terrible damage sustained by most of these small-scale societies. While reliable numbers are elusive, particularly for earliest postcontact times, the reality of serious demographic declines in later generations is generally clear (Green 1993; Ramenofsky 1987, for example). Furthermore, however pristine tribal social boundaries might once have been, they were repeatedly breached as social orders staggered to find new balances in the accelerated flux of theretofore unprecedented challenges. Strangers met and recoiled or amalgamated in unanticipated ways. Omahas married Kaskaskias or Peorias, Osages adopted Delawares, every second or third family had French or Metis relatives. Even before the tide of displaced easterners hit the Mississippi Valley, south of Lake Ontario some Iroquois towns had more alien than native residents.

Contemplate the populations of the Siouan tribes considered in this chapter, for which generally loose estimates prevail early, tighter estimates and even census counts later. Omitted here are extremely early, and probably fanciful, estimates and rebounding numbers from the end of the nineteenth century inflated in good part by in-marrying non-tribesmen, white as well as Indian. Unless otherwise noted, all of these figures are taken from the tribal chapters in the Smithsonian Institution's *Handbook of North American Indians*, Volume 13, published in 2001.

The Iowas (M. M. Wedel 2001:444 and 445, Table 2) are thought to have numbered more than a thousand people in the eighteenth century. How many more is anybody's guess. They were at most half the estimated minimum of that unknown range by the middle of the following century. The nadir of their decline was in 1875, at which time they comprised only 219 members. What is unknown, of course, is how many of that relict population were by then "mixed-bloods" and how many could not be counted because they had dispersed and melted into the general population. But it is clear that the tribe had suffered enormous losses in the first three-quarters of the nineteenth century. Similarly, the Kansa tribe (Bailey and Young 2001:472, Table 2) dwindled from something on the order of 1,400 to 1,600 people during the first half of the nineteenth century and then plummeted before 1860 to a mere 198 by 1890.

Succumbing to smallpox epidemics in the middle to late 1700s, in 1800–1801, 1831, 1835, and, combined with cholera, again in 1851 and struck by a measles outbreak in 1874, the Omahas (Liberty et al. 2001:412, 415, Table 2) lost two-thirds of their reported late-eighteenth-century population by the middle of the nineteenth. My appraisal of 6,200–7,200 Osage Indians for the late eighteenth to the early nineteenth centuries is derived by multiplying the reported 1,800 "warriors" for that period by the anthropologically conventional four so as to include women and children. That population had been reduced to approximately 5,000 by the middle of the new century. During the following three decades, they declined to less than half of *that* number, and they were only some 1,500 by the century's last decade. As with most of the other tribes, this latest figure would have been smaller still but for "mixed-bloods" having been added to the tribal role (Bailey 2001:492–493). The Otos and Missouris ("Otoe and Missouria") have been combined in Schweitzer's (2001:453, Table 2) tabulation of their likely numbers. The earliest figures are for men only, but I have again employed the multiplier four in order to approximate total population. If truly reflective of original conditions, these show a two-thirds drop from 1,600 people at the very end of the eighteenth century to only 520 to 560 a decade later. Despite an apparently strong recovery by circa 1830, numbers again quickly fell to their nadir of 358 at the century's end. Figures for the Poncas (Brown and Irwin 2001:430, Table 1) and Quapaws (Young and Hoffman 2001:501, Table 2) exhibit more or less similar sad configurations. And most of them—in all of the tribes—incorporate unknown proportions of outsiders through cohabitation, with or without marriage, and adoption. Thus the "Quapaw" counts for the nineteenth and twentieth centuries include members originally hailing in whole or in part from the Michigameas, Peorias, Choctaws, Cherokees, Caddos, Osages, Poncas, Wyandots, and "New York Indians" (Iroquois and Munsees)—not infrequently with white, especially French, relations. Except for ethnohistorical allusions to demographic collapse in early postcontact time, little is really known of Winnebago (Ho-Chunk) population history (Green 1993; Lurie 1960, 1978; C. Mason 1976:344–347, 1988:65–67).

Smallpox, cholera, influenza, and other alien microbial scourges took especially heavy toll of the very young and the old. The latter, of course, were quintessentially the conveyers of lineage, clan, and tribal lore from each generation to the next. One must therefore wonder how much of that successively reiterated verbal legacy escaped extinction on its precarious way to fossilization in writing. How authentic—that is, how truly representative of their oral progenitors—are the renditions thus preserved? How much genuine history contra "this is the way it was" tales survived the passage? However remote the chances of unimpeachable answers (see Chapter 2 for the parallel case of the Catawbas), the known historical circumstances prompting the questions must nevertheless give pause to categorical acceptance or rejection of the traditions as received. Estimations of trustworthiness regarding what came to be recorded must rely on extraneous considerations that accordingly circumscribe their justified enlistment as independent sources of historical information.

If the migrations described in the recorded traditions cannot be accommodated within the compass of recency as just delimited, logic suggests that the migration traditions, qua traditions, can be. With the hitherto unparalleled changes brought about by the European invasions coetaneous with recency, some salient catalysts of which have just been mentioned, Native American belief systems no less than their social and material cultures were coerced to adapt or expire. If the former, personal identities and social cohesion, inescapably bound up in this epochal chaos, correspondingly required reinforcement or at least tolerable adjustment. Looking to the ancestors, of course, can secure some sense of legitimacy when it is most needed. As the invasion progressed, shared traumatic experiences, rapidly mutating oral histories, and legendary tales, especially when compared among linguistically related peoples thrown together, offered a hope to resecure a sense of continuity with the ancestors. Shared fates could be rationalized even as the traditions, as always in times past, although rarely with such pressured alacrity, were refurbished afresh to fit with the latest contingencies. Given the conditions of this situation, in the absence of independent evidence it is simply impossible for anyone not committed a priori to the veracity or falsity of those oral traditions to confidently assert or deny their historical worth *as authentic stand-alone information*. In this sense they are marginal to the truth-testing evidential arena of science and critical historiography and should be treated accordingly. To the archaeologist, they are tantalizingly fascinating but pragmatically dangerous. As Robert Lowie and Lord Raglan concluded many years ago, except as spur for investigation, they are essentially irrelevant to credible attempts at culture history reconstruction. To this may be added the qualification that this is especially so when they are beyond the temporal grasp of Vansina's oral tradition recency.

Prudence requires searching for intersecting lines of evidence—for maximum convergence of the least ambiguous information. Uncertainty not infrequently survives even this, however. Oral traditions of an ostensibly historical disposition, or that make reference to characters or events that might be interpreted in such a manner, may take on enhanced persuasiveness in a given situation if other cases of like nature can be shown via autonomous information to have been reliable. To change the earlier metaphor of the "kernel of truth" for another, the danger of throwing out a possible baby with the bathwater is apropos of the need to consider all rational possibilities.

Evaluating the reliability of oral traditions for purposes of tracing past tribal migrations in prehistory and in early historical times invites attention to a range of considerations with which the traditions must be reconcilable. These considerations include data from ethnohistoric sources that can be assayed for reliability independently of the traditions on which they are thought to bear, ethnographic culture trait distributions and the continuities subsisting between them and those recoverable from thought-to-be-related archaeological assemblages, spatial patterning of art styles or motifs, folktale distributions, mapping of language distributions, historical linguistics and the reconstruction of protolanguages, biological relationships between the posited ethnographic and archaeological populations, and clues from landmarks and place names. Each of these requires discretion in its handling.

How much archaeological credence should be given traditional stories about migrations is complicated by a number of considerations, as already seen. Not least of these is the problem of correctly identifying the ethnic group or groups represented by the physical debris sloughed off by now-extinct generations. Entailed in such identifications are correctly distinguishing truly single-component sites, which are relatively rare in my experience, from multicomponent ones and, to the extent possible, dissecting the latter to recover the original integrity of the several occupational episodes. Critical in both situations, especially with respect to protohistoric and early historic sites, is sensitivity to the fluidity of many ethnic or tribal cultural markers during times of depopulation, territorial displacements, and conjoining fragments of formerly independent ethnicities. Complicating variables are tribal intermarriages; the sometimes hyperpermeable nature of social and cultural boundaries; rates and pervasiveness of acculturation; ambiguous or mistaken attributions by traders, missionaries, explorers, and other Indians of living or defunct communities—including long-abandoned localities—to named groups; and the ethnic masking effect caused by accumulating and accelerating replacement of native manufactures by European or Euroamerican goods. And not least to be considered, although far too often it is, is the potentially false lead awaiting archaeologists when they encounter in an ethnography or historical document *the* lineage, *the* clan, or *the* tribal migration or other historical legend when in fact the probability is high of originally multiple, and not always compatible, stories—or even none at all remotely like the one or two that happened to be recorded.

But nuts and bolts and other methodological issues aside, hearing or reading an oral tradition can be like consulting an oracle or a sibyl. They each possess a fondness for obliquity and answering questions with riddles. Nevertheless, what has issued from the present interrogation is a general compatibility of the Central Siouan traditions of a trans-Mississippi westerly migration or migrations with independent sources of information pertinent thereto. That extramural information, derived from language distributions, archaeology, and the other kinds of data just enumerated, is sufficient, especially when taken together, to indicate former population movements even if the traditions had never existed. This being the case, the latter, whatever their true geneses, are dependent variables. Regardless of their indigenous prestige, their extra-parochial historical authority derives as wholly from external information sources as, on the other hand, do rejections of claims of Pawnee and Arikara residence east of the Mississippi Valley (see above) or of postcontact-period Ponca sightings of live hairy elephants and 40-foot-long monsters in Nebraska (Chapter 7). With regard to the time of the migration or migrations, in toto they appear suspended between the floating gap and the lower limits of recency as defined in Vansina's hourglass metaphor. There is at present no way of gauging the historicity, let alone temporality, of the alleged *pre*-trans-Mississippi migration traditions. Standing alone, traditions utter historical truth enigmatically.

10

Conclusions

In midwinter of 2004–2005, herded by two border collies, my wife, our daughter, and I were trudging along a snow-covered dirt and gravel back-country road ascending higher terrain just west of U.S. Highway 93 between Salmon and North Fork, Idaho. From atop successively higher rises affording vistas of the Salmon River valley and the bluffs sculpting its eastern margin, I saw the even more awesome Beaverhead Mountains of the Bitterroot Range puncture the sky, their loftiest farthest-off peaks defining the continental divide separating Idaho and Montana. Lagging behind at a couple of those lookouts, I slipped from the consciousness of space, magnificent as it was, to the contemplation of time, finding myself conjuring up the Lemhi Shoshonis, who were here when Meriwether Lewis and William Clark arrived with Sacajawea, and, before them, the now nameless people whose archaeological traces attest centuries and even millennia of precedence. What successions of names and significances had been linked with those peaks and valleys and the creeks that here and there venture out of the uplands to join the river? What personal experiences and social memories had formerly given identities to each of those places I saw but whose meanings had vanished with their bestowers? Had this steep declivity at my feet or that dramatic cliff at the river's bend once—or, more likely, more than once—been sentient? What spirits had quickened these places now silently occupied by inanimate sandstones and conglomerates, basalts, and the tracery of pegmatite and diabase sills and dikes in walls of granite? Whole peoples come and gone! The same places but different worlds! How enriched is our modern vision—and how impoverished! Perhaps the Canadian novelist Anne Michaels (1998:210) came closest when she answered her own question, "What is the true value of knowledge?" by suggesting that it "makes our ignorance more precise."

Knowledge, even so modestly conceived, is no mean thing. If achieved, its necessary and welcome corollary is a more generous conception: an expanded acquaintance with the world as it is and even as it once was. But a bittersweet companion corollary is the sloughing off of incompatibilities with such knowledge. That delimitation of ignorance whereby the petrology and mineralogy and geological history of the country I have just described—and something as well about its prehistoric inhabitants—have come to be knowable, and even to some degree known, is the same process whereby sentience left the landscape and spirits went into exile. To acknowledge this is painful and maybe even impossible for many people still committed to respected traditional stories about the world and their place in it. This is a dilemma shared by reflective anti-evolution Christian biblical-literalists as well as non-Christian religious fundamentalists in addition to many tribal or recently tribal people the world over. Nevertheless, even cherished stories cannot remain immune to challenge *if and as* they are extracted from their cultural milieu and intruded into or offered as a surrogate for missing or inadequate scientific or critical historiographic information. The effort that "makes our ignorance more precise" is daunting as it is, without proscribing the questioning of traditional knowledge. The evolution of the right to freedom of inquiry and the pursuit of new knowledge has had many causes, has met with much resistance, and has inevitably undercut the influence of religious and other traditional restrictions on their exercise. That process and resulting tension continue.

To question traditional beliefs about history or anything else can be a touchy business. Even with every effort at tact, it can elicit resentment. Especially when coming from an outsider, hints of anything perceived as more negative than neutrality can be taken as effrontery, as disrespect for the individual or society concerned. People's pasts, after all, form to a greater or lesser degree a component of their self-identification, expressing, indeed validating, who they are. But while most Native Americans in their everyday activities are no more concerned with their history than are average non–Native Americans, both being caught up in their more pressing current affairs, many do take their cultural heritage, history included, very seriously. There are also, of course, opportunists who seize upon history as a political weapon. Ranging from firebrands to Uriah Heeps, these thrust or insinuate concern for "respect for the ancestors" into any discussion of "who owns the past?" This can be a smokescreen to disarm people or, as Alice Kehoe (1998:214) has labeled it, a red herring that distracts attention from their real concern: power and the issue of tribal sovereignty. Nevertheless, it remains true that many American Indians take seriously the heritage stories with which they grew up. Questioning that legacy can be seen as an unwelcome intrusion, as indeed it would be if the intention of such questioning is to challenge what is properly part of a sovereign conceptual system that is none of the questioner's business. But those oral traditions *become* the business of archaeologists when they are proffered by Indians or other advocates as deserving of equal epistemological status with propositions derived from the assumptions and procedures of scientific and systematic historiographic inquiry.

If the preceding two paragraphs seem to have labored over the elementary distinction between respect for people as fellow human beings and respect for their beliefs, which become properly subject to critical examination when plucked from their autonomous cultural sphere and injected unmodified into another, experience has proved it necessary. For example, in a previous *archaeological* publication I addressed my misgivings explicitly to *archaeologists* about the willingness of many *archaeologists* as well as Native Americans to

grant co-equal status to myths, folktales, spiritual insights, and other "traditional knowledge" along with archaeological (scientific) knowledge in searching out and making sense of the past. Admonishments to "respect" and "acknowledge" the "validity of oral history and traditional knowledge"—something apart from the respect due persons, I would stipulate—are commonplace in the discipline today.

"Traditional knowledge" has produced flat earths, geocentrism, mice spontaneously generated out of piles of rubbish, women arising from mens' ribs, talking ravens, polygenesis, the superiority or inferiority of this group or that, and the historically latest "first people" of the Black Hills upwelling from holes in the ground. Science, by its very nature, must challenge, not "respect" or "acknowledge as valid," such folk renditions of the past. I do wonder if the same calls for accommodation of oral history, "traditional knowledge," and "other ways of knowing" would be considered as equally appropriate and binding on the archaeological community if their proponents were not themselves (or others speaking for) Native American or First Nations people but were, for example, Anglo-Saxon Christian fundamentalists pushing their own knowledge claims.

Common decency requires respect for people holding a pre-scientific metaphysics. But it does not require compromising the systematic and interdependent axioms, postulates, corollaries, and methodologies that hard-won experience has demonstrated as most responsible for whatever advancement of knowledge archaeology can boast. NAGPRA is the law of the land and its true intellectual costs are yet to be computed. More costly yet will be acquiescence in the re-mystification of the past [Mason 1997b].

Although these words received a few more favorable than unfavorable responses, one distinguished archaeologist either failed to grasp, or would not concede, the distinction I was trying to make between respect owed persons and that appertaining to the evaluation of ideas. So touchy and morally self-assured was he on this subject that he felt no compunction in publicly classifying me with other, but unnamed, archaeologists allegedly sharing "Indiana Jones" self-images. We were portrayed as exhibiting personality traits characterized by, among other named deficiencies, "brashness and insensitivity . . . with one archaeologist [me] even going so far as to declare that our job is to challenge peoples' oral traditions!" Fortunately, he wrote, "most archaeologists are not so insensitive" (Zimmerman 2003:12). Regarding the latter offence, many other scholars, though perhaps not many enough in archaeology, to judge by Zimmerman's shocked sense of propriety, are equally indictable. As just two eminent examples already cited in preceding pages, I offer the authors of the following asseverations. First, by not challenging sources of information—and here I paraphrase—be those sources oral traditions, eyewitness accounts, or other scholarly authorities, the student of the past surrenders "his autonomy as an historian" and, in effect, turns over to others the task that, "if he is a scientific thinker, he can only do for himself" (Collingwood 1946:236). Second, if sources are allowed "to stand uncriticized, he [their user] abdicates his role as critical historian. He is no longer a seeker of knowledge but a mediator of past belief; not a thinker but a transmitter of traditions" (Harvey 1966:42).

Aside from the raising of hackles, the search for a universal (in the sense of cross-cultural) historiography acceptable to everyone is doomed by definition. Universality could only be achieved by the subordination of innumerable parochial "ways of knowing." It still has not been realized in science, or at least medicine, as a visit to the local health stores in any American city, let alone many other places in the world, will attest. That different peoples have rights to maintain and celebrate their accustomed lineage or tribal histories is axiomatic. So also is the certainty of collisions with the science paradigm of archaeology. Balancing coexistence of the epistemologically unequal in a pluralistic society should not be an aspiration unworthy of pursuit. Finding that equilibrium, however, is a sham exercise if it requires or results in dilution of the essential distinctions by which each has its identity. The gestalt of a special place as "perceived" by, say, a Western Apache (Basso 1996), while rightly a subject for anthropological inquiry, is no more contingent on a scientific exposition of the geomorphology of that place than the reverse, they each being independent realms, neither beholden to the other.

Alice B. Kehoe (1998), in an erudite and impassioned history of American archaeology, attempts with mixed results to grapple with this problem. In that attempt she labels as an unwarranted "hegemonic assumption" the proposal that a "rigorously scientific" archaeology had in 1995 been recommended by the conveners of the Society for American Archaeology's ethics workshop as the path for "enriching our collective understanding of the past." This recommendation, typical, she says, of an outmoded positivist philosophical era, is asserted to have echoed the now-defunct closed elitist club that had controlled the profession into the mid-twentieth century; its demise was precipitated by the democratization of opportunity engendered by passage of the G.I. Bill, the Civil Rights Act, expansion of federally and state-mandated cultural resource management (CRM) programs, and enactment of the Native American Graves Protection and Repatriation Act (NAGPRA), even though some of the consequences of the latter she explicitly deplores. The changes thus wrought eventually led, Kehoe argues, to a shifting of some of the funding for archaeology from the National Science Foundation, where incorporating Native American historiographies into grant proposals was alleged to be discouraged, to the National Endowment for the Humanities, where, it is supposed, it is not. "Accountability"—the envisioned result of the passage of NAGPRA and the "stricter" compliance requirements of CRM projects (fortunately not always but all too often satisfied by little more than dollars-and-cents form-filling reports devoid of substance)—has "*pushed archaeologists into a postmodern realization that the discipline's known pasts may not necessarily override others' versions of the past*" (Kehoe 1998:212–213; my emphasis). NAGPRA, especially, "galvanized American archaeologists into accepting a post-colonial position." But, then, they were "already coming down from the veranda of the colonial officer" (Kehoe 1998:212–213). If the ambiguous use of the phrase "postmodern realization" simply refers to recognition of current political reality, as it does in this instance (Kehoe, personal communication, 2005), rather than the assayed merits of an intellectual repositioning, there can be no gainsaying it.

The complaint about "rigorously scientific" and "collective understanding of the past" focuses on archaeologists' alleged exclusion of how native peoples, American Indians in this instance, think about their past, the means through which they know it, and what it is they know as history. That exclusion is the "hegemony" of the complaint. In reality, as I understand it, what is being complained of is not the exclusion, in the sense of ignoring, of those considerations, but their non-incorporation into the theoretical structure of scientific archaeology. Furthermore, as Kehoe herself points out, there is no monolithic indigenous *history*, there are indigenous *histories*. But the exclusionary point, however one reads it, resonates in the postmodern ethos of much contemporary archaeology. The innuendoes of politically loaded labels like "hegemonic" and "colonialist" (tags conjuring up spec- ters of tyranny, oppression, and exploitation) aside, expunging the values and practices to which such terms have been and are being applied man- dates the surrender of not inconsequential components of the archaeological discipline's intellectual autonomy. As expressed in the words of the afore- mentioned Larry Zimmerman, here taken out of strict context but not spirit, "consultation and involvement of nonarchaeologists puts at least some of the control of research into hands other than ours. Are we really willing to do this? If you say yes, you have agreed to an approach that will funda- mentally change archaeology" (quoted in Kehoe 1998:214). Kehoe approv- ingly cites Zimmerman's "yes" to the question he poses in the foregoing quotation. As an example of the benefits of that change, the reader is told of non-Indian archaeologists and an ethnohistorian, working at the direction of Hopi clan elders and priests, who "align" their "rigorous scientific and historiographic practices . . . with oral history and Hopi interpretations of data, not deforming but enriching the prehistory and conventional [?] his- tory." However, this assertion is immediately preceded by another: "The contracted professionals document a Hopi past frequently colliding with the national [conventional?] American past" (Kehoe 1998:214). It would thus appear that in Hopiland, anyway, it is possible to eat one's cake and have it, too.

Apropos of the foregoing, although addressed to problems in the South- east rather than the Southwest, but relevant to all culture areas, are the ob- servations of David S. Brose (1993:13–14):

> The rise of what has been politely called "folk archaeology" now claims that each ethnic group is . . . given license to discover its own interpretation of what it loosely believes to be the archaeological texts of its past. If the Cherokee claim to have only recently come east of the Mississippi River, which Anglo-American archaeologist is free enough of racial biases to say they are wrong? If the Creek believe that their ancestors built Poverty Point, there are surely archaeological data that can be interpreted to fit this belief. Accepting this paradigm will hold little future for southeastern archaeology, for only compara- tive literary aesthetics can legitimately evaluate alternative mythic histories.

The often-made complaint of American Indians, and of many non- Indians who presume to speak for them, that they have been excluded from, indeed "robbed" of, their own histories by anthropologists generally and archaeologists particularly has been mentioned many times in this book, most immediately in the present chapter. It has become an increasingly strident charge that plays on the inchoate guilt of a great many Americans and Canadians who agree that great wrongs were perpetrated by the present majority's forebears on the continent's native peoples, peoples whose descendants still labor under serious social and economic disadvantages. Most archaeologists working in North America, being a part of that majority population, and having in addition a professional investment in their land's first peoples, are doubly vulnerable to allegations of culpability. Some, as previously cited, have confessed to guilt, a few with startling enthusiasm. But the charge is a sham. However honestly made and accepted, it is a populist appeal that, to be truly meaningful, covertly introduces expectations of change in theory and practice inimical to honest inquiry. Intentionally or not, it is a disguised attempt, not unlike that of so-called scientific creationists or intelligent design advocates, to breach the divide between science and traditional beliefs. Repeatedly enunciated, however, it captures newspaper columns and the attention of alert politicians ("We are certainly not going to return anything of *real* value, so why not give them back the stuff in museums—and who cares about their history anyway?"). Although the previously quoted Larry Zimmerman would not concur with all of my concerns, his prediction of a "fundamentally change[d] archaeology" is inarguable.

It being hardly credible that all of the archaeologists who have pleaded guilty to the Indian history thievery charge are naive about the intellectual implications for their own discipline, one must suppose the interposition of an overriding consideration. While a marginal few may have nothing more in mind than promoting or preserving access to CRM contracts requiring Native American approval, I believe the others to be more honorably motivated. If I understand the latter correctly, a paramount concern for human rights, as manifested in this instance by reluctance to interfere with a people's prerogative to identify themselves by whatever lawful means they think appropriate, even if it devolves on appeal to myth, seems implicit if it is not offered directly. Sometimes, as in the Kehoe rendering, that appeal is couched in more political terms invoking the principle of tribal sovereignty. Although I am sympathetic to both renditions of this argument, it fails to address two countervailing ones. The first of these maintains that publicly enunciating the results of free and honest inquiry into any question, howsoever unpopular they may be, is also a fundamental human right—the repression of which has understandably been a characteristic of authoritarian regimes the world over. The second repudiates any implication that by conceding the autonomy of Indian "ways of knowing" their incorporation into the structure of archaeological knowledge is thereby warranted.

American Indians are of course free to conceive their histories any way they see fit. They do, frequently in ways anathema to any philosophy of science. Indeed, a common Indian theme is that they already know their pasts (that is, those aspects of the past that they regard as worth knowing): "Archaeologists are interested in learning about the past. Native Americans are interested in maintaining the cultural traditions they inherited from their ancestors who lived in the past" (Anyon et al. 1997:78, 83–84). They may, as in litigation over land rights, or may not, as in spiritual matters or, usually, in learning about their ancestors, be interested in archaeological knowledge. That is their privilege. Incongruities with archaeological or ethnohistorical information may be ignored or resolved in favor of their own cultural traditions. To the extent allowed by law and the elasticity of professional conscience, on reservation lands Indians have license to set the conditions by which archaeologists may conduct surveys, excavate or avoid specified sites, and question the modern residents about beliefs and practices possibly relevant to the archaeology. Certain areas or culturally proscribed features (burials, precincts regarded as sacred) or topics (clan traditions, ritual practices) may be declared off limits to outsiders of any stripe. It is the right of Native Americans to prohibit any archaeological investigations whatsoever on their own lands or, on the other hand, to fund strictly delimited projects as determined by tribal authorities instead of granting permission for programs designed by and for professional interests alone. Arapahoes in Colorado, Hoopas in California, Haidas in British Columbia, Mashantucket Pequots in Connecticut, Navajos in Arizona, Senecas in New York, Seminoles in Florida, and scores of other tribes have established museums in which they curate, exhibit, and interpret their cultural legacies in accordance with traditional knowledge, augmented or not with archaeological or ethnographic perspectives. The National Museum of the American Indian in Washington, D.C., attempts to do the same. There being a considerable range in Native Americans' receptiveness to the contributions the latter perspectives have made to their culture histories, tribal museums are hardly uniform in their messages to visitors. Trying to reconcile the two in public museum storage and exhibition programs can be very expensive and draining of patience on both sides (e.g., Evers and Toelken 2001; Holm and Pokotylo 1997).

Critical to understanding that lack of uniformity as well as the ambivalence about archaeological pertinence to customary folk beliefs is facing up to questions either not asked or fudged if they are. Traditionally minded people are caught between two worlds as, in a sense, are archaeologists who want to know the past as objectively as they can even while trying to comprehend the native view of that same past. But are they the *same* pasts? Do they both, each incompletely or unequally, reflect the "past as it was," à la Leopold von Ranke or as in William Dray's (1993:1) "certain stratum of reality which historians make it their professional business to study," as earlier discussed in Chapter 2? Or is what is at stake mutually impervious *conceptions* of the past?

As much of this book documents, cultural relativists abound who would condemn claims for the superiority of any—perhaps most particularly the Western mainstream historical profession's—construction of history over any other. After all, they argue, history is a cultural product; it is therefore whatever it is made out to be in each such context. And in part because each society must know its own history better than outsiders can possibly know it, it is only prudential, let alone humane and democratically fair, that such other histories be regarded as having equal value, however different the forms they may take (see, for examples, Anyon et al. 1997 [in Swidler et al. 1997]; Dongoske et al. 1997; Echo-Hawk 1997, 2000; Handsman and Richmond [in Schmidt and Patterson 1995:87–117]; Martin 1987; Miller 1998; Whiteley 2002 [the last with some reservations]).

Ceding to indigenous conceptions of history, each embedded in its own traditional epistemology, immunity from scholarly challenges is a respectable exercise of the venerable anthropological doctrine of cultural relativism. Anthropology, however, is charged with more than respect for the unique. It has nomothetic, generalizing, interests. And only at the cost of irrelevance does it forfeit its responsibility to "translate" or "decipher" the experience, terms, and ideas of other peoples into the language of modern scientific and historiographic discourse. These additional pursuits require suspension, not rescission, of cultural relativism. If a universal history—one, that is, that aspires to comprehend all histories in a minimally ethnocentric intelligible whole—is ever to be constructed, the primacy of the authoring society's historiography over all others must be granted *for that cosmopolitan purpose.* That purpose requires challenging historiographic ethnocentrisms, not excluding our own. Only conjoined Western science and historiography have developed the tools to undertake that effort. To say this is not cultural arrogance; it simply states the necessary precondition for such a project. It is also a historical fact. Without this concession and actuality, mankind would be hopelessly condemned to perpetuate the "interpretive Tower of Babel" of which Peter Whiteley (2002:406) despairs. While Pimas and Maricopas may show some interest in or at least a casual awareness of each other's traditions, and Zunis and Comanches are mutually indifferent, only Western-educated social scientists and historians possess the interest and analytical tools to engage them all.

Alleviating his Babelian angst somewhat, recent strides in anthropological and historical studies, Whiteley (2002:407) says, are revealing "indigenous histories as *genuinely* historical" (my emphasis). As he draws on ideas from Claude Lévi-Strauss and Marshall Sahlins that, as he quotes them, in effect deny the possibility of knowing any past as it was but only as refracted by cultural and other biases, Whiteley's finding of "genuine" history anywhere is contradictory. But, then, Sahlins himself, although in a different part of the world, seems to have grasped the same logical tar baby in his struggles to come to grips with the histories of the Maoris, Fijians, Hawaiians, and other Polynesians. In the lives of those peoples, he maintains, their "schemes of cosmological proportions . . . may be even more significant historically" than *"what actually happened"* (Sahlins 1985:76; my emphasis). Given the insistence that histories—*all histories*—are relative to, and thus inevitably distorted (refracted) by, social purposes and cultural ethos, how can what *genuinely happened anywhere* possibly ever be determined? What culture-free correction exists for refraction? Whiteley certainly fails to find it in archaeology, for that discipline, he says, is "just one kind of [Lévi-Straussian] 'history-for' [that is] as attached to forms of social interest, that are indeed often ideological, as [are] others" (Whiteley 2002:407). Nevertheless, he says:

> If we are to move closer to historical understanding, we must first reject the great scholastic fiction of "mythic" vs. "historic" societies. *Myth discernibly includes empirical descriptions of objectively historical events and practices* (cf. Bloch 1989). The bible, for example, is a classic case of *a mythological text, with historical elements* embedded in it (e.g., Leach and Aycock 1983). Notwithstanding its originally oral basis, the bible's very textuality enables it to be conceptualized as including history more easily than is the case with oral mythology, owing to *engrained— though largely unexamined—ideas about the supposed instability and unreliability of oral narratives in the Western cult of the written word* [Whiteley 2002:407; my italicizations of non sequiturs and gross exaggeration].

Some of Whiteley's pronouncements on oral traditions and archaeology were briefly introduced in Chapter 2, along with the views of Peter Nabokov and others. Nabokov, despite acknowledging the general Native American "prioritizing" of cultural values over factual accuracy, their not infrequent injection of "myth-time" characters and agencies into the present world, and their common indifference to "incompatibilities between the world of facts and that of dreams," nevertheless urges Western scholars to "somehow weave Native historicities into the bedrock of their accounts" (Nabokov 1996:54). Mixed metaphor aside, one must wonder how this is to be done while respecting the integrity of fundamentally incompatible historical philosophies. They who recommend so daunting a task should feel more of an obligation to specify the steps whereby it is to be accomplished. Many of the obstacles to be dealt with, some already encountered in earlier chapters, defy resolution.

How, for example, does a would-be "bedrock weaver" accommodate the Western ideal of openness of inquiry to Hopi oral tradition gatekeepers who alone will judge what is and is not to be talked about with researchers (Anyon et al. 1997:85)? Or make it compatible with the Zuni proscription of outsiders having access to material that may encroach on "tribal cultural sensitivities" (Anyon et al. 1997:86)? Or with the Hualapais' similar secretiveness (Anyon et al. 1997:86)? Or with the now three-decades-long prohibition of non-native persons, researchers or not, to witness an Iroquois Longhouse ceremony either in Canada or in the United States (Michelson 2003:17)? Or reconcile it with Calvin Martin's (1987:9) finding that "the two core philosophies [of Indian and Western history] . . . are fundamentally antagonistic and irreconcilable," even though he too is a would-be "bedrock weaver"? Or with Keith Basso's following characterization of Western Apache historiography, one that is in essentials not atypical of many others:

It is history constructed in spurts, in sudden bursts of imaginative activity, and it takes the form of stories delivered in spoken Apache, the language of the ancestors and most of their modern descendants. Answering the question "What happened here?", it deals in the main with single events, and because these are tied to places within Apache territory, it is pointedly local and unfailingly episodic. It is also extremely personal, consistently subjective, and therefore highly variable among those who work to produce it. For these and other reasons, it is history without authorities—all narrated place-worlds, provided they seem plausible, are considered equally valid—and the idea of compiling "definitive accounts" is rejected out of hand as unfeasible and undesirable. Weakly empirical, thinly chronological, and rarely written down, Western Apache history as practiced by Apaches advances no theories, tests no hypotheses, and offers no general models. What it does instead, and likely has done for centuries, is fashion possible worlds, give them expressive shape, and present them for contemplation as images of the past that can deepen and enlarge awareness of the present [Basso 1996:32].

Urging ethnographers to also examine how *they* imagine history even while they "try to discern how history gets imagined by the people whom they study," Basso (1996:154–155n7) warns that they must "allow for the possibility—which the Apache case affirms—that the two may differ in far-reaching ways and perhaps be incompatible and even irreconcilable."

Recognizing some of the sorts of problems just reviewed, Peter Nabokov (2002:233) has argued at length that in order for non-Indians to study Indian "ways of history" they must learn to understand and respect the "centrality of symbols," for they are important in establishing (revealing) the values common to a given culture. However, it is also important to appreciate that "these *master* symbols and *root* metaphors [my italics] have almost certainly undergone transformations" (Nabokov 2002:233). Although he maintains that these transformations have been constrained by a high value placed on consistency, they sometimes require "adjusting the facts" and making "retroactive enhancement" of traditions "*in order for history to make sense in Indian terms*" (Nabokov 2002:233–234; my italics). One must wonder what transformations the *lesser* symbols and metaphors experienced and in which "transformation," "adjustment," and "retroactive enhancement" non-Indians are to find history "in Indian terms" that is intelligible as history in non-Indian terms.

Indians, says Nabokov, do not share "the pastness of the past" that Goody and Watt (1968:33–34) describe as characteristic of literate societies. Rather, the past transcends time and is actively coextensive with the contemporary and, indeed, future worlds, into which the ancestors "may even put in their two cents' worth" (Nabokov 2002:234). Furthermore, "their historical traditions have rarely seen any incompatibilities between the world of facts and that of dreams" (Nabokov 2002:234). To deal with puzzles like these, he recommends that non-Indians wanting "to do" Indian history should, in effect, "apprentice" themselves to anthropology, the scholarly discipline best equipped, in Nabokov's quotation from Mildred Mott Wedel and Raymond J. DeMallie, to "discern the clouded facts, correctly analyze the misleading commentary, or extract significant cultural information that appears incidentally in documents written for quite different purposes" (Nabokov 2002:236). Ideally, Nabokov (2002:235) advises inviting Indians to participate as full and equal partners in such endeavors. He says nothing, however, about the qualifications of such partners beyond their being Indians.

Native Americans, we are told, have their own intellectual legacies that must be acknowledged. Of critical importance in this connection is recognition of the underlying assumptions influencing Indian and non-Indian views of themselves and of each other (Nabokov 2002:237). There should be a concerted effort, Nabokov urges, to produce multivoiced cross-cultural "alternative, parallel, or altogether Other [*sic*] viewpoints" that will be a "liberating challenge" to what has gone before in representations of history (Nabokov 2002:238).

Unless that envisioned "liberating challenge" is to result in a reinvigorated Babelian cacophony of "parallel" histories, that is to say, the fiction of histories publicly separate but equal, the only viable alternatives are reduced to the nonsense of a logically unintelligible melding of the incompatible and the single-voiced anti-Babelian historiography I regard as inevitable in its ascendancy (see above). Like the archaeological data that Lewis R. Binford (1983:19) has long insisted require "translating" or "decoding" through testable inferences in order to become statements about the past, so too the multitude of parochial histories. There must be a way of testing applicable to all, one voice, so to speak, one historical epistemology—one that can encompass what the others have to say when they can be translated, decoded, into its more cosmopolitan terms. For all its transient lapses into ideological extremes, Western historiography is so far the sole candidate for that universalizing role.

A century and a quarter ago Edward B. Tylor, in his monumental *Primitive Culture,* concluded:

> Even the fragments of real chronicle found embedded in the mythic structure are mostly in so corrupt a state, that, far from their elucidating history, they need history to elucidate them. Yet unconsciously, and as it were in spite of themselves, the shapers and transmitters of poetic legend have preserved for us masses of sound historical evidence . . . [that is] their own ancestral heirlooms of thought and word . . . the operations of their own minds . . . the philosophy and religion of their own times, times of which formal history has often lost the very memory. Myth is the history of its authors, not of its subjects [Tylor 1920 (1871):1:416].

That Tylor's conclusions remain defensible even after the passage of 125 years of vastly expanded research is a modern endorsement of the late nineteenth century's identification of anthropology as "Mr. Tylor's science." His name remains honored notwithstanding his proneness, along with most of his contemporaries, to overesteem the myths, legends, folklore, customs, and so forth then known to science as faithful reflections of ancient cultural traits and to underestimate their evolving adaptations to the, à la Leslie White, "one damn thing after another" of history. Tylor, unlike many of his modern successors, knew there was a distinction between history and myth.

This essential latter distinction along with how to recognize its manifestations across cultural and temporal boundaries represented in oral traditions and archaeology has been, of course, the paramount concern of this book. While the focus of that concern has been on aboriginal North America, it early became apparent that the field of vision had to be widened so as to take advantage of pertinent work done elsewhere. In parts of Chapters 2 through 5 I have made modest attempts to do that by drawing on germane contributions of historians, archaeologists, and ethnographers in Africa, the Aegean, the Levant, and some other parts of the world beyond the Americas and by enlisting the contributions of psychologists, classicists, folklorists, sociologists, and biblical scholars. That widening could readily have gone even further, to examine even more of the sometime tension between history as written, for example, and history as archaeologically adduced. The former, for all its advantages as a checkable permanent record, is not uncommonly as mythical in whole or in part as the contents of much of oral tradition. The highly disputaceous field of academic historians gives ample proof of that. With more archaic historical texts typically dedicated to tasks transcending disinterested reportage, as in ancient Egypt, Mesopotamia, India, or China, the incongruities archaeology reveals with what was written can be enormous. Modern readers can no doubt supply titles of recently published "histories" in similar service.

It is also true, of course, that archaeology is itself a quarrelsome enterprise, being often ambiguous, usually tentative, and sometimes flatly wrong (e.g., Kehoe 1998; Trigger 1989; Willey and Sabloff 1993). But it has additionally proved capable of intervening decisively in many controversies like those concerning the coexistence of humans and elements of the Pleistocene megafauna, as well as settling the insubstantiality of related claims that such animals had survived as late as or to just before the coming of Europeans to America; questions about the identity of the Mound Builders; debates about whether more than feud-level warfare and scalping were indigenous or had been introduced by Europeans; whether prehistoric Indian cultures had been static or had significantly changed over centuries and even millennia; questions regarding the independent origin of New World plant domestication and the rise of an American "Neolithic Revolution"; and the uncertainty that the Vikings really did reach America. And although it did not seem necessary to further the argument in another direction, it would not have been inappropriate to have examined the discrepancies between what modern Americans and Canadians *say they do* in their consumption habits (thus potentially inaugurating future oral traditions) and what they *actually, really, truly do* as testified by the household garbage they throw out (thus creating an independent and in many ways more reliable archaeological record of their consumption behavior; Rathje and Murphy 1992).

An old and often repeated adage has it that what people believe about the past is more important than whatever actually took place. As argued in the first two chapters, most people, most of the time the world round, have not had reason, means, or leisure to question the possibility of a difference. Since long before the rise of nation-states, family, or other traditional storytellers, and additionally thereafter political and religious clerisies, sometimes less than innocently, have taken advantage of this human foible. Twentieth- and now twenty-first-century propagandists with their hitherto unparalleled means of mass public access have thrived on it. Professional historians and archaeologists, however, cannot, or should not, lose sight of the difference even if they are unable to distinguish it in specific instances. Oral traditions thought of as true statements about the past by their narrators lose their authority when extracted from their generative context. They are justly subject to critical appraisal if and when they are so extracted and considered as scientific or historical evidence in the modern Western sense. Certain Northwest Coast Indians may believe their forebears were created separately from the rest of humanity near or where they, their descendants, presently live. They may recount "memories" of life in the Ice Age. Their ancestral traditions, as Dell Hymes (1990:601) observes, may be said to have predicted the coming of Europeans, show that Jesus and the trickster were somehow one and the same, or tell how Coyote flew "out over the ocean in an airplane." Rather than oral traditions, or at least mythology, being "a relic of the past . . . narrative creativity did not end with the arrival of outsiders" (Hymes 1990:601). These tellings of the past are useful for connecting that realm, even as it mutates, to the present. As Robert Borofsky (1987:145), writing about the Polynesian Pukapukan islanders, so succinctly put it, "traditional knowledge must continually adjust to changing circumstances . . . What is at stake is a pragmatic rather than correspondent sense of truth—meaningfulness to the living rather than precise accuracy to the past." Or, as another ethnographer concluded for Oceania as a whole, "it is debatable whether any indigenous Pacific narrative form can be identified with the Western model of 'history,'" although, as she suggests, bits of history, in the Western sense, may be embedded in some of the narratives (Linnekin 1997:16–20). It is just this possibility, as raised also in Asia, Africa, and elsewhere besides America, as previously seen, that tantalizes students of the past desperate for any help they can get.

Chapter 4 reviews how it was the possibility of such help that stimulated the search for Homer's Troy, and, however creditable that venture may be judged, the result has been significant contributions to Aegean archaeology and culture history. It was oral traditions as rendered in the Norse sagas that fostered the field investigations culminating in Newfoundland at L'Anse aux Meadows. And regardless of what one thinks of particular outcomes, it was the desire to "illustrate" the historicity of the traditions that saw their ultimate shape in the Bible that was responsible for much of the pioneering archaeology undertaken in the Holy Land, thus contributing to secular knowledge quite apart from whatever its spiritual value may be. Other chapters have shown instances of oral traditions' usefulness in offering things to think about vis-à-vis certain prehistoric Inuit tool distributions in the high Canadian Arctic, Iroquoian ceramic design motifs in Ontario, the meanings of effigy mound shapes in Wisconsin and Iowa and the symbolism of Ohio Valley earthworks, the ethnic identifications of certain southwestern archaeological assemblages, the possible linkages of selected artifact assemblages with prairie and plains Siouan tribal groups, provisional interpretations of pictographs and the message content of Mississippian ear ornaments, the signaling of northern Plains petroforms. This, it seems to me, is the quintessential role for oral traditions in archaeological practice: to spark the imagination about matters not accessible by other means and to give impetus to thoughts of testing them. Without the support of independent checks, claims for oral tradition historicity must be held in abeyance, being neither confirmable nor disconfirmable. Untested, they are irrelevant for the history-retrieving purposes of archaeology and sister disciplines, however vital they may remain in their natal system of discourse. Occasionally testing may be inadvertent, as with the prehistoric "magician" at the Ridge Ruin site in Arizona discussed in Chapter 8. Apropos of that celebrated instance, there is a parallel one from the Pacific: two "chiefly" graves excavated on Aneityum, a Polynesian "outlier" in the Vanuatu or New Hebrides islands in Melanesia, yielded assemblages of ornaments in agreement with descriptions of chiefly burial rites in oral traditions. One of the burials has been dated to 300–400 B.P. (Denoon 1997:67).

Although, as Robert Lowie (1915, 1917) argued almost a century ago, the sometime concordance of traditions with archaeological or other autonomous evidence can mean little; the veracity of the former being a function of compatibility with the latter, the possibility of something more is not necessarily excluded. Genuine history, in the modern Western sense, verified by unimpeachable independent data, has been shown to reside in some of the oral traditions of non-Western as well as Western societies. Because every independent species of evidence has its own peculiar limitations, redundancy has its uses. What is sometimes referred to as the "method of convergent verification" stresses the desirability of access to as many autonomous lines of investigation as possible. Generally, in any historical or scientific investigation, what is affirmed by multiple methods is to be preferred to something reliant on one alone. If one of those multiple methods in a particular case is provided by oral tradition analysis, and it proves compatible with all, or most, or the best of the other lines of evidence regarded as reliable, it would be difficult to deny it evidential status in other instances where it can be shown to have a bearing.

Nevertheless, given all of the previously reviewed reasons for regarding with skepticism oral traditions, especially those purporting to go back a century and a half or more, as tantamount to Western-style history spoken in a foreign tongue, prudence militates against its endorsement as reliable stand-alone proof or disproof of anything. The after-the-fact demonstration of oral tradition's reliability in particular instances is not an argument for its a priori acceptance in others. There are too many disconfirming examples, usually ignored by those preoccupied with the exceptions, to justify the genre's methodological elevation to comparable status with cross-culturally applicable research tools such as radiometric assays, stratigraphic ordering, or seriational analysis. Nevertheless, when an oral tradition does prove historically confirmable, it is apt to lower stringency requirements on others. As earlier suggested, therein lies much of the abuse present in the literature. Enlisting oral traditions in support of a particular thesis, without laying the necessary and sufficient foundations for doing so, parallels other bad archaeological habits like the once more popular global picking and choosing of isolated culture traits by hyperdiffusionists and the still too frequently encountered affection for uncritical appeals to ethnographic analogies.

As earlier noted, calling into question the citing of Native American oral traditions as if they spoke for themselves as historical data has become more than an academic concern. In today's so-called culture wars, to raise that question risks charges of insensitivity, chauvinism, cultural repression or theft, or other sins. But if the question is unaddressed, its proscribers should acknowledge the consequences. To maintain, as is frequently the case, that traditions in oral societies are as *historically* true and trustworthy *in their own way* as modern archaeological or historical evidence—only more translucent or even opaque because of metaphor, indifference to chronology, interweaving of fictive and taken-to-be historical personages, and so on—insinuates conclusions that such tradition-as-history defenders are apt to find discomforting. These imply either (1) an ontological difference in subject matter, thus raising the issue of fundamental incomparability, or (2) simple incompetence in how the past is rendered in traditions on the order of "when they said *this,* they really meant *that.*" If the latter, a type of assertion typically unescorted by substantiating argument, the correction is a tacit acknowledgment of tradition's inadequacy as a vehicle for the transmission of history.

History as reconstructed by professional historians and archaeologists, and by historical geologists, paleontologists, palynologists, astronomers, and so on, epitomizes a philosophy of knowledge qualitatively distinct from that embedded in oral traditions. Their underlying assumptions, operational priorities, methodologies, and standards of truth telling are fundamentally at odds with each other. Neither should be confused with nor found wanting for not being a substitute for the other. That they at times have been found to touch at certain points, even to coincide in what they say or seem to say about specific past events, does not obliterate their essential differences. Those differences are essential to the understanding and proper appreciation of both. Even given their occasional congruences, it is best to proceed warily before recruiting either of the genres to stand in for lacunae in the other. The migration legend of the Cherokees—actually, there is more than one—does not substitute for an archaeological record. The same is true if the terms are reversed. Arising from disparate worldviews, they do not address the same problems; neither do they answer, or even recognize, the same questions. Of a similar nature are the Bitterroot Mountains and their history as seen by modern eyes and by those of Sacajawea's Lemhis. It is not in this sense that one is right and the other wrong. It is that they are incongruous in the same explanatory scheme. Not only does neither need the other, they are more often than not incompatible if forced into epistemic cohabitation. They inhabit different explanatory worlds.

Demonstrated instances of compatibilities, of course, capture imagination and raise hope of additional examples awaiting discovery. Nominating oral traditions as historical in Western terms, however, should result from testing, not a priori acceptance. If the aim is to get as close to the past as it was, or as close to that goal as mortals can get, beliefs about history must be put to the test. But testing propositions about the past for confirmation or disconfirmation is not the province of oral tradition. It is, in fact, its greatest danger—and the greatest ally of reliable history. Ignorance about the human past is vast enough without inviting its further diffusion when some precision in its delimitation has been shown to be within our reach. As with Leonard Thompson's (1978:4) understanding of the Bible, Native American oral traditions speak to a "more fantastic country," one that "is not to be confused with the ancient world in which it arose."

Historically factual content retained in *oral history,* that is, in the recountings of past events as they were experienced by witnesses who reported them, is generally conceded to be substantially greater than that in *oral tradition,* the latter being the product of renditions of subsequent generations about what their predecessors had told them. For all their known deficiencies, firsthand testimonies err less than secondhand. However, as with the somewhat parallel distinction in the Vansina hourglass metaphor, that of recency and the floating gap specifically, the disparity in genuine historicity between the contrasted pairs is less sharp than their descriptions might be taken to suggest. Given that detailed remembrances in oral history tend gradually rather than precipitously to degrade over time, although there are proven instances of its acceleration sometimes attending inventions of traditions (Clifton 1990; Hobsbaum and Ranger 1983), annihilation of all historicity is probably less common in oral tradition than its dilution. Indeed, some corroborating examples of this contention have been presented in previous chapters: the Norse sagas bearing on the discovery of America; the Hopi prediction of burial paraphernalia at the Ridge Ruin site; the fact, if not the details, of Central Siouan westward migrations. That being so, it is hardly surprising that many archaeologists hope to find and employ additional examples to help in reconstructing cultural histories.

Many students of oral societies now accept as a truism that the historical traditions that have survived for them to record are in any given case likely to constitute a fortuitous rather than a definitive sample. Furthermore, those survivors have been subject to volitional alteration, as with chiefly genealogies, as well as the unselfconscious drift of memory erosion and the attention demands of changing circumstances. A commitment to disinterested objectivity is not one of the cultural universals. Moreover, judgments of what is historically significant and thus worth remembering vary among different societies. A literally graphic illustration of this fact, one alluded to in previous chapters, is provided by the pictographs on buffalo-robe "winter counts" or calendars. As James Mooney pointed out in his late-nineteenth-century study of the pictographic calendars of the Kiowas, their selection of what to commemorate in each year was frequently puzzling to people of European or Euroamerican background. For instance, whereas no notice was taken of the epochal 1868 Custer attack on the Kiowa, Cheyenne, and other Indian encampments along the Washita River in western Oklahoma, the result of which compelled the defeated tribes to accept removal to reservations, some years were memorialized by ideograms representing such "trivial" happenings as a woman's elopement or the theft of a horse (Mooney 1898:145–146). Memorable to Indians and non-Indians alike, however, was the "winter that the stars fell." This November 1833 meteor shower was depicted on many Indian calendars as the sign of that year (Mooney 1898:260–261). And certainly not trivial by any human standard were the awful years whose painted signs recorded visitations of measles, smallpox, and cholera.

As earlier cited examples have shown, possible historical insights are by no means the only interest oral traditions have for archaeologists, ethnographers, ethnohistorians, or folklorists. They have been valued as "windows" into the psyches of their tellers and the societies of which they are presumed to speak. In this sense, they are often treated as though they are autoethnographies of memorized pasts. As such, they are seen as facilitating insights into a people's way of thinking about themselves and as offering clues about their worldview, values, social organization, religious beliefs, identification of "place-worlds," and so on. They are regarded as sources of information on the meanings of ancient symbols and on the functions of perplexing artifacts and site features. There are, however, a priori reasons for caution when peering through such windows. Just who are they whose worldviews, values, and place-worlds are so revealed? Are "they" the deceased people talked about in the traditions, or are "they" really the people reciting the traditions? Or a hybrid of both? Scholarly users of the traditions need always remind themselves that such autoethnographies or "memory cultures" have multiple functions and relatively shallow time depths. They speak to recent generations, not time immemorial, as some venerable ethnographies and archaeological borrowings therefrom are apt to imply. While the possibility must be acknowledged that some information pertinent to times of archaeological interest may be retained in those sources, it is also a certainty that much of it has drifted away from what it once was and more properly resides near the recent end of oral tradition's tenure.

It is curious how many archaeologists who inveigh against the stereotype of "the" American Indian as unchanged through centuries and millennia are nevertheless comfortable accepting what amounts to the same travesty in its foregoing window-peeping guise. This enticing appeal to assumed authority so conveniently accessed is not to be recommended for any discipline having serious historiographic or scientific aspirations. Although ideas derived thereby ought freely to be investigated for whatever they are worth, the price paid in inconsistency should be acknowledged, and whatever findings are made must be paid for in the foreign coin of independent data.

References Cited

Albright, William Foxwell
  1963   *The Biblical Period from Abraham to Ezra*. Harper and Row, New York.
  1983   From the Patriarchs to Moses. II. Moses Out of Egypt. In *The Biblical Archaeologist Reader*, 2nd edition. Vol. 4, edited by Edward F. Campbell, Jr., and David Noel Freedman, pp. 35–64. Almond Press, Sheffield England.

Alex, Lynn M.
  2000   *Iowa's Archaeological Past*. University of Iowa Press, Iowa City.

Alexander, Hartley Burr
  1916   North American [Mythology]. In *The Mythology of All Races*, edited by Louis Herbert Gray, vol. 10. Archaeological Institute of America. Marshall Jones, Boston.

Allen, Barbara, and William Lynwood Montell
  1981   *From Memory to History, Using Oral Sources in Local Historical Research*. The American Association for State and Local History, Nashville, Tennessee.

Allison, John
  2000   Letter to the Editor. *Society for American Archaeology Bulletin* 18(5):3–4.

Allport, Gordon W., and Leo Postman
  1947   *The Psychology of Rumor*. Holt, Rinehart and Winston, New York.

Andrews, David, and Joseph Flanagan (editors)
  1999   *The Federal Archeology Program 1996–97, Secretary of the Interior's Report to Congress*. National Park Service Archeology and Ethnography Program, Washington, D.C.

Anyon, Roger, T. J. Ferguson, Loretta Jackson, Lillie Lane, and Philip Vicenti
  1997   Native American Oral Tradition and Archaeology, Issues of Structure, Relevance, and Respect. In *Native Americans and Archaeologists, Stepping Stones to Common Ground*, edited by Nina Swidler, Kurt E. Dongoske, Roger Anyon, and Alan S. Downer, pp. 77–87. AltaMira Press, Walnut Creek, California.

Ashley Montagu, M. F.
  1944   An Indian Tradition Relating to the Mastodon. *American Anthropologist* 46(4):568–571.

Bahr, Donald

1971   Who Were the Hohokam? The Evidence from Pima-Papago Myths. *Ethnohistory* 18(3):245–266.

1998   Mythologies Compared: Pima, Maricopa, and Yavapai. *Journal of the Southwest* 40(1):25–66.

2001   Bad News: The Predicament of Native American Mythology. *Ethnohistory* 48(4):587–612.

Bahr, Donald, Juan Smith, William Smith Allison, and Julian Hayden

1994   *The Short Swift Time of Gods on Earth: The Hohokam Chronicles.* University of California Press, Berkeley and Los Angeles.

Bailey, Garrick A.

2001   Osage. In *Plains,* edited by Raymond J. DeMallie, pp. 476–496. Handbook of North American Indians, vol. 13, Part 1, William C. Sturtevant, general editor. Smithsonian Institution, Washington, D.C.

Bailey, Garrick A., and Gloria A. Young

2001   Kansa. In *Plains,* edited by Raymond J. DeMallie, pp. 462–475. Handbook of North American Indians, vol. 13, Part 1, William C. Sturtevant, general editor. Smithsonian Institution, Washington, D.C.

Barber, Elizabeth Wayland, and Paul T. Barber

2004   *When They Severed Earth from Sky: How the Human Mind Shapes Myth.* Princeton University Press, Princeton, New Jersey.

Bartlett, Frederick C.

1920   Some Experiments on the Reproduction of Folk Stories. *Folklore* 31:30–47.

1977   *Remembering: A Study in Experimental and Social Psychology.* Cambridge
[1932]   University Press, London.

Bascom, William

1957   The Myth-Ritual Theory. *Journal of American Folklore* 70:103–114.

1958   Rejoinder to Hyman. *Journal of American Folklore* 71:155–156.

Basso, Keith H.

1996   *Wisdom Sits in Places: Landscape and Language Among the Western Apache.* University of New Mexico Press, Albuquerque.

Beck, David R. M.

2002   *Siege and Survival: History of the Menominee Indians, 1634–1856.* University of Nebraska Press, Lincoln.

Beck, Jane C.

1972   The Giant Beaver: A Prehistoric Memory? *Ethnohistory* 19(2):109–122.

Behm, Jeffery A.

· 1992   *The 1990 and 1991 Archaeological Survey and Evaluation of the Bellhaven Estates Property, Section 7, Town of Algoma, Winnebago County, Wisconsin.* Reports of Investigation No. 1, Archaeology Laboratory, University of Wisconsin-Oshkosh.

Benedict, Ruth

1955   *Patterns of Culture.* New American Library of World Literature (Mentor
[1934]   Book), New York.

1969   *Zuni Mythology,* 2 vols. AMS Press, New York. Originally published in Co-
[1935] lumbia University Contributions to Anthropology, No. 21, New York.
Benn, David W.
1995   Woodland *People* and the Roots of Oneota. In *Oneota Archaeology: Past,
Present, and Future,* edited by William Green, pp. 91–139. Office of the State
Archaeologist, University of Iowa, Report 20, Iowa City.
Bernardini, Wesley
2005   *Hopi Oral Tradition and the Archaeology of Identity.* University of Arizona
Press, Tucson.
Bienkowski, Piotr
1990   Jericho Was Destroyed in the Middle Bronze Age, Not the Late Bronze Age.
Biblical Archaeology Review 16(5):45–46, 69.
Bierhorst, John (editor)
1976   *The Red Swan: Myths and Tales of the American Indians.* Farrar, Straus and
Giroux, New York.
1985   *The Mythology of North America.* William Morrow, New York.
Binford, Lewis R.
1983   *In Pursuit of the Past: Decoding the Archaeological Record.* Thames and Hudson,
London.
Biolsi, T., and Larry Zimmerman (editors)
1997   *Indians and Anthropologists: Vine Deloria Jr. and the Critique of Anthropology.*
University of Arizona Press, Tucson.
Birmingham, Robert A., and Leslie E. Eisenberg
2000   *Indian Mounds of Wisconsin.* University of Wisconsin Press, Madison.
Blair, Emma Helen (editor)
1911– *The Indian Tribes of the Upper Mississippi Valley and Regions of the Great Lakes,
1912   as Described by Nicolas Perrot, French Commandant in the Northwest; Bacqueville
de la Potherie, French Royal Commissioner to Canada; Morrell Marston, American Army Officer; and Thomas Forsyth, United States Agent at Fort Armstrong,*
vols. 1 and 2. Arthur H. Clark, Cleveland.
Blegen, Carl W.
1963   *Troy and the Trojans.* Frederick A. Praeger, New York.
Blegen, Carl W., C. G. Boulter, J. L. Caskey, M. Rawson, and J. Sperling
1950– *Troy: Excavations Conducted by the University of Cincinnati, 1932–1938,* 4 vols.
1958   Princeton University Press, Princeton, New Jersey.
Boas, Franz
1888   The Central Eskimo. In *Sixth Annual Report of the Bureau of Ethnology
for 1884–1885,* pp. 399–669. U.S. Government Printing Office, Washington, D.C.
1910   *Kwakiutl Tales.* Columbia University Contributions to Anthropology, No.
2, New York.
1969   *Kwakiutl Tales,* new series, 2 parts. AMS Press, New York. Originally pub-
[1935– lished in Columbia University Contributions to Anthropology, No. 26,
1943] New York.

Boas, Franz, and George Hunt

1975a   *Kwakiutl Texts.* AMS Press, New York. Originally published in Publications
[1902–   of the Jesup North Pacific Expeditions, Vol. 3, Nos. 1–3 (Memoirs of the
1905]   American Museum of Natural History No. 5, New York).

1975b   [1906] *Kwakiutl Texts,* second series. AMS Press, New York. Originally pub-
lished in Publications of the Jesup North Pacific Expeditions, Vol. 10, No. 1
(Memoirs of the American Museum of Natural History No. 14, pp. 1–269,
New York).

Bonnefoy, Yves (compiler)

1991   *Mythologies,* 2 vols. University of Chicago Press, Chicago.

Bordewich, Fergus M.

1996   *Killing the White Man's Indian: Reinventing Native Americans at the End of the
Twentieth Century.* Anchor Books, Doubleday, New York.

Borofsky, Robert

1987   *Making History, Pukapukan and Anthropological Constructions of Knowledge.*
Cambridge University Press, New York.

2000   An Invitation. In *Remembrance of Pacific Pasts: An Invitation to Remake History,* edited by Robert Borofsky, pp. 1–30. University of Hawaii Press,
Honolulu.

Boszhardt, Robert F.

2004   Blind Dates and Blind Faith: The Timeless Story of the "Emergent"
Oneota McKern Phase. *The Wisconsin Archeologist* 85(1):3–30.

Bourgeois, Arthur P. (editor)

1994   *Ojibwa Narratives of Charles and Charlotte Kawbawgam and Jacques LePique,
1893–1895.* Wayne State University Press, Detroit.

Bower, Gordon H.

2000   A Brief History of Memory Research. In *The Oxford Handbook of Memory,*
edited by Endel Tulving and Fergus I. M. Craik, pp. 3–32. Oxford University Press, New York.

Boyd, C. Clifford, Jr.

2004   Monacans as Moundbuilders? *American Antiquity* 69(2):361–363.

Bradley, James W.

1987   *Evolution of the Onondaga Iroquois: Accommodating Change, 1500–1655.* Syracuse University Press, Syracuse, New York.

Bradley, Richard

2003   The Translation of Time. In *Archaeologies of Memory,* edited by Ruth M.
Van Dyke and Susan E. Alcock, pp. 221–227. Blackwell, Malden, Massachusetts.

Bray, Robert T.

1991   The Utz Site: An Oneota Village in Central Missouri. *The Missouri Archaeologist* 52.

Bray, Tamara

2001   *The Future of the Past: Archaeologists, Native Americans and Repatriation.*
Routledge, New York.

Bringhurst, Robert

1999   *A Story as Sharp as a Knife: The Classical Haida Mythtellers and Their World.* University of Nebraska Press, Lincoln.

Brose, David S.

1993   Changing Paradigms in the Explanation of Southeastern Prehistory. In *The Development of Southeastern Archaeology,* edited by Jay K. Johnson, pp. 1–17. University of Alabama Press, Tuscaloosa.

2001   Penumbral Protohistory on Lake Erie's South Shore. In *Societies in Eclipse: Archaeology of the Eastern Woodland Indians, A.D. 1400–1700,* edited by David S. Brose, C. Wesley Cowan, and Robert C. Mainfort, Jr., pp. 49–65. Smithsonian Institution Press, Washington, D.C.

Brown, Donald N., and Lee Irwin

2001   Ponca. In *Plains,* edited by Raymond J. DeMallie, pp. 416–431. Handbook of North American Indians, vol. 13, part 1, William C. Sturtevant, general editor. Smithsonian Institution, Washington, D.C.

Brown, Douglas Summers

1966   *The Catawba Indians: The People of the River.* University of South Carolina Press, Columbia.

Brown, James A.

1990   Ethnohistoric Connections. In *At the Edge of Prehistory: Huber Phase Archaeology in the Chicago Area,* edited by James A. Brown and Patricia J. O'Brien, pp. 155–159. Published for the Illinois Department of Transportation by the Center for American Archeology, Kampsville, Illinois.

1997   The Archaeology of Ancient Religion in the Eastern Woodlands. *Annual Review of Anthropology* 26:465–485.

Buettner-Janusch, John

1973   *Physical Anthropology: A Perspective.* John Wiley and Sons, New York.

Burns, Louis F.

2004   *A History of the Osage People.* University of Alabama Press, Tuscaloosa.

Butterfield, Herbert

1981   *The Origins of History.* Basic Books, New York.

Calder, William M. III, and David A. Traill (editors)

1986   *Myth, Scandal, and History: The Heinrich Schliemann Controversy and a First Edition of the Mycenaean Diary.* Wayne State University Press, Detroit.

Carneiro, Robert L.

2000   *The Muse of History and the Science of Culture.* Kluwer Academic/Plenum, New York.

Catlin, George

1913   *North American Indians, Being Letters and Notes on Their Manners, Customs, and*
[1841] *Conditions, Written During Eight Years' Travel Amongst the Wildest Tribes of Indians in North America, 1832–1839,* 2 vols. Leary, Stuart, Philadelphia. Originally published by the author.

Chadwick, John

1976   *The Mycenaean World.* Cambridge University Press, Cambridge.

Chaney, William A.

1970   The Cult of Kingship in Anglo-Saxon England: The Transition from Paganism to Christianity. University of California Press, Berkeley.

Chapman, Carl H.

1946   A Preliminary Survey of Missouri Archaeology, Part 1: Historic Indian Tribes. The Missouri Archaeologist 10(1):1–56.

1959   The Little Osage and Missouri Indian Village Sites, ca. 1727–1777 A.D. The Missouri Archaeologist 21(1):1–67.

Chatters, James C.

2001   Kennewick Man and the First Americans. Simon and Schuster, New York.

Clark, Geoffrey A.

1998   NAGPRA, the Conflict Between Science and Religion, and the Political Consequences. Society for American Archaeology Bulletin 16(5):22, 24–25.

Cleland, Charles E.

1992   Rites of Conquest: The History and Culture of Michigan's Native Americans. University of Michigan Press, Ann Arbor.

Cleland, Charles E., and G. Richard Peske

1968   The Spider Cave Site. In The Prehistory of the Burnt Bluff Area, assembled by James E. Fitting, pp. 20–60. University of Michigan Museum of Anthropology, Anthropological Papers 34, Ann Arbor.

Cleland, Charles E., Richard D. Clute, and Robert E. Haltinger

1984   Naub-cow-zo-win Discs from Northern Michigan. Midcontinental Journal of Archaeology 9(2):235–249.

Clifton, James A.

1977   The Prairie People: Continuity and Change in Potawatomi Indian Culture 1665–1965. Regents Press of Kansas, Lawrence.

Clifton, James A. (editor)

1990   The Invented Indian: Cultural Fictions and Government Policies. Transaction, New Brunswick, New Jersey.

Cobb, Charles R., and Brian M. Butler

2002   The Vacant Quarter Revisited: Late Mississippian Abandonment of the Lower Ohio Valley. American Antiquity 67(4):625–641.

Collingwood, R. G.

1946   The Idea of History. Oxford University Press, Oxford.

Cook-Lynn, Elizabeth

2001   Anti-Indianism in Modern America: A Voice from Tatekeya's Earth. University of Illinois Press, Urbana and Chicago.

Cowgill, George L.

1993   Distinguished Lecture in Archeology: Beyond Criticizing New Archeology. American Anthropologist 95(3):551–573.

Cruikshank, Julie

1998   The Social Life of Stories: Narrative and Knowledge in the Yukon Territory. University of Nebraska Press, Lincoln.

2002   Oral History, Narrative Strategies, and Native American Historiography:

Perspectives from the Yukon Territory, Canada. In *Clearing a Path: Theorizing the Past in Native American Studies,* edited by Nancy Shoemaker, pp. 3–27. Routledge, New York.

Cushing, Frank Hamilton

1901   The Cock and the Mouse. In *Zuni Folk Tales,* pp. 411–422. G. P. Putnam's Sons, New York. Reprinted in *The Study of Folklore* (1965), edited by Alan Dundes, pp. 269–276, Prentice-Hall, Englewood Cliffs, New Jersey.

Custer, Jay F.

2001a   Working Together. Who Cares? *The Society for American Archaeology Archaeological Record* 1(4):21–22, 38.

2001b   Henry Deisher, His Baskets and George Byron Gordon, Part 1. *Pennsylvania Archaeologist* 71(2):72–87.

Custred, Glynn

2000   The Forbidden Discovery of Kennewick Man. *Academic Questions* 13(3): 12–30.

2002   The Case of Kennewick Man: Linguistic Evidence and Cultural Affiliation. *Mammoth Trumpet* 17(2):1–3, 17–20.

Dansie, Amy

1999   Working Together—International Implications of the Impact of Repatriation in Nevada Museums. *Society for American Archaeology Bulletin* 17(3): 30–32.

Davies, Philip

1992   *In Search of "Ancient Israel."* Journal for the Study of the Old Testament Press, Sheffield, England.

2000   What Separates a Minimalist from a Maximalist? Not Much. *Biblical Archaeology Review* 26(2):24–27, 72–73.

Day, Gordon M.

1972   Oral Tradition as Complement. *Ethnohistory* 19(2):99–108.

Dean, Patricia A., and Clayton F. Marler

2001   Shoshone Spirituality and Enhancing Archaeological Interpretation in Southeast Idaho. *The Society for American Archaeology Archaeological Record* 1(2):34–36.

Deloria, Philip J.

2002   Historiography. In *A Companion to American Indian History,* edited by Philip J. Deloria and Neal Salisbury, pp. 6–24. Blackwell, Malden, Massachusetts.

Deloria, Vine, Jr.

1997a   *Red Earth, White Lies: Native Americans and the Myth of Scientific Fact.* Fulcrum, Golden, Colorado. Originally published in 1995 by Scribners, New York.

1997b   Conclusion: Anthros, Indians, and Planetary Reality. In *Indians and Anthropologists: Vine Deloria, Jr., and the Critique of Anthropology,* edited by Thomas Biolsi and Larry Zimmerman, pp. 209–221. University of Arizona Press, Tucson.

DeMallie, Raymond J.

1980   Touching the Pen: Plains Indian Treaty Councils in Ethnohistorical Perspective. In *Ethnicity on the Great Plains,* edited by Frederick C. Luebcke, pp. 38–53. University of Nebraska Press, Lincoln.

1984   *The Sixth Grandfather: Black Elk's Teachings Given to John G. Neihardt.* University of Nebraska Press, Lincoln.

2001a   Sioux Until 1850. In *Plains,* edited by Raymond J. DeMallie, pp. 718–760. Handbook of North American Indians, vol. 13, part 2, William C. Sturtevant, general editor. Smithsonian Institution, Washington, D.C.

2001b   Teton. In *Plains,* edited by Raymond J. DeMallie, pp. 794–820. Handbook of North American Indians, vol. 13, part 2, William C. Sturtevant, general editor. Smithsonian Institution, Washington, D.C.

DeMallie, Raymond J., and Douglas R. Parks

2001   Tribal Traditions and Records. In *Plains,* edited by Raymond J. DeMallie, pp. 1062–1073. Handbook of North American Indians, vol. 13, part 2, William C. Sturtevant, general editor. Smithsonian Institution, Washington, D.C.

Dening, Greg

2000   Possessing Tahiti. In *Remembrance of Pacific Pasts: An Invitation to Remake History,* edited by Robert Borofsky, pp. 112–132. University of Hawaii Press, Honolulu.

Denoon, Donald

1997   Human Settlement. In *The Cambridge History of the Pacific Islanders,* edited by Donald Denoon, Stewart Firth, Jocelyn Linnekin, Malama Meleisea, and Karen Nero, pp. 37–79. Cambridge University Press, Cambridge.

de Vaux, Roland

1970   On Right and Wrong Uses of Archaeology. In *Near Eastern Archaeology in the Twentieth Century: Essays in Honor of Nelson Glueck,* edited by James A. Sanders, pp. 64–80. Doubleday, Garden City, New York.

Dever, William G.

1985   Syro-Palestinian and Biblical Archaeology. In *The Hebrew Bible and Its Modern Interpreters,* edited by D. Knight and G. M. Tucker, pp. 31–74. Fortress, Philadelphia.

1990   *Recent Archaeological Discoveries and Biblical Research.* University of Washington Press, Seattle.

2000   Save Us from Postmodern Malarkey. *Biblical Archaeology Review* 26(2):28–35, 68–69.

Dewdney, Selwyn

1975   *The Sacred Scrolls of the Southern Ojibway.* University of Toronto Press, Toronto.

Dewdney, Selwyn, and Kenneth E. Kidd

1967   *Indian Rock Paintings of the Great Lakes,* 2nd ed. University of Toronto Press, Toronto.

Dixon, Roland B.

1915   Dr. Dixon's Reply. *American Anthropologist,* n.s., 17:599–600.

Dobyns, Henry F.

1983   *Their Number Become Thinned: Native American Population Dynamics in Eastern North America.* University of Tennessee Press, Knoxville.

Dockstader, Frederick J.

1979   Hopi History, 1850–1940. In *Southwest,* edited by Alfonso Ortiz, pp. 524–532. Handbook of North American Indians, vol. 9, William C. Sturtevant, general editor. Smithsonian Institution, Washington, D.C.

Dongoske, Kurt, Mark Aldenderfer, and Karen Doehner (editors)

2000   *Working Together: Native Americans and Archaeologists.* Society for American Archaeology, Washington, D.C.

Dongoske, K. E., M. Yeatts, R. Anyon, and T. J. Ferguson

1997   Archaeological Cultures and Cultural Affiliation: Hopi and Zuni Perspectives in the American Southwest. *American Antiquity* 62:600–608.

Dorsey, J. Owen

1886   Migrations of Siouan Tribes. *The American Naturalist* 20(3):211–222.

1888   Osage Traditions. In *Sixth Annual Report of the Bureau of Ethnology for 1884–1885,* pp. 377–397. U.S. Government Printing Office, Washington, D.C.

Dorsey, J. Owen, and Cyrus Thomas

1910   Omaha. In *Handbook of American Indians North of Mexico,* edited by Frederick Webb Hodge, pp. 119–121. Bureau of American Ethnology Bulletin 30, Part 2. U.S. Government Printing Office, Washington, D.C.

Dorson, Richard M.

1963   Current Folklore Theories. *Current Anthropology* 4(1):93–112.

1972   *Folklore: Selected Essays.* Indiana University Press, Bloomington.

Dray, William H.

1993   *Philosophy of History,* 2nd edition. Prentice-Hall, Englewood Cliffs, New Jersey.

Drews, Robert

1993   *The End of the Bronze Age: Changes in Warfare and the Catastrophe ca. 1200 B.C.* Princeton University Press, Princeton, New Jersey.

Driver, Harold E.

1961   *Indians of North America.* University of Chicago Press, Chicago.

Du Bois, Cora (editor)

1960   *Lowie's Selected Papers in Anthropology.* University of California Press, Berkeley and Los Angeles.

Dumas, Alexandre

1997   *La Reine Margot.* Oxford University Press, Oxford.

Duncan, James R., and Carol Diaz-Granados

2000   Of Masks and Myths. *Midcontinental Journal of Archaeology* 25(1):1–26.

Dundes, Alan

1965   *The Study of Folklore.* Prentice-Hall, Englewood Cliffs, New Jersey.

1999   *Holy Writ as Oral Lit, the Bible as Folklore.* Rowman and Littlefield, Lanham, Maryland.

Easton, Donald
1985   Has the Trojan War Been Found? *Antiquity* 59:189–196.

Echo-Hawk, Roger C.
1997   Forging a New Ancient History for Native America. In *Native Americans and Archaeologists, Stepping Stones to Common Ground,* edited by Nina Swidler, Kurt E. Dongoske, Roger Anyon, and Alan S. Downer, pp. 88–102. AltaMira Press, Walnut Creek, California.

2000   Ancient History in the New World: Integrating Oral Traditions and the Archaeological Record. *American Antiquity* 65(2):267–290.

Eiseley, Loren C.
1943   Archaeological Observations on the Problem of Post-Glacial Extinction. *American Antiquity* 8(3):209–217.

1945   Myth and Mammoth in Archaeology. *American Antiquity* 11(2):84–87.

Emerson, Thomas E., and James A. Brown
1992   The Late Prehistory and Protohistory of Illinois. In *Calumet and Fleur-de-Lys, Archaeology of Indian and French Contact in the Midcontinent,* edited by John A. Walthall and Thomas E. Emerson, pp. 77–128. Smithsonian Institution Press, Washington, D.C.

Emmons, G. T.
1911   Native Account of the Meeting Between La Perouse and the Tlingit. *American Anthropologist,* n.s., 13:294–298.

Engelbrecht, William
2003   *Iroquoia: The Development of a Native World.* Syracuse University Press, Syracuse, New York.

Erdoes, Richard, and Alfonso Ortiz (editors)
1984   *American Indian Myths and Legends.* Pantheon Books, New York.

Evers, Larry, and Barre Toelken (editors)
2001   *Native American Oral Traditions: Collaboration and Interpretation.* Utah State University Press, Logan.

Faulkner, Charles H.
1972   *The Late Prehistoric Occupation of Northwestern Indiana: A Study of the Upper Mississippi Cultures of the Kankakee Valley.* Indiana Historical Society, Prehistoric Research Series 5(2), Indianapolis.

Feder, Kenneth L.
1990   *Frauds, Myths, and Mysteries: Science and Pseudoscience in Archaeology.* Mayfield, Mountain View, California.

Fenton, William N.
1962   This Island, the World on the Turtle's Back. *Journal of American Folklore* 75:283–300.

1998   *The Great Law and the Longhouse: A Political History of the Iroquois Confederacy.* University of Oklahoma Press, Norman.

Finkelstein, Israel, and Neil Asher Silberman

2001 *The Bible Unearthed: Archaeology's New Vision of Ancient Israel and the Origin of Its Sacred Texts.* Free Press, New York.

Finley, Moses I.

2000 *Ancient History: Evidence and Models.* Pimlico, London. Originally published 1985.

Finley, M. I., J. C. Caskey, G. S. Kirk, and D. L. Page

1964 The Trojan War. *The Journal of Hellenic Studies* 84:1–20.

Finnegan, Ruth

1970 *Oral Literature in Africa.* Clarendon Press, Oxford.

Fischer, David Hackett

1970 *Historians' Fallacies: Toward a Logic of Historical Thought.* Harper and Row, New York.

Fletcher, Alice C., and Francis La Flesche

1911 The Omaha Tribe. In *Twenty-Seventh Annual Report of the Bureau of American Ethnology for 1905–1906,* pp. 17–672. U.S. Government Printing Office, Washington, D.C.

Foley, John Miles

1990 *Traditional Oral Epic: The Odyssey, Beowulf, and Serbo-Croatian Return Song.* University of California Press, Berkeley.

Ford, Richard I. (editor)

1985 *The Ethnographic American Southwest, a Source Book: Southwestern Society in Myth, Clan, and Kinship.* Garland, New York.

Forsdyke, E. J.

1956 *Greece Before Homer.* Max Parrish, London.

Fowler, Loretta

1987 *Shared Symbols, Contested Meanings: Gros Ventre Culture and History, 1778–1984.* Cornell University Press, Ithaca, New York.

Funk, Robert E.

2001 Letter to the Editor. *The Society for American Archaeology Archaeological Record* 1(4):3–4.

Gallatin, Albert

1836 A Synopsis of the Indian Tribes Within the United States East of the Rocky Mountains, and in the British and Russian Possessions in North America. *Archaeologia Americana: Transactions and Collections of the American Antiquarian Society* 2:1–422. Cambridge, Massachusetts. Reprinted in 1973 by AMS Press, New York.

Gatschet, Albert S.

1884 *A Migration Legend of the Creek Indians,* vol. 1. Brinton's Library of Aboriginal American Literature, No. 4. D. G. Brinton, Philadelphia.

Gehring, C. T., and W. A. Starna (editors)

1988 *A Journey into Mohawk and Oneida Country, 1634–1635: The Journal of Harmen Meyndertsz van den Bogaert.* Syracuse University Press, Syracuse, New York.

Gellner, Ernest

1985　*Relativism and the Social Sciences.* Cambridge University Press, Cambridge.

1988　*Plough, Sword, and Book: The Structure of Human History.* University of Chicago Press, Chicago.

German, Carlos

1998　Saskatchewan Effigy Sites Repatriated. *Canadian Archaeological Association Newsletter* 18(2):16–17.

Gibbon, Guy

1989　*Explanation in Archaeology.* Basil Blackwell, Oxford.

Gill, Sam D.

1983　*Native American Traditions: Sources and Interpretations.* Wadsworth, Belmont, California.

1987　Mythic Themes. In *Native American Religions: North America,* edited by Lawrence E. Sullivan, pp. 157–166. Macmillan, New York.

Gillespie, Beryl C.

1970　Yellowknives: *Quo Iverunt?* In *Migration and Anthropology,* edited by Robert F. Spencer, pp. 61–71. Proceedings of the 1970 Annual Spring Meeting of the American Ethnological Society. University of Washington Press, Seattle.

1981　Yellowknife. In *Subarctic,* edited by June Helm, pp. 285–290. Handbook of North American Indians, vol. 6, William C. Sturtevant, general editor. Smithsonian Institution, Washington, D.C.

Goddard, Ives

1996　Introduction. In *Languages,* edited by Ives Goddard, pp. 1–16. Handbook of North American Indians, vol. 17, William C. Sturtevant, general editor. Smithsonian Institution, Washington, D.C.

Goldenweiser, Alexander A.

1915　The Heuristic Value of Traditional Records. *American Anthropologist,* n.s., 17:763–764.

Goodman, Nelson

1955　*Fact, Fiction, and Forecast.* Harvard University Press, Cambridge, Massachusetts.

Goody, Jack

1972　*The Myth of the Bagre.* Oxford University Press, Oxford.

1987　*The Interface Between the Written and the Oral.* Cambridge University Press, Cambridge.

2000　*The Power of the Written Tradition.* Smithsonian Institution Press, Washington, D.C.

Goody, Jack, and Ian Watt

1968　The Consequences of Literacy. In *Literacy in Traditional Societies,* edited by Jack Goody, pp. 27–68. Cambridge University Press, New York.

Green, Thomas, and Cheryl A. Munson

1978　Mississippian Settlement Patterns in Southwestern Indiana. In *Mississippian Settlement Patterns,* edited by Bruce D. Smith, pp. 293–330. Academic Press, New York.

Green, William

1993   Examining Protohistoric Depopulation in the Upper Midwest. In *Exploring the Oneota-Winnebago Direct Historical Connection,* edited by David F. Overstreet, pp. 290–323. *The Wisconsin Archeologist* 74(1-4).

Griffin, James B.

1937   The Archaeological Remains of the Chiwere Sioux. *American Antiquity* 2:180–181.

1960   A Hypothesis for the Prehistory of the Winnebago. In *Culture in History: Essays in Honor of Paul Radin,* edited by Stanley Diamond, pp. 809–865. Columbia University Press, New York.

1995   The Search for Oneota Cultural Origins: A Personal Retrospective Account. In *Oneota Archaeology: Past, Present, and Future,* edited by William Green, pp. 9–18. Office of the State Archaeologist, University of Iowa, Report 20, Iowa City.

Griffin, James B. (editor)

1952   *Archeology of Eastern United States.* University of Chicago Press, Chicago.

Griffin, James B., David J. Meltzer, Bruce D. Smith, and William C. Sturtevant

1988   A Mammoth Fraud in Science. *American Antiquity* 53(3):578–582.

Gubser, Nicholas J.

1965   *The Nunamiut Eskimos: Hunters of Caribou.* Yale University Press, New Haven, Connecticut.

Halbwachs, Maurice

1992   *On Collective Memory,* edited, translated, and with an introduction by Lewis A. Coser. University of Chicago Press, Chicago.

Hall, Robert L.

1976   Ghosts, Water Barriers, Corn, and Sacred Enclosures in the Eastern Woodlands. *American Antiquity* 41(3):360–364.

1993   Red Banks, Oneota, and the Winnebago: Views from a Distant Rock. *The Wisconsin Archeologist* 74(1-4):10–79.

1997   *An Archaeology of the Soul: North American Indian Belief and Ritual.* University of Illinois Press, Urbana.

2003   Rethinking Jean Nicolet's Route to the Ho-Chunks in 1634. In *Theory, Method, and Practice in Modern Archaeology,* edited by Robert J. Jeske and Douglas K. Charles, pp. 238–251. Praeger, Westport, Connecticut.

2004   Comment on "Blind Dates and Blind Faith: The Timeless Story of the 'Emergent' Oneota McKern Phase." *The Wisconsin Archeologist* 85(1): 31–35.

Hallberg, Peter

1962   *The Icelandic Saga.* Translated with introduction and notes by Paul Schach. University of Nebraska Press, Lincoln.

Hallowell, A. Irving

1937   Temporal Orientation in Western Civilization and in a Pre-Literate Society. *American Anthropologist* 39(4):647–670.

Hanks, Christopher C.

1997   Ancient Knowledge of Ancient Sites: Tracing Dene Identity from the

Late Pleistocene and Holocene. In *At a Crossroads: Archaeology and First Peoples in Canada,* edited by George P. Nicholas and Thomas D. Andrews, pp. 178–189. Archaeology Press Publication No. 24, Simon Fraser University, Burnaby, British Columbia.

Harris, Heather

1997   Remembering 10,000 Years of History: The Origins and Migrations of the Gitksan. In *At a Crossroads: Archaeology and First Peoples in Canada,* edited by George P. Nicholas and Thomas D. Andrews, pp. 190–196. Archaeology Press Publication No. 24, Simon Fraser University, Burnaby, British Columbia.

Harvey, Van Austin

1966   *The Historian and the Believer: The Morality of Historical Knowledge and Christian Belief.* Macmillan, New York.

Hassrick, Royal B.

1964   *The Sioux: Life and Customs of a Warrior Society.* University of Oklahoma Press, Norman.

Hatch, Sharon

1999   The Footprints of Our Ancestors. In *The Federal Archeology Program 1996–97, Secretary of the Interior's Report to Congress,* edited by David Andrews and Joseph Flanagan, pp. 20–21. National Park Service Archeology and Ethnography Program, Washington, D.C.

Helm, June

2000   *The People of Denendeh.* University of Iowa Press, Iowa City.

Helm, June, and Beryl C. Gillespie

1981   Dogrib Oral Tradition as History: War and Peace in the 1820s. *Journal of Anthropological Research* 37(1):8–27.

Henige, David P.

1974   *The Chronology of Oral Tradition: Quest for a Chimera.* Clarendon Press, Oxford University Press, Oxford.

1982   *Oral Historiography.* Longman, New York.

1986   Primary Source by Primary Source? On the Role of Epidemics in New World Depopulation. *Ethnohistory* 33(3):293–312.

1990   Their Numbers Become Thick: Native American Historical Demography as Expiation. In *The Invented Indian: Cultural Fictions and Government Policies,* edited by James A. Clifton, pp. 169–191. Transaction, New Brunswick, New Jersey.

Henning, Dale R.

1993   The Adaptive Patterning of the Dhegiha Sioux. *Plains Anthropologist* 38(146):253–264.

2001   Plains Village Tradition: Eastern Periphery and Oneota Tradition. In *Plains,* edited by Raymond J. DeMallie, pp. 222–233. Handbook of North American Indians, vol. 13, part 1, William C. Sturtevant, general editor. Smithsonian Institution, Washington, D.C.

Henning, Dale R., and Thomas D. Thiessen
2004   Central Siouans in the Northeastern Plains: Oneota Archaeology and the Blood Run Site. *Plains Anthropologist* 49(192), Memoir 36, Part 2.

Hewitt, J. N. B.
1903   Iroquoian Cosmology, First Part. In *Twenty-First Annual Report of the Bureau of American Ethnology for 1899–1900,* pp. 127–339. U.S. Government Printing Office, Washington, D.C. Reprinted in 1974 by AMS Press, New York.
1928   Iroquoian Cosmology, Part Two. In *Forty-Third Annual Report of the Bureau of American Ethnology for 1925–1926,* pp. 449–819. U.S. Government Printing Office, Washington, D.C. Reprinted in 1974 by AMS Press, New York.

Hickerson, Harold
1962   *The Southwestern Chippewa: An Ethnohistorical Study.* American Anthropological Association Memoir 92. Menasha, Wisconsin.
1988   *The Chippewa and Their Neighbors: A Study in Ethnohistory,* revised edition, edited by J. S. H. Brown and L. L. Peers. Waveland Press, Prospect Heights, Illinois. Originally published 1970 by Holt, Rinehart and Winston, New York.

Hobsbawm, Eric, and Terence Ranger (editors)
1983   *The Invention of Tradition.* Cambridge University Press, Cambridge.

Hodder, Ian (editor)
1982   *Symbolic and Structural Archaeology.* Cambridge University Press, Cambridge.
1987a   *The Archaeology of Contextual Meanings.* Cambridge University Press, Cambridge.
1987b   *Archaeology as Long-Term History.* Cambridge University Press, Cambridge.

Hoffman, Michael P.
1990   The Terminal Mississippian Period in the Arkansas River Valley and Quapaw Ethnogenesis. In *Towns and Temples Along the Mississippi,* edited by David H. Dye and Cheryl Anne Cox, pp. 208–226. University of Alabama Press, Tuscaloosa.

Hoffman, Walter J.
1891   The Mide-wi-win or Grand Medicine Society of the Ojibwa. In *Seventh Annual Report of the Bureau of Ethnology for the Years 1885–1886,* pp. 143–300. U.S. Government Printing Office, Washington, D.C.
1896   The Menomini Indians. In *Fourteenth Annual Report of the Bureau of Ethnology for the Years 1892–1893,* part 1, pp. 3–328. U.S. Government Printing Office, Washington, D.C.

Holden, Constance
2005   U.S. Government Shifts Stance on Claims to Ancient Remains. *Science* 309(5736):861.

Hollow, Robert C., Jr., and Douglas R. Parks
1980   Studies in Plains Linguistics: A Review. In *Anthropology on the Great Plains,*

edited by W. Raymond Wood and Margot Liberty, pp. 68–97. University of Nebraska Press, Lincoln.

Holm, Margaret, and David Pokotylo
1997   From Policy to Practice: A Case Study in Collaborative Exhibits with First Nations. *Canadian Journal of Archaeology* 21(1):33–43.

Hooke, S. H.
1963   *Middle Eastern Mythology.* Harmondsworth (Penguin Books), Middlesex, England.

Hoppe, Leslie J.
1984   *What Are They Saying About Biblical Archaeology?* Paulist Press, New York.

Howard, James H.
1965   *The Ponca Tribe.* Bureau of American Ethnology Bulletin 195, Smithsonian Institution. U.S. Government Printing Office, Washington, D.C.

Hreinsson, Vidar (general editor)
1997   *The Complete Sagas of Icelanders.* 5 vols. Leifur Eiriksson, Reykjavik, Iceland.

Hudson, Charles
1966   Folk History and Ethnohistory. *Ethnohistory* 13(1):52–70.
1990   *The Juan Pardo Expeditions: Exploration of the Carolinas and Tennessee, 1566–1568.* Smithsonian Institution Press, Washington, D.C.

Hunter, Ian M. L.
1984   Lengthy Verbatim Recall (LVR) and the Mythical Gift of Tape-Recorder Memory. In *Psychology in the 1990s,* edited by K. M. J. Lagerspetz and P. Niemi, pp. 425–440. North Holland, Amsterdam.
1985   Lengthy Verbatim Recall: The Role of Text. In *Progress in the Psychology of Language,* edited by A. Ellis, vol. 1, pp. 207–235. Erlbaum, Hillsdale, New Jersey.

Hyde, George E.
1937   *Red Cloud's Folk: A History of the Oglala Sioux Indians.* University of Oklahoma Press, Norman.

Hyman, Stanley Edgar
1955   The Ritual View of Myth and the Mythic. *Journal of American Folklore* 68:462–472.
1958   Reply to Bascom. *Journal of American Folklore* 71:152–155.

Hymes, Dell
1990   Mythology. In *Northwest Coast,* edited by Wayne Suttles, pp. 593–601. Handbook of North American Indians, vol. 7, William C. Sturtevant, general editor. Smithsonian Institution, Washington, D.C.

Ingstad, Anne Stine
1977   *The Discovery of a Norse Settlement in America: Excavations at L'Anse aux Meadows, Newfoundland, 1961–1968.* Universitetsforlaget, Oslo, Bergen, Tromso, Norway.

Ingstad, Helge
1964   Vinland Ruins Prove Vikings Found the New World. *National Geographic* 126(5):708–734.

1969　*Westward to Vinland: The Discovery of Pre-Columbian Norse House-Sites in North America.* St. Martin's Press, New York.

Jamieson, Susan M.
1999　When Natives and Archaeologists Meet: Cooperative Archaeology as a Vehicle for Awareness and Education. *Arch Notes* (Ontario Archaeological Society), n.s., 4(3):8–11.

Johnson, Alfred E.
1991　Kansa Origins: An Alternative. *Plains Anthropologist* 36(133):57–65.

Jordy, William H.
1952　*Henry Adams: Scientific Historian.* Yale University Press, New Haven, Connecticut.

Kehoe, Alice Beck
1998　*The Land of Prehistory: A Critical History of American Archaeology.* Routledge, New York.

Kehoe, Thomas F., and Alice B. Kehoe
1959　Boulder Effigy Monuments in the Northern Plains. *Journal of American Folklore* 72(284):115–127.

Keller, Werner
1995　*The Bible as History,* 2nd rev. ed. Barnes and Noble Books, New York.

Kenyon, Kathleen M.
1993　Jericho. In *The New Encyclopedia of Archaeological Excavations in the Holy Land,* edited by Ephraim Stern, vol. 2, pp. 674–681. The Israel Exploration Society and Carta, Jerusalem. Simon and Schuster, New York.

Kidd, Kenneth E.
1965　Birch-bark Scrolls in Archaeological Contexts. *American Antiquity* 30(4): 480–483.
1981　A Radiocarbon Date on a Midewiwin Scroll from Burntside Lake, Ontario. *Ontario Archaeology* 35:41–43.

Kidwell, Clara Sue
2002　Native American Systems of Knowledge. In *A Companion to American Indian History,* edited by Philip J. Deloria and Neal Salisbury, pp. 87–102. Blackwell, Malden, Massachusetts.

King, Thomas F.
1998　*Cultural Resource Laws and Practice: An Introductory Guide.* AltaMira Press, Walnut Creek, California.

Kirk, G. S.
1976　*Homer and the Oral Tradition.* Cambridge University Press, Cambridge.

Krajick, Kevin
2005　Tracking Myth to Geological Reality. *Science* 310(5749):762–764.

Krech, Shepard III
1999　*The Ecological Indian: Myth and History.* W. W. Norton, New York.

Kroeber, Alfred L.
1940　Conclusions: The Present Status of Americanistic Problems. In *The Maya and Their Neighbors,* compiled by Clarence L. Hay et al., pp. 460–487.

D. Appleton-Century, New York. Reprinted in 1962 by University of Utah Press, Salt Lake City.

1951   A Mohave Historical Epic. *University of California Anthropological Records* 11(2):71–176.

1976   *Yurok Myths.* University of California Press, Berkeley and Los Angeles.

Kuhn, Robert D., and Martha L. Sempowski

2001   A New Approach to Dating the League of the Iroquois. *American Antiquity* 66(2):301–314.

Kuhn, Thomas S.

1970   *The Structure of Scientific Revolutions,* 2nd edition, enlarged. International Encyclopedia of Unified Science, Vol. 2, No. 2. University of Chicago Press, Chicago.

Kurten, Bjorn, and Elaine Anderson

1980   *Pleistocene Mammals of North America.* Columbia University Press, New York.

Kuznar, Lawrence A.

1997   *Reclaiming a Scientific Anthropology.* AltaMira Press, Walnut Creek, California.

Lance, H. Darrell

1981   *The Old Testament and the Archaeologist.* Fortress Press, Philadelphia.

Lankford, George E. (editor)

1987   *Native American Legends—Southeastern Legends: Tales from the Natchez, Caddo, Biloxi, Chickasaw, and Other Nations.* The American Folklore Series, W. K. McNeil, general editor. August House, Little Rock, Arkansas.

Lapham, Increase A.

1855   *The Antiquities of Wisconsin as Surveyed and Described.* Smithsonian Contributions to Knowledge, vol. 7, article 4, pp. 1–92 plus plates. Smithsonian Institution, Washington, D.C.

Latacz, Joachim

2004   *Troy and Homer: Towards a Solution of an Old Mystery.* Translated from German by Kevin Windle and Rosh Ireland. Oxford University Press, New York.

Laughlin, John C. H.

2000   *Archaeology and the Bible.* Routledge, London and New York.

Lazarus, Edward

1991   *Black Hills/White Justice: The Sioux Nation Versus the United States, 1775 to the Present.* HarperCollins, New York.

Leach, Edmund R.

1954   *Political Systems of Highland Burma: A Study of Kachin Social Structure.* Harvard University Press, Cambridge, Massachusetts.

Lepper, Bradley T.

2000   Working Together—Or Serving Two Masters? *Society for American Archaeology Archaeological Bulletin* 18(4):22–25.

2004   Kennewick Man Decision Upheld by Court of Appeals. *Mammoth Trumpet* 19(2):1–2, 18–19.

Leveillee, Alan
2002   Applied Archaeology Influencing Native Traditions: A Case from Rhode Island. *Archaeology of Eastern North America* 30:21–28.

Lévi-Strauss, Claude
1969   *The Raw and the Cooked.* Translated from the French. J. and D. Weightman, New York.

Levy, Thomas E.
2000   Remember Marcellus's Warning. *Science* 289(5482):1145–1146.

Liberty, Margot P., W. Raymond Wood, and Lee Irwin
2001   Omaha. In *Plains,* edited by Raymond J. DeMallie, pp. 399–415. Handbook of North American Indians, vol. 13, part 1, William C. Sturtevant, general editor. Smithsonian Institution, Washington, D.C.

Liljeblad, Sven
1986   Oral Tradition: Content and Style of Verbal Arts. In *Great Basin,* edited by Warren L. D'Azevedo, pp. 641–659. Handbook of North American Indians, vol. 11, William C. Sturtevant, general editor. Smithsonian Institution, Washington, D.C.

Linnekin, Jocelyn
1997   Contending Approaches. In *The Cambridge History of the Pacific Island- ers,* edited by Donald Denoon, Stewart Firth, Jocelyn Linnekin, Malama Meleisea, and Karen Nero, pp. 3–36. Cambridge University Press, Cam- bridge.

Lippert, Owen (editor)
2000   *Beyond the Nass Valley: National Implications of the Supreme Court's* Del- gamuukw *Decision.* The Fraser Institute, Vancouver.

Loftus, Elizabeth F., and Katherine Ketcham
1991   *Witness for the Defense, the Accused, the Eyewitness, and the Expert Who Puts Memory on Trial.* St. Martin's Press, New York.

Loftus, Elizabeth F., and Geoffrey R. Loftus
1980   On the Permanence of Stored Information in the Human Brain. *American Psychologist* 35(5):409–420.

Lord, Albert B.
1960   *The Singer of Tales.* Harvard University Press, Cambridge, Massachusetts.

Lottinville, Savoie (editor)
1980   *A Journal of Travels into the Arkansas Territory During the Year 1819,* by Thomas
[1821]   Nuttall. University of Oklahoma Press, Norman. Originally published by Thomas N. Palmer, Philadelphia.

Lowie, Robert H.
1915   Oral Tradition and History. *American Anthropologist,* n.s., 17:597–599.
1917   Oral Tradition and History. *The Journal of American Folk-Lore* 30(116): 161–167.
1942   *Studies in Plains Indian Folklore.* University of California Publications in American Archaeology and Ethnology, Vol. 40. Berkeley.

Luce, John Victor

1998   *Celebrating Homer's Landscapes: Troy and Ithaca Revisited.* Yale University Press, New Haven, Connecticut.

Lurie, Nancy O.

1960   Winnebago Protohistory. In *Culture in History: Essays in Honor of Paul Radin,* edited by Stanley Diamond, pp. 790–808. Columbia University Press, New York.

1978   Winnebago. In *Northeast,* edited by Bruce G. Trigger, pp. 690–707. Handbook of North American Indians, vol. 15, William C. Sturtevant, general editor. Smithsonian Institution, Washington, D.C.

Lyons, Patrick D.

2003   *Ancestral Hopi Migrations.* University of Arizona Press, Tucson.

McClellan, Catherine

1970   Indian Stories About the First Whites in Northwestern America. In *Ethnohistory in Southwestern Alaska and the Southern Yukon: Method and Content,* edited by Margaret Lantis, pp. 103–133. University Press of Kentucky, Lexington.

McGee, W J

1897   The Siouan Indians: A Preliminary Sketch. In *Fifteenth Annual Report of the Bureau of Ethnology for 1893–1894,* pp. 153–204. U.S. Government Printing Office, Washington, D.C.

McGhee, Robert

1977   Ivory for the Sea Woman: The Symbolic Attributes of a Prehistoric Technology. *Canadian Journal of Archaeology* 1:141–149.

1984   Contact Between Native North Americans and the Medieval Norse: A Review of the Evidence. *American Antiquity* 49(1):4–26.

McGovern, Thomas H.

1981   The Vinland Adventure: A North Atlantic Perspective. *North American Archaeologist* 2(4):285–308.

McGregor, John C.

1943   Burial of an Early American Magician. *Proceedings of the American Philosophical Society* 86(2):270–298. Philadelphia.

McIlwraith, T. F.

1992 [1948]   *The Bella Coola Indians,* 2 vols. University of Toronto Press, Toronto.

McKern, Will C.

1945   Preliminary Report on the Upper Mississippi Phase in Wisconsin. *Milwaukee Public Museum Bulletin* 16:109–285.

McKusick, Marshall

1970   *The Davenport Conspiracy.* Office of the State Archaeologist of Iowa First Report. University of Iowa, Iowa City.

Magnusson, Magnus, and Hermann Palsson

1966   *The Vinland Sagas, the Norse Discovery of America: Graenlendinga Saga and Eirik's Saga.* New York University Press, New York.

Malinowski, Bronislaw

1926   *Crime and Custom in Savage Society.* Kegan Paul, Trench, Trubner, London.

Mallery, Garrick

1886   Pictographs of the North American Indians. In *Fourth Annual Report of the Bureau of Ethnology for 1882–1883,* pp. 3–256. U.S. Government Printing Office, Washington, D.C.

Marriott, Alice, and Carol K. Rachlin

1968   *American Indian Mythology.* Thomas Y. Crowell, New York.

Martin, Calvin (editor)

1987   *The American Indian and the Problem of History.* Oxford University Press, New York.

Martin, Thomas R.

2000   *Ancient Greece from Prehistoric to Hellenistic Times.* Yale University Press, New Haven, Connecticut. Originally published 1996.

Mason, Carol I.

1976   Historic Identification and Lake Winnebago Focus Oneota. In *Cultural Change and Continuity: Essays in Honor of James Bennett Griffin,* edited by Charles E. Cleland, pp. 335–348. Academic Press, New York.

1985   Archaeological Analogy and Ethnographic Example: A Case from the Winnebago. In *Indians, Colonists, and Slaves: Essays in Memory of Charles H. Fairbanks,* edited by Kenneth W. Johnson, Jonathan M. Leader, and Robert C. Wilson, pp. 95–104. Florida Journal of Anthropology Special Publication No. 4. Gainesville.

1988   *Introduction to Wisconsin Indians: Prehistory to Statehood.* Sheffield, Salem, Wisconsin.

1993   Historic Pottery and Tribal Identification in Wisconsin: A Review of the Evidence and the Problems. *The Wisconsin Archeologist* 74(1–4):258–271.

Mason, J. Alden

1946   *Notes on the Indians of the Great Slave Lake Area.* Yale University Publications in Anthropology No. 34. Yale University Press, New Haven, Connecticut.

Mason, Ronald J.

1976   Ethnicity and Archaeology in the Upper Great Lakes. In *Cultural Change and Continuity: Essays in Honor of James Bennett Griffin,* edited by Charles E. Cleland, pp. 349–361. Academic Press, New York.

1986   *Rock Island, Historical Indian Archaeology in the Northern Lake Michigan Basin.* Midcontinental Journal of Archaeology Special Paper No. 6. Kent State University Press, Kent, Ohio.

1993   Oneota and Winnebago Ethnogenesis: An Overview. *The Wisconsin Archeologist* 74(1–4):400–421.

1997a   Archaeoethnicity and the Elusive Menominis. *Midcontinental Journal of Archaeology* 22(1):69–94.

1997b   Letter to the Editor. *Society for American Archaeology Archaeological Bulletin* 15(1):3.

2000 Archaeology and Native North American Oral Traditions. *American Antiquity* 65(2):239–266.

Mazar, Amihai

1990 *Archaeology of the Land of the Bible, 10,000–586 B.C.E.* Anchor Bible Reference Library, Doubleday, New York.

Meltzer, David J., and William C. Sturtevant

1983 The Holly Oak Shell Game: An Historic Archaeological Fraud. In *Lulu Linear Punctated: Essays in Honor of George I. Quimby,* edited by Robert C. Dunnell and Donald K. Grayson, pp. 325–352. University of Michigan Museum of Anthropology, Anthropological Paper 72, Ann Arbor.

Merrell, James H.

1989 *The Indians' New World: Catawbas and Their Neighbors from European Contact Through the Era of Removal.* University of North Carolina Press, Chapel Hill.

2000 The Indians' New World: The Catawba Experience. In *American Encounters: Natives and Newcomers from European Contact to Indian Removal, 1500–1850,* edited by Peter C. Mancall and James H. Merrell, pp. 27–50. Routledge, New York. Originally published 1984 in *William and Mary Quarterly,* 3rd series 41:537–565.

Meyer, David, and S. J. Smailes

1975 *Archaeology.* Saskatchewan Department of the Environment, Churchill River Study, Final Report 19, Regina.

Meyerhoff, Hans (editor)

1959 *The Philosophy of History in Our Time: An Anthology.* Doubleday Anchor Books, Garden City, New York.

Michaels, Anne

1998 *Fugitive Pieces.* Vintage Books, New York. Originally published 1996.

Michelson, Gunther

2003 Midwinter at Two Onondaga Longhouses. *Northeast Anthropology* 65:17–29.

Millard, Alan

2000 How Reliable Is Exodus? *Biblical Archaeology Review* 26(4):51–57.

Miller, Jay

1998 Tsimshian Ethno-Ethnohistory: A "Real" Indigenous Chronology. *Ethnohistory* 45(4):657–674.

Mills, Antonia

1994 *Eagle Down Is Our Law: Witsuwit'en Law, Feasts, and Land Claims.* University of British Columbia Press, Vancouver.

Mooney, James

1894 *The Siouan Tribes of the East.* Bureau of American Ethnology Bulletin 22. U.S. Government Printing Office, Washington, D.C.

1898 Calendar History of the Kiowa Indians. In *Seventeenth Annual Report of the Bureau of American Ethnology for 1895–1896,* part 1, pp. 129–445. U.S. Government Printing Office, Washington, D.C.

Moorey, P. R. S.
1991   *A Century of Biblical Archeology.* Westminster/John Knox Press, Louisville,
        Kentucky.

Morgan, Lewis Henry
1962   *League of the Ho-de-no-sau-nee or Iroquois.* Corinth Books, New York. Origi-
[1851] nally published by Sage, Rochester, New York.

Morison, Samuel Eliot
1971   *The European Discovery of America: The Northern Voyages A.D. 500–1600.*
        Oxford University Press, New York.

Morse, Dan F.
1990   The Nodena Phase. In *Towns and Temples Along the Mississippi,* edited by
        David H. Dye and Cheryl A. Cox, pp. 69–97. University of Alabama Press,
        Tuscaloosa.

Morse, Dan F., and Phyllis A. Morse
1983   *Archaeology of the Central Mississippi Valley.* Academic Press, New York.

Mott, Mildred
1938   The Relation of Historic Indian Tribes to Archaeological Manifestations
        in Iowa. *Iowa Journal of History and Politics* 36(3):227–314.

Muller, Jon
1986   *Archaeology of the Lower Ohio River Valley.* Academic Press, Orlando, Florida.

Nabokov, Peter
1996   Native Views of History. In *The Cambridge History of the Native Peoples of
        the Americas,* vol. 1: *North America,* part 1, edited by Bruce G. Trigger and
        Wilcomb E. Washburn, pp. 1–59. Cambridge University Press, Cambridge.
2002   *A Forest of Time: American Indian Ways of History.* Cambridge University
        Press, New York.

Nadel, Siegfried F.
1937   A Field Experiment in Racial Psychology. *British Journal of Psychology*
        28:195–211.

Nagel, Thomas
1986   *The View from Nowhere.* Oxford University Press, New York.

Nagy, Gregory
1996   *Homeric Questions.* University of Texas Press, Austin.

Nassaney, Michael S.
1994   An Epistemological Enquiry into Some Archaeological and Historical In-
        terpretations of Seventeenth Century Native American-European Rela-
        tions. In *Archaeological Approaches to Cultural Identity,* edited by Stephen
        Shennan, pp. 76–93. Routledge, New York.

Neihardt, John G.
1979   *Black Elk Speaks: Being the Life Story of a Holy Man of the Ogalala.* Univer-
        sity of Nebraska Press, Lincoln. Originally published in 1932 by William
        Morrow, New York.

Neisser, Ulric
1981   John Dean's Memory: A Case Study. *Cognition* 9:1–22.

Neisser, Ulric (editor)

1982   *Memory Observed: Remembering in Natural Contexts.* W. H. Freeman, San Francisco.

Neisser, Ulric, and Ira E. Hyman, Jr. (editors)

2000   *Memory Observed, Remembering in Natural Contexts,* 2nd edition, revised, with deletions and additions. Worth, New York.

Nelson, S. N., and Alice B. Kehoe (editors)

1990   *Powers of Observation: Alternative Views in Archeology.* Archeological Papers of the American Anthropological Association 2. American Anthropological Association, Arlington, Virginia.

Nicastro, Nicholas

2000   Kennewick and Repatriation. *Archaeology* 53(3):69–71.

Nicholas, George P., and Thomas D. Andrews (editors)

1997   *At a Crossroads: Archaeology and First Peoples in Canada.* Archaeology Press Publication No. 24. Simon Fraser University, Burnaby, British Columbia.

Nielsen, Eduard

1954   *Oral Tradition: A Modern Problem in Old Testament Introduction.* Studies in Biblical Theology No. 11. SCM Press, London.

Novick, Peter

1988   *That Noble Dream: The "Objectivity Question" and the American Historical Profession.* Cambridge University Press, New York.

1999   *The Holocaust in American Life.* Houghton Mifflin, Boston.

O'Brien, Michael J., and W. Raymond Wood

1998   *The Prehistory of Missouri.* University of Missouri Press, Columbia.

Offer, Daniel

2000   Untitled study reported in *Science* 288:1961 (16 June).

Ong, Walter J.

1982   *Orality and Literacy: The Technologizing of the Word.* Methuen, London and New York.

Opler, Marvin K.

1940   The Southern Ute of Colorado. In *Acculturation in Seven American Indian Tribes,* edited by Ralph Linton, pp. 119–203. D. Appleton-Century, New York.

Ortiz, Alfonso (editor)

1979   *Southwest.* Handbook of North American Indians, vol. 9, William C. Sturtevant, general editor. Smithsonian Institution, Washington, D.C.

Osgood, Cornelius

1936   *The Distribution of the Northern Athapaskan Indians.* Yale University Publications in Anthropology No. 7. Yale University Press, New Haven, Connecticut.

O'Shea, John M., and John Ludwickson

1992   *Archaeology and Ethnohistory of the Omaha Indians: The Big Village Site.* University of Nebraska Press, Lincoln.

Oswalt, Wendell H.
2002 *This Land Was Theirs: A Study of Native Americans,* 7th edition. McGraw-Hill, Mayfield, New Jersey.

Overstreet, David F.
1993 McCauley, Astor, and Hanson—Candidates for the Provisional Dandy Phase. *The Wisconsin Archeologist* 74(1-4):120-196.
2001 Dreaded Dolostone and Old Smudge Stories—A Response to Critiques of Emergent Horizon Oneota 14C Dates from Eastern Wisconsin. *The Wisconsin Archeologist* 82(1-2):33-85.

Parkin, Alan J.
1993 *Memory: Phenomena, Experiment, and Theory.* Blackwell, Oxford.

Parks, Douglas R., and Robert L. Rankin
2001 Siouan Languages. In *Plains,* edited by Raymond J. DeMallie, pp. 94-114. Handbook of North American Indians, vol. 13, part 1, William C. Sturtevant, general editor. Smithsonian Institution, Washington, D.C.

Parry, Adam (editor)
1971 *The Making of Homeric Verse: The Collected Papers of Milman Parry.* Oxford University Press, Oxford.

Parry, Milman, Albert B. Lord, and D. E. Bynum
1974 *Serbo-Croatian Heroic Songs,* vol. 3: *Avdo Medjedovic: The Wedding of Smailagic Meho.* Translation with introduction and commentary by Albert B. Lord. Harvard University Press, Cambridge, Massachusetts.

Peabody, Berkley
1975 *The Winged Word: A Study in the Technique of Ancient Greek Oral Composition as Seen Principally Through Hesiod's "Works and Days."* State University of New York Press, Albany.

Pendergast, David M., and Clement W. Meighan
1959 Folk Traditions as Historical Fact: A Paiute Example. *Journal of American Folk-Lore* 72(284):128-133.

Phillips, Philip, and James A. Brown
1978 *Pre-Columbian Shell Engravings from the Craig Mound at Spiro, Oklahoma,* parts 1 and 2. Peabody Museum Press, Harvard University, Cambridge, Massachusetts.

Pike, Kenneth
1954– *Language in Relation to a Unified Theory of the Structure of Human Behavior,*
1960 vols. 1-3. Summer Institute of Linguistics, Glendale, California.

Powell, J. W.
1881 On Limitations to the Use of Some Anthropologic Data. In *First Annual Report of the Bureau of Ethnology for 1879–80,* pp. 73-86. U.S. Government Printing Office, Washington, D.C.

Prange, Gordon W.
1982 *At Dawn We Slept: The Untold Story of Pearl Harbor.* Penguin Books, New York.

Price, Barbara J.

1980   The Truth Is Not in Accounts but in Account Books: On the Epistemological Status of History. In *Beyond the Myths of Culture: Essays in Cultural Materialism,* edited by Eric B. Ross, pp. 155–180. Academic Press, New York.

Radin, Paul

1923   The Winnebago Tribe. *Thirty-Seventh Annual Report of the Bureau of American Ethnology for the Years 1915–1916.* U.S. Government Printing Office, Washington, D.C.

1948   *Winnebago Hero Cycles: A Study in Aboriginal Literature.* Indiana University Publications in Anthropology and Linguistics, Memoir 1, Bloomington.

Raglan, Lord

1949   *The Hero: A Study in Tradition, Myth, and Drama.* Watts, London. Originally published 1936 by Methuen, London.

1957   Reply to Bascom. *Journal of American Folklore* 70:359–360.

Rajnovich, Grace

1994   *Reading Rock Art: Interpreting the Indian Rock Paintings of the Canadian Shield.* Natural Heritage/Natural History, Toronto.

Ramenofsky, Ann F.

1987   *Vectors of Death: The Archaeology of European Contact.* University of New Mexico Press, Albuquerque.

Ramsey, Jarold

1977   *Coyote Was Going There: Indian Literature of the Oregon Country.* University of Washington Press, Seattle.

Rathje, William, and Cullen Murphy

1992   *Rubbish! The Archaeology of Garbage.* HarperCollins, New York.

Reff, Daniel T.

1992   Contact Shock in Northwestern New Spain, 1518–1764. In *Disease and Demography in the Americas,* edited by John W. Verano and Douglas H. Ubelaker, pp. 265–276. Smithsonian Institution Press, Washington, D.C.

Rescher, Nicholas

1997   *Objectivity: The Obligations of Impersonal Reason.* University of Notre Dame Press, Notre Dame, Indiana.

Richards, Patricia B.

1993   Winnebago Subsistence—Change and Continuity. *The Wisconsin Archeologist* 74(1-4):272–289.

Robb, John E.

1998   The Archaeology of Symbols. *Annual Review of Anthropology* 27:329–346.

Rosnow, Ralph L.

1991   Inside Rumor: A Personal Journey. *American Psychologist* 46(5):484–496.

Rubin, David C.

1995   *Memory in Oral Traditions: The Cognitive Psychology of Epic, Ballads, and Counting-Out Rhymes.* Oxford University Press, New York.

Rudes, Blair A., Thomas J. Blumer, and J. Alan May

2004   Catawba and Neighboring Groups. In *Southeast,* edited by Raymond D.

Fogelson, pp. 301–318. Handbook of North American Indians, vol. 14, William C. Sturtevant, general editor. Smithsonian Institution, Washington, D.C.

Sabo, George III

2000 The Quapaw Indians of Arkansas, 1673–1803. In *Indians of the Greater Southeast,* edited by Bonnie G. McEwan, pp. 178–203. University Press of Florida, Gainesville.

Sahlins, Marshall

1985 *Islands of History.* University of Chicago Press, Chicago.

Salzer, Robert J.

1987 Preliminary Report on the Gottschall Site (47Ia80). *The Wisconsin Archeologist* 68(4):419–472.

1993 Oral Literature and Archaeology. *The Wisconsin Archeologist* 74(1–4):80–119.

1997 Wisconsin Rock Art. In *Wisconsin Archaeology,* edited by Robert A. Birmingham, Carol I. Mason, and James B. Stoltman, pp. 48–77. *The Wisconsin Archeologist* 78(1–2).

Salzer, Robert J., and Grace Rajnovich

2001 *The Gottschall Rockshelter: An Archaeological Mystery.* Prairie Smoke Press, St. Paul.

Salzman, Philip Carl

2002 On Reflexivity. *American Anthropologist* 104(3):805–813.

Sasso, Robert F.

1993 La Crosse Region Oneota Adaptations: Changing Late Prehistoric Subsistence and Settlement Patterns in the Upper Mississippi Valley. *The Wisconsin Archeologist* 74(1–4):324–369.

Schlesinger, Arthur M., Jr.

2000 *A Life in the Twentieth Century: Innocent Beginnings, 1917–1950.* Houghton Mifflin, Boston.

Schliemann, Henry (Heinrich)

1881 *Ilios, the City and Country of the Trojans; The Results of Researches and Discoveries on the Site of Troy and Throughout the Troad in the Years 1871–72–73–78–79.* Harper and Brothers, New York.

Schmidt, Peter R., and Thomas C. Patterson (editors)

1995 *Making Alternative Histories: The Practice of Archaeology and History in Non-Western Settings.* School of American Research Press, Santa Fe, New Mexico.

Schoolcraft, Henry R.

1851– *Information Respecting the History, Condition and Prospects of the Indian Tribes*
1857 *of the United States,* 6 vols. Collected and prepared under the direction of the Bureau of Indian Affairs. Lippincott, Grambo, Philadelphia.

Schwartz, Barry

2000 *Abraham Lincoln and the Forge of National Memory.* University of Chicago Press, Chicago.

Schweitzer, Marjorie M.

2001 Otoe and Missouria. In *Plains,* edited by Raymond J. DeMallie, pp. 447–

461. Handbook of North American Indians, vol. 13, part 1, William C. Sturtevant, general editor. Smithsonian Institution, Washington, D.C.

Science

2000   Bones Decision Rattles Researchers. *Science* 289(5488):2257.

Secoy, Frank Raymond

1953   *Changing Military Patterns on the Great Plains, Seventeenth Century Through Nineteenth Century.* Monographs of the American Ethnological Society, No. 21. J. J. Augustin, Locust Valley, New York.

Sekaquaptewa, Emory, and Dorothy Washburn

2004   They Go Along Singing: Reconstructing the Hopi Past from Ritual Metaphors in Song and Image. *American Antiquity* 69(3):457–486.

Shanks, Michael, and Christopher Tilley

1992   *Re-constructing Archaeology: Theory and Practice,* 2nd ed. Routledge, London.

Sheridan, Thomas E.

2002   Arizona State Museum and Hopi Collaboration. *Anthropology News* (American Anthropological Association) 43(2):17.

Shrimpton, Gordon S.

1997   *History and Memory in Ancient Greece.* McGill-Queen's University Press, Montreal and Kingston.

Siebert, F. T., Jr.

1937   Mammoth or "Stiff-Legged Bear." *American Anthropologist* 39(4):721–725.

Silberman, Neil Asher

1989   *Between Past and Present: Archaeology, Ideology, and Nationalism in the Modern Middle East.* Henry Holt, New York.

Silverberg, Robert

1968   *Mound Builders of Ancient America: The Archaeology of a Myth.* Ohio University Press, Athens.

Speck, Frank G.

1935   Mammoth or "Stiff-Legged Bear." *American Anthropologist* 37(1):159–163.

1938   The Question of Matrilineal Descent in the Southeastern Siouan Area. *American Anthropologist* 40(1):1–12.

Speck, Frank G., and C. E. Schaeffer

1942   Catawba Kinship and Social Organization with a Resume of Tutelo Kinship Terms. *American Anthropologist* 44(4):555–575.

Springer, James W., and Stanley R. Witkowski

1982   Siouan Historical Linguistics and Oneota Archaeology. In *Oneota Studies,* edited by Guy E. Gibbon, pp. 69–83. University of Minnesota Publications in Anthropology No. 1. University of Minnesota, Minneapolis.

Stapp, Darby C., and Julie Longenecker

2000a   The Times, They Are A-Changin: Can Archaeologists and Native Americans Change with the Times? *Society for American Archaeology Archaeological Bulletin* 18(2):18–20, 27.

2000b   Dr. Lepper Is Wrong. *Society for American Archaeology Archaeological Bulletin* 18(4):22–24.

Stothers, David M.

2000   The Protohistoric Time Period in the Southwestern Lake Erie Region: European-Derived Trade Material, Population Movement, and Cultural Realignment. In *Cultures Before Contact: The Late Prehistory of Ohio and Surrounding Regions,* edited by R. A. Genheimer, pp. 52–95. Ohio Archaeological Council, Columbus.

Strong, William Duncan

1934   North American Indian Traditions Suggesting a Knowledge of the Mammoth. *American Anthropologist* 36(1):81–88.

Sturtevant, William C.

1966   Anthropology, History, and Ethnohistory. *Ethnohistory* 13(1):1–51.

Swann, Brian (editor)

1992   *On the Translation of Native American Literatures.* Smithsonian Institution Press, Washington, D.C.

2004   *Voices from the Four Directions.* University of Nebraska Press, Lincoln.

Swanton, John R.

1911   *Indian Tribes of the Lower Mississippi Valley and Adjacent Coast of the Gulf of Mexico.* Bureau of American Ethnology Bulletin 43. U.S. Government Printing Office, Washington, D.C.

1915   Dr. Swanton's Reply. *American Anthropologist,* n.s., 17:600.

1922   *Early History of the Creek Indians and Their Neighbors.* Bureau of American Ethnology Bulletin 73. U.S. Government Printing Office, Washington, D.C.

1952   *The Indian Tribes of North America.* Bureau of American Ethnology Bulletin 145. U.S. Government Printing Office, Washington, D.C.

Swidler, Nina, Kurt E. Dongoske, Roger Anyon, and Alan S. Downer (editors)

1997   *Native Americans and Archaeologists: Stepping Stones to Common Ground.* AltaMira Press, Walnut Creek, California.

Tailhan, Jules (editor)

1864   *Mémoire sur les moeurs coustumes et relligion des sauvages de l'Amérique septentrionale.* Leipzig and Paris.

Teague, Lynn S.

1993   Prehistory and the Traditions of the O'Odham and Hopi. *Kiva* 58(4): 435–454.

Thomas, Cyrus

1887   Burial Mounds of the Northern Sections of the United States. *Fifth Annual Report of the Bureau of Ethnology for 1883–84,* pp. 9–119. U.S. Government Printing Office, Washington, D.C.

1894   Report of the Mound Explorations of the Bureau of Ethnology. *Twelfth Annual Report of the Bureau of American Ethnology for 1890–91.* U.S. Government Printing Office, Washington, D.C.

1910   Quapaw. In *Handbook of American Indians North of Mexico,* edited by Frederick Webb Hodge, pp. 333–336. Bureau of American Ethnology Bulletin 30, part 2. U.S. Government Printing Office, Washington, D.C.

Thomas, David Hurst

2000   *Skull Wars: Kennewick Man, Archaeology, and the Battle for Native American Identity.* Basic Books, New York.

Thompson, Leonard L.

1978   *Introducing Biblical Literature: A More Fantastic Country.* Prentice-Hall, Englewood Cliffs, New Jersey.

Thompson, Stith

1951   *The Folktale.* Holt, Rinehart, and Winston, New York. Originally published 1946 by Dryden Press, New York.

1953   The Star Husband Tale. *Studia Septentrionalia* 4:93–163. Reprinted in Dundes 1965:414–474.

1955–   *Motif-Index of Folk-Literature; A Classification of Narrative Elements in Folk-*
1958   *tales, Ballads, Myths, Fables, Mediaeval Romances, Exempla, Fabliaux, Jest-Books, and Local Legends,* revised and enlarged edition. Indiana University Press, Bloomington.

1967   *Tales of the North American Indians.* Indiana University Press, Bloomington.

[1929]   Originally published by Harvard University Press, Cambridge.

Thompson, Thomas L.

1974   *The Historicity of the Patriarchal Narratives.* W. de Gruyter, Berlin and New York.

1999   *The Mythic Past, Biblical Archaeology and the Myth of Israel.* Basic Books (Perseus), London and New York.

Thorsson, Ornolfur, and Bernard Scudder (editors)

2000   *The Sagas of Icelanders,* with preface by Jane Smiley and introduction by Robert Kellogg. Viking Penguin, New York.

Thwaites, Reuben Gold (editor)

1896–   *The Jesuit Relations and Allied Documents: Travels and Explorations of the Jesuit*
1901   *Missionaries in New France, 1610–1791.* 73 vols. Burrows Bros., Cleveland.

1902   *The French Regime in Wisconsin, I: 1634–1727.* Collections of the State Historical Society of Wisconsin, Vol. 16. Wisconsin State Historical Society, Madison.

1904–   *Early Western Travels, 1748–1846: A Series of Annotated Reprints of Some of the*
1907   *Best and Rarest Contemporary Volumes of Travel, Descriptive of the Aborigines and Social and Economic Conditions in the Middle and Far West, during the Period of Early American Settlement. With Notes, Introduction, Index, etc.* 32 vols. Arthur H. Clark, Cleveland. Reprinted in 1966 by AMS Press, New York, and in 1974 by Arthur H. Clark, Cleveland.

Trevelyan, G. Otto

1876   *The Life and Letters of Lord Macaulay,* 2 vols. Harper and Brothers, New York.

Trevor-Roper, Hugh

1983   The Invention of Tradition: The Highland Tradition of Scotland. In *The Invention of Tradition,* edited by Eric Hobsbawm and Terence Ranger, pp. 15–41. Cambridge University Press, Cambridge.

Trigger, Bruce G.

1976   *The Children of Aataentsic: A History of the Huron People to 1660.* McGill-Queen's University Press, Montreal and London.

1989   *A History of Archaeological Thought.* Cambridge University Press, Cambridge.

Tulving, Endel, and Fergus I. M. Craik (editors)

2000   *The Oxford Handbook of Memory.* Oxford University Press, New York.

Tylor, Edward B.

1920   *Primitive Culture: Researches into the Development of Mythology, Philosophy, Re-*
[1871]   *ligion, Language, Art and Custom,* 6th edition, 2 vols. John Murray, London.

Upham, Steadman

1992   Population and Spanish Contact in the Southwest. In *Disease and Demography in the Americas,* edited by John W. Verano and Douglas H. Ubelaker, pp. 223–236. Smithsonian Institution Press, Washington, D.C.

Vansina, Jan

1985   *Oral Tradition as History.* University of Wisconsin Press, Madison.

Van Stone, James W.

1965   *The Changing Culture of the Snowdrift Chipewyan.* National Museum of Canada Bulletin, No. 209, Ottawa.

Vecsey, Christopher

1983   *Traditional Ojibwa Religion and Its Historical Changes.* The American Philosophical Society, Philadelphia.

Vecsey, Christopher (editor)

1990   *Religion in Native North America.* University of Idaho Press, Moscow.

Vehik, Susan C.

1993   Dhegiha Origins and Plains Archaeology. *Plains Anthropologist* 38(146): 231–252.

Vennum, Thomas, Jr.

1978   Ojibwa Origin-Migration Songs of the Mitewiwin. *Journal of American Folklore* 91:753–791.

von Gernet, Alexander

1996   *Oral Narratives and Aboriginal Pasts: An Interdisciplinary Review of the Literature on Oral Traditions and Oral Histories,* 2 vols. Research and Analysis Directorate, Indian and Northern Affairs Canada, Ottawa.

2000   What My Elders Taught Me: Oral Traditions as Evidence in Aboriginal Litigation. In *Beyond the Nass Valley: National Implications of the Supreme Court's Delgamuukw Decision,* edited by Owen Lippert, pp. 103–129. The Fraser Institute, Vancouver.

von Gernet, Alexander, and Peter Timmins

1987   Pipes and Parakeets: Constructing Meaning in an Early Iroquoian Context. In *Archaeology as Long-Term History,* edited by Ian Hodder, pp. 31–42. Cambridge University Press, Cambridge.

Wahlgren, Erik

1969 Fact and Fancy in the Vinland Sagas. In *Old Norse Literature and Mythology: A Symposium,* edited by Edgar C. Polome, pp. 19–80. University of Texas Press, Austin.

1986 *The Vikings and America.* Thames and Hudson, London.

Walker, James R.

1982 *Lakota Society,* edited by Raymond J. DeMallie. University of Nebraska Press, Lincoln.

Wallace, Anthony F. C.

1958 The Dekanawideh Myth Analyzed as the Record of a Revitalization Movement. *Ethnohistory* 5(2):118–130.

Warren, William W.

1984 *History of the Ojibwa People.* Minnesota Historical Society Press, St. Paul.

[1885] Originally published in *Collections of the Minnesota Historical Society,* vol. 5, St. Paul.

Watkins, Joe

1998 Native Americans, Western Science, and NAGPRA. *Society for American Archaeology Archaeological Bulletin* 16(5):23, 25.

2000 *Indigenous Archaeology, American Indian Values and Scientific Practice.* AltaMira Press, Walnut Creek, California.

Watson, Burton (translator and editor)

1964 *Chuang Tzu: Basic Writings.* Columbia University Press, New York.

Wauchope, Robert

1962 *Lost Tribes and Sunken Continents: Myth and Method in the Study of American Indians.* University of Chicago Press, Chicago.

Wedel, Mildred Mott

1959 Oneota Sites on the Upper Iowa River. *The Missouri Archaeologist* 21(2–4).

1986 Peering at the Ioway Indians Through the Mist of Time: 1650–circa 1700. *Journal of the Iowa Archeological Society* 33:1–74.

2001 Iowa. In *Plains,* edited by Raymond J. DeMallie, pp. 432–446. Handbook of North American Indians, vol. 13, part 1, William C. Sturtevant, general editor. Smithsonian Institution, Washington, D.C.

Weiss, Harvey, and Raymond S. Bradley

2001 What Drives Societal Collapse? *Science* 291(5504):609–610.

White, Andrew D.

1955 *The Warfare of Science with Theology in Christendom.* George Braziller, New
[1895] York.

White, Richard

2000 The Winning of the West: The Expansion of the Western Sioux in the Eighteenth and Nineteenth Centuries. In *American Encounters, Natives and Newcomers from European Contact to Indian Removal—1500–1850,* edited by Peter C. Mancall and James H. Merrell, pp. 542–561. Routledge, New York. Originally published in *Journal of American History* 65(2):319–343.

Whiteley, Peter M.

1997   The End of Anthropology (at Hopi)? In *Indians and Anthropologists, Vine Deloria, Jr., and the Critique of Anthropology,* edited by Thomas Biolsi and Larry J. Zimmerman, pp. 177–207. University of Arizona Press, Tucson.

1998   *Rethinking Hopi Ethnography.* Smithsonian Institution Press, Washington, D.C.

2002   Archaeology and Oral Tradition: The Scientific Importance of Dialogue. *American Antiquity* 67(3):405–415.

Whitley, David S. (editor)

2001   *Handbook of Rock Art Research.* AltaMira Press, Walnut Creek, California.

Willey, Gordon R., and Jeremy A. Sabloff

1993   *A History of American Archaeology,* 3rd edition. W. H. Freeman, New York.

Williams, Stephen

1957   The Island 35 Mastodon: Its Bearing on the Age of Archaic Cultures in the East. *American Antiquity* 22(4):359–372.

1990   The Vacant Quarter and Other Late Events in the Lower Valley. In *Towns and Temples Along the Mississippi,* edited by David H. Dye and Cheryl A. Cox, pp. 170–180. University of Alabama Press, Tuscaloosa.

2001   The Vacant Quarter Hypothesis and the Yazoo Delta. In *Societies in Eclipse: Archaeology of the Eastern Woodlands Indians, A.D. 1400–1700,* edited by David S. Brose, C. Wesley Cowan, and Robert C. Mainfort, Jr., pp. 191–203. Smithsonian Institution Press, Washington, D.C.

Wittry, Warren L.

1963   The Bell Site, Wn9, an Early Historic Fox Village. *The Wisconsin Archeologist* 44(1):1–57.

Wonderley, Anthony

2000   The Elm-Antone Creation Story in Comparative and Historical Context. In *The Oneida Creation Story,* by Demus Elm and Harvey Antone, translated and edited by Floyd G. Lounsbury and Bryan Gick, pp. 7–27. University of Nebraska Press, Lincoln.

Wood, Bryant G.

1990   Dating Jericho's Destruction: Bienkowski Is Wrong on All Counts. *Biblical Archaeology Review* 16(5):47–49, 68–69.

Wood, Michael

1985   *In Search of the Trojan War.* Facts on File Publications, New York/Oxford.

Wright, G. Ernest

1983   What Archaeology Can and Cannot Do. *The Biblical Archaeologist Reader,* vol. 4, edited by Edward F. Campbell, Jr., and David Noel Freedman, pp. 65–72. Almond Press, Sheffield, England.

Wright, James V.

1974   *The Nodwell Site.* Mercury Series, Archaeological Survey of Canada Paper 22. National Museum of Man, Ottawa.

Wright, Joyce M.

1999   *Numbers: A Message from the Past.* London Museum of Archaeology Bulletin 16, University of Western Ontario, London, Ontario.

Wylie, M. Alison

   1982   Epistemological Issue Raised by a Structuralist Archaeology. In *Symbolic and Structural Archaeology,* edited by Ian Hodder, pp. 39–46. Cambridge University Press, Cambridge.

   2002   *Thinking from Things: Essays in the Philosophy of Archaeology.* University of California Press, Berkeley and Los Angeles.

Young, Gloria A., and Michael P. Hoffman

   2001   Quapaw. In *Plains,* edited by Raymond J. DeMallie, pp. 497–514. Handbook of North American Indians, vol. 13, part 1, William C. Sturtevant, general editor. Smithsonian Institution, Washington, D.C.

Young, M. Jane

   1988   *Signs from the Ancestors: Zuni Cultural Symbolism and Perceptions of Rock Art.* University of New Mexico Press, Albuquerque.

Zimmerman, Larry J.

   2003   *The Archaeologist's Toolkit,* vol. 7: *Presenting the Past.* AltaMira Press, Walnut Creek, California.

Index